INSIDERS' GUIDE® TO
EL PASO

HELP US KEEP THIS GUIDE UP TO DATE

We would love to hear from you concerning your experiences with this guide and how you feel it could be improved and kept up to date. Please send your comments and suggestions to:

editorial@GlobePequot.com

Thanks for your input, and happy travels!

INSIDERS' GUIDE® SERIES

INSIDERS' GUIDE® TO
EL PASO

FIRST EDITION

MEGAN EAVES

INSIDERS' GUIDE

GUILFORD, CONNECTICUT
AN IMPRINT OF GLOBE PEQUOT PRESS

All the information in this guidebook is subject to change. We recommend that you call ahead to obtain current information before traveling.

To buy books in quantity for corporate use
or incentives, call **(800) 962–0973**
or e-mail **premiums@GlobePequot.com.**

INSIDERS' GUIDE ®

Copyright © 2010 Morris Book Publishing, LLC

ALL RIGHTS RESERVED. No part of this book may be reproduced or transmitted in any form by any means, electronic or mechanical, including photocopying and recording, or by any information storage and retrieval system, except as may be expressly permitted in writing from the publisher. Requests for permission should be addressed to Globe Pequot Press, Attn: Rights and Permissions Department, P.O. Box 480, Guilford, CT 06437.

Insiders' Guide is a registered trademark of Morris Book Publishing, LLC.

Editor: Kevin Sirois
Project Editor: Lynn Zelem
Layout Artist: Kevin Mak
Text Design: Sheryl Kober
Maps: Design Maps Inc. © Morris Book Publishing, LLC

Library of Congress Cataloging-in-Publication Data is available on file.
ISBN 978-0-7627-6014-5

Printed in the United States of America
10 9 8 7 6 5 4 3 2 1

CONTENTS

Directory of Maps

ABOUT THE AUTHOR

Born and raised in New Mexico and West Texas, Megan Eaves is proud to call the Southwest home. She began traveling at a young age, finishing her B.A. at the University of New Mexico and going on to earn her M.A. in Intercultural Studies from Dublin City University in Ireland. In between, Megan spent a significant amount of time in Asia and there penned her first book, *This Is China: A Guidebook for Teachers, Backpackers and Other Lunatics* (Lulu Press, 2009).

After years abroad, Megan recently returned home to the sunny Southwest and, newly married to a wonderful man from Ireland, she is enjoying exploring her old stomping grounds with new eyes. When not working furiously on guidebooks, Megan is a freelance writer and publishes a number of articles and blog entries on the Web about the many places around the world that she has visited. Megan is especially fond of El Paso for its unique cultural mix and great food.

Visit Megan Eaves online at her Web site, www.meganeaveswriting.com, where you can check out her personal blog, follow her daily musings on Twitter (@megoizzy) or catch up with her via Facebook.

ACKNOWLEDGMENTS

This book was a labor of love. I owe thanks to my family, friends, and particularly my husband, who put up with what seemed like endless days of writing and researching and who laughed along when I accidentally began replacing daily words with "El Paso" towards the end. I must thank El Paso Convention and Visitors Bureau for providing me with copious amounts of information about the city (and for keeping their Web site so well updated), and also the many businesses and individuals around the city that welcomed me and provided information—especially those who responded quickly!

Special thanks are due to Amy Lyons, senior editor at Globe Pequot Press, for giving me the gig and trusting my skills, and to Kevin Sirois, my acquisitions editor, for his sunny disposition and constant flow of encouraging words, without which I would never have completed this book.

Paseños, you have an amazing city. I hope I managed to capture it.

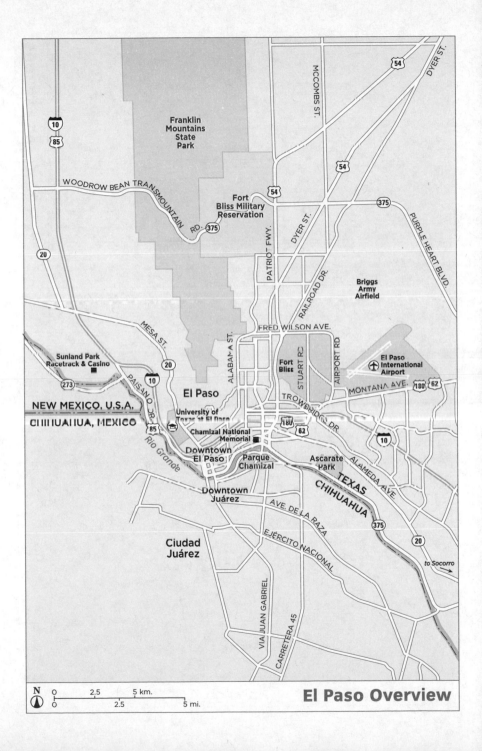

El Paso Overview

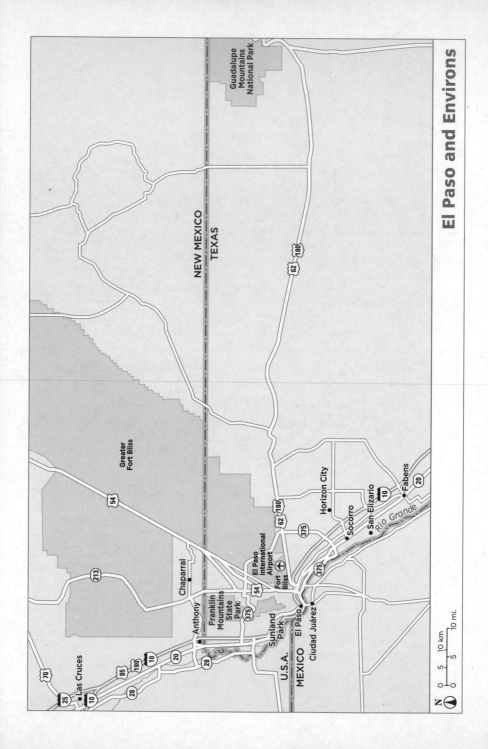

El Paso and Environs

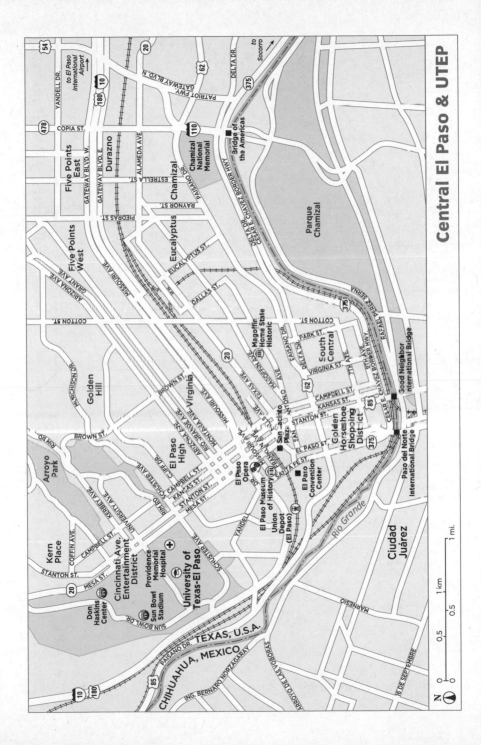

Central El Paso & UTEP

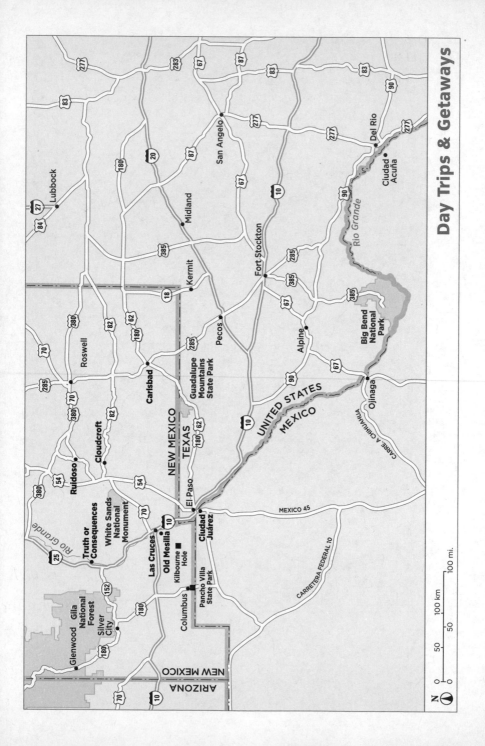

Day Trips & Getaways

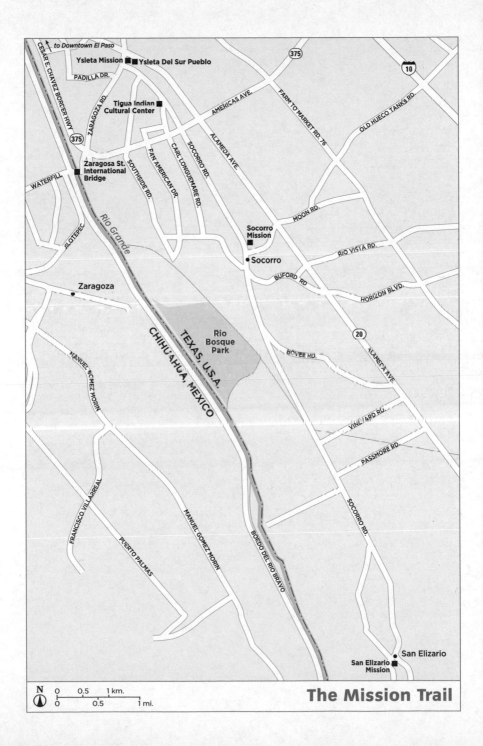

to Downtown El Paso

Ysleta Mission ■ ■ Ysleta Del Sur Pueblo

375

10

CESAR E. CHAVEZ BORDER HWY

PADILLA DR.

ZARAGOZA RD.

Tigua Indian ■
Cultural Center

AMERICAS AVE.

FARM TO MARKET RD. 76

OLD HUECO TANKS RD.

375

Zaragosa St. ■
International
Bridge

WATERFILL

PAN AMERICAN DR.

SOUTHSIDE RD.

CARL LONGUEMARE RD.

SOCORRO RD.

ALAMEDA AVE.

Rio Grande

JILOTEPEC

MOON RD.

Socorro
Mission ■

RIO VISTA RD.

● Socorro

BUFORD RD.

HORIZON BLVD.

Zaragoza ●

TEXAS, U.S.A.

CHIHUAHUA, MEXICO

Rio
Bosque
Park

20

HOVEE RD.

ROMERA AVE.

MANUEL SCHEZ MORIN

VINEYARD RD.

PASSMORE RD.

FRANCISCO VILLABREAL

MANUEL GOMEZ MORIN

BORDO DEL RIO BRAVO

SOCORRO RD.

PUERTO PALMAS

San Elizario ●

San Elizario ■
Mission

N

0   0.5   1 km.

0   0.5   1 mi.

The Mission Trail

PREFACE

I am a travel writer. My job is not to make places sound good; it is to uncover whatever the most unique and wonderful aspects of a place are and report on them. It is to find out how a city breathes and describe the inhalations and exhalations for others. It is to pinpoint the rare corners of the world and bring them to life on a page.

When I first started writing this book, my knowledge of El Paso was shallow: a few good restaurants, the main tourist sites, the bridges to Juárez (and why not to cross them), the best areas of town for shopping. But through this process, I have come to understand that El Paso is not like Santa Fe (my hometown) or Tucson or even Los Angeles. Its charms bubble far below the surface and you have to dive deep to see them. El Paso is not a shallow city—it is not a place of glowing magnetism and it certainly isn't a tourist trap. What I have uncovered here is the lifeblood of a true American city. If you ever want to understand the earliest beginnings of this country or get a sense of what life in the Southwest is really about, minus the turquoise jewelry and faux Navajo rugs, then you absolutely must spend some time getting to know El Paso.

If you've picked up this book or even casually flipped through the pages in a bookstore, you have at least some interest in the Sun City. Maybe you are passing through on your way to somewhere else (as many of El Paso's visitors are). Perhaps you are being relocated here or stationed at Fort Bliss. You might even be an incoming college student enrolling at UTEP. And you might be simply interested in learning about the American Southwest through its last authentic outpost. If you are of that last group, congratulations, for you are a rare and important breed. No matter what brings you to El Paso, though, you will find something in this book to help you get around, from relocation advice to accommodation listings and sightseeing spots.

Despite spending the better part of four months every day living and breathing El Paso, I'm still not sure I completely understand it, for it is a city that takes an incredible length of time to reveal itself. The layers of culture, heritage, background, socioeconomics, politics, and language here are so thick that it would perhaps take a lifetime of living here to really *get* El Paso. But that doesn't mean that the average visitor can't experience some of the city's finest and most authentic aspects, whether they be shopping for cowboy boots or discovering the nation's oldest churches, on even the most casual of trips.

I hope you will find this book useful and inspiring on your journey into El Paso, and I truly hope that you can, as I did, find something here worth writing home about.

HOW TO USE THIS BOOK

Welcome to the *Insiders' Guide to El Paso*. This book has everything you'll need to know before setting out to discover all the fantastic things that the Sun City has to offer. Within these pages, you'll find a selection of listings, stories, and general information to help you get around, whether you're visiting for a short weekend or staying in El Paso for awhile. What makes this book different from a visitors guide or tourism pamphlet is that we are allowed to have opinions. All of the information presented in this book was gathered from personal experience, and the author allowed herself to remain anonymous while doing this research, seeing the city just like you—as a visitor. The end result is a set of travel guidelines that do not pander to specific businesses, but rather present a true-to-life collection of listings that will help you make your decisions about how to best experience El Paso.

Where you start reading this book will depend largely on your purpose in El Paso. If you are coming for a vacation, you'll find an excellent overview of the accommodations, restaurants, and sightseeing opportunities on offer here. If you are relocating or being stationed at Fort Bliss, you can dive into the relocation-specific chapters toward the back of the book. One of the wonderful things about this guide is that you can start almost anywhere you like—you don't necessarily need to begin at the beginning.

The chapters at the front of the book will get you started in your vacation plans. Before you jump in the car or head to the airport, you might want to take a look at the Getting Here, Getting Around chapter, which will give you an idea about how El Paso is laid out and help you find your way through the city when you first arrive.

The Accommodations and Attractions chapters should be your next stop as you begin to decide where you'd like to stay and what you'd like to see while you're here.

If you're sitting on a plane or in an airport lounge, I would recommend diving into the History chapter, for understanding El Paso's history is one of the keys to understanding the city itself. This chapter is presented in summary form and includes the major events that shaped El Paso from its founding in the 1500s. With such a long span of time to cover, this is also the densest chapter in the book and you may find yourself needing to take your time and read it section by section.

For a quick cultural overview of El Paso, you'll want to check out the Borderlands chapter, which describes the Sun City's unique collection of cultural backgrounds, heritages, and languages, and describes a bit about what life is like along the U.S.–Mexico border.

There are also chapters about El Paso's restaurants and nightlife, and a family-friendly chapter entitled Kidstuff with lots of great places that are sure to keep the young ones entertained. All of these chapters are presented in listings format, with information about the part of the city in which each business is located. If you are here on business or have a specific part of town in mind, you'll be able to pinpoint the perfect hotel or place to eat nearby; otherwise, you can use the maps at the front of the book to help you decide in what part of El Paso you might like to stay. Shopping is one of the most delightful things to do in El Paso, and so the Shopping chapter covers everything from modern malls to Mexican *mercados*.

The Sun City's beautiful weather makes outdoor recreation and sports a joy here. The Franklin Mountains, the Rio Grande, and the Chihuahuan Desert come together in providing a plethora of unique and beautiful places to spend the day outside. The Parks and Recreation chapter will tell you all about El Paso's many city parks, as well as where to go bicycling, mountain biking, hiking, camping, and more. And if you'd like to take in a game, the multitude of spectator sports on offer in El Paso are listed here, too.

El Paso is also an artistic city, so you won't be surprised to find specific chapters dedicated to The Arts and Annual Events and Festivities, and from these pages you can begin to explore the many art museums, galleries, bookshops, and cultural activities available here throughout the year. The Annual Events and Festivities chapter presents a month-by-month listing of some of El Paso's most popular events, from rodeos to film festivals.

Fancy an overnight soak in the hot springs of New Mexico or a quick weekend ski trip? You'll find a wealth of places to explore within a day's drive of El Paso in the Day Trips and Getaways chapter. Many of the places covered delve deeper into Southern and Central New Mexico, as well as nearby areas to the east in Texas, such as Guadalupe National Park and Big Ben. It would take weeks to explore them all, so if you are relocating to El Paso, take your time and go through each one. Those just traveling through may have some tough decisions to make about which of these numerous amazing nearby spots to visit.

Moving to El Paso or already live here? Be sure to check out the blue-tabbed pages at the back of the book, where you will find the **Living Here** appendix that offers sections on relocation, retirement, education, health and wellness, and media. If you have children, you'll want to take a look at the Education and Child Care chapter, which provides an overview of the city's daycare options, school systems, and colleges. Likewise, the Health and Wellness chapter will point you toward the wonderful hospitals and care centers in El Paso, as well as a number of spas and gyms.

Of course, this book is not a phonebook, so the information here is just a choice selection of places to go and things to see. We encourage you to stray from these pages, particularly as regards restaurants and nightlife—El Paso has so many wonderful places to eat and drink that it would be impossible to list them all. One of the best parts about traveling is discovering things for yourself, so by all means, blaze new trails, using this book as your starting point.

It must be said that businesses come and go with El Paso's rapid expansion, so information can change quickly. Even Web sites can be wrong if they aren't updated regularly. As such, the information provided here has been kept to generalities rather than specifics, and it is always a good idea to call beforehand to confirm the hours of operation or entrance fees.

The *Insiders' Guide to El Paso* will be updated regularly, so if on your explorations you find some of the information within to be wrong, or if you have suggestions of your own about El Paso's best and most interesting, we would love to hear from you. You may write to us at Globe Pequot Press, P. O. Box 480, Guilford, CT 06437-0480 or at editorial@globepequot.com.

AREA OVERVIEW

Welcome to El Paso, the sixth largest city in Texas and a true western frontier town and vibrant modern city in the sunny Southwest. For many, just the name "El Paso" conjures up images of Old West gunfights, saloon brawls, and rattlesnakes, and though there are plenty of the latter that lurk in the desert mountains surrounding the city, with a population of more than 600,000, El Paso is truly a modern metroplex with all the amenities and amusements on offer in any of America's best cities. Make no mistake, though, El Paso is one of America's oldest towns. Decades before the British landed on Plymouth Rock, El Paso was already an established settlement and burgeoning trade center along the Spanish Camino Royal. Once a part of Spain, then Mexico and finally the United States, El Paso has seen its share of tumultuous battles, devastating natural phenomena, and of course, saloon brawls. And while Santa Fe and Tucson have unceremoniously sold their souls to the turquoise masses, El Paso retains its authentic flavor that is rustic, outlawish, and just a little bit gritty.

The fact that El Paso has changed hands a number of times, being at one time Spanish, then Mexican, New Mexican, and finally Texan, means that El Pasoans carry on that heritage. The mix of cultures here is as diverse as anywhere you'll find in the United States, and people here are proud of their colors and backgrounds. Spanish flows freely on El Paso's streets and sidewalks, and vivid murals flash portrayals of local flavor and history around the city as colorful as the spicy dishes served in the best of its restaurants.

El Paso has a unique "live and let live" policy that distinguishes it from the rest of Texas. Indeed, El Paso is closer to Santa Fe than its own capital city, Austin, and sometimes the locals joke that El Paso should secede from Texas and join New Mexico. Considering the shared heritage—the fact that El Paso was at one time part of New Mexico and that it is the only city in Texas operating on Mountain Time—it's a notion that isn't difficult to fathom. You might find that *Paseños* aren't as openly friendly as people in other West Texas towns, but give it time and you'll soon come to find that the locals will open up to you in a very real and welcoming way.

ENVIRONMENT

El Paso's environment is striking and unusual. Known as the Sun City, El Paso sees more than 300 days of sunshine a year and gets only about 9 inches of rainfall annually. While this presents unique challenges, especially regarding water conservation and water supply, of which there is almost always a shortage, it also makes El Paso an absolutely beautiful place to visit or live. Golf is understandably popular here; so is outdoor recreation of all kinds.

El Paso's winters are fairly mild, drop-

What's Your Pleasure?

There is something for everyone in this outpost town, and here, so far away from the fancy suits of Washington and the hippie shops of San Francisco, almost anything goes. Whatever your lifestyle and interests may be, you'll find an outlet in El Paso. Outdoorsy types will discover plenty of mountain biking and camping to keep them busy year round, and the amazing sunshine here helps make that possible, too. Culture vultures will go for El Paso's museums, from which there are more than a dozen to choose, ranging from art galleries to modern art museums, history museums, and more. If you're a foodie, welcome to paradise—El Paso has an absolutely unparalleled underground food scene that includes mom 'n' pop joints, tiny Mexican holes-in-the-wall, and upscale gourmet bistros. And down home sports fans can pull up a stool in one of El Paso's scores of homey sports bars to catch a game or cheer on the local UTEP Miners college athletics.

take one summer day's heat inside your car and a nearly melted steering wheel scalding your hands before you invest in a cheap but oh-so-necessary windshield shade.

Another aspect of El Paso's environment is its altitude. At slightly under 3,800 feet, it is just high enough to be arid but rarely presents a problem for newcomers. El Paso also sits at the very northern edge of the Chihuahuan Desert, so it is home to a wonderful array of flora and fauna, including the aforementioned rattlesnakes, as well as coyotes, mountain lions, and scorpions, which can be both beautiful and dangerous.

i If you are bitten by a snake or attacked by a wild animal, contact 911 emergency response and/or the West Texas Regional Poison Center at (800) 764-7661 immediately.

When hiking or enjoying the numerous outdoor activities around El Paso, several things are important to keep in mind. First, always wear sunscreen and protective clothing, especially in the summer when you might sunburn. It is very easy to become a victim of heat exhaustion, dehydration, and sunstroke, so always be sure to drink extra amounts of water, especially as you are newly adjusting to El Paso's climate. When walking or camping in the wilderness, there are several amazing but deadly creatures that you might encounter, including rattlesnakes and scorpions, so stay away from small holes and underbrush.

The Rio Grande flows right through the middle of El Paso and creates the international boundary between the United States and Mexico. Traditionally, the river has been the lifeblood of the area and it created a lush, fertile valley where it was possible to

ping to an average low of about 35°F at night, but staying at a mild 55°F on most winter days. The city sees a few snows during the winter, which rarely last long and often melt off once the sun begins to shine again—usually within half a day. The summers can be scorchingly hot at around 90°F during the day, but the dry heat makes that temperature much more tolerable than in other locations with humidity. It will only farm a number of produce and fruits. Some of the earliest settlers here were vintners from Spain who found the area to be ideal for growing grapes. As such, El Paso was the first winemaking region in the United States.

One thing is for sure: El Paso is stunningly beautiful. The Franklin Mountains, which jut south into the city and curve El Paso into a horseshoe shape, comprise the largest urban park in the United States and provide a stunning backdrop to downtown El Paso's skyline. They are also the masters of creating blazing sunsets that light up the sky almost nightly in beautiful hues of orange, pink, purple, and violet. And if you still aren't convinced, just spend an evening sipping a margarita on one of the city's obligatory patios watching that sunset and you'll be on board. ¡Bienvenidos!

EL PASO NEIGHBORHOODS

Central

The area known as Central El Paso is the oldest part of the city and includes the downtown district and the University of Texas at El Paso, as well as South El Paso, which is a less economically developed area of the city. While Central has arguably some of the most beautiful and historic neighborhoods in the city, in recent years, many El Pasoans have opted to move to the newer developments on the East and West sides, favoring more modern homes in suburban developments over the compact and historic feel of Central El Paso.

If you are looking for a historic, centrally located place to live in a vibrant, colorful, and multicultural district, then Central El Paso is the place. The streets here comprise a diverse array of distinct neighborhoods, some of them unfortunately neglected, and all of them once part of a lively city center

Visitor Information

El Paso Convention & Visitors Bureau
One Civic Plaza
(915) 534-0600
(800) 351-6024
www.elpasocvb.com
You can request free information about El Paso, including a welcome packet and an official visitors guide, from the El Paso Convention and Visitors Bureau. Likewise, stop in to their offices downtown once you arrive for a free map, pamphlets, and lots of great advice about what to do and where to go in the Sun City.

Texas Welcome Center
I-10 at Exit 0 in Anthony
(915) 886-3468
This tourist office is located right at the Texas–New Mexico border in Anthony as you cross the state line. If you're driving into town from the west or north, this makes an easy stop for a few maps or pamphlets.

Airport Welcome Center
El Paso International Airport
(915) 534-0658

Fort Bliss Visitors Center
Inside the PX Mall
(915) 534-0657

Juárez Tourist Center
Avenida Lerdo
Just south of the Bridge of the Americas.

atmosphere of a bygone era. Central, too, is the leafiest district of El Paso, with large lumbering tree-lined streets and an interesting variety of unique brick architecture. Most of the homes in Central were once prized mansions, and though many are now inhabited by the older generations of El Pasoans still clinging to a time in the city's past, this can be an absolutely charming, convenient, and not all too expensive area to live in.

Eastside

The fastest growing area of El Paso is the Eastside, a sprawling swath of city bordered on the north by US 10/62 and on the southwest by I-10. The Eastside's flat desert land was ideal for affordable housing construction, which allowed many large developers to move in over the past decade, resulting in a massive boom of new subdivisions here, and the Eastside now accounts for more than half the city's new homes each year. In 1999, the City of El Paso annexed nearly 2,400 acres of land on the Eastside, which continues to be developed into suburban neighborhoods by large housing companies. Most of the homes and neighborhoods on the Eastside are modern suburban housing complexes and subdivisions, as well as some gated communities. The Eastside thus has become one of the most expensive places in terms of El Paso real estate, with homes selling for upwards of $200,000 in subdivisions like Vista Hills and El Dorado. If you are looking for a modern home built within the past 10 years in a cutely sculpted suburban area with good schools, the Eastside is an ideal choice, as homes here are not as expensive as those in similar developments on the Westside.

Northeast Side

The laid back lifestyle of the Northeast Side is popular with nature lovers and retirees for its beautiful views and proximity to Transmountain Road and the Franklin Mountains.

This narrow district is bordered to the east by US 54 and Fort Bliss and backed by the mountains to the west, and is easily accessible via Loop 375 and US 54. The Transmountain Road provides very scenic access to the Westside in about 20 minutes. At Cohen Stadium, you can take in an AA baseball game or a summer concert. Also, because the area is not far from Fort Bliss, many military families and retirees choose to reside here. Homes on the Northeast Side are not old, though the area is not expanding at the rate of the East- or Westside. Homes here are much more reasonably priced, averaging around $122,000 and topping out at $225,000 in the luxurious Angel's Triangle neighborhood, probably because the area is further afield from downtown. However, it is still well-served with plenty of shops, grocery stores, churches, and fast food restaurants.

Lower Valley

The Lower Valley is made up of a series of independent communities that are among the oldest in the area. Comprised of Ysleta, Socorro, and San Elizario, the Lower Valley is a string of once-thriving farming communities where most businesses still carry a family name and it is not unusual to farm chickens in your backyard. Life in the Lower Valley is a unique combination of rural and urban, being only a few minutes' drive from downtown and yet still characterized by pecan orchards and family farms. Most of the homes in the Lower Valley are older, some with expansive backyards, gardens, and facilities for livestock. Though certainly not the most pristine or modern part of El Paso, the Lower Valley has a charm and culture all its own, as a mixture of well-established Native American and Mexican cultures com-

🔍 Close-up

Kern Place

Considered by many to be El Paso's earliest suburb, the beautifully historic Kern Place neighborhood, which sits to the east of the UTEP campus, was created in 1914 by a local entrepreneur by the name of Peter Kern. When Kern arrived to El Paso in the 1880s, he established his own business in the jewelry trade and eventually bought a large piece of land in what was, at the time, the very outer limit of El Paso. It wasn't until after his return from an extended trip to Alaska in 1914 that Kern, together with New York engineer W. I. Rider, began drawing up plans for the unique neighborhood that would become Kern Place.

No longer a suburb, Kern Place is now deeply set in Central El Paso and is recognized for its lawns and gardens, historic homes, lush parks, and a lively entertainment district. The houses and architecture of Kern Place are unlike any in El Paso. Among the most recognized homes in the neighborhood is Paul Luckett's house at 1201 Cincinnati Ave., which is constructed of rock gathered from the area and is fondly referred to as "The Castle" because of its round walls and crenellated rooftop. The Hoover House at 711 Cincinnati Ave. is another well-known home in Kern Place. The Hoover House was originally built for El Paso Mayor Richard M. Dudley and was eventually bought by businessman Robert Thompson Hoover, whose wife later deeded the house to UTEP. Since 1965, the Hoover House has been home to the university's presidents.

By far, the neighborhood's most popular spot is the Cincinnati Avenue Entertainment District, located at the intersection of Mesa Street and Cincinnati Avenue just east of the UTEP campus. The city's greatest concentration of bars, clubs, and restaurants is located here along Cincinnati Ave., and it is a popular nightlife spot among El Paso's younger set, especially UTEP students.

Kern Place is also home to a number of green spaces. Among them, Madeline Park, which was named after Peter Kern's estranged daughter, is located off of Kern Drive and Baltimore Drive. With a lovely gazebo, children's playground, and basketball court, this oblong-shaped park is a great place to take in a picnic or get outdoors on a sunny El Paso afternoon. Just east of Kern Place is Arroyo Park, a natural desert open space with a large *arroyo* (dry riverbed) running through it. Arroyo Park is popular with nature walkers and mountain bikers and offers a lovely view of downtown and Ciudad Juárez from the base of the Franklin Mountains.

prise the breadth of the population here. The community rests between I-10 and the Border Highway, with the Rio Grande running along the southern strip of the valley, creating natural border between El Paso and Juárez. The Tigua Indian reservation, one of the El Paso's biggest tourist attractions and site of the Ysleta Mission, built in 1680, is located within the Lower Valley.

Many of the homes in the Lower Valley are priced below $70,000, representing an incredible value for an area that is more rural than economically underdeveloped. There are also a few pockets of new development along the far eastern ends of the valley, where higher value homes are being built. The Lower Valley is served by Ysleta Independent School District, which offers both traditional schools and magnet school programs with specialized curricula in fine arts, science, and technology.

Westside/Upper Valley

The Westside (also known as the Upper Valley) is a rapidly expanding concoction of modern homes, shopping malls, chain restaurants, and department stores that extends north and west of downtown, bordered by the Rio Grande and Mexico to the west and the Franklin Mountains to the east. The most pricey real estate area in El Paso, homes on the Westside average in the $300,000 to $400,000 range, with the most expensive on the market peaking out at upwards of $600,000 in posh neighborhoods like Country Club and Festival Hills. Particularly the area south of Mesa Street/Country Club Road and west of I-10, homes are spread out onto larger tracts of land in open, leafy neighborhoods that are less cramped than the tightly packed new subdivisions of the Eastside. Like the Eastside, though, the Westside is one of the fastest growing and most sought-after real estate markets in the city, and is well served with all types of shopping and dining options.

TEXAS SUBURBS
Canutillo

Canutillo (pronounced *can-uh-tee-yo*) is a community on the east bank of the Rio Grande and on US 80 and 85 about 12 miles northwest of downtown El Paso in northwestern El Paso County. The community also was on the Atchison, Topeka, and Santa Fe Railway and was the site of the historic homestead of Joseph Magoffin in the 1800s. Sandwiched between the river and the mountains, Canutillo represents an interesting mix of urban El Paso and the surrounding rural communities. Here you will find slightly older homes built on suburban style streets and surrounded by a similar rural desert quality of the Lower Valley, but lacking the charming farms and scenic pecan groves of some of the New Mexico suburbs.

Homestead Meadows

Homestead Meadows is an eastern suburb of El Paso and is split into two sections by US 180/62: Homestead Meadows North and Homestead Meadows South. Neither area is particularly well developed; at present, it is a sparsely populated ranching community with large tracts of desert land that have yet to be built upon. Life in Homestead Meadows is a pleasant and quiet alternative to the bustle of the more suburban and central areas of the city, while still only a short drive to downtown El Paso. Homestead Meadows is served by the Clint Independent School District, a small district with three high schools, three middle schools, and three elementary schools. This as yet mostly untapped suburban community will, no doubt, see a lot of growth during the coming decade.

Horizon City

Listed as one of CNN *Money's* 2007 best places to live, Horizon City is located around 20 miles east of El Paso in El Paso County and has a population of around 15,000 people. This tidy suburban town has a number of beautiful parks, extremely low crime rates, and good schools served by the small Clint Independent School District. Horizon City has comparably low home prices averaging at just over $100,000 for most places, and it is an ever-expanding suburb (much like the rest of East El Paso) where many of the homes are newly built within the last 10 years. Horizon City is located a few miles off I-10 along Horizon Road.

NEW MEXICO SUBURBS

Anthony

Known locally as "the best little town in two states," Anthony is located literally on the border between Texas and New Mexico. It is a quiet small suburban town located about 15 miles north of El Paso. As of July 1, 2010, Anthony is officially incorporated as its own town with an elected mayor, a city council, and a judge. Anthony has a similar rustic feel not unlike the Lower Valley of El Paso, which is dotted with pecan orchards, farms, cotton fields, and horse ranches. Like much of New Mexico, Anthony is noted for scenic sunsets with views of the desert mountains. The main part of town is characterized by little *adobe* (mud) storefronts lined up one next to the other in a multitude of yellows, browns, and reds. On the Texas side, Anthony is served by its own Independent School District, while students on the New Mexico side attend schools in the Gadsden ISD.

Chaparral

Eleven miles across the mountain through Anthony Gap east of Anthony is Chaparral, another small rural suburb of El Paso. In *Place Names of New Mexico* it is described as a "rural subdivision whose name means 'overgrown with scrub oak,'" a fairly apt description of Chaparral, which is characterized by a scrubby desert landscape. Many manufactured homes and mobile homes are scattered over a wide expanse of land here and housing is cheap, though it is certainly not the most modern or beautiful area of El Paso. Because the eastern boundary of Chapar-

ral is Fort Bliss, some military personnel choose to live here. There is some business in Chaparral, but it is primarily a "bedroom community" for El Paso and Las Cruces workers. Chaparral is served by the Gadsden Independent School District of New Mexico.

Sunland Park

Formerly known as Anapra, Sunland Park was renamed for its most popular attraction, the Sunland Park Racetrack and Casino. Sunland Park sits northwest of downtown El Paso under the watchful eye of Mount Cristo Rey, a huge Christ statue located on a mountain peak a few miles from town. The racetrack is, of course, the biggest draw to Sunland Park, as well as the recently relocated Western Playland Amusement Park, where many El Paso families come for a bit of roller coaster excitement during the summer. Sunland Park, like the other nearby New Mexico suburbs, is served by Gadsden Independent School District and is considered part of the Las Cruces municipal area, even though it is much closer to El Paso. Sunland Park is a quiet, clean little suburb with rows of affordable homes tucked onto several neatly gridded streets.

LANGUAGE

While neither Texas nor El Paso has an official language, both Spanish and English are used here on a regular basis. Of course, English tends to be the language of choice for most daily activities and most El Pasoans are native English speakers. However, you are certain to encounter Spanish, as El Paso is home to one of the largest Spanish-speaking populations in the U.S., and one of the most literate Spanish populations at that. The city has also developed its own unique combination of the two—a kind of "Spanglish" combination of both Spanish and English words, chosen at will for whichever word is most appropriate at the time. If you plan to stay awhile or are relocating, you'll certainly want to brush up on your Spanish—it will endear you to the locals and provide you some of the best meals on offer in El Paso.

In addition to English and Spanish, you might also hear a number of other languages around the city. Thanks to Fort Bliss, each year El Paso plays host to a number of German soldiers undergoing Air Force training here. There are also quite a few Chinese, Thai, and Vietnamese people in the city, many of whom are second and third generation family members of railroad workers who arrived in the 1880s.

i Piñata Publishing, which produces the *El Paso Visitors Guide* magazine, also maintains a useful visitors' Web site with plenty of helpful information at www.elpasosouthwest .com.

TIME ZONE

El Paso operates as part of the Mountain Time zone, quite apart from the rest of Texas, which uses Central Time, so El Paso is always one hour behind Houston, Austin, and Dallas. This time zone includes two Texas counties—El Paso and its neighbor to the west, Hudspeth—and the rest of the state operates as usual on Central Time. The change of time zone can be a little confusing if you are driving through or traveling between Texas cities, so once you reach El Paso, be sure to move your clock one hour behind Central Time or one hour ahead of Pacific Time. Conversely, if you are coming from Arizona

or anywhere in New Mexico, you'll keep your clock on the same time zone.

i Daylight Savings Time begins at 2 a.m. on the second Sunday in March and reverts to Standard Time at 2 a.m. on the first Sunday in November. El Pasoans set their clocks one hour forward in March and back one hour in November.

CURRENCY AND ECONOMY

Being so proximal to Mexico presents unique challenges for El Paso's economy. Prior to the 1994 signing of the North American Free Trade Agreement (NAFTA), much of El Paso's economy relied on industrial manufacturing, as many large companies had factory headquarters here. However, NAFTA changed all of that, allowing free trade across both the Mexican and Canadian borders. Many of El Paso's longtime economic contributors then chose to move their factories south of the border, where they found less expensive operating costs and a plethora of cheap labor. Known as *maquiladoras*, or assembly factories, many of these plants are now located in Ciudad Juárez and have taken on a controversial reputation for employing underpaid, overworked (mostly women) laborers. And of course, these relocations adversely affected many El Paso workers, putting hundreds of people out of jobs. This, in turn, has spurred the establishment in recent years of several dozen technical colleges and trade schools that formed to educate displaced workers, arming them with technical skills for a newly developing jobs market.

Nonetheless, El Paso is a working town and some of its biggest employers continue to be manufacturing facilities and industrial plants. Western Refining, for instance, has offices in El Paso, as do a number of mechanical parts companies, such as Boeing, Hoover, and Delphi auto parts. Perhaps surprisingly, the city's largest employer is El Paso Independent School District, with Fort Bliss taking an unsurprising second-place seat, employing some 6,800 civilian workers. Other major employers in the city include the other school districts and the University of Texas at El Paso, as well as the city itself.

i Did you know that Fort Bliss is the largest air defense center in the world? More than 8,000 people live and work on Fort Bliss, and the base contributes around $2 billion every year to the local economy.

Being firmly a part of the United States for more than 150 years, El Paso of course operates on the U.S. dollar. However, its proximity to Mexico means that there is a presence of the Mexican peso and plenty of *bureaus de change* and banks where one can exchange currency, especially downtown near the international bridges. On the Mexican side, of course the peso is in full use, but most shops and markets in Juárez will gladly accept U.S. dollars, too.

CITY HIGHLIGHTS

To orient yourself in El Paso, the first thing you must remember is that the city is almost split in two by the Franklin Mountains. The Westside is El Paso's most affluent and quickly developing area, with lots of large, beautiful homes, expansive new shopping centers, and chain restaurants going up in spades. The Eastside is home to the Texas sprawl, which is fitting considering that it is the area most closely connected to the rest of the state. The downtown area is a narrow, hilly strip that falls at an incline from the foothills above the University of Texas at El Paso (UTEP) down to the Rio Grande and the international bridges. Most of downtown operates on a grid, luckily, with many of the streets traveling as one-ways either east or west. The rest of the city is fairly easy to maneuver, with several major roads and highways providing access to both sides of the city in a matter of minutes. Thus, El Pasoans don't hesitate to skirt across town for a quick bite to eat or an evening out.

Many of the city's highlights are concentrated in the downtown area, including the major museums, great shopping, international flavor, beautiful hotels, tasty restaurants, and good nightlife. In the event that you are just passing through or have arrived by bus or train, you should have no problem exploring the main sites on foot, and there are upscale hotels, cheap motels, and even a backpacker hostel to accommodate all types of travelers.

One of the Sun City's main tourist draws is its history, most of which is concentrated outside of downtown in the Lower Valley along the Mission Trail. Here, you can visit a series of historic churches that were among the first buildings erected in the area some 350 years ago. Here, too, you can visit the only Native American pueblo in Texas. The Ysleta del Sur pueblo is home to the Tigua Indian tribe, one of three federally recognized Native American tribes in the state. In addition to taking in the historic beauty of the mission churches here, you can also get to know the rich traditions of this Native American culture at the Tigua Indian Cultural Center.

If it's outdoorsy delights that you are after, you'll have no trouble spotting the massive, craggy Franklin Mountains from pretty much any vantage point in the city.

Vital Statistics

Founded: 1659 (incorporated 1873)

Area codes: 915, El Paso; 432, El Paso County; 575, nearby New Mexico

Population: 751,296 (2009 estimate); Ciudad Juárez, 1,512,354

County: El Paso County

State capital: Austin

Area cities: Ciudad Juárez, Mex.; Las Cruces, NM; Horizon City, Socorro, Ysleta, Sunland Park, Anthony, Canutillo, Homestead Meadows

Area: 250.9 sq. mi.

Elevation: 3,762 ft.

Nickname: The Sun City

Average temperatures:
January: 55°F (high); 28°F (low)
July: 95°F (high)

Annual rainfall: 8.75 inches

Average days of sunshine: 302

Colleges and universities: University of Texas at El Paso, Texas Tech University Health Sciences Center El Paso Campus, Park University Fort Bliss, Texas Tech College of Architecture at El Paso, El Paso Community Colleges, Doña Ana Community College, Texas Tech University— Paul Foster School of Medicine

Time zone: Mountain Standard Time, Mountain Daylight Time

Major area employers: El Paso Independent School District, Fort Bliss, Ysleta Independent School District, City of El Paso, University of Texas at El Paso, Socorro Independent School District, Sierra Providence Health Network, El Paso Community College, Wal-Mart, El Paso County, Las Palmas and Del Sol Regional Health Care System, Echostar

Famous *Paseños*: Eddie Guerrero (pro-wrestler), Vikki Car (singer), Debbie Reynolds (singer), Stevie Nicks (singer), Jeff Bingaman (senator), Patrick G. Forrester (NASA astronaut), Sandra Day O'Connor (retired Supreme Court Justice), George S. Patton (U.S. Army general), John J.

In this, the largest urban park in the nation, you'll find plenty of campsites, hiking paths, and mountain biking trails to explore. If you prefer the comfort of your car, Transmountain Road runs a circular loop through the Franklins providing amazing views of the city below. And the Wyler Aerial Tramway will take you from the foothills to the peaks in just a matter of minutes, with an interesting guided talk as you soar your way up.

El Paso is a city that reveals itself in folds and not one that can be easily understood in a few short hours. Though its charms are not always present at first glance, as you come to a greater understanding of this truly authentic Southwestern city, you will begin

Pershing (U.S. Army general), Pat Garrett (Western lawman), Thomas Haden Church (actor), Anthony Quinn (actor), Sam Donaldson (former ABC news anchor), Jack Handey (comedian), Frank Castillo (MLB player), Don Haskins (UTEP basketball coach), Lee Trevino (professional golfer)

Major airports: El Paso International Airport

Public transportation: Sun Metro (700-A San Francisco St.; 915-533-3333; www.ci.el-paso.tx .us/sunmetro)

Military bases: Fort Bliss

Driving laws: Seatbelts are mandatory for all passengers. No open alcohol containers are allowed in vehicles. Children up to four years must be in a child safety seat. New drivers must obtain a Texas driver's license within 90 days of arrival. Young drivers must be 15 years old to obtain a Hardship License.

Alcohol laws: The drinking age in the state of Texas is 21 years. Open alcohol containers are prohibited from motor vehicles and streets and sidewalks in the central business district, and public intoxication is a fineable offence. Last call at bars across Texas is 2 a.m.

Tobacco laws: The minimum age for the purchase of tobacco products is 18 years. In 2002, El Paso instituted a stringent smoke-free indoor air ordinance that banned smoking in all workplaces, restaurants, and bars. Many businesses have outdoor patios for smoking.

Daily newspapers: *El Paso Times, El Diario de El Paso* (Spanish language)

City sales tax: 1.0 percent

State sales tax: 6.25 percent

Time and temperature: (915) 532-9911

Important phone numbers: 911 emergency; (915) 779-1800, Crisis help line; (800) 764-7661, West Texas Regional Poison Center; (915) 772-8894, weather service

City Web site: www.ci.el-paso.tx.us

Chamber of commerce: Greater El Paso Chamber of Commerce (10 Civic Center; 915-534-0500; www.elpaso.org); El Paso Hispanic Chamber of Commerce (2401 East Missouri Ave.; 915-566-4066; www.ephcc.org)

to love it more and more. Take your time. Explore everything. Do some reading about El Paso's amazing history. And use this book as a jumping off point from which to begin your explorations. If you truly invest the time to understand this little corner of the world, you will learn that it is one of the most unique and authentic places left on earth.

i Compared to other U.S. cities of its size, El Paso has a considerably low cost of living. El Pasoans pay only 94 percent of the national average for all items, and pay no state, county, or city income tax.

SAFETY

In their 2008/09 City Crime Rankings study, CQ Press ranked El Paso as having the third lowest crime rate among cities of 500,000 people or more, and with only about three murders a year on average, it is easily one of the safest places to live in the United States. This is often surprising to people, given the city's locale along the border. El Paso's low crime rate stands in stark contrast to its neighbor across the border, Ciudad Juárez, which is now considered the most dangerous city on earth. Increasing drug cartel violence over the past decade has transformed Juárez's reputation as a seedy-but-loveable border town into an all out war zone. The more than 2,000 homicides in 2009 combined with Ciudad Juárez's population of 1.5 million give it an estimated murder rate of 133 per 100,000 people—and it is believed that more people die in Juárez a year than do soldiers stationed in Iraq. When compared with El Paso's three murders per year, the situation in Juárez is both appalling and shocking, and has led to many El Pasoans' unwillingness to cross the border—an activity that, just a few years ago, would have been a regular Sunday outing.

The effects of Juárez's drug war, though, have really only touched El Paso through reputation, and it is honestly a safe, clean city that lives quite apart from the raging violence to the south. Of course, a large portion of Mexican drug trafficking does occur through the El Paso/Juárez ports, but it seems that once on U.S. soil, most traffickers are keen to keep their heads down and noses clean. And so the violence, for the moment, appears to be confined to Mexico.

Certainly, El Paso suffers from the types of petty crime that plague most American cities—theft and robbery being among the worst that go on here. While shopping in the downtown areas, it is smart to keep a watch on your wallet or purse, as pickpockets may target tourists, especially in crowds. It is wise to always keep your doors locked and to avoid leaving tempting items inside your car overnight, as auto break-ins and theft are not uncommon.

For the most part, though, you will find El Paso a safe place to be. The Westside and Eastside, where rapid urban development is occurring, are particularly suburban, while downtown sees its share of cross traffic. The lowest income areas of the city are in the Lower Valley, which sadly does correspond to crime rate in most cases, and several rough neighborhoods lie just along the border between downtown and the Lower Valley, including Chihuahuita, or "Little Chihuahua"—a group of streets right near the border crossings south of downtown. No matter where you are, you will want to avoid walking around late at night, especially in areas that may seem or look unsavory.

GETTING HERE, GETTING AROUND

E l Paso has long been a transportation hub. Starting as early as the 16th century, El Camino Real ("The Royal Road"), a busy trading route that connected Mexico City to Santa Fe, New Mexico, brought traffic to the El Paso region. Situated smack dab in the middle of El Camino Real, El Paso, which was officially founded in 1659, served as a halfway point along the route, where traders, conquistadors, politicos, and the Spanish army could rest and refuel. In modern history, El Paso's air industry has often been at the forefront of technology. In 1968, El Paso International Airport was the first in the United States to install a 130-foot air traffic control tower; in 2000, it was the first airport in the country to begin utilizing the high-tech STARS radar system.

Despite its historic role as a connecting place, El Paso is uniquely situated as the western-most point of Texas along a domestic boundary with New Mexico and an international border with Mexico. This rare geographic placement has helped form El Paso's identity as a binational, multicultural city. Additionally, El Paso's far west location dictates that it has always been a bit of an outpost. It is the only major city in Texas that operates on Mountain Time (the rest of Texas is on Central Time), and the city's rich Spanish heritage, mix of Hispanic cultures, and a shared history mean that El Paso often identifies more with its neighbor state, New Mexico, than with Texas. Indeed, New Mexico's capital city, Santa Fe, is only 328 miles from El Paso, while its own state capital, Austin, is a whopping 618 miles away.

Since the founding of El Paso in the 17th century, the city's layout has been shaped largely by the natural surroundings. Running mostly on an east-west axis, El Paso forms a U shape around the Franklin Mountains, which make up the southern tip of the North American Rockies. The stark desert mountains rising behind the El Paso skyline give the city a striking backdrop and a number of fantastic outdoor recreational areas, and make it the only major metropolitan area in Texas with a mountainous cityscape.

OVERVIEW

As most El Pasoans will tell you, it is pretty much impossible to get lost in the Sun City. I-10 forms the major east-west artery through the city, and the U.S.–Mexico border, comprised of a concrete ditch through which the Rio Grande flows, makes up the city's southern boundary. The general rule of thumb is: if you come to a bridge, you're leaving the United States!

Generally speaking, El Paso is a driving city. There is a fairly extensive public transport network, Sun Metro, which utilizes buses and trolleys, but most locals opt to drive. Parking is rarely a problem, even in the central areas, and it is also possible to walk, as long as you stick to the downtown and University of Texas at El Paso (UTEP) areas of town. Walking across the bridges to Ciudad Juárez in Mexico was a popular pastime among tourists (although in recent years, tourism numbers to Juárez have dwindled because of the city's increasing crime rates). A combination of taxis, shuttle buses, and city buses transports travelers to and from El Paso International Airport, which is a mere 6 miles from downtown. Across the board, El Paso is an extremely easy and scenic city to maneuver and offers visitors the chance to explore the special Borderlands culture unique to the area.

BY PLANE

EL PASO INTERNATIONAL AIRPORT
6701 Convair Rd.
(915) 780-4749
www.elpasointernationalairport.com
Situated just 6 miles from downtown along US Highway 180/62, El Paso International Airport is a bustling transportation hub that sees more than 60 commercial flights a day. In operation three quarters of a century, El Paso International Airport was originally opened as a small municipal airport in 1928. Since then, the airport has gone through multiple changes of name and location.

Today, El Paso International Airport, abbreviated as ELP, sits on 6,800 acres and is home to 15 gates in two concourses. Gates A1 and A2 service American Airlines, which runs nine flights a day to and from Dallas and Chicago. In Concourse B, the rest of the gates are shared between US Airways, Continental, Delta, Frontier, New Mexico Airlines, Southwest, and United Express/SkyWest. By

far, the largest commercial carrier operating at El Paso International Airport is Southwest Airlines, with 34 flights a day to nine destinations including Albuquerque, Austin, Dallas–Love, Houston–Hobby, Las Vegas, Los Angeles, Phoenix, San Antonio, and San Diego. In 2008, El Paso International served more than 3 million passengers on its two carrier runways.

Having undergone major renovations over the past decade, El Paso International is well set up to accommodate travelers with a range of services. A variety of restaurants and lounges is available in the airport, including Burger King, Starbucks, a snack bar, and three restaurants. There are also several gift shops throughout the airport, both before and after the security checkpoints. A Travelex business center, located on the lower level next to the Information Booth, provides currency exchange, fax and photocopying services, and postage, and sells phone cards and travel insurance. There is also Wi-Fi Internet coverage provided by Opti-Fi throughout the airport, with fees of $7.95 for a 24-hour period or $21.99 a month. Travelers that don't have a laptop or other wireless device can get online at the Travelex Business Center in the main lobby.

Commercial Airlines

AMERICAN AIRLINES
(800) 433-7300
www.aa.com

US AIRWAYS
(800) 428-4322
www.usairways.com

CONTINENTAL AIRLINES
(800) 523-3273
www.coair.com

DELTA AIRLINES
(800) 325-1999
www.delta.com

FRONTIER AIRLINES
(800) 432-1359
www.frontierairlines.com

SOUTHWEST AIRLINES
(800) 435-9792
www.southwest.com

Regional/Commuter Airlines

NEW MEXICO AIRLINES
(888) 564-6119
www.flynma.com

UNITED EXPRESS/SKYWEST
(800) 864-8331
www.unitedexpress.com

i There is a courtesy hotel phone bank located directly in front of the baggage claim area. Use this phone to contact local hotels to arrange ground transportation.

From the Airport to the City

Car Rentals

Driving is the easiest way to get around El Paso and there are several major attractions located some distance apart, so a rental car is one of the best ways to travel during your visit. Car rental desks are located in the baggage claim area on the lower level of El Paso International Airport. The rental car companies operate free shuttles to and from the terminal to the car pickup points, which are located off-site.

ALAMO
(800) 462-5266
www.alamo.com

AVIS
(800) 831-2847
www.avis.com

BUDGET
(800) 527-0700
www.budget.com

DOLLAR
(800) 800-3665
www.dollar.com

ENTERPRISE
(800) 736-2260
www.enterprise.com

HERTZ
(800) 654-3131
www.hertz.com

NATIONAL
(800) 227-7368
www.nationalcar.com

THRIFTY
(800) 847-4389
www.thrifty.com

Airport Shuttles

There are several bus and shuttle options operating between El Paso International and the surrounding areas. Shuttle companies provide ground transport ranging from service to nearby Las Cruces, New Mexico, to private charters farther afield in Texas, Arizona, and California. Twenty-four-hour courtesy shuttles run between the airport terminal and the long-term parking lot every

Hotels Offering Airport Shuttle Service

- **Camino Real Hotel,** (915) 534-3000; www.caminoreal.com (see p. 47)
- **Chase Suites Hotel,** (915) 772-8000; www.chasehotelelpaso.com (see p. 50)
- **Comfort Inn,** (915) 594-9111; www.comfortinn.com (see p. 46)
- **Hampton Inn & Suites,** (915) 833-7000; http://hamptoninn1.hilton.com (see p. 48)
- **Hawthorn Inn & Suites,** (915) 778-6789; www.hawthorn.com (see p. 52)
- **Holiday Inn Airport,** (915) 778-6411; www.hielpasoairport.com (see p. 53)
- **Howard Johnson Inn,** (915) 591-9471; www.hojoelpaso.com (see p. 48)
- **Hyatt Place,** (915) 771-0022; www.elpasoairport.place.hyatt.com (see p. 53)
- **La Quinta Inn,** (915) 585-2999; www.lq.com (see p. 48)
- **Marriott Hotel,** (915) 779-3300; www.marriott.com (see p. 54)
- **Radisson Suite Hotel,** (915) 772-3333; www.radisson.com (see p. 54)
- **Ramada Inn & Suites,** (915) 591-9600; www.ramada.com (see p. 50)
- **Wyndham El Paso Airport,** (915) 778-4241; www.wyndham.com/hotels/elpht (see p. 54)

day. In addition, many local hotels operate free shuttle services to and from the airport to their locations throughout the city.

AMIGO SHUTTLE
Sergio Camacho
6869 Enid Ct., #11
(915) 355-1739
www.amigoshuttle.info
Offering a wide range of services in and around El Paso and Ciudad Juárez, Amigo Shuttle is a private company that can be hired for just about anything, from basic airport ground transportation to local apartment hunting services and tours. Services offered in English and Spanish.

LAS CRUCES SHUTTLE & TAXI SERVICE
P.O. Box 3172
Las Cruces, NM 88003
(800) 288-1784
www.lascrucesshuttle.com
This extremely reliable shuttle van service operates regular schedules between El Paso International Airport and downtown, as well as several destinations across southern New Mexico, including Las Cruces, Deming, Silver City, and Anthony. Reservations are required and can be made by calling their reservation line. A one-way fare between El Paso and Las Cruces runs $43, while trips further afield to Deming and Silver City cost $60 and $80 respectively. Discounts are offered for companion fares, as well as same-day trips and bulk ticketing.

Public Transportation
Public bus Route 33, run by the municipal bus company, Sun Metro, services passengers between El Paso International and downtown, with stops at Five Points Terminal, where passengers can transfer to a wide

variety of other lines, as well as Bassett Place Mall. Buses depart from the airport Mon to Fri from 5:40 a.m. to 8:45 p.m., Sat from 6:40 a.m. to 8:45 p.m., and Sun and holidays from 7:50 a.m. to 6:40 p.m.

At the airport, you can board the bus outside of baggage claim on the lower level of the terminal building, near the taxi rank. At the Downtown Transfer Center, Route 33 boards at Bay 14. The journey takes approximately half an hour, but be sure to take potential traffic problems into account when planning your journey, and leave at least two hours in advance of your flight to avoid mishaps.

Taxis and Limos

Several taxi and limousine services operate at El Paso International Airport, giving visitors a range of options for travel to and from the city. All taxis are licensed by the city and metered, and taxi ranks are located just outside the terminal building near the baggage claim area. Taxi services operate 24/7, but it is up to the individual limo services to decide their hours of operation.

ADVANCED LIMOUSINE SERVICE
4720 Dyer St.
(915) 562-5466
www.advancedlimos.net
Offering the largest fleet of SUVs and stretch vehicles in El Paso, including a stretch Hummer, Jaguar S-Type, Rolls Royce Phantom, and Excalibur Classic Conversion, this service has a wide range of interesting vehicles for hire. Standard airport pickup/dropoff services are available; otherwise a basic hire of two to three hours is required.

CITY LIGHTS LIMOUSINE SERVICE
(915) 590-5944
www.citylightslimo.com

Taxi Fare Information

Some specific destinations in and around El Paso have set taxi fares as follows:

- From El Paso International Airport to Ciudad Juárez (excluding Colonias, Juárez Bus Terminal, and Juárez Airport): $42 per carload

- From El Paso International Airport to Juárez Bus Terminal: $48 per carload

- From El Paso International Airport to Juárez Airport: $60 per carload

- To zones within the city limits, the fare is either $10 per carload, or the fare shown on the taxi meter, whichever is higher.

There are three taxi companies with permits to service El Paso International Airport:

- Border Cab Co., (915) 533-4245
- Sun City Cab Co., (915) 544-2211
- United Independent Cab Co., (915) 590-8294, www.590taxi.com

This extensive car service has a huge fleet of vehicles, including basic limousines, stretch limos, luxury SUVs and sedans, executive sedans, passenger vans, and limo buses. They offer hourly rates and have several vehicles dedicated solely to airport transfers. Advance reservations are required.

L & M LIMOUSINE

P.O. Box 547
Organ, NM 88052
(800) 786-0518
www.landmlimo.com
This private car service offers both limousine and private car hire 24 hours, every day of the year, including airport transfers. In addition to their several new model limos, they also keep a fleet of vehicles that includes luxury SUVs and sedans. Reservation bookings are accepted by phone or via their Web site.

BY CAR

Driving is far and away the easiest way to get into and around El Paso and the city is set up for cars. Most El Pasoans drive to get where they're going, rather than relying on mass transit, which is only offered on a fairly limited basis. You will also find that many of the attractions and listings in the El Paso area are fairly spread out, so having or renting a car will benefit you in getting to some of the more out-of-the-way spots.

I-10 and I-25

The city's main interstate highway is I-10, which runs in an east-west swath across the city, cutting El Paso directly in half before jutting north to Las Cruces, New Mexico, where it intersects with I-25, the major north-south thoroughfare. I-10 provides direct access to Phoenix, Arizona and Los Angeles in the west, as well as San Antonio and Houston, Texas, New Orleans, and Jacksonville, Florida in the east. On 1-25, you can cruise due north to Albuquerque and Santa Fe, New Mexico, and further afield to Colorado, Wyoming, and Montana.

Main Roadways

Several highways provide access to El Paso from the surrounding areas. Highway 54, officially titled the Patriot Freeway and known locally as the North-South Freeway, runs north to the New Mexico destinations of Alamogordo and Ruidoso, while Highway 180/62 cuts east to the Guadalupe Mountains and Carlsbad Caverns in New Mexico, and eventually, the Dallas/Fort Worth Metroplex.

Within the city, Loop 375 encircles El Paso, providing quick access to most of the city, as well as connections to I-10 and the Patriot Freeway/54. Most notably, in its southernmost stretch, Loop 375 runs along the U.S.–Mexico border, where it is more commonly referred to as the Cesar E. Chavez Border Highway. It is across here that several major bridges provide easy access between El Paso and Ciudad Juárez, by car and on foot.

International Crossings

Four bridges connect the El Paso metro area with Ciudad Juárez and Mexico. Highway 62, or Santa Fe Street as it runs through downtown, crosses into Juárez via the Paso del Norte International Bridge, where visitors can either drive or walk across the border. The nearby Good Neighbor International Bridge connects South Stanton St. with Lerdo in Juárez. Further east, the Bridge of the Americas connects El Paso's Paisano Drive with Parque Chamizal on the Juárez side. The fourth and final cross-border bridge is located in the southern suburb of Ysleta. Known as the Ysleta-Zaragoza International Bridge, this crossing can be accessed easily by heading southeast on Loop 375.

Parking

El Paso is a surprisingly easy place to park. The heavy amount of urban sprawl has allowed the construction of ample parking lots at most large stores and malls. Downtown, there is plenty of metered parking, as well as several large private parking garages that offer decent daily rates. The parking meters downtown only accept quarters, so you will need to have a supply of change on hand in order to pay for your parking time. If you work or do business downtown, or plan to be parking there often, you can buy a SMART Card, which acts as a debit card that can be used in all downtown parking meters. SMART Cards can be purchased from any Sun Metro ticket office, at the municipal cashier on the first floor of City Hall, or from the Central Business Association located at 201 East Main on the 16th floor. Cards cost $4 to buy and can be filled in increments of $25, $50, $75, or $100.

BY TRAIN OR BUS

UNION DEPOT
700 San Francisco Ave.
(915) 545-2247
www.amtrak.com
El Paso's train station, Union Depot, is a beautiful historic building that is worth seeing in its own right, even if you aren't in transit through it. Although this stately red stone building was once the region's most bustling transport center, it is now mostly quiet: The weekly train service saw only about 9,605 rail passengers in 2008. Designed by architect Daniel H. Burnham, who also designed Washington D.C.'s Union Station, El Paso's Union Depot opened 1906 and was added to the National Register of Historic Places in 1971. Amtrak services El Paso with two

railroad lines running east and west: Sunset Limited and Texas Eagle (www.amtrak.com). Service east toward Chicago goes weekly on Tues, Wed, and Sat, while service west to Los Angeles runs Sat, Sun, and Mon. Local Sun Metro buses stop nearby, and there is ample parking, both in the short term parking lot near the station, as well as long term parking, which is available at El Paso Civic Center around the block.

> **i** Local legend says that Pancho Villa used the Union Depot bell tower as a lookout point during an attack on Ciudad Juárez during the Mexican Revolution.

GREYHOUND
200 West San Antonio Ave.
(915) 533-5921
www.greyhound.com
TNM&O merged with Greyhound, limiting long distance bus service in and out of El Paso. The Greyhound bus station is located downtown, around the corner from El Paso Convention Center and just down the street from several museums, cafes, theaters, and hotels, making it a convenient stop for those passing through to see a bit of El Paso.

SUN METRO
(915) 533-3333
www.elpasotexas.gov/sunmetro
The city's mass transit system, Sun Metro, operates an extensive network of public buses and trams throughout El Paso, including the suburban community of Sunland Park, New Mexico. Standard one-way bus fare is $1.25 and must be paid in exact change upon boarding the bus. Discounts are offered to seniors and those with stu-

dent or military ID cards. Prepaid passes are available on a monthly, weekly, and daily basis and provide unlimited rides. Daily and weekly passes can be purchased directly on board any Sun Metro bus, but monthly passes must be purchased at a Sun Metro ticketing office (these are main bus stops, transfer centers, and terminals), through the post, or at any public library in El Paso.

It costs an additional 25 cents to transfer bus lines. If you need to transfer, be sure to request a transfer slip upon boarding your first bus and use the transfer within two hours.

i Routes 4 and 9 are free downtown circulator routes. Route 4, known as the Golden Horseshoe Circulator, goes around Union Plaza, while Route 9 goes from Anthony Street to the Downtown Transfer Center every 35 minutes.

WALKING AND BICYCLING

Despite the creeping suburban sprawl that is slowly expanding El Paso's borders, the downtown areas of the city are extremely walkable. Many of the main attractions and museums can be reached on foot or bicycle. That said, the city is not a bike-friendly place and most El Pasoans opt to drive rather than bike. There are a few bike paths dotted around the city, with plans to construct more over the next few years, but commuting by bicycle is very difficult, as the traffic is heavy and drivers aren't conscientious of cyclists. However, mountain biking is an extremely popular pastime and a lovely way to enjoy the Franklin Mountains, if you are so inclined. More information about recreational cycling, including where to rent bicycles in El Paso, can be found in the Parks and Recreation chapter of this guide.

HISTORY

To talk about the history of El Paso is to talk about the history of America itself. When most people think of our country's beginnings, they imagine the pilgrims landing on the shores of Massachusetts in 1620. But time travels much farther back than that in the Southwest. The Spanish arrived here sometime in the 1580s and the settlement that would become El Paso was founded in 1598 by the Spanish explorer, Don Juan de Oñate. The "first Thanksgiving" was celebrated here, on the banks of the Rio Grande, some 23 years before the pilgrims feasted at Plymouth Rock. Millennia before that, native tribes already occupied the region around what is now El Paso. In essence, the story of El Paso is the story of America's beginnings. It is one of intrigue, of fortune seeking, of growth, and of depression, and sometimes it is a story of lawlessness.

To many, El Paso is the picture of the Wild West, and indeed, it once was (and in certain ways, still is) the quintessential Wild West town, where outlaws and lawmen had shootouts and drank whiskey in saloons with swinging doors, and where cowboys and *vaqueros* fought cattle wars, smuggling herds back and forth across the border. Some hold the belief that El Paso has already seen its glory days in those lawless moments. Others hold that the city has yet to see its best years as it expands into a modern metropolis.

OVERVIEW

As you read on in this book, and as you explore the Sun City for yourself, one thing you may notice is that many of the attractions, the best restaurants, the important places, and the interesting tidbits here are tied together by a historical connection. History is deeply part of El Paso's culture and it is a city connected to its surrounding areas in ways that transcend the timelines and borderlines of political geography. Some, in fact many, of the areas that are now part of the United States once thrived under the umbrella of Mexico, and vice versa. Indeed, El Paso and its Mexican sister city, Ciudad Juárez, were at one time hardly distinguishable from one another, carrying the same name: El Paso del Norte. So, lines here, both cultural and geopolitical, are fuzzy.

In the following pages, you will find only the highlights of El Paso's history, for it is a story so lengthy that historian W. H. Timmons needed 366 pages to tell it from start to finish in his fantastic work, *El Paso: A Borderlands History*. Instead, I have attempted to capture what I think are the most important dates in El Paso's history, the ones that have defined it as a city and shaped it into the place it is today. You will also discover biographies of some of El Paso's most intriguing and famous characters, like Mexican revolutionary Pancho Villa and notorious gunslinger John Wesley Hardin. And as you explore

(Q) Close-up

El Paso Timeline

Pre-history: For millennia Indians traversed the El Paso area.

1581: The Rodriguez-Chamuscado expedition arrives, becoming the first Europeans to reach the Pass of the North.

1598: The Juan de Oñate expedition celebrates the first Thanksgiving, La Toma, on what would become United States soil, marking the beginning of continuous inhabitants in the El Paso area.

December 8, 1659: The Mission Nuestra Señora de Guadalupe de los Manos del Paso del Norte was founded by Fray García de San Francisco on the south bank of the Rio Grande, marking the official founding of what would become El Paso.

1680: The Pueblo Revolt in New Mexico forces Spanish and Indian groups south to the Rio Grande. Many settled along the river at the Pass of the North, primarily on the south side of the river. That same year, El Paso becomes the base for Spanish governance of its territories in the Southwest.

1680: The Ysleta del Sur and Socorro pueblos are established, Ysleta taking a new name to indicate their status as the Isleta tribe "of the south." The Mission de Corpus Christi de San Antonio de la Ysleta del Sur is built by Antonio de Otermín and Fray Francisco de Ayaeta, and Nuestra Señora de Limpia Concepcion de los Piros de Socorro del Sur is constructed for the Piro tribe of Socorro Pueblo.

1685: Post-revolt peace is restored and the original five settlements at the Pass of the North are founded.

1700–1720: El Camino Real flourishes as a trade route and supply trail, with El Paso del Norte at its center.

1783: The royal postal service of New Spain arrives in El Paso del Norte.

1789: The Spanish military presidio of San Elizario, including the San Elizario Mission, is founded to help in the defense of the El Paso settlements against the Apaches.

1790s: Peace with the Apaches is achieved by Bernardo de Gálvez, viceroy of New Spain.

1821: Mexico gains its independence from Spain, bringing the entire American Southwest, including El Paso, under its control.

1829–1831: The Rio Grande floods its banks and runs drastically off-course, forming a new channel south of the settlements of Ysleta, Socorro, and San Elizario, stranding them on an island.

1836: The Texas Revolution breaks out.

May of 1846: Disputes over the Texas/Mexico boundary lead to a subsequent invasion of Mexico by U.S. military forces, and the start of the Mexican-American War.

February 2, 1848: Treaty of Guadalupe Hidalgo is signed, ending the Mexican-American War and making El Paso officially part of the United States.

1850: The Compromise of 1850 is signed, drawing the Texas/New Mexico border and putting El Paso into Texas. El Paso County is established with San Elizario as its first seat.

1854: The Post Opposite El Paso is established as the early predecessor of Fort Bliss.

1862: The Union California Column captures El Paso and it is used as the headquarters for the 5th Regiment California Volunteer Infantry.

1873: The town of Franklin, which would later become El Paso, is officially incorporated, encompassing the small area communities that had developed along the river.

1877: The Salt War of San Elizario causes mayhem and murder for several months around San Elizario.

1881: The railroads arrive in El Paso and Joseph Magoffin is elected mayor.

1883: The first church in El Paso, St. Mary's Chapel, is erected.

1884: El Paso's first public school is opened.

1888: El Paso del Norte officially changes its name to Ciudad Juárez, ending decades of confusion between El Paso and Juárez.

1905: Ordinances are passed that end gambling and prostitution in El Paso.

1906: The Union Depot train station is opened.

1910–1911: The Mexican Revolution begins, resulting in a flood of refugees from across the border into El Paso.

1914: The Texas State College of Mines and Metallurgy, now the University of Texas at El Paso, is founded.

September 12, 1930: The Plaza Theater is opened in downtown El Paso, showing the movie *Follow Through* to a crowd of more than 2,000 people.

1936: Standard Airport, which would later become El Paso International Airport, opens to commercial flight traffic.

1939–1945: World War II.

1967: The Chamizal Agreement that verified the boundary and the exact course of the Rio Grande through the city is signed.

1974: Chamizal National Memorial is established on both sides of the border as a museum to commemorate resolution of the border conflict.

1979: The Franklin Mountain State Park is created and becomes the largest urban park in the United States, with exceptional geologic history and the highest structural point in Texas.

1990s: El Paso's economy declines as many factories are moved to cheaper markets abroad.

1994: North American Free Trade Agreement is signed, opening trade between the United States and Mexico.

1999: El Paso's largest copper smelter closes.

September 11, 2001: Terrorist attacks of 9/11 prompt increased security along the U.S.–Mexico border.

2006: Completion of a multimillion-dollar renovation of the Plaza Theater.

2007: Increased drug violence in Ciudad Juárez escalates.

2008: Initiative is passed to revitalize and redevelop all of downtown El Paso.

El Paso on your own, you will notice that much of the history you read in these pages still exists in the form of place names of old buildings, restaurants, and roads.

EARLIEST HISTORY

The El Paso region has had human settlement for thousands of years. Around the Hueco Tanks, geologists and archaeologists have found Folsom points, more commonly known as arrowheads, as well as thousands of petroglyphs left behind by the hunting-gathering Jornada people, who roamed the area for about a thousand years. At the time of the arrival of the Spanish, the Manso, Suma, Jocome, and Jumano tribes populated the area, living in small villages that the Spanish termed *rancherías* and cultivating maize, squash, and beans using fairly primitive agricultural methods. These groups would form the basis of what is today known as the *Mestizo* culture in the area, a racially mixed group of both European and Native American decent. The Mescalero Apache roamed the region as well and were renowned for being extremely violent.

The first Spanish to arrive in Texas were fortune seekers who had heard about the "Seven Lost Cities of Gold" and wanted to try their hands at finding riches in the New World. Some arrived through what is now Central America and Mexico, while others came across from Florida. The most famous of these was Alvar Núñez Cabeza de Vaca who, in the 1530s along with three companions, escaped from an ill-fated Florida expedition that had blown off course on its way back to Cuba and landed on the Gulf Coast of Texas. For about two years, this quartet wandered across the area that is now southern and western Texas, exploring the region, meeting local tribes, and tasting the indigenous food. In the Rio Grande area, perhaps very near what is now El Paso, they encountered Indians who told them of a number of rich cities to the north. This, of course, fueled the Spaniards' imaginations about the mythic Seven Cities of Cíbola, and this would later coax many more parties back to the area in search of riches.

When he finally returned to Mexico City a couple of years later, Cabeza de Vaca spread the news of his findings across the city, and the idea of the supposed cities made of gold piqued the interest of several Spanish officials. A number of parties were sent north from Mexico in search of the Seven Cities of Cíbola during that period, the most well known of which was led by Francisco Vásquez de Coronado in 1540. For two years, he searched most of what is now New Mexico and West Texas in search of the riches, but of course, never found more than small pueblos that were home to local, and sometimes hostile, Indians.

For almost 50 years after the Coronado expedition, Spain's interest in the Southwest dwindled and the area was left dormant of explorers. It wasn't until the 1560s that interest was again piqued for fortune seeking when silver veins were found in what is now southern Chihuahua, Mexico. In 1567, the town of Santa Bárbera was established there for silver mining, and Spain was once again on the bandwagon of searching for the Lost Cities of Gold. In 1581, a new expedition set out, led by three Spanish friars: Augustín Rodríguez, Francisco López, and Juan de Santa María, who were sent as missionaries to proselytize the area. Accompanying them was an armed escort commanded by Francisco Sánchez Chamuscado; thus the mission today is known as the Rodríguez-Chamuscado expedition.

In 1581, the Rodríguez-Chamuscado expedition became the first group of explorers ever to reach the Pass of the North, what is now El Paso, staying for several months to explore the region. When they arrived in the El Paso area, they saw a huge mountain range and a long river, with a narrow swath of land traveling north up the middle, and they called the area *El Paso del Norte*, or "the Pass of the North"—a name that would stick with Ciudad Juárez into the 19th century. This first visit laid the foundations for European settlement in the El Paso region, and after the group returned to Mexico, Philip II, the monarch of Spain, became extremely interested in exploring and colonizing the New Mexico territory, which at that time was known as Nueva España, or New Spain, and covered a large swath of what is now the American Southwest.

DON JUAN DE OÑATE ARRIVES

For several decades, the viceroy of New Spain searched for a suitable leader to implement Philip II's plans for New Mexico and finally, in 1595, Don Juan de Oñate was awarded the honor. Oñate was perfect for the job. He came from good stock as the son of a rich silver miner, and his wife was the granddaughter of the famous explorer to Mexico, Cortez, and her great-grandfather was none other than the Aztec emperor, Montezuma. Though it took quite awhile for the expedition to come together, in January of 1598 the party finally headed north from Santa Bárbera. The expedition consisted of a colony of 400 men, 130 of whom had brought along families, as this was to be not only a party of conquest, but of colonization. About a third of the group had signed up to stay on and settle the lands that they discovered, and so the party also carried a hefty amount of baggage, wagons, and livestock.

When the Oñate expedition reached the Rio Grande on April 30, 1598, they named it *El Río del Norte* (the Northern River), and immediately built a small chapel and held High Mass under the lofty cottonwood trees along its banks. Then, on the site of present-day San Elizario just south of what is now downtown El Paso, Oñate held a formal ceremony in which he took possession of the entire region in the name of Philip II. This act was known as *La Toma* ("the taking") and is often referred to around El Paso as the "original Thanksgiving." *La Toma* was one of the single most important moments in not only the history of El Paso, but also the history of the United States, because it symbolized for the first time a European colonial presence in what is now the United States more than 20 years before the British arrived on the East Coast.

After performing this symbolic act, some of the expedition party (including Oñate himself) continued north, following the river as far as Santa Fe. Just north of the present-day city, they established a colony and officially founded New Mexico. However, after several years of searching and conquest, the New Mexico region failed to yield the type of riches and wealth that Oñate and his monarch had hoped for, and in 1608 the commander resigned his post and left for good. The Spanish crown held on to the New Mexico territory, though, appointing Don Pedro de Peralta as its governor the following year.

FOUNDING OF EL PASO DEL NORTE

The traditional date for the founding of El Paso del Norte (the present-day Ciudad Juárez) is December 8, 1659, when the Mission Nuesta Señora de Guadalupe de los

Mansos del Paso del Norte was founded by Fray García de San Francisco on the south bank of the Rio Grande. The Guadalupe Mission, which today sits in downtown Juárez, was a small adobe structure where a number of baptisms, marriages, and burials were performed. The mission as it appears today was constructed later, in 1668, and eventually became a way station of sorts for travelers along the route between Mexico and Santa Fe. The amazing little church has rested for the last 300 years in the same spot and has in modern times become a popular tourist stop for visitors to Juárez.

Several other mission churches were founded around the same time as the Guadalupe Mission. The San Francisco de los Sumas Mission was built some twelve leagues to the southeast of the Guadalupe site, and a third mission named Nuestra Señora de la Soledad was built at Janos, near Casas Grandes (Mexico). Together, these three missions made up the only permanent settlements in the El Paso area at that time.

PUEBLO REVOLT

1680 was a landmark year in El Paso's history. It all started in August of that year, when Indian discontent with Spanish rule in New Mexico erupted into full on violence in pueblos across the territory. This skirmish has come to be known as the Pueblo Revolt of 1680 and is considered one of the greatest disasters in the history of Spanish colonial rule in the Americas. As things worsened in the pueblos, communication between the main colonies in Santa Fe and Isleta became impossible, so two Spanish commanders, along with a small group of various Indian tribes that were loyal to Spain, decided to flee southward. After traveling for some six weeks, the parties arrived at La Salineta, and

created five settlements: El Paso del Norte, San Lorenzo, Senecú, Ysleta, and Socorro, and the Pass of the North has been continuously inhabited since then. Thus, 1680 also marks the time that El Paso became the base for Spanish governance of the territory of New Mexico, since the main Spanish commanders had ordered the party to flee south and established their settlements around the Pass of the North. From El Paso, the Spaniards, led by Don Diego de Vargas, regrouped and began their recolonization efforts of the Spanish territory that centered around Santa Fe and stretched from Socorro northward to Taos.

Over the next few years after the Pueblo Revolt, the state of the northern territories was precarious at best. Indian hostilities were still very high and anger against Spanish rule was rampant, even in the missions in and around El Paso that were once loyal to the Spanish. Several outbreaks of hostilities and revolts left local livestock and food supplies, including precious grain stores, depleted and buildings ruined. Even after peace was restored in 1685, the settlers suffered from food and clothing shortages, drought, and famine. The poor conditions, though, were too much for many of the settlers, who finally chose to flee the area, resulting in population drops throughout the 1690s. Nonetheless, the five settlements at the Pass of the North remained steadfastly intact, bringing El Paso del Norte into the 18th century.

EL CAMINO REAL

For the next few decades, the Spanish settlements along the border flourished as El Paso became the southernmost locality of the Provincia de Nuevo Mexico (New Mexico). It communicated with Santa Fe and Mexico City by the Camino Real, or the Royal Road.

The Camino Real was a major trade route and had at its heart El Paso del Norte, which proved to be an invaluable stopping point for weary travelers and traders. According to historian W. H. Timmons, "For more than two centuries, the Camino Real from Mexico City to Santa Fe and Taos, New Mexico was the lifeline of the Spanish northern frontier." Thus began a theme of El Paso being used as a stopover point that would continue into modern times, and still persists today.

The Camino Real got its start as a supply route for the missions and, during those early years, was most often traversed by wagon trains and caravans that were controlled by the local friars. New Mexico traded cattle, wool, textiles, animal hides, salt, and nuts with the mining towns of Chihuahua, most of which were moved along the Camino Real. Few foreign travelers, outside of Spanish merchants and officials, ventured so far north, as it typically took six months for a trading caravan to travel from one end to the other of the 1,500-mile route. All told, a trip along the Camino Real, including disbursement of goods and return time, would have taken a year and a half. El Paso's fortunate locale almost exactly mid-way between Mexico City and Santa Fe ensured the city's development from a few scattered riverside settlements into a thriving 18th-century town.

Most of the goods and supplies moved along the Camino Real were brought by traders from the south, but some of the goods were also grown locally. El Paso at that time had a vibrant agricultural industry, much of which was dominated by wine making. Some of the first vintners in North America established their vineyards at El Paso del Norte and found the region to be well suited to winemaking because of its high, dry climate and lush, fertile land along the Rio Grande. A large dam and a series of irrigation ditches known as *acequias* were installed to provide thriving agriculture for the area. Vineyards flourished, producing wine and brandy that ranked in quality with the best in the entire region.

By the mid-1700s, somewhere between 2,500 and 5,000 people lived in the El Paso area, including Spaniards, *Mestizos*, and Indians, comprising the largest and most complex population on the Spanish northern frontier. In 1789, the Spanish military presidio of San Elizario was founded to help in the defense of the El Paso settlements against the Apaches. This complex included the San Elizario Mission, which was built to minister to local military that were stationed there.

During the last decade of 18th century, peace was finally gained with Apache tribes due to an administrative restructuring and change of strategies. Bernardo de Gálvez, viceroy of New Spain, issued his *Instrucción*, which called for a new approach to dealing with both hostile and friendly Indian tribes. The plan was threefold and included continued military pressure, building of alliances with the friendlier tribes, and the fostering of a dependent relationship between Indians and the Spanish. The fact that the Apaches were no longer a viable threat, combined with the newly developed vaccine for smallpox, led to a steady increase in El Paso del Norte's population at the end of the 18th century. This period also saw the establishment of a public school system in El Paso and the arrival of the royal postal service of New Spain in 1783. El Paso was on its way.

TREATY OF GUADALUPE HIDALGO

In 1821, Mexico gained its independence from Spain after 11 years of fighting, which brought the entirety of what is now the American Southwest under Mexican rule. Thus, the El Paso settlements were all incorporated into the Mexican state of Chihuahua and El Paso became a *cabecera*, or capital, and elected its own local government. The Camino Real played an important part as a communication highway, as travelers carried information about events in central Mexico to the pueblos and villas in the internal provinces.

Throughout the years, the spinal cord of the El Paso area had always been the Rio Grande. A fickle river, it often overflowed its banks and, over the span of the several hundred years of Spanish and Mexican rule, the *Río* had changed its course several times. Between 1829 and 1831, though, the river ran more drastically off-course than ever before, forming a new channel that flowed south of the settlements of Ysleta, Socorro, and San Elizario, stranding the three on an island that was about 20 miles long and 4 to 5 miles wide. This flood had widespread effects. It caused severe damage to the Ysleta and Socorro missions (both of which were later rebuilt) and it also caused a boundary dispute that would forever alter the international border between Mexico and the United States.

In 1836, the Texas Revolution broke out between the settlers in Texas and Mexico, and resulted in the establishment of the Republic of Texas; although in El Paso, which didn't become part of Texas until 1848, the war was not felt as strongly. It did result, though, in a feeling of animosity between Americans and Mexicans, and brought a general air of suspicion to the El Paso area, where both cultures lived and worked together in high concentrations.

Then, just a decade later, in May of 1846, the dispute over the boundary of Texas between Mexico and the United States led to a subsequent invasion of Mexico by U.S. military forces, resulting in the Mexican-American War. During the War, Col. Alexander Doniphan and a force of American volunteers defeated Mexican fighters at the battle of Brazito, taking El Paso del Norte. The Treaty of Guadalupe Hidalgo was signed on February 2, 1848, ending the dispute and again changing the boundary between the two nations, with provisions that Mexico should cede most of its northern territories, including the present-day states of New Mexico, Colorado, Arizona, and California. This brought the entire El Paso region under the blanket of the United States, ending nearly 200 years of Spanish and Mexican rule over the area.

The present Texas–New Mexico boundary, which placed El Paso on the Texas side, was not drawn until the Compromise of 1850, so for several years, El Paso remained part of the New Mexico territory. El Paso County was established in March 1850, with San Elizario as the first county seat.

WILD WEST YEARS (LATE 1800S)

The latter half of the 19th century was a boomtown time for El Paso, and it was the era of cowboys and Indians, shootouts and swinging saloon doors. Just two weeks before the signing of the Treaty of Guadalupe Hidalgo, which brought El Paso into the United States, gold was discovered in California, and so this period saw a rush of crazy and interesting characters into the area, on their way to or from a search for riches on the West Coast. Virtually overnight, the quiet adobe buildings and dusty streets of the El Paso settlements were transformed into a bustling, brawling frontier town, home to soldiers and army deserters, fortune seekers, ranchers, and wife deserters, comprising a largely male population. Most of the women of El Paso were of Mexican or *Mestizo* descent, save for the town's only Anglo (white) female: a 6-foot-tall Amazon woman known as "the Great Western." By 1848, a number of settlements were flourishing north of the river, many of them the homesteads of local movers and shakers like James Wiley Magoffin, Benjamin Franklin Coons, Hugh Stephenson, and Simeon Hart. And in 1850, after months of deliberation, the U.S. Senate voted to approve a plan that decided the boundary lines of Texas and New Mexico, bringing El Paso under the jurisdiction of Texas once and for all.

By the early 1850s, Benjamin Franklin Coons' ranch was known as Franklin, presumably after his middle name, and was one of several thriving settlements in the area that would become present-day El Paso. The settlement at Franklin would end up becoming the nucleus of the future El Paso, and a year later, pioneer and retired Army officer Anson Mills laid out a plan for the town, calling it El Paso, which for years afterward would cause much confusion between the U.S. El Paso and El Paso del Norte (present-day Juárez) on the Mexican side of the river. A military post called the Post Opposite El Paso (meaning opposite El Paso del Norte, across the Rio Grande) was established in 1854, which provided the foundation for Fort Bliss. It would later be moved several times before arriving at its current location.

During the Civil War, the Confederate cause was met with great support from Franklin residents, but the area was never a Confederate stronghold. Though El Paso's alliance was to the South, the Union presided here and local Southern sympathizers eventually received pardons. In 1862, the Union California Column captured the town and it was used as the headquarters for the 5th Regiment California Volunteer Infantry until December 1864. From that time on, El Paso was part of the Union. After the war was over, the area's population began to grow and, in 1873, El Paso finally incorporated as a town, encompassing all of the small nearby communities that had developed along the river.

In 1877, Texans and Mexicans became embroiled in a bitter local civil war, the Salt War of San Elizario, which lasted six months and was fought over control of several salt flats located east of El Paso, not far from San Elizario. When Judge Charles Howard proclaimed that the hundreds of acres of salt beds were his personal property and that he would charge a fee to anyone who wished to collect salt, Italian immigrant Luis Cardis took the chance to increase his own political standing by rallying the local Mexican population against Howard. What followed were several months of violence that started as fistfights and escalated to pillaging and gun murders. Fort Bliss was closed for a time, and when it finally reopened, peace was established and Mexican families were once again allowed to haul salt from the flats, this time for a fee.

The Southern Pacific, the Texas and Pacific, and the Atchison, Topeka and Santa Fe railroads arrived in El Paso in 1881, which transformed the village into a lively frontier community and caused the population to soar, attracting newcomers that ranged from businessmen and priests to gunfighters and prostitutes. By 1890, some 10,000 people called El Paso home, and it became known as the "Six Shooter Capital" and "Sin City" because of its lawlessness. Prostitution and gambling flourished and every corner of town was dotted with a gambling hall, saloon, or dance hall. The beginnings of downtown El Paso were formed, with brick structures going up along El Paso Street and San Antonio Street, both of which were in the lively center of town. A number of Chinese shops and laundries sprang up as Chinese workers arrived in El Paso with the railroad, and a number of brothels and whorehouses were strung along Utah Street (what is now South Mesa Street).

It was a time of mayhem and fun. Most of the residents of El Paso had not meant to end up there, but found themselves there escaping something else—a bad marriage, lost fortunes, the strict laws of the northeast. Joseph Magoffin, who had been elected mayor in 1881, faced myriad problems in cleaning up the city and establishing infrastructure, but made significant progress in developing a water system, fire protection, and utilities and providing public transport in the form of mule-drawn street cars on the town's two main streets. Though the Mexican government had unsuccessfully tried to institute a public school system in El Paso during the late 18th century, in 1884 the first American public school was opened. Only one year earlier, the first church in El Paso had been erected—St. Mary's Chapel for the Catholic congregation.

Years of confusion ended in 1888 when the Mexican city across the border changed its name from El Paso del Norte to Ciudad Juárez after Mexican president Benito Juárez. By 1890, El Paso's citizens were tiring of the city's sinful atmosphere and lawlessness and demanding reform, and so in 1905, El Paso passed ordinances that banned gambling and prostitution. At the turn of the century, El Paso's frontier image was fading and its fresh start as a modern city began.

EARLY 20TH CENTURY (MINING AND OIL)

The turn of the century finally saw El Paso reform. In 1905, the local Citizen's Reform League got a petition signed to outlaw gambling, and in November of that year, the mayor closed all the dance halls, brothels, and gambling halls. El Paso went silent as its prostitutes and gamblers headed south into Juárez. To counteract the deficit caused by the loss of these lucrative businesses, a program of civic improvements was introduced that included an electric streetcar service and a street paving initiative that would allow the new Ford Model T horseless carriages to grace the streets of El Paso. This decade also saw the building of the city's first hospitals, high schools, libraries, and the impressive Union Depot train station in 1906, which cost $260,000 to construct. In 1914, the Texas State School of Mines and Metallurgy (now University of Texas at El Paso) was founded with its first 27 students exploring mines and metals in the Franklin Mountains.

In 1911, the Mexican Revolution, led by the infamous Francisco "Pancho" Villa, saw thousands of refugees streaming into El Paso, as the outbreaks and epicenter of the revolution were situated along the border in and around Ciudad Juárez, where supplies and munitions were easily gotten and where more liberal and revolutionary ideas flowed freely between the two countries. During the height of the war, El Paso residents would often sit on the roofs of their houses, or go to the tops of downtown buildings to watch shots being fired across the border in Juárez, and many El Paso buildings became revolutionary headquarters for Mexican fighters. When the fighting finally died down, some of the refugees went home, but most remained, contributing to

🔍 Close-up

Pancho Villa (1878–1923)

Born as José Doroteo Arango Arámbula on June 5, 1878 in Río Grande, Mexico, this famous Mexican revolutionary is better known by his pseudonym, **Francisco "Pancho" Villa.** The eldest of five children, Villa, along with his family, worked on one of the largest haciendas in the state of Durango. At the age of 16, the young Villa purportedly shot and killed one of the hacienda's administrators who had tried to rape his sister. Escaping, he joined a bandit gang and changed his name to Francisco Villa after his grandfather.

It is then that Villa's Robin Hood story began. While living as a fugitive, Villa joined Francisco Madero's successful uprising against the Mexican dictator, Porfirio Díaz, and because of his skills as a fighter and a leader he was made a colonel, signifying his historical transition from *bandito* to *revolucionario*. A charismatic figure, Villa was able to recruit an army of thousands, including a substantial number of Americans, some of whom were made captains in his own military force, División del Norte. For a number of years, he was involved in a series of clashes with other Mexican military groups and even fought against U.S. troops from 1916 to 1917.

During the mid-1910s, Villa became something of a folk hero in the United States. Hollywood filmmakers as well as U.S. newspaper photographers flocked to northern Mexico to record his battle exploits, many of which were staged for the benefit of the cameras. Villa's forces were based in Chihuahua, where he ruled over northern Mexico like a medieval warlord. Villa financed his army by stealing from cattle herds in northern Mexico. Faced with a failing economy, he issued his own money, and if merchants refused to take it, they risked being shot. Villa often ordered executions on a whim, but left the dirty deed to his friend Rodolfo Fierro, best known by the nickname "El Carnicero" ("the Butcher"). In true Robin Hood style, he broke up the vast land holdings of local *hacendados* and parceled them out to the widows and orphans of his fallen soldiers. During fiestas, he would purportedly dance all night with female camp followers even though he didn't drink. He was an avid swimmer and would run to stay in shape. According to one of Villa's last surviving widows, he officially married 26 times.

When the U.S. government came out openly in support of the Carranza presidency in Mexico, Villa retaliated by raiding U.S. border towns, most notably Columbus, New Mexico, where he took out an army fort and killed several soldiers. This prompted a U.S. Army "punitive expedition" into Mexico in 1916, led by General John J. Pershing. Along with 4,800 troops, Pershing chased Villa around Mexico for nine months to no avail, and finally the Mexican government accepted Villa's surrender and retired him on a general's salary to Canutillo, Durango. In 1923, Villa was assassinated while returning from bank business in Parral, Chihuahua.

Today, many Mexicans remember Pancho Villa with pride for having victoriously led important revolutionary campaigns across the country. Because of Villa's escapade in Columbus, New Mexico, and subsequent evasion of U.S. troops, he is also often cited as the only foreign military personage ever to have "successfully" invaded continental United States territory.

the character, economy, and cultural heritage of El Paso.

During Prohibition in the 1920s and '30s, El Paso became a popular train stopover for transcontinental travel because of its proximity to alcohol-saturated Juárez, and as tourism increased, so did the hospitality industry. Large hotels were built, including a Conrad Hilton hotel that eventually became the Plaza Hotel. The nation's finest entertainment troupes, anticipating a layover in El Paso, booked shows and concerts in advance and El Paso burgeoned into a city of theaters. On September 12, 1930, the grandiose Plaza Theater opened, showing the movie *Follow Through* to a crowd of more than 2,000 people. El Paso International Airport, then known as Standard Airport, was constructed in 1929 to facilitate transcontinental mail service, and in 1936 it became a commercial airport serving American Airlines.

World War II accelerated the town's growth, with downtown El Paso transforming into a sea of military uniforms and soldiers who were stationed at Fort Bliss or came through for training. Between 1900 and 1925, the city's population grew from just under 16,000 to almost 77,600—a remarkable increase in such a short period. However, the Depression era hit the city hard, causing the population to decline somewhat at the end of World War II. Following the war, military expansion in the area, as well as oil discoveries in the Permian Basin, facilitated a rapid economic expansion, as copper smelting, oil refining, and the abundance of low wage industries such as garment making bolstered the city's growth. The expansion slowed again in the 1960s but the city has continued to grow, in large part because of the increased importance of trade with Mexico.

Census reports from 1930 showed about 102,500 residents in El Paso. Development after the war brought new residents, and in 1950, there were around 130,000 people in the Sun City. El Paso's population nearly doubled in the following decades, and by 1970 the population was up to nearly 340,000. Fort Bliss, too, saw a lot of growth in the 1940s and 1950s. By the mid-1980s, Fort Bliss' military personnel and family members made up nearly a quarter of the city's population, and by that time, petroleum, textiles, tourism, metals, cement, and food processing made up the bulk of El Paso's industry.

CHAMIZAL NATIONAL MEMORIAL

One major point of contention throughout El Paso's history as a city was the border between the U.S. and Mexico, which runs right through the city and creates a distinction between El Paso and Juárez. From 1852 to 1868, the Rio Grande, which marks the border, had continually shifted south, with the most radical shift occurring after the flood in 1864, which created an island that stranded three settlements. By 1873, the river had moved approximately 600 acres, more than two square kilometers, cutting off Mexican land that was, in effect, made United States territory. The newly exposed land came to be known as *El Chamizal*, and eventually the land was settled and incorporated as part of El Paso; however, both Mexico and the United States claimed the land. In 1895, Mexican citizens filed suit in the Juárez Primary Court of Claims to reclaim the land.

At the time that the Mexican-American War ended with the Treaty of Guadalupe Hidalgo, another treaty was put into effect to resolve the border dispute. The Treaty of

1884 specified that the middle of Rio Grande was to be the border between the two countries, irrespective of any alterations in the channels or banks. The Treaty went on to maintain that any alterations had to result from gradual natural causes.

In 1910, Mexico and the United States agreed on rules of arbitration to settle the ongoing dispute and a tribunal was created to investigate and deliberate over whether the change in the river's course had been gradual, whether the boundaries set by the treaties were fixed, and whether the 1884 treaty applied. Mexico felt that the boundary had never changed and therefore that the Chamizal was technically Mexican territory, while the United States held that the 1884 convention applied, meaning that the boundary was the result of gradual erosion, and thus the land belonged to the United States. The tribunal made several recommendations, all of which were eventually rejected by one government or the other, fuelling an ongoing dispute between the two and fostering ill will. During this period of indecision, the tract of land located in the middle of the river came to be known as Cordova Island, and it became a haven for crime and illegal crossings because it was essentially a swath of Mexican land inside U.S. territory, so there was very little control by any local authorities.

For several decades between 1911 and 1963, attempts were made by a number of presidents to solve the Chamizal problem. Suggested compromises included forgiving debt, exchange of other territory along the Rio Grande, direct purchase of the tract, and inclusion of the Chamizal in the Rio Grande Rectification Project. The matter was unresolved until January 14, 1963, when U.S. President John F. Kennedy decided to agree

on the 1911 arbitration recommendations. The agreement awarded Mexico 366 acres of the Chamizal area and 71 acres east of the adjacent Cordova Island. The United States received 193 acres of Cordova Island from Mexico, and the two nations agreed to share equally the cost of rechanneling the river. On September 17, 1963, the U.S. Congress introduced the American-Mexican Chamizal Convention Act of 1964, which settled the matter once and for all, and in 1964, Presidents Adolfo López Mateos of Mexico and Lyndon B. Johnson of the United States met on the border to officially end the dispute.

One of the aims of the Chamizal Convention was to build a man-made channel to prevent the Rio Grande from going off course or overflowing its banks in the future and blurring the international boundary. The cost of the channel, which was constructed of concrete about 170 feet wide and 15 feet deep, was footed by both governments, as well as the cost of three new bridges to facilitate crossing between the two countries. The Chamizal National Memorial was established on both sides of the channel in 1974 as a museum and parkland dedicated to the history of the dispute and to increasing visitor awareness of cooperation, diplomacy, and cultural values as a basic means to conflict resolution.

MODERN DEVELOPMENT

During the 1990s, El Paso's economy suffered under the weight of major competition from factories and businesses abroad with low labor rates, particularly ever-present Juárez. In 1994, passage of the North American Free Trade Agreement (NAFTA) helped local service and transportation firms to expand their businesses, but hurt the city's industrial sector, as most major refineries and factories

⊙ Close-up

John Wesley Hardin (1853–1895)

John Wesley Hardin was an outlaw and gunslinger rumored to be so mean that he once shot a man for snoring. Born May 26, 1853, in Bonham, Texas, Hardin's father was a Methodist minister who named his boy after the founder of his religion. John grew to be a slightly built, good-looking boy, but it wasn't long before he displayed an uncontrollable rage that would set his course as one of the West's most notorious gunfighters. At age 14, he got into a fight with a schoolmate, stabbing him twice with a knife, and the following year he shot a black man to death. Hardin fled the law following that murder, killing at least one of the Union soldiers who were attempting to apprehend him.

As a cowboy on the Chisholm Trail in 1871, Hardin killed at least seven people, and shortly after his return to Texas, he met Wild Bill Hickok in Abilene. The two got on well, but a split between them came one night when Hardin shot holes through the wall of his hotel room to get the man next door to stop snoring. The second bullet killed the man. Knowing that Hickok would be out to get him, Hardin ran from his room and hid the rest of the night in a haystack. The next day he fled, determined to get as far away from Hickok as he could.

Finally, Hardin married his long time love, Jane Bowen. Despite their love and the fact that she bore him two children, Hardin couldn't keep away from his life as a wandering troublemaker. The murder that would finally see Hardin brought to justice occurred on May 26, 1874—his 21st birthday. Hardin had just won big at the horse races in Comanche, Texas, and set off on a celebratory crawl of the local saloons. Meanwhile, local Deputy Charles Webb was on a hunt to capture the outlaw. When he caught up with Hardin at one of the saloons, the lawman pulled his gun when Hardin's back was turned. The ensuing shot grazed Hardin but didn't prevent him from firing back at Webb. The bullet hit Webb squarely in the face, killing him instantly.

Hardin hightailed it out of town, evading the law for the next two years, and he finally arrived in Florida, where he took on a new identity. But on July 23, 1877 the gig was finally up when Texas Rangers cornered him in the smoking car of a train in Pensacola, Florida. Hardin was convicted of killing Deputy Webb and sentenced to 25 years in jail. After several unsuccessful escape attempts, he settled down in Huntsville Prison where he studied theology and the law. In 1894, the governor of Texas pardoned him of his crimes.

After his release, Hardin opened a law practice in El Paso, but ever the gunslinger, it wasn't long before he was in trouble again after getting into an argument with policeman John Selman. On August 19, 1895, Selman walked up behind Hardin in the Acme Saloon in El Paso while he was playing dice and shot him in the back. Legend has it that Hardin's last words were, "Four sixes to beat, Henry." Thus, one of the deadliest gunslingers in Texas history was dead at the age of 42. Within that time he had sent 44 men to their graves, and despite that, Hardin had a reputation as a gentleman among those who knew him, and he always claimed that he never killed anyone who didn't need killing. John Wesley Hardin was laid to rest in El Paso's Concordia Cemetery, where he still resides to this day.

moved their industrial plants south of the border where operating costs were much cheaper. Closure of the city's main copper smelter in 1999 was driven largely by crashing copper prices around the world and affected a large number of jobs.

Since El Paso is sensitive to changes in Mexico's economy, the devaluation of the Mexican peso in the 1990s and the border traffic controls instituted after the September 11, 2001 terrorist attacks both affected El Paso's economy. As well, El Paso has the unpleasant distinction of being one of the main entry points for drug smuggling into the United States, an attribute that has plagued the area's reputation for decades, although it has seemingly not affected the city's crime rate. But since 2007, Ciudad Juárez has erupted into a state of almost uncontrollable violence by drug gangs fighting over control of smuggling areas. Sadly, El Paso's reputation has suffered by proxy, despite its virtual lack of involvement, aside from being a favorite entry point of smugglers.

Still, the area is recovering from these incidents. The year 2006 saw the completion of a $38 million renovation to the historic Plaza Theatre, which spurred the decision in 2008 to pass a redevelopment initiative for revitalization of the entire downtown area. Modern El Paso breathes with a fantastic mix of cultures that have long historical connections to the area, as well as a strong military presence and the excitement of a border town, and today, the El Paso–Juárez international metropolitan area is the largest binational community on an international border anywhere in the world. As a crossroads and the main port of entry into and out of Mexico, as well as the largest town on the American side of this international border, there are no limits to El Paso's growth.

THE BORDERLANDS

Trying to understand the Borderlands is trying to understand a 1,960-mile length of land that runs from San Diego and Tijuana in the west to McAllen, Harlingen, and Heroica Matamoros in the southeast. As it travels from end to end, *La Frontera*—the U.S.–Mexico border—touches dozens of cultures and hundreds of years' worth of history. The stories here are of struggle—struggle to find an identity, a sense of place, a common ground. For many, the border is blurred by time, culture, and ethnicity. For others, it is ever more real as a 700-mile-long fence continues to be constructed, furthering the physical sense of "us versus them" and forcing many people to watch their homes, land, and cultures be physically yet unnaturally divided.

The Borderlands have always been a difficult place to define, for the border itself was constantly changing for most of its history. Ever since the Spaniards arrived in the mid-1500s and began to colonize what is now the American Southwest, they relied on the Rio Grande and other natural barriers to define their borders, natural barriers that were often fickle and changing. The Rio Grande changed its course half a dozen times or more over the course of the Southwest's history, blurring the lines between countries, states, and cultures as it flooded.

For El Pasoans, or *Paseños* as they are known in Spanish, the border is quite simply a way of life. It literally cuts in half the historic Pass of the North, creating two cities—El Paso and Ciudad Juárez—and the largest binational metroplex on earth. As you drive into El Paso on I-10 heading east, you are shocked with the expansive view of shanty homes rising crustily up along the desert mountains, providing the stark realization that there is Mexico, a literal stone's throw away.

In the 1960s, the Rio Grande border was finally put to rest with the Chamizal Convention Act of 1964. Mexico and America agreed on the final line, trenches were dug, concrete was poured, and the *Río* was put into its coffin, never to change course again. Bridges were erected to facilitate movement between the two cities—movement that was, for most of history, as fluid as the river's water that had to be crossed. The identities of the two cities were one, as were the metros themselves—joined like Siamese Twins of the Southwest.

OVERVIEW

The land that lies between the Gulf of Mexico and Baja California was first inhabited by a number of Native American societies. Later, Spaniards took ownership of this land, and then out of this mix came *Mestizos*, whose lifestyles mirrored their ancestry of combined Indian and Hispanic heritage. Finally, Anglo citizens of the U.S. arrived, bringing with them the English language and their ideas of land ownership, informed by commercial capital and manifest destiny. And so the Borderlands are usually thought of as composed of these main groups, who were landowners, former landowners, and workers. But the environment of *La Frontera* is one of opportunity that has attracted many other types of people, and their presence continues to transform the socio-cultural life of the region.

Here, then, is the difficulty that *Paseños* (and indeed all Texans that live along the border, as well as New Mexicans, Arizonans, and Southern Californians, and Mexican citizens on the other side) have always faced in understanding their cultural heritage. Are we Mexican? Spanish? Native American or Anglo? The answer is, of course, a mix of them all, if not ethnically then indeed culturally. Borderlands scholar Olivia Cadaval called El Paso and Ciudad Juárez a "crucible of cultural identities, in which shared border personas are created, exported, re-imported, and transformed." Some scholars even consider the Borderlands region to be the massive, confusing meeting point of Hispanic South American cultures and Anglo North American ones—the place on earth where this change in backgrounds, heritage, language, and culture takes place.

So, to understand what makes El Paso and its people tick, we must somehow take in the entire blend of backgrounds and heritage that has shaped the city, both good and bad, and let them be together in spirit and in practice. In truth, El Paso is a remarkable place where people of strongly different backgrounds live and let live, and where who you are is okay, no matter where you're from or what your outlook on life may be.

THE U.S.–MEXICO BORDER

According to the Migration Policy Institute (www.migrationpolicy.org), of the 11,000 Border Patrol officers working in the United States, 89 percent are stationed along the U.S.–Mexico Border—a strong indication of the sensitive situation that this lengthy strip of land actually presents. It has traditionally been an area of poverty, low income work in *maquiladoras* (duty-free assembly factories), industrial economies, and crime, and it is a place where, in recent years, drug violence has all but overtaken the local populations, especially in towns south of the border, and particularly in El Paso's next door neighbor, Ciudad Juárez. Although these problems tend to be less evident in El Paso itself, many of the more rural counties and towns along the border, known as *colonias* ("neighborhoods" in Spanish), face the harsh realities of life in substandard conditions without basic infrastructure, such as drinking water. Even though El Paso as a city does not face such issues today, the culture and attitude that is developed out of life in the *colonias* definitely pervades a part of the city's culture, and indeed the entire identity of the peoples that live along the U.S.–Mexico border.

At nearly 2,000 miles, *La Frontera* is the longest international border on the planet, and life here tends to be characterized by dichotomies and polarization: one of the most developed nations in the world versus one of the least, capitalism versus stark industrialization, violence versus peace and rich versus poor, and it is these dichotomies that make truly understanding an El Pasoan's identity and way of life nearly impossible. The fact is that, unless you are from here, you probably just won't get it—at least that is the way *Paseños* tend to perceive and interact with newcomers.

Historically, the cultural and economic conflict that still plagues the Borderlands can be traced to the decades following the

Mexican-American War (mid-1800s), when American cattle ranchers and other opportunists arrived from the East and Midwest and began to dominate U.S.–Mexican trade across the river. As they grew richer, these largely Anglo merchants started acquiring tracts of land and finally arrived at a situation where they exerted dominion over the earlier settlers of Spanish and Mexican descent. This created an environment of cultural and economic conflict that still characterizes the Borderlands and has further polarized society here for centuries.

i If you do a lot of business in Mexico or plan to cross into Ciudad Juárez (or other Mexican border towns) regularly, you may apply for a U.S. Passport Card—a wallet-sized passport substitute that grants the bearer access to cross to and from Mexico by land and sea ports-of-entry easily. The Passport Card cannot be used for air travel, however. More information, including an application, is available from www .travel.state.gov/passport.

Further complicating things has been the rise in the past decade of the drug cartels' power in Mexico and the extreme violence that has accompanied drug trafficking through the Juárez/El Paso ports. While the violence has largely been contained to south of the border, mostly because once the drug traffickers reach U.S. soil they prefer to stay undetected, its effects can still be felt in the Sun City. Many longtime Mexican residents of El Paso now refuse to go across the border, even for family events like funerals and weddings, where even 10 years ago, a trip to Juárez would have been a relaxed Sunday family outing. The weight of Juárez's

drug violence problem can be felt in a kind of eerie silence that sometimes overwhelms downtown El Paso on a weeknight—a feeling that there is no imminent danger but violence is only a sniff away.

One can only hope that the drug violence will dampen in coming days and years and that the symbiotic relationship that Ciudad Juárez and El Paso have historically maintained will be revived once again.

HISPANIC CULTURE

In the 2000 census, 80 percent of El Paso's population claimed to be of partial or total Hispanic descent, and much of El Paso's local culture, architecture, food, and surface identity can be derived from this fact. Make no mistake, Hispanic does not necessarily equal Mexican, but many El Pasoans do come from either direct or mixed Mexican descent. Mostly, though, Hispanic culture here has its own set of cultural metaphors that truly reflect the mixed heritage of Spanish and Mexican influences throughout history.

Traveling around El Paso, one of the first things you will notice is that many signs are in Spanish, and there is a prevalence of Spanish-language media here, too. While some who misunderstand the Borderlands consider this a recent development or a result of an imagined influx of people from south of the border, in fact, Spanish has always been the dominant language in the Borderlands region, and it was the English-speaking Anglos that arrived near the turn of the 20th century who brought a foreign language and culture with them. Truthfully, though, language, like most elements of cultural mixing here, is fluid. Most people speak both Spanish and English and use them for different purposes and to convey different feelings and ideas in context.

Hispanic culture is also evident in much of El Paso's artwork, including the many murals that color the city's vacant walls and concrete spaces. These murals depict the struggles of border life and are one of the most direct lines into the culture of El Paso. Recurring symbols in *los murales* include religious iconography handed down all the way from the Spanish, gang warfare and poverty that have stricken this part of the world for decades, feasts, and family time, as well as stark political statements about the harsh realities of life along *La Frontera*.

As you turn on your radio, dine in one of the city's finest restaurants, or meander through the shops downtown, you are likely to hear the cheerful rhythms of *la musica Norteña*. This "northern style music" developed in the 1830s and '40s out of Bohemian and immigrant influences derived from European polkas brought by miners and immigrant workers who arrived during the early 1800s. Tejano music, too, can be heard. This unique Tex-Mex style of music takes its name from a word that literally means "Texan of Spanish heritage," and was the music of pre-American settlers who formed the basis of the tunes from traveling ranch musicians who played flute, guitar, and drums. Tejano music sounds a little bit polka and a little bit mariachi, and often now incorporates an accordion—an obvious influence of the Northern European settlers who first came to Texas from the Czech Republic and Germany.

NATIVE AMERICAN INFLUENCE

Long before there were Anglos, Mexicans, or even Spaniards in El Paso, there were Native Americans who called the Pass of the North home. Some 8,000 years ago, a society of primitive hunters lived in the area around Hueco Tanks, finding refuge among the hollows there. They hunted large game with Folsom point arrowheads, which archaeologists have discovered all around the Hueco Bolson. An ancient village dating to 4,500 years ago was also discovered at the Keystone Archaeological Site (Keystone Heritage Park), at which time archaeologists believe that the local population had evolved from a society of mobile hunter-gatherers to sedentary farmers.

i To get a real understanding of the history and culture of the Ysleta del Sur pueblo, visit the Tigua Indian Cultural Center, located along the Mission Trail. Here, you'll explore a museum dedicated to Tigua history, peruse a number of native handmade items in the gift shop, and if you're lucky, catch a dance or song performance in the plaza. Find it at 305 Yaya Lane; (915) 859-7700, www.ysletadel surpueblo.org.

The next era of population saw Formative sedentary villages crop up sometime between 100 and 1100 AD, probably around the beginning of the Christian period in Europe. Evidence of this includes the ruins of small agricultural villages, many of which were pit houses that had structures belowground. Even early man knew the value of a basement! By 1200 AD, these so-called pit houses had developed into large villages with mazes of mud-constructed buildings, not unlike the Native American pueblos still in existence today. These peoples began the first cultivation of corn, beans, and squash that would become the foundation for Native American cuisine in the years to come. Then, suddenly, in 1400 AD, the El Paso area was completely abandoned.

When the first Europeans arrived some 1,500 years later, they did encounter Native American tribes: the hunter-gatherer Sumas, Mansos, Jocomes, and Jumanos. These tribes lived in what the Spanish termed *rancherías*—small villages that accommodated around 100 people. As the Spanish traveled north over the next two centuries, they would see a lot of contact with the tribes of northern New Mexico, including many that were quite friendly and welcomed Christianization, and others that were extremely hostile, namely the Mescalero Apaches, who were known for their aggressive tactics and tendency to war.

For decades, the Spanish and Native American tribes got along fairly well. Many of the Native tribes welcomed the Spanish, who offered them the chance to further develop their small villages and brought their native Catholic religion. The Spanish established missions (churches) for the Native Americans that they met and protected the tribes from warring tribes that might exploit them. However, as time wore on, some of the tribes—particularly those living under strict Spanish rule in the northern part of the New Mexico territory—became disgruntled and, in 1680, the tribes began to revolt in an uprising that has come to be known as the Pueblo Revolt of 1680. The revolt lasted several months, finally forcing the Spanish governors to flee south, taking with them the few tribes that were still loyal to them.

The journey south was a long and difficult one, but after six weeks, the Spanish and loyal tribes arrived to La Salineta, near modern day El Paso, establishing new missions and new tribal homelands for the fleeing Native groups, which included the tribes of Senecú, Socorro, Alamillo, Sevilleta and Tiwa.

And so El Paso's oldest missions were formed to cater to the Indian refugees who had left their homes in the north, and these three have remained in the area ever since, calling it home and going to great lengths in those early years to distinguish themselves from the tribes that had left. The Tiwa tribe from Isleta began using the Spanish terms *Ysleta* and *Tigua* to create their own identity in their new home. In 1680, the same year that they had fled the Pueblo Revolt, the Ysleta del Sur *pueblo* ("town" in Spanish) was established, its new name *del Sur* indicating they were the tribe "of the south." The Mision de Corpus Christi de San Antonio de la Ysleta del Sur, which stands today on Ysleta tribal lands southwest of downtown El Paso, is still the oldest continuously active parish in the state of Texas. Likewise, the Socorro Mission was founded by some 60 Piro Indian families of Socorro who were displaced after the 1680 Revolt. The third group, the Piros of Senecú, had moved south from their original home that had been located just north of where Elephant Butte Lake now sits in Central New Mexico, abandoning that entire pueblo and replanting near El Paso.

Despite Spain's insistence on keeping the groups segregated, Spanish settlers had begun intermarrying with local Christianized Indians, marking the beginnings of the mixed *Mestizo* populations, which are still an integral part of El Paso's cultural heritage today. The poor conditions, though, were too much for many of the settlers, who finally chose to flee the area, resulting in population drops throughout the 1690s. Nonetheless, the five settlements at the Pass of the North remained steadfastly intact throughout history.

Today, Ysleta del Sur is the only tribe that remains actively intact in El Paso. It also holds the distinction of being one of three federally recognized tribes in Texas, and the state's only pueblo. The tribe operates as a sovereign nation, with its own traditional government system, laws, and ceremonial practices. The tribe participates in the local economy by operating its own entertainment center and gas station and employs some 400 tribe members on pueblo lands. Visiting the Ysleta del Sur pueblo, you might encounter a ceremonial dance being performed in front of their sacred mission church, which was established in 1680—the year that the Tiguas arrived from the north—and is still the oldest continually active Catholic parish in Texas. This church marks the beginning of the Mission Trail, a historic sightseeing route that leads to the three missions that were constructed here for the relocated tribes in or after 1680. The Socorro Mission and the San Elizario Mission, established much later, are the other two sites along the trail. Of the other groups that relocated here, many Piro people still claim their ancestry and heritage but do not operate an active pueblo, while the Senecú tribe became part of Mexico during the Mexican Revolution in the early 1900s. This tribe formerly had a mission that would be, today, located along the Mission Trail if it had not been destroyed by the Rio Grande flood in 1832.

ACCOMMODATIONS

During your stay in El Paso, you'll find no shortage of accommodations. Hotels and motels are plentiful here, or if you have your own home on wheels, you'll find plenty of suitable RV parks to accommodate you. If you like the comfort of knowing just what to expect, you'll find plenty of national hotel and motel brands to choose from in El Paso. Conversely, if you're the type of traveler who prefers to stay in truly unusual accommodations that are unique to the local surrounds, you'll find a few hidden gems around the Sun City as well. The beautiful and historic El Camino Hotel downtown is almost as old as El Paso itself and is one of the city's premier places to stay. There is also a small selection of boutique hotels and historic motels, as well as plenty of clean, cozy national chains to choose from. Best of all? Accommodations in El Paso are cheap. Compared to other cities in Texas and around the country, you'll find you can book the perfect hotel room for a very reasonable price.

Where you choose to stay in El Paso depends largely on your purpose in the city. Are you visiting friends or just passing through? Are you on business here or being stationed at Fort Bliss? Is this purely a pleasure trip? Once you've figured out what your goals are, you can choose an area of town that best suits your needs. Listings for hotels and motels in this chapter have been provided by area of town, and additional sections are devoted solely to RV parks and budget options in El Paso. If you wish to be convenient to Fort Bliss, several hotels and motels are listed that give you the option to stay in the northeast part of the city. If you're sightseeing or prefer the ambiance of a luxury hotel, you'll find several options downtown. Most of the national chain hotels, which represent the best value for quality, are located along the major highways like I-10 and Loop 375, giving you easy access if you're driving through.

If you choose to stay downtown, be aware that parking can present a problem here, as many hotels do not have their own parking lots and merely suggest that you park on the street, which is fine for a few hours, but may be risky overnight. Top-end hotels, such as El Camino Hotel and the Doubletree, do have their own underground parking lots and offer free parking to guests. When in doubt, always double check before reserving if you're going to be driving.

Price Code

The following price code has been included to give you a rough idea of what one regular double occupancy room or overnight stay will cost at each of the following places. When choosing a hotel, it is important to bear in mind that costs can vary greatly from high season to low, so you may be pleasantly surprised to find a lower price when you actually go to make the reservation. Additionally, many of the hotels and accommodations listed here offer special rates and sales, so be sure to check around before you book.

$.................. Less than $70
$$ .... $70 to $100
$$$ .... $101 to $200
$$$$$ .... More than $200

HOTELS AND MOTELS
Central/Downtown

THE ARTISAN HOTEL $$–$$$
325 North Kansas St.
(915) 225-9100
www.artisanelpaso.com
El Paso's only boutique hotel, the Artisan Hotel is the picture of chic. Located right downtown, this deluxe hotel is artsy, cozy, and hip. The black tiled entrance creates an almost art deco feel, and as you enter the hotel, the first things you notice are paintings displayed prominently throughout the lobby, lounge, and even on the ceiling. Dim lighting and antique mirrors create an opulent atmosphere and as you check in, the "Mona Lisa" gives a wry look from behind the lobby desk. Every room here is themed, displaying works of master artists backset by wallpapers in richly lavish colors and atypical striped bedspreads. The hotel's Artisan Cafe and Lounge has a design inspired by the watering hole in Las Vegas which shares its namesake. The fifth floor pool will make you feel like you're in LA rather than El Paso, with incredible views of downtown from pillow topped sun chairs. Valet parking is available for a daily fee.

DOUBLETREE HOTEL $$$–$$$$
600 North El Paso St.
(866) 539-0036
http://doubletree1.hilton.com

This 3.5-star property is one of the few high rises that grace the skyline of downtown El Paso. Situated right on El Paso Street, from here you have the Golden Triangle shopping district and all of downtown on your front doorstep. The airy lobby is adorned with dark wood and leather lounge chairs, while the rooms boast large cushy beds contrasted against solid-colored accent walls for a clean, modern feel. Each room has a plasma TV and designer bathroom toiletries. A business-friendly hotel, the Doubletree has a business center and meeting rooms equipped with all of the standard audio/visual equipment, as well as free Wi-Fi Internet throughout the hotel. Or, if you're just here to play, there is also a nice indoor pool and a fitness facility that overlooks downtown El Paso through a large picture window. The Liquid Bar, an outdoor rooftop bar, is one of the cooler features of the hotel, and often attracts locals who come in for an evening of swanky cocktails with a nice view. A complimentary airport shuttle is available on request, as well as a complimentary area shuttle within 3 miles and a train station pickup service. Free parking is offered in an underground garage.

HILTON GARDEN INN $$
111 West University Ave.
(915) 351-2121
www.hiltongardeninn.com
UTEP parents and sports fans love this hotel because it is located on the southeast corner of the UTEP campus and is within walking distance to the entire campus, including the Don Haskins Center and Sun Bowl Stadium. If you're a proud parent coming to watch your child graduate from UTEP or are here to catch a Miners football game, this is the place to stay. As you approach the hotel, you'll notice that it is designed with the

ACCOMMODATIONS

same Bhutanese-style architecture as many of the buildings on UTEP's campus. Inside, you'll find a cleanly decorated front lobby with slate floors and pleasant, bright, comfy guest rooms. The outdoor pool is lined with palm trees and overlooks downtown El Paso, providing a nice space to unwind under the El Paso sun, and there is a fitness center equipped with several weight machines and treadmills. Some 40 restaurants, bars, and nightclubs are located within walking distance along the Cincinnati Avenue Entertainment District, so this is also a good hotel option if you're traveling on a budget and want to explore El Paso's nightlife. On site, the Great American Grill serves breakfast, lunch, and dinner, with both indoor and outdoor seating. Self-parking is available in a number of outdoor and covered spaces around the hotel.

**HOLIDAY INN EXPRESS
CENTRAL** $$$
409 East Missouri Ave.
(915) 544-3333
www.hiexpress.com
The peach and yellow exterior of this brightly painted downtown hotel is hard to miss. A nine-story high rise, it is very centrally located with easy access to all the downtown shopping areas and the Mexican border. The rooms here are fairly spacious, with either a king size bed or double queen beds available, 25-inch TVs, in-room coffee, and other standard amenities. There is an included free breakfast that takes place in a rather drab breakfast room off the lobby, and the smallish outdoor pool, though well-kept, is nothing to write home about. The hotel offers a complimentary shuttle to the Juárez border, the airport, and other transportation terminals. Free parking is available to guests

in a large outdoor parking lot. Though certainly not the best value downtown, this is a good option if everything else is full.

Westside

BEST WESTERN—OASIS OF SUN $$
9401 South Desert Blvd.
(915) 886-3333
www.bestwestern.com
Snuggled on the border of Texas and New Mexico, this Anthony hotel has basic amenities typical of the Best Western name. Clean and comfortable, the Oasis of Sun is only 19 miles from Las Cruces, New Mexico and 23 miles from downtown El Paso, providing easy access to nearby recreation areas and points of interest in the Franklin Mountains and Mesilla Valley. The hotel was recently renovated, and each room includes a microwave, refrigerator, free high-speed Internet access, a workspace, and cable television. Upgraded whirlpool rooms are also available. A complimentary full breakfast and free copy of *USA Today* are provided during your stay, and recreation amenities include an on-site fitness center, swimming pool, and hot tub.

COMFORT SUITES $$
949 Sunland Park Dr.
(915) 587-5300
www.comfortsuites.com
Although touting itself as "Comfort Suites University," this hotel is several miles away from UTEP on the Westside. An all-suite hotel, the rooms here are spacious for the price, most with a microwave, refrigerator and DVD player. A stay here includes a free continental breakfast, a copy of *USA Today*, and access to a basic indoor pool and spa. They also have a business center with a free computer kiosk, as well as copy, fax, and

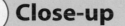 **Close-up**

Old World El Paso at the Camino Real

As soon as you step into the Camino Real Hotel in downtown El Paso, you know that it has history. Established in 1912, this landmark is located in the heart of El Paso's revitalized downtown area, adjacent to the convention center and the Plaza Theater. In many ways, the Camino Real is a shining testament to the city's colorful past and vibrant future. Listed in the National Historic Register, this hotel is classically beautiful, from the most photographed grand staircase in the Southwest and the exquisite crystal chandeliers in the lobby and ballrooms to the marble installed by skilled Italian craftsmen almost a hundred years ago. The hotel and particularly the Dome Bar inside are tourist must-sees in and of themselves. Wander in to the circular bar, past the lobby desk, and look up. The extraordinary Tiffany cut glass dome, 25 feet in diameter and suspended by wires, sheds a colorful halo of light over the historic circular wooden bar. You can almost imagine cowboys and outlaws of the olden days ponying up here for a whiskey.

The hotel's builder, Zach T. White, was drawn to El Paso by its magical name, "Pass of the North." After the Gran Central Hotel, which stood on the site of the present day Mills Building, burned in 1892, White dreamed of building an elegant hotel that would be both the center of El Paso social life and a gathering place for tourists. Together with local architectural firm, Trost and Trost, a structurally sound and fireproof design for the hotel was formed of brick, steel, and terra cotta, with the interior walls made of gypsum from the nearby White Sands National Monument. The hotel was built at a cost of $1.5 million and christened the Hotel Paso del Norte, opening on Thanksgiving Day 1912 with a lavish ball.

No detail was spared in the construction of the elegant hotel. The cherrystone, golden scagliola, and black serpentine marble features that grace the lobby, mezzanine, and dining rooms were installed by Italian artisans. Twelve gold leaf cages with live parakeets adorned pillars in the main dining area, and the Tiffany glass dome, still in place today, crowned the lobby. All woodwork was solid mahogany. In its early days, the hotel supported its own bakery, ice factory, butcher shop, laundry, and a lavishly stocked bar. A ballroom and patio on the roof were the scene of many dinner dances and Sunday tea parties, and during the Mexican Revolution, many locals gathered there to watch the gunfire just a few miles across the border. In time, the hotel became the headquarters for cattlemen and ranchers, and legend has it that more heads of cattle were bought and sold in the lobby than at any other single location in the world. The hotel remained in the White family until 1970, when TGK Investment Co. Ltd. bought it and promised to refurbish and modernize it, while preserving the Western atmosphere. Over the years, the hotel has undergone several renovations, including the addition of the 17-story tower in 1986 and a $4.2 million renovation in mid-2004.

Today, the Camino Real offers 359 Texas-sized rooms and suites, and often does great specials that can make a room here affordable even if you haven't got lots of cash to blow. The rooms have a genuine historic feel and are absolutely massive—twice the size of most modern hotel rooms, even for a standard king. In addition to a beautiful stay, guests can enjoy the taste of regional Mexican cuisine in Azulejos, an on-site restaurant, or indulge their tastebuds in the extremely elegant Dome Restaurant. Parking is available in the Camino's underground lot for a fee and complimentary Wi-Fi Internet is provided in all the guest rooms. 101 South El Paso St.; (915) 534-3000; www.caminoreal.com; $$$–$$$$.

printing services. This hotel is a good option for access to local points of interest on the Westside, like Sunland Park Racetrack and Casino and Sun Bowl Stadium , and nearby dining options include Olive Garden, Red Lobster, and TGI Friday's.

HAMPTON INN & SUITES WEST $$
6411 South Desert Blvd.
(915) 833-7000
http://hamptoninn1.hilton.com

Like most Hampton Inns, this hotel is clean and basic. Its 139 rooms are sparsely decorated and have cable TV with movies and clean bathrooms. If you're looking for a bit more luxury, you can opt for one of the hotel's one- and two-room suites, which include refrigerators and microwaves. There is a basic selection of meeting rooms, a small outdoor pool, a fitness room, and a gift shop. A complimentary continental breakfast comes with the price of the room and there is free on-site parking around the hotel's perimeter. The hotel's courtesy car will take you to sights and restaurants within a several mile radius, as well. Dining options nearby include Landry's Seafood, Jaxon's Brewpub, Forti's Mexican, and several others.

HOWARD JOHNSON INN $
8887 Gateway West
(915) 591-9471
www.hojoelpaso.com

This is a barebones hotel with prices to match, and even in the high season you'll be able to find a room here to fit your budget. The 120 rooms come in two different types here: a standard room with either two queen beds or a king bed, and a deluxe room that is among their "home office" rooms with a large work desk and chair for business travelers. All of the standard amenities are on offer here, and pets are welcomed. Located nearby is a large shopping mall, as well as several dining options, including Olive Garden, Cattle Baron, Hooters, and Landry's Seafood & Steakhouse.

LA QUINTA INN BARTLETT $
7620 North Mesa St.
(915) 585-2999
www.lq.com

The 102 cheap and cheerful guest rooms at La Quinta Inn Bartlett may just be one of the best bargains in El Paso. Sunny and uncomplicated, this hotel has a number of room options, from a basic double room to a deluxe king suite with a microwave and refrigerator. There is a heated outdoor pool surrounded by a large sundeck, and Nintendo gaming systems are available upon request. If you are a business traveler, this hotel is convenient to the Mesilla Valley Training Institute, Hoover, Compumedics, Cingular Wireless, and Vista Corrugated. There is ample free parking and the hotel sits adjacent to a Chili's Bar & Grill, with Famous Dave's and the Ranchers Grill not far away.

SPRINGHILL SUITES $$$
7518 Remcon Circle
(915) 845-7400
www.marriott.com/elpse

Operated by Marriott, this chain hotel is located just off of I-10 on the Westside, on a circular loop adjacent to a Wal-Mart. All 103 rooms are studio suites that feature a pantry and small kitchen area. There are two types of suites: a larger queen studio with two queen beds and a sofa bed, or a slightly smaller king suite with a king bed and a sofa bed. In both rooms, spacious living areas are separated from the bedroom by a partial wall. Most notably, the decor is colorful and modern, in contrast to many of the more drab business hotels. A number of dining options are nearby, including Leo's Mexican Restaurant next door.

STUDIO PLUS $$
990 Sunland Park Dr.
(915) 833-7731
www.studioplus.com

If you plan to be on the road for awhile, this hotel is a decent option because it is designed for longer stays, and each of the 73 rooms is a suite that features a separate kitchen with a miniature stovetop where you can cook homemade meals. You can even request a room with a dishwasher to totally complete the home experience, and unlike many hotels these days, Studio Plus still offers a few smoking rooms. The property also has a swimming pool and a fitness center, as well as free parking. While the location is nothing special, a number of popular dining options are located just across I-10 near the Sunland Park Mall, including PF Chang's China Bistro, Red Lobster, and others.

WINGATE BY WYNDHAM $$$-$$$$
6351 Gateway West
(915) 772-4000
www.elpasowingate.com

Located right along I-10 near Geronimo drive, the best thing about this hotel is its location not far from the airport. With an emphasis on modernity, the hotel's rooms are decorated with contemporary furnishings and outfitted with all the most high-tech amenities, such as free Wi-Fi Internet, lighted work desks and premium cable. If you're looking for something a little more luxurious, they also offer a few "choice" suite rooms which have huge garden tubs and separate areas for working and relaxing. The

hotel offers a full range of recreation options and a free breakfast, and there is ample free parking in both covered and open spaces around the hotel. Taco Cabana, a fast food restaurant, is located next door.

Eastside

COMFORT INN AIRPORT EAST $$
900 North Yarbrough Dr.
(915) 594-9111
www.comfortinn.com

Despite its name, this hotel is located several miles from the El Paso airport along I-10 on the Eastside. With 200 rooms, this hotel has all the basic but convenient elements that you would expect from a Comfort Inn. All of the rooms feature a computer port and cable, with the unexpected bonus of a Nintendo gaming system, while several of the more deluxe rooms also have refrigerators, microwaves, work desks, and whirlpool baths. The decor of the rooms leaves a little to be desired, but for the price, it is extremely comfortable and clean. On the property there is an outdoor pool with a few sparse palm trees and a tiny hot tub. Complimentary breakfast is offered each morning and there is a free airport shuttle and plenty of parking. Next door are several restaurants, such as Rudy's Country Store & BBQ and Lin's Chinese Buffet.

DAYS INN EAST $
10635 Gateway West
(915) 595-1913
www.daysinn.com

Days Inn is a solid option for weary travelers on a budget who just need a basic room to sleep in. Even in high season, rooms here are not expensive, and the style and size of the 122 rooms reflect the reasonable price. All of the rooms open onto exterior corridors, many overlooking the sheepish swimming pool and its retro patio furnishings. However basic, though, you can expect a clean room and a free breakfast in the bright lobby breakfast room. There is plenty of free parking here and the hotel is just a stone's throw from a Wal-Mart Supercenter and several restaurants, such as Texas Roadhouse.

RAMADA INN & SUITES $-$$
8250 Gateway East
(915) 591-9600
www.ramada.com
If you are looking for a little more luxury that won't break the bank, the Ramada Inn & Suites represents a surprisingly good deal for the price. This recently renovated hotel features 124 rooms, all of which are suites. One of the best features of the new rooms are the comfortable mattresses and modern showers, and be sure to look out for the nice toiletries provided in the bathrooms. There are two types of rooms on offer with either a king bed or two double beds. Ramada does a decent but unremarkable free continental breakfast each morning from 6 to 10 a.m., and there is free Wi-Fi Internet throughout the hotel, including in every room. Recreational features include a rather austere outdoor pool and an exercise room with a few windows that have nice views of the city. A number of restaurants are nearby, including Denny's, Tony Roma's, and Cheddars.

SLEEP INN $-$$$
5640 East Paisano Dr.
(915) 775-9880
www.sleepinn.com
For a basic chain hotel, this Sleep Inn has a bit more pizzazz. Though self-titled as a "university" hotel, the Sleep Inn is still a few miles from UTEP. The decor in the rooms is stylish,

with gold bedding, rich red carpeting, and unique wall hangings. The standard rooms are small but liveable, while the suites have an additional blandly colored sofa bed and a small desk, separated from the sleeping area by a partial wall. You can also request a deluxe room that has a whirlpool bath, which is strangely placed right in the room, where the sofa would be in one of the suites. Other freebies here include a continental breakfast and Wi-Fi Internet,, and access to a nearby full-service health club, which is a nice addition if you're trying to stay fit while you're traveling. On-site, there is a small but clean outdoor pool with connected hot tub. Nearby dining options are sparse if you don't have a car, but there is a Popeye's Chicken across the street if you're desperate.

Airport

CHASE SUITES HOTEL $$-$$$
6791 Montana Ave.
(915) 772-8000
www.chasehotelelpaso.com
This is a true airport hotel that doesn't feel like one at all. While it's just half a mile from El Paso airport, once inside the rooms of this all-suite hotel, you'll feel right at home. Both inside and out, Chase Suites seems more like an apartment complex, distinguished by a series of meandering walkways that connect the staircased entrances, which are lit with iron lampposts. Inside, the rooms have small full kitchens that look and feel like those in a real apartment, rather than a hotel's attempt at an in-room kitchen. The large bedrooms have colorful paintings and luxury bedding, while the living rooms have vaulted ceilings and corner windows that suggest anything but "hotel." Two types of rooms are available here: a classic studio suite on one level and a split-level two-bedroom loft. Working wood

fireplaces complete the warming experience here and make you feel like you're right at home. Most surprising about this hotel are the prices, which seem like they should be more expensive for what is on offer.

Outside of the normal breakfast and coffee amenities, the hotel hosts a weekly manager's reception, and weeknight happy hours. For corporate travelers, fully equipped meeting rooms and express office bars with computer terminals and printers are available, and the property has free Wi-Fi access throughout. Two outdoor pools, a basketball court, and barbecue areas are all on site, and guests are given free access to the nearby Powerhouse Gym.

Among other amenities, the staff here provides a complimentary grocery shopping service to help fill the full-sized fridge in your suite, as well as a free shuttle service to local areas within a 3-mile radius. Nearby eating options include Cattle Baron and Applebee's one block away, and Dominic's Italian next door.

CORAL MOTEL $
6420 Montana Ave.
(915) 772-3263
www.coralmotel.net

If you're looking for a truly retro Southwest motel experience, look no further than the Coral Motel. In business for over 30 years, the Coral offers clean accommodation decorated in the Spanish style that is so unique to the El Paso area. The owners and staff of the Coral might just be some of the friendliest around, too. Don't come expecting any extras like bathroom toiletries, but what you will get is a clean, spacious room in a wonderfully restored, classic kitschy motel next to the El Paso airport. The rooms are located along a one-level corridor strip where you

can drive up to your door, and inside you'll find two queen-size beds and a wealth of charming old 1950s decor. You can also request a room with a fridge, microwave, and sofa.

During your stay, look out for some of the wonderfully retro details around the property, like the tile mosaics located on some of the outer walls and the Mexican floral detailing on the doors. Free Wi-Fi Internet is available throughout the motel. The Coral is located about 10 minutes' drive from downtown El Paso, along an old U.S. highway strip that is full of great restaurants that are seemingly unchanged since 1955, serving excellent Texas-style barbecue, Tex-Mex, and American comfort food. Considering the dirt cheap prices and unique El Paso feel of the place, the Coral is definitely one of the coolest spots to stay in the city.

i If you're planning to stay at the Coral Motel, check their Web site, which, at the time of writing, featured a printable coupon for an even cheaper overnight rate.

COURTYARD BY MARRIOTT $$-$$$
6610 International Dr.
(915) 772-5000
www.marriott.com

This 90-room Courtyard has pretty much everything you might expect from the Marriott name. Though there are definitely better bargains to be had elsewhere in El Paso, for many, the quality and reliability of a Marriott hotel can't be beat. Among the rooms on offer here are standard king and queen bed rooms, a spa king room with a whirlpool bath that fits two, and a king suite that sleeps four people and has two TVs. The lobby and decor here are nothing special, with an average assortment of green carpeting and wood and marble fixtures, but the service is friendly and the rooms are clean. The property also houses an outdoor pool and a fitness center, free parking, complimentary newspapers, and a variety of the standard business and meeting facilities. The Courtyard Café provides an on-site (but not free) breakfast, while nearby dining options include Dominguez Mexican, Jaxon's Brewpub, and more.

EXTENDED STAY AMERICA $–$$
6580 Montana Ave.
(915) 772-5754
www.extendedstayamerica.com
The best thing about this non-descript suite hotel is its location across the street from the Lucchese Cowboy Boot outlet. As its name suggests, Extended Stay America is designed with long-term travelers in mind, and all of the rooms are suites with studio layouts. Prices here are extremely reasonable, especially for suites, but the decor is an unmemorable and unfortunate brown. However, the studios do offer the convenience of full kitchens with a refrigerator, microwave, utensils, and a stovetop, as well as plenty of workspace.. The rooms also have fairly comfy recliners and complimentary movie channels. Parking is free but the wireless Internet is not, and at a steep $4.99 per stay, you may want to rethink your options if your trip is short.

There are few dining options nearby with the exception of Dos Nidos Mexican Café, which is a short walk away.

GUESTHOUSE SUITES $$–$$$
1940 Airway Blvd.
(915) 772-0395
www.elpasoguesthouse.com

Perhaps the most unique thing on offer at this all-suite hotel, which is just a mile from El Paso airport, are a number of special package deals that include a weekend pizza package, the Stay Park N Fly package that allows you to leave your vehicle overnight if you've stayed at least one night, a Sunland Park Racetrack & Casino package for gamblers, and the Stay N Play for One, which includes a reserved tee time at Butterfield Trail Golf Club. There are a number of different bed options available and the hotel emphasizes its Accessibility Rooms, which are designed for handicap access. Though the decor in the rooms is bland, the layout is cozy, with a unique island kitchenette separating the living and sleeping spaces. The addition of a four-seat dining table is particularly useful, and the plain but comfortable couches and coffee tables in each room provide a small measure of homey feel.

HAWTHORN INN & SUITES $–$$$
6789 Boeing St.
(915) 778-6789
www.hawthorn.com
A great option for overnight travelers or anyone that has an early plane to catch, the 191 rooms at Hawthorn Suites are about as close to the airport as you can get.

Touting itself as an "affordable extended stay hotel," this chain is run by Wyndham and shares a parking lot with two restaurants. This hotel offers 18 suites with kitchens and balconies, six of which boast working fireplaces, although the decor and furnishings are a bit outdated. Every room has free Wi-Fi and, among the nicer features of the rooms are the sweet breakfast bars with stools. There is a complimentary shuttle service that runs to and from the terminal regularly, and a variety of other standard amenities from a business center to fitness options.

Monday through Thursday there is a Manager's Reception featuring snacks, beverages, and a mini meal on Wednesday, and weeknights from 5 to 7 p.m. there is a happy hour. There is plenty of free parking, as well as a courtesy car that will take you to nearby places if you wish to get out and see a bit of El Paso. In the parking lot of this inn you'll find Cattle Baron and Applebee's, and other nearby dining options include Chili's Bar & Grill and Village Inn.

HOLIDAY INN AIRPORT $$–$$$
6655 Gateway West
(915) 778-6411
www.hielpasoairport.com
The most striking thing about this Holiday Inn is the airy lobby, which is decked out in colorful Southwestern decor. From large geometric patterned area rugs to the cartoonish cowboys and Indians mural depicting El Paso's history on one wall, you will definitely know you're in the Southwest when staying here. The rooms, too, feature Southwestern motifs, with the superior rooms being extremely large and featuring floor-to-ceiling windows along one side that provide quite a lot of light. Perhaps the best aspect of a stay in this hotel is the chance to participate in one of the weekly activities that are offered, such as Tequila Tasting Class, How to Make the Perfect Margarita, and Salsa Dancing Lessons.

Among the more standard amenities on offer here are a morning paper that is delivered to your door, high-speed Internet, and in-room coffee makers. There are also two pools here: an indoor/outdoor pool with a swim-under window and an indoor hot tub, as well as an outdoor pool with green umbrellas and plenty of leafy trees offering shade during the summer months.

In the lobby, you can enjoy a meal or cocktail in the Atrium Bar, the name of which reflects the hotel's high ceilings and bright airy space. Two other dining and drinking options are located on site: Teddy's Lounge and the Cactus Rose Grill.

HYATT PLACE $$
6030 Gateway East
(915) 771-0022
www.elpasoairport.place.hyatt.com
Of all the chain hotels on offer in El Paso, this one wins for interior décor, with a warm design that looks and feels more like a boutique hotel than a national chain. . All 111 of the rooms have an Asian-inspired design that incorporates soft lighting and matte furnishings. A Japanese-style screen forms the partial wall that separates the bedroom from the living area, which is equipped with a flat screen HDTV. One unique and useful feature of this hotel is the plug panel, which gives you a variety of ways to plug your media into the TV. The entire hotel is covered in free Wi-Fi Internet and the lobby also houses a cute grab-and-go area, where you can get a Starbucks espresso or a muffin, and there is also a 24-hour guest kitchen that cooks made-to-order dishes, which is a nice option if you're arriving late and just want a fresh meal. The hotel also has a fitness center, outdoor swimming pool, and an e-room with complimentary computers and a printer. Free parking and an airport shuttle are both offered, as well. Just a short walk away, you will find El Nido Mexican Restaurant.

MARRIOTT HOTEL $$–$$$
1600 Airway Blvd.
(915) 779-3300
www.marriott.com

This Marriott recently underwent a multi-million-dollar renovation and it shows. The decor is fully updated, with cushy beds, sleek furniture, and tasteful carpeting. There are two room options: a standard king or double room, or a concierge level room. If you stay on this deluxe floor, you get the added bonus of a lounge, which offers cocktails and business services, but with little else on offer, it hardly seems worthwhile for the extra price. As with most luxury chain hotels, this Marriott delivers a newspaper to your door and has an unremarkable selection of onsite dining options, including a bistro and a sports bar. The standard group of indoor/outdoor pool, sauna, whirlpool, and exercise facility are available, with the pleasant addition of a spa offering a small menu of facials and massages. The only trouble with Marriott is the myriad of extra fees that you encounter—cocktails and business services cost extra, even on the Concierge Floor, and the Internet is not complimentary, which seems shocking when so many hotels these days have jumped on the bandwagon of offering free Wi-Fi to their guests.

RADISSON SUITE HOTEL $$$
1770 Airway Blvd.
(915) 772-3333
www.radisson.com
This hotel is situated just south of El Paso Airport's long term parking lot, making it one of the closest options for accommodation available to air travelers in the Sun City. There are 239 standard or deluxe studio suites, as well as one-bedroom suites, on offer here, but unfortunately, the decor in the rooms seems sparse and slightly dated. The rooms feature either a king bed or two full beds, as well as an in-room coffee station, mini-fridge, microwave, and DVD player, and for busi-

ness travelers, there is an ample work desk and free high-speed Internet throughout the hotel. Radisson's "Print Me" functionality, which allows you to print documents using the local network, can be convenient.

Other amenities on offer at the Radisson include a quaint outdoor swimming pool surrounded by cabana umbrellas, a fairly sizeable exercise room that includes weight machines and several treadmills, and a completely undecorated small indoor pool and hot tub. A complimentary shuttle goes to and from the airport terminal and to other sites within a 3-mile radius.

There is a nightly manager's reception from 4 to 7 p.m. in the hotel lounge, which welcomes guests with free cocktails and snacks, and on-site dining is available in Olive's Restaurant, which offers a free breakfast for up to two registered hotel guests. Adjacent restaurants include Cattle Baron Steak House and Applebee's.

WYNDHAM EL PASO AIRPORT $$–$$$
2027 Airway Blvd.
(915) 778-4241
www.wyndham.com/hotels/elpht
There are two things to recommend this Wyndham: its proximity to the airport and its on-site waterpark! There is no other hotel closer to the El Paso airport terminal than this one, which is nearly within walking distance of the terminal; though, of course, there is a free shuttle back and forth between the terminal building and the hotel. Bright and clean, this hotel has a classic feel that helps detract from the fact that you're sleeping next door to the airport tarmac. The best features are outdoors, though, with a leafy tropical style pool area where a 200-foot waterslide rockets into a small, dedicated

kiddie pool. There are 121 rooms overlooking the green courtyard, while all of the other rooms are "Club Level" two-room suites on a key access only floor. Guests on this level are invited to evening hors d'oeuvres, and they are also the only ones in the hotel that receive a free breakfast. The property is covered with free Wi-Fi Internet, and there are also two specialty suites that feature a full-sized Jacuzzi in a separate room.

In the lobby, there are a number of plush red sofas and area rugs that cozy up to a shiny black grand piano, giving the whole room an airy, classic feel. Dining options here include Magnim's Restaurant, which serves international and Southwestern style cuisine, and Magnim's Lounge, a sleek steely bar that has regular happy hour specials. Also on-site are a salon, a gift shop, and a 24-hour business center.

Fort Bliss

ARMED SERVICES YMCA HOTEL
7060 Comington St.
(915) 562-8461
www.asymcaelpaso.com
The Armed Services YMCA (ASYMCA) is a non-profit organization and a national member association of the YMCA that works with the Department of Defense to provide support services to military service members and retirees, veterans, and their families. The ASYMCA's El Paso branch operates a hotel and accommodation services for servicemen and women and their families who are visiting or relocating to Fort Bliss. Their aim is to provide you with a clean, safe, and distinctive stay at minimal cost. The 52 rooms at this ASYMCA hotel, 14 of which are pet friendly rooms, are basic but comfortable, with king size beds in each single room. In addition, each room comes with a private bath and is

fully carpeted. All of the rooms have Internet service, coffee makers, microwaves, cable TV, and a refrigerator, and several rooms are available with a kitchenette. Every morning, a local newspaper will be delivered to your room, and there are complimentary copy and fax services located inside the hotel, in case you need to send an e-mail or take care of some paperwork. The hotel has ample free parking and an outdoor basketball court. Guests are treated to a continental breakfast each morning. Guests of all kinds are welcomed to the hotel, including active duty military and their families, retirees, veterans, and civilians.

11 AM FORT BLISS LODGING
www.blissmwr.com/lodging
Fort Bliss Lodging Services is a department of Family and Morale, Welfare and Recreation on Fort Bliss. They have several lodging facilities throughout the post for your stay at Fort Bliss. You can have your choice of one of the Southwestern designed rooms, available with double, queen, or king-size beds, each of which is equipped with a microwave, a mini-refrigerator, an in-room coffee station, and ironing necessities to make your stay feel more like home. The executive suite is available for those looking for a relaxing atmosphere with a luxurious feel and features a work desk, PC hook-up, and dial-up online access. A centralized front desk operation provides check-in and check-out services for soldiers with PCS or TYD travel orders, as well as unofficial travelers. Located just a block away from the PX and Commissary areas, this central check-in office is extremely convenient and can get you settled into any of the comfortable rooms on base. Here, you'll also find a lobby with a magnificent courtyard, an outdoor swim-

ming pool, and a fitness room. There is also a playground area for the children and a business center with computers, printers, and a copy machine, and there is free Wi-Fi Internet in the lobby and Pace Hall. One handy feature is the free DVD check-out station. Fort Bliss Lodging also offers an afternoon movie matinee every Saturday at noon in the lobby of the Inn at Fort Bliss. Guests are treated to a movie and free popcorn, and are welcome to bring their own snacks.

They also operate a free shuttle service to and from El Paso airport seven days a week from 7 a.m. to 11 p.m.

BED AND BREAKFASTS

CASA DE SUEÑOS $$$
405 Mountain Vista Rd. South
La Union, NM
(575) 874-9164
www.casaofdreams.com

With a name that means "house of dreams" in Spanish, Casa de Sueños touts itself as "a touch of Santa Fe just outside El Paso." With all the Southwest charm that you'd expect from a local bed and breakfast, Casa de Sueños is a hacienda-style home with four guest rooms available. This adobe ranch house is decorated in quaint Southwestern themes, and the tiled floors and wooden furnishings that welcome you upon entering give it an authentically rustic feel. Much of the decor centers around the mythology of the Mimbres Indians, who were indigenous to the southwestern portion of New Mexico. Outside, a shaded center courtyard is surrounded by a variety of desert plant life and old wagon wheels are propped against the uneven stone wall.

Casa de Sueños sits on a high mesa overlooking the Rio Grande River Valley.

Three sets of mountain ranges—in New Mexico, Texas, and Mexico—are visible from the expansive guest patio. The nighttime views of twinkling city lights and the swath of stars among the Milky Way Galaxy overhead are unforgettable. Guests can relax on the glider or swing on the patio, with a latte in hand, and watch the sunrise or the moon rising over the Franklin Mountains. The stillness and quiet of the rural surroundings provide a wonderful rest after the end of a long cross-country trek or a hectic day of work. A Meditation Circle, based upon the indigenous people's Medicine Wheel design, sits off off the back patio, which overlooks the dusty *arroyo*. This sweet casa isn't all rustic, though. The guest house is covered in Wi-Fi Internet that is available free to guests, while Abi and Peanut, the happy resident concierge dogs, welcome guests with wagging tails and a tour of the grounds.

Of course, the guest rooms are the central attraction of Casa de Sueños. Each of the four boasts a Spanish name—Pajaritos, Oso, Kokopelli, and Tortugas—and is decorated with unique Southwestern decor and wooden furnishings. Two of the rooms, Pajaritos and Oso, are located in the guesthouse and offer much seclusion, each with a large four-poster queen bed, rawhide lamps, and unique wall hangings. The other two rooms are more centrally located in the main house. Kokopelli is a two-room suite with a king bed, rocking chairs, and a dresser in the main room, and a small single bed in an adjoining alcove. The last of the four, Tortugas, is the smallest of them, with a queen bed and a shared living space with the suite.

Casa de Sueños has an ideal location that provides the feeling of seclusion while still being connected to the metro area. It is situated about 12 miles from downtown

El Paso, so exciting nightlife, restaurants, shopping, and sightseeing, as well as air and train connections, are just a short drive away. Meanwhile, the full experience of rural desert life is the point of a stay at the bed and breakfast, and it certainly delivers just that.

HILLTOP HACIENDA $$$
2600 Westmoreland Ave.
Las Cruces, NM
(575) 382-3556
www.zianet.com/hilltop

Located a few miles north of Las Cruces, New Mexico, this secluded, romantic retreat is not exactly proximal to El Paso, but it's completely worth the drive. The property sits on 18 acres overlooking the Las Cruces basin, and the patios that surround the house offer 360-degree views of mountains and valleys. The inn itself is a unique two-story arched adobe brick home with three guest rooms on offer. Each of the rooms has a distinctly homey feel, with country wallpaper, floral bedspreads, and antique furnishings, but the overall atmosphere at Hilltop Hacienda is more luxurious than rustic. All of the rooms have their own ensuite baths that are more like the bathrooms you would find in a fancy home than a hotel, decorated with luscious hand soaps, seashells, and fresh flowers. All visitors have access to a cozy living area with a TV, movie library, and a library of Southwestern books, and every room has a view of the surrounding gardens.

The true stars here are the decadent gardens that encircle the house. Colorful flowers spring up through a sea of green plants and trees of all kinds. A rose garden offers a meandering path that makes for a romantic walk. Guests often walk along graveled garden paths where they are greeted by the local wildlife: hummingbirds, quail,

roadrunners, and an occasional jackrabbit. A variety of delicate patio tables and benches offer a few moments of repose among the gorgeous plants and make for a good place to dig into one of the inn's offered books. Along one side, a stunning upper level patio breezeway is fitted with comfy deck chairs and provides amazing views of the surrounding desertscape through a series of brick archways.

A stay here includes a full country breakfast every day, which is served either in the sunny dining room or outside on the terraces when weather permits. There is also a fully equipped private kitchen available, in case you would like to cook your own meals. Free Wi-Fi Internet is also offered throughout the inn.

Hilltop Hacienda is located about 5 miles northeast of Las Cruces, New Mexico at the foot of the Organ Mountains. A drive to El Paso from here would take about half an hour, and many amenities are also available in the city of Las Cruces. If you choose to stay here and wish to drive to El Paso, consider taking NM 28 as an alternative to I-10, which travels through the scenic Mesilla Valley.

SUNSET HEIGHTS INN $$$
717 West Yandell Ave.
(915) 544-1743

This charming Victorian inn is the only bed and breakfast of its kind actually located in El Paso. Situated in the historic Sunset Heights neighborhood at the base of the Franklin Mountains, this bed and breakfast is within walking distance of downtown El Paso and the University of Texas, and makes a great base for exploring the Sunset Heights neighborhood, a fantastic collection of Victorian homes. The house itself is a wonderful example of the architecture of its time, and offers a quiet and secluded alternative to the bustle of El Paso's more conventional accommodation options. With four guest rooms available, it is the intricacies of this inn that make it charming and also mean that nothing is exactly standardized here. Expect homey mattresses, rustic furnishings, and unusual decor, all of which come together to create a wonderfully cozy atmosphere. From the outside, the three-story house sits on beautifully landscaped lawns, with cute gabled windows and a number of lush palm trees welcoming you into the front door. An outdoor pool and hot tub are available for guests to use and the proprietress upon request will cook a gourmet evening meal at a reasonable price.

BUDGET OPTIONS

GARDNER HOTEL AND EL PASO YOUTH HOSTEL $–$$
311 East Franklin Ave.
(915) 532-3661
www.gardnerhotel.com
www.elpasohostel.com

Although these two are often listed as separate accommodations, and they have separate Web sites, the Gardner Hotel and El Paso Youth Hostel are more or less one and the same. Situated in the same building, which is in fact the oldest continually operating hotel in the city of El Paso, you can either book into the hotel or the hostel and are roomed accordingly. The hotel costs more and is situated on a different set of floors than the hostel (which is El Paso's only), and many of the rooms in the hotel section still have their original antique furniture, although cable TV and new telephones have been added. An interesting tidbit is the fact that, in the 1930s, the notorious gangster John Dillinger stayed at the Gardner Hotel, which is situated right

downtown, just before his capture in Tucson, Arizona. The lobby boasts a beautiful antique stairwell with lush red carpeting, and a smattering of antique phones and knickknacks scattered around gives the place a very old-world feel, as does the antique elevator which has a very heavy accordion door. But that is where the charm of this place ends.

There is very little difference between the hotel and hostel, except that the hotel rooms are slightly better appointed, while upon check-in to the hostel, which houses four- and two-bed dorm rooms, you're given a tatty set of sheets and a grubby blanket for use on the barebones bunks. Not uncommon practice in hostels the world over, but if you're used to staying in the friendly backpacker hostels of Europe, you may be in for a bit of a shock here. This hostel-cum-hotel is sorely lacking in flavor and the convivial atmosphere that one often expects when backpacking, and the rooms are questionably unclean to the point that you might not want to take off your shoes. Some of the hostel rooms are equipped with a tiny sink, while shared bathrooms are located down the hall. Another nuisance while staying here is the nightclub downstairs, which those that are relegated to rooms at the west end of the building must endure hearing late into the night.

All in all, the Gardner Hotel and El Paso Youth Hostel is an interesting historical landmark but leaves a lot to be desired on the accommodation front. The staff is friendly and helpful, and for those dyed-in-the-wool backpackers that aren't bothered by not having a super clean accommodation, this might be an okay option. Furthermore, the price for a dorm room here is only a bargain for solo travelers, but for two sharing, you'll pay the same amount for much better at other hotels in the area. It should also be noted that this hotel does not offer parking of any kind, but it is convenient to the train and bus stations for those just traveling through.

RV PARKS

ARVEY'S PARK $
11200 Montana Ave.
(915) 598-7522
This friendly little RV park is situated along the southern border of Fort Bliss, not far from the airport, in East El Paso. While the amenities here are somewhat lacking, the park is suitable for self-sufficient RVs. The welcoming managers and the owners live on the premises and are always willing to help, and overall, the staff is friendly and attentive. One of the best aspects about this park are the prices, which are among the most reasonable in the area. It is a quiet little place, not luxurious but definitely quaint. In addition to being an RV park, Arvey's is also a very popular campground among folks in El Paso. There are plenty of spots for enjoying the local natural scenery along the Rio Bosque Wetlands Park Trails here, as well as hiking opportunities on the Wilderness Park Museum Trail. One of El Paso's largest recreational areas, Ascarate Park, as well as the Lone Star Golf Club, are also both not far away.

FORT BLISS RV PARK &
FAMILY CAMPGROUND $
Fort Bliss, Building 4130
(915) 568-0106
www.blissmwr.com/rvpark
This well kept RV park located on Fort Bliss is run by the base's Family and Morale, Welfare and Recreation department. On-site, there are 73 full service trailer hookups

complete with water, electricity, and sewer conveniences. There are also a number of amenities on offer for entertainment and travel needs, including a family room that is equipped with a full kitchen, TV, and free Wi-Fi Internet access. A small fitness room, which is home to a stair stepper, bike, two ellipticals, and two treadmills, helps you keep in shape while you're on the road, and there is a small outdoor playground for children. Two outside pavilion areas with built-in grills are provided for parties or small get-togethers, and a doggie walk is available; however patrons may walk their pets wherever they wish. Other useful amenities include a laundry room, shower facilities and public restrooms, and a dump station. Although the park is mainly open to service-men and women, active duty members of the military and retirees can now sign in their family members or friends who might want to utilize the Fort Bliss RV Park on a space-available basis. The RV Park office is open from 8 a.m. to 3 or 4 p.m. daily and offers an after-hours night host to assist late arrivals.

FRANKLIN MOUNTAINS
STATE PARK $
1331 McKelligon Canyon Rd.
(512) 389-8900
www.tpwd.state.tx.us/spdest/findadest/
parks/franklin
If you are interested in parking yourself in a secluded mountain recreation area for a few days, make for the Tom Mays Recreation Area in the Franklin Mountains State Park. The best part of this mountainous camp-ground and recreational area is the stunning view over El Paso from high above. The Tom Mays section of the park is a public day use area that has a number of shaded picnic/barbecue sites, self-composting toilets, sev-

eral miles of gentle hiking trails through the foothills of the Franklins, and camping areas. There are two types of campsites available here: a limited number of primitive tent-camping sites, which have space for tents placed on the ground, as well as developed sites that feature tables and grills for cooking out. Meanwhile, five self-contained RV sites are scattered throughout the park as well, but they are for use by self-sufficient RVs only and have no water or electrical hookups.

All potential campers should be fore-warned: ground fires are not allowed within the park boundaries and there is no water or electricity available, so be sure to pack supplies, food, and water before you go. If you want to have a barbecue or cookout, you must light your fire only in designated fire pits. Reservations for the campsites and RV sites are recommended, and those desiring to reserve a campsite must contact the park office.

LAS CRUCES KOA $
814 Weinrich Rd.
Las Cruces, NM
(575) 526-6555
www.lascruceskoa.com
This campground in nearby Las Cruces, New Mexico, is famous for its views to the east, which feature a panorama of Las Cruces, the Mesilla Valley, and the surrounding mountains. There are a number of accommodation options here, including tent sites, cabins, and pull-through RV sites. Kamping Kabins are a series of one-room cabins designed for camping-like overnight stays. A number

of campsites offer more traditional camping opportunities on sodded, shaded tent areas with beautiful romantic views. And there is a wide array of pull-through RV sites with 30- and 50-amp hookups, up to 80 feet long to accommodate large rigs and tow vehicles. In addition to the amazing views, this KOA offers a number of special amenities, such as a heated pool that is open in season, an onsite grocery shop, recently remodeled restrooms and shower facilities that are kept clean, a children's playground, and a pet walk area. You can also access cable TV and free Wi-Fi Internet across the grounds. If you don't have a computer with you, there is a dedicated guest computer available for use in the office.

MISSION TRAIL MOBILE
 HOME PARK $
8479 Alameda Ave.
(915) 859-0202
www.missiontrailmhc.com
This small RV park and mobile home village has 15 pull-through sites with 30- and 50-amp hookups, in addition to its semi-permanent mobile home sites. The park is located along the Mission Trail in El Paso's Lower Valley, convenient to a number of historic sightseeing areas, including the Mission Trail itself. Rates here are extremely reasonable, and the park has secure, lighted streets, as well as a clubhouse with laundry facilities and bathroom and shower facilities. Many of the hookup spaces here also boast shady trees, which can be a welcome relief from the intense El Paso sun during the summer.

RESTAURANTS

If there's one thing El Paso's got going for it, it is an amazing food scene. The centuries of cultural mixing here have produced an amazing local food culture that incorporates elements of Mexican, Native American, and Anglo-American cooking styles. Tex-Mex cuisine was virtually invented in El Paso and other Texas towns along the border, and New Mexican cooking, with its spicy chile sauces, is ever-present. So, the variety of dishes and cuisines here spans across the hundreds of Mexican, Tex-Mex, and New Mexican restaurants to be found in the city.

Beyond Southwestern cuisine, you are bound to bump into a number of international restaurants throughout the city. Fort Bliss has long been a training center for the German Air Force, which has led to the existence of several excellent, authentic German restaurants around town. And the arrival of immigrants from around the world during the city's boomtown years means that there is plenty to choose from ethnically, like Italian, Chinese, Vietnamese, and Thai foods. Furthermore, El Paso's haute culinary scene is now beginning to grow as several El Paso chefs are making their way into the cooking world with a few dynamic, upscale restaurants. And if it's just plain, good old American food you're after, well, there's no shortage of burger joints, barbecue pits, and pizzerias to soothe your hometown hankerings.

OVERVIEW

The restaurants in this chapter are presented by style of cuisine and range from local Mexican holes in the wall and low-key rib joints to upscale steakhouses and fancy wine bars. A price code has been incorporated to help you find just the meal you're looking for; of course, there are literally thousands of eateries, diners, restaurants, and delis across the city, so this is just a sampling of some local favorites and the most popular or well-known places to eat in the Sun City.

In 2002, El Paso instituted a stringent city ordinance that banned smoking in all workplaces, restaurants, and bars, so you will not find smoking sections in any of El Paso's restaurants. However, many bars and restaurants around town have opened their patios and gardens to smokers, and the city's great weather means that these types of outdoor spaces are open year-round in many places.

Of course everyone will have his or her favorites and I've attempted to include many of mine. By all means, check with local friends and family for their recommendations about El Paso's best places to eat, and use this chapter as simply a starting point for exploring the thousands of amazing restaurants that the Sun City has to offer.

Price Code

The following price code has been included to give you a rough idea of what an average

RESTAURANTS

dinner of entrees for two will cost, excluding cocktails, wine, appetizers, desserts, tax and tip. El Paso has restaurants that range from the very cheap to extremely fine dining, so there is sure to be something in this chapter that caters to your budget. Unless otherwise noted, all restaurants accept major credit cards.

$................. Less than $10
$$ .... $10 to $30
$$$ .... $31 to $50
$$$$ ....$51 and up

AMERICAN
Central/Downtown

CRAVE KITCHEN & BAR $$$
300 Cincinnati Ave.
(915) 351-3677
www.cravekitchenandbar.com
Crave is a yuppie foodie's delight, with a trendy menu that offers new takes on old homey favorites and a cozy, bright atmosphere. The restaurant is tiny but often packed and the service is always reliably good. Inside, the decor is sleek with bright colors, large windows, and a huge mirror, all of which go a long way to disguising the comparatively small dining area. The casually dressed staff offset the general air of upscale about Crave, which boasts prices to match.

The menu concept at Crave takes old favorites, like your mother's mac and cheese, southern fried chicken, and turkey sandwiches—all the stuff you enjoyed as a kid—and turns them into a hodgepodge of delicious upscale mains that include tasty sandwiches like Turkey, Brie and Bacon, or their BLTA, which adds avocado to the traditional lineup of bacon, lettuce, and tomato. Buttermilk Fried Chicken, a grilled ribeye steak with an ancho-espresso rub, and New-

castle Fish and Chips served with salt and vinegar kettle chips are among the unique offerings at Crave.

Inside, the menu is scrawled across a huge chalkboard along the back wall, and leather stools at the bar counter are shaped to fit your seat for a comfy dining experience. Alternately, you can sit at one of the high tables with a larger party, or enjoy an intimate dinner at a traditional table for two under the exposed brick wall. Warm track lighting and a teeny but well-stocked bar add to the cozy atmosphere here. While this isn't the restaurant to head to if you're in a hurry, Crave would make for a great long lunch or a cozy dinner treat.

MESA STREET BAR AND GRILL $$$–$$$$
2525 North Mesa St.
(915) 532-1881
www.mesastreetgrill.com
This moderately fancy restaurant is an El Paso staple for a special night out. The traditional restaurant atmosphere is heavy on theme, with lots of lamps, indoor plants, and old paintings and photographs that make you settle into the surroundings. The decor here nods to some 1950s New York Italian lounge without being smoky or stale. Highly decorated by several well-known wine publications, Mesa Street Bar and Grill has an extensive wine list that includes both local New Mexico and Texas wines, as well as a great selection of American and international wines for almost every budget. They also have a cigar room with a menu of both vintage and infused cigars.

The food here, too, is traditional, with their steaks and seafood the crowning points of the menu, while the salads and greens feel a bit more like an afterthought. You'll get great service that is neither overwhelming nor lacking, and they do monthly six-course wine tasting dinners. An excellent executive chef and pastry chef make all desserts in-house, including homemade ice cream. If you aren't in the mood for a full meal (or don't have the budget for it), you can opt to have a drink in the classic bar or on the cozy patio, where a limited (and more reasonably priced) bar menu boasts a few tasty offerings.

Westside

AJ'S DINER $$
7120 North Mesa St.
(915) 584-2514
www.ajsdiner.com

Opened in 1986, this true 1950s-style diner was designed to bring the good ole days back for new generations and for those who want to remember the past with fondness. Even though, situated in an unremarkable strip mall, the restaurant doesn't look like much from the outside, inside AJ's comes alive with 1950s decor. A row of red pleather booths sits along one side, overseen by numerous old photos of antique cars and Mickey Mouse memorabilia. The counter takes up the other half of AJ's, where stools with red pleather padding to match the booths cozy up to the silver bar. Behind, a number of servers dressed in period costumes are busy making shakes and malts at one of the few true soda fountains in El Paso. An old working jukebox stands as a centerpiece in the diner, crowned by painted musical notes and the word "music" written in red neon lettering.

The menu at AJ's is admittedly not as interesting as its decor, but is full of 1950s greats: burgers and sandwiches, platters, onion rings and fries. There is a huge selec-

tion of 18 burgers, many named after 1950s music icons like Little Richard, Fats Domino, and Buddy Holly, and all can be substituted with a chicken patty instead. The menu proudly proclaims that all of the food at AJ's is made fresh with original recipes that have been handed down in the family through history.

Though not a culinary revolution, AJ's is a great place to go for a burger and a malt with a side of nostalgia.

ARDOVINO'S DESERT CROSSING $$$
1 Ardovino Dr.
Sunland Park, NM
(505) 589-0653
www.ardovinos.com

Though the menu here is decidedly Italian, the ambiance and overall atmosphere at Ardovino's Desert Crossing is much more than that. A truly hip restaurant, Ardovino's is nestled in the foothills of Mt. Cristo Rey and has been in operation since 1949. The Mecca Lounge at Ardovino's is a throwback to the swanky lounges of the 1950s, offering fabulous cocktails and an extensive selection of fine wines, scotch, and beer. Dinner items here are created with garden-grown herbs, and the menu entrees combine traditional Italian staples like pasta and gnocchi with unusual Southwestern-inspired ingredients to form mains like the gnocchi with Spanish chorizo. Other items are more traditional, such as the lamb rack, which features New Mexico raised lamb loin chops rubbed with rosemary and served with raisin chipotle chutney and a parmesan polenta.

Every Saturday morning in the summer through fall, there is a farmers' market with fresh local produce, and breakfast is served on the patio. Full service banquet facilities are available for private events from

10 to 350 guests. They also often have live entertainment on the patio and host special brunches and tasting events.

Eastside

GESKE'S $$
1506 North Lee Trevino Dr., Suite C
(915) 593-3473

This fresh restaurant is a great option for anyone looking for a tasty, no-nonsense meal with plenty of vegetarian options. The food here is extremely fresh and the ingredients are combined together to form unusual offerings, such as the ahi tuna steak sandwich and margarita french fries. Geske's crab cakes are renowned for being some of the best in the city, and they also pour up a mean mojito. The dining experience here is of a fresh American style. The dining area surrounds a small bar and looks into the open kitchen with a full view. Other menu items include hand-cut steaks, fresh seafood, and bone-in pork chops, all of which are prepared on an open grill. Their sauces and salad dressings are unique and homemade and all of the vegetables are extremely fresh. Try the ribs, which are so succulent that they literally fall off the bone! Closed Sundays.

HINEY'S $$
1-10 at Lomaland
(915) 590-0115
www.hineys.net

Even if you aren't into sports bars, you will probably think Hiney's is pretty cool. This all-American true blue bar is all about the sports . . . and great food. The large, no-frills dining room is equipped with tons of booths, all of them sporting their own individual 22-inch flat screen TVs, which means you can sit and enjoy any game you want without having to crane your neck or bother watching someone else's team win. They show all the major sports games, including the NFL, NBA, NHL, and MLB games, as well as most college sports in season. If you want a real experience, head to Hiney's on a UTEP game night—just be sure to get there early!

While the food at most sports bars leaves much to be desired, Hiney's actually has a decent menu that is fairly evolved. In addition to the sports bar grub basics, like mozzarella sticks and chicken strips, Hiney's offers a large selection of really fresh hot wings with a variety of sauces to choose from. Their variety of burgers and sandwiches, too, transcends the average bar food menu, from the spicy Buffalo chicken sandwich to the unusual Hawaiian burger, which sports a ring of pineapple. Beyond these sports fan favorites, Hiney's offers a selection of homespun American dishes like chicken fried steak, pork chops, and a number of reasonably priced steaks.

They also have a breakfast menu that includes homemade menudo and huevos rancheros.

JAXON'S $$
Eastside
1135 Airway Blvd.
(915) 778-9696
www.jaxons.com

Anyone that is interested in craft beers and great food must pay a visit to Jaxon's. Established in 1973, this restaurant and microbrewery serves up tasty Southwestern food and a rotating selection of their own house-made beers. Signature dishes here include homemade potato green chile and tortilla soups, Santa Barbara beef, a specially seasoned grilled sirloin served sliced with Jaxon's own barbecue sauce, gourmet hamburgers, and more. Tried and true spicy lovers and even the odd New Mexican will be impressed with Jaxon's green chile sauce, and their "King" margaritas and signature cocktails are acclaimed as some of the best in the region. (see the entry in the Nightlife chapter, p. 89) A second and third location are located far Northwest at 4799 North Mesa St. (915-544-1188), and on the Westside at 7410 Remcon Circle (915-845-6557). All three locations have a bar and free wireless Internet access.

Northeast Side

ROSCO'S BURGER INN   **$–$$**
3829 Tompkins Rd.
(915) 564-9028
Rosco's Burger Inn is an El Paso hamburger institution. In business for more than 50 years, not much about the place has changed since its opening, including the food. The menu at Rosco's, which is posted on the wall to the right as you walk in, could fit onto their business card: hamburgers, cheeseburgers, hot dogs, grilled cheese, caldillo, chili bowls, meat burritos, fries, and onion rings. And this is pretty much the only reason to go there, as the place is completely atmosphere-less, a fact much beloved by the locals who frequent the joint. The burgers are basic and look and taste as if they came right out of the '50s—huge, juicy patties covered in all the fixings (onions, pickles, lettuce, tomatoes, ketchup, and mustard) plus cheese, on a greasy white bun. If one patty isn't enough for you, you can ask for a double or even triple burger.

The draw of Rosco's, which boasts a tiny dining room with a few ancient plastic tables and chairs that all sport an excellent view of the huge grill behind the counter where the burgers are made, is the layers of history that you can see (and smell) inside. It is not a polished corporate burger joint, and its old school mentality beat In 'N' Out Burger to the punch. Rosco's only accepts cash—no credit cards or checks—and there is often a line out the door during lunchtime, but the burgers here are definitely worth the wait.

ASIAN
Central/Downtown

PHO TRE BIEN   **$$**
6946 Gateway East
(915) 598-0166
www.photrebien.com
This newly remodeled Vietnamese restaurant has a warm and inviting atmosphere with a spacious dining room and bar counter seating. The walls here are painted in a deep red color and decorated with traditional Asian instruments, while low pendant lights hang over individual tables. An elegant grand piano sits on an elevated corner stage and the lovely outdoor garden is adorned with seated Buddha statues and lotus flowers.

The menu at Pho Tre Bien consists of traditional Vietnamese cuisine. The spring rolls here are particularly fresh and delicious, while the restaurant's namesake, pho, a fresh noodle dish with lime and bean sprouts, is indeed trè bien. The staff are extremely polite staff and there is rarely a wait to be seated, as there is ample room in the dining area and on the patio.

TARA THAI   **$$–$$$**
2606 North Mesa St.
(915) 533-1300
www.tarathairestaurant.com
Though many people consider Pad Thai to be the dish by which to measure any Thai

restaurant, for me, it is Tom Kha Gai, a deli-cious coconut milk soup with chicken, gin-ger, and chilis. For this dish, Tara Thai gets my total approval. Whole pieces of lemongrass float invitingly in Tara Thai's spicy yet sweet version of this unforgettable soup. The Pad Thai, too, is not too syrupy and comes with a traditional selection of garnishes, including crushed peanuts and lime.

The menu at Tara Thai is typical of most Thai restaurants you've been in before. They boast heavily about their Drunken Noodles, which are a house favorite. They also serve complimentary Thai flat bread with spicy green dipping sauce—a unique addition. The interior is subdued, with calming colors and about a dozen well-spaced tables that invite intimate conversation. Tara Thai was started in 2008 by Sai Pituk, who is of full Thai decent. Regulars to the restaurant are often greeted by name, and first-time customers enjoy a personalized introduction to the restaurant and its menu. The restaurant is bolstered by an upscale air that is brought home with the addition of beer and wine, including a lovely house cabernet sauvi-gnon. Top off your meal with the Thai Flan, an authentic sweet Thai dessert, made of rice pudding and coconut.

Westside

KOZE TEPPAN GRILL $$$
6127 North Mesa St.
(915) 584-1128
www.kozeteppangrill.com
Teppan, or teppanyaki, is a style of Japanese cooking that involves fast frying on an open iron grill. Most teppan restaurants in the United States involve sitting at a large communal table, watching a trained chef toss morsels of food around in an almost

juggler-style performance before serving it up onto your plate. Pronounced like Jose with a K, Koze Teppan Grill has two sections: the more traditional teppan-style grill, and a regular restaurant side with a sushi bar. Its clean, hip interior is decorated in pleas-ant industrial, east-meets-west contempo-rary Japanese decor, with dim lighting and upbeat music. Dining areas are sectioned off by wood dividers and glass windows that allow you to view the surroundings and also minimize some of the ambient noise from surrounding tables. The sushi bar is the foremost feature to greet arrivals with an array of popular sushi, prepared beautifully in the authentic Japanese way, while the teppan grillers are very skilled spatulateers, and their rhythmic clacking is sure to amaze and entertain guests. Among some of the better menu items is the soft shell crab, which is served with fried sweet potato strips and green onions, as well as a delectable New York steak with shiitake mushrooms.

OKAZURI FLOATING SUSHI $$–$$$
865 North Resler Dr., Suite C
(915) 581-7733
www.okazuri.com
This small sushi bar is a boatload of fun—literally. The sushi they serve is solid, but the real novelty here is the service, where sushi is floated to you in a little boat at the sushi bar. Because of its size, Okazuri can get crowded and sometimes the service is slower than you might hope for, so it's a good idea to come here when you intend to enjoy the ambiance over a leisurely evening meal. The sushi here is an elaborate offering with a variety of fish and other very fresh seafood placed over rice and seaweed. Other

dishes include tempura, where seafood or vegetables are breaded and fried and served hot and crunchy, and a variety of other traditional Japanese dishes, some prepared with unique methods in order to adapt to the local style of cuisine.

Eastside

SHAN DONG CHINESE
RESTAURANT $$
3125 North Lee Trevino Dr.
(915) 590-2999
Shan Dong Chinese Restaurant, which takes the name of one of China's northeastern provinces, was started by an experienced Chinese chef who brought some flavorful, innovative recipes to the menu. It quickly became popular as stories of Shan Dong appeared in the food feature sections of local newspapers, and people flocked to the restaurant in a desperate attempt to find an alternative to the many mediocre buffet restaurants in the city. Although the restaurant was eventually sold, the food at Shan Dong continues to be as good as it was when the founding chef was there. There is no buffet here, so all of the dishes offered on the somewhat unchanging menu are cooked fresh when ordered.

One of the best features about the food here is the presentation. All of the items have a deep, rich color and are served garnished with an orange. At lunch, you have your choice of either hot and sour soup or egg drop soup, both of which are delicious. Most dishes are also served with a colorful array of condiments that include plum sauce, hot mustard, and chile oil.

The menu at Shan Dong is a little different than most Chinese restaurants. Many of the dishes are typical of China's northeastern

cuisine, with plenty of noodles, dumplings, and homey items, including lots of excellent chicken dishes. Most items come in either full or half orders and are available all day, so there is no specific lunch menu. Shan Dong's chicken egg rolls are particularly notable, and other excellent offerings include the spicy Home Style Tofu, General Tsao's Chicken, Double Cooked Chicken, Crispy Chicken, or Lemon Chicken.

SHOGUN JAPANESE
STEAKHOUSE $$
1201 Airway Blvd.
(915) 775-1282
This traditional Japanese steakhouse is El Paso's oldest teppanyaki restaurant, serving up typical hibachi grilled favorites. They are known for both their delicious food and the real showmanship used in its preparation, with friendly, humorous teppan chefs who use their considerable spatula skills to put on a great show. Their menu boasts a selection typical of most Japanese teppanyaki restaurants: steaks, chicken, lobster, and shrimp that are prepared right before your eyes by your very own chef at a hot grill in the middle of your table. The food is less the star here than the chefs, and the real purpose of going here is not for a no-frills meal, but for the prep show, which is really a lot of fun to watch. The restaurant also features a large sushi bar with some 25 varieties of sushi, including maki rolls, sashimi, and nigiri. They also have a selection of desserts, including Japanese ice cream. They have a full bar with Japanese beer and exotic cocktails on offer. Lunch here is only served Mon through Fri, but they are open every day for dinner.

BARBECUE
Central/Downtown

RIB HUT $$
2612 North Mesa St.
(915) 532-7427
www.ribhutelpaso.com

In business since 1984, Rib Hut is famous for one thing and one thing only: ribs, of course! They have a variety of different options, from big beef ribs to baby-back pork ribs, and the sauces vary from their special barbecue sauce to mesquite smoked with a honey glaze. Ribs here are slow-cooked in a Texas style, which makes them mouth-watering and falling off the bone. Their menu selection also includes barbecue brisket, which is lean, smoked, and thinly sliced, as well as juicy sausages, chicken-fried steak, and a number of steaks, including a charbroiled sixteen-ounce T-bone. Their burgers are also worth a mention—the half-pound Angus steakburger is a local favorite—but are certainly not the best reason to come here.

Wednesday night is the time to come to Rib Hut, if you can get in the door, as they offer $1.25 rib night, which means you can pack in just about as many ribs as you can eat without breaking the bank. They also offer a selection of beer and wine, which means you can enjoy your barbecue the way it was meant to be eaten: over a cold beer in a relaxed, friendly atmosphere.

TONY'S THE PIT BAR-B-Q $–$$
1700 Myrtle Ave.
(915) 546-9140
www.tonysthepitbbq.com

This popular barbecue restaurant was the first to introduce a mesquite-smoking pit to the El Paso barbecue scene back in the early 1960s. Family owned and operated for three generations, they have been in business since, serving up excellent combination platters and barbecue sandwiches, along with the staple side dishes like baked beans, potato salad, and coleslaw. All of the barbecue items here are mesquite-smoked, giving them that unique, woodsy flavor so important in Texas-style barbecue. Their specialty is a huge, juicy barbecue beef sandwich that comes smothered in their own special house barbecue sauce. Other menu items include ham, chicken, and sausage—it's all about the meat here! This is a great place to bring the family, as they also offer barbecue beef by the pound, which could literally feed an army. A second location is at 6101 Gateway West on the Eastside (915-775-0535).

Eastside

SMITTY'S $$
6219 Airport Rd.
(915) 772-5876

Smitty's has been in business since 1955, making it one of the oldest barbecue joints in El Paso. They serve a selection of barbecue items cooked in an old-fashioned firebrick pit after marinating for two days, resulting in flavorful, tender, and juicy meat. Smitty's was actually started by Mr. Smith, who ran it until 1976, when it was bought by the Payan family. Eddie Payan, the second-generation owner, began working here at age 16 and still runs it today. Among their best menu items are the smoked pork ribs, the barbecue brisket, and the corned beef sandwiches, which are an unusual but delicious addition to a barbecue list, and of course, cold beer, which is a staple for any barbecue restaurant. Smitty's also does tea the right way: one order of iced tea gets you a full glass and a full pitcher, so you'll never have to ask for refills. A successful restaurant, Smitty's is known for its consistent quality. A trip here is all about the barbecue.

BREAKFAST, BAKERIES, AND CAFES

Central/Downtown

THE PERCOLATOR $$
217 North Stanton St.
(915) 351-4377
www.myspace.com/thepercolator915
This downtown café and gallery is one of the more unique restaurant experiences in El Paso. Here, you will experience a dining option that combines art, music, film, and culture, and of course coffee and food. If a full-service coffeeshop mated with an art center, the result would be the Percolator. On offer here are the standard variety of specialty drinks at a full service espresso bar, as well as a number of classic deli sandwiches and fresh pastries. What makes the Percolator so unique, though, are its cultural tendencies. It often hosts events that include live music, cultural presentations, and independent films, and they have a 17-seat projection theater that is available for presentations. If you're hankering for that truly cultural hangout or just a great place to go and sip a strong espresso in the presence of some great El Paso artwork, this is definitely the place to be.

Westside

INTERNATIONAL BAKERY & DELI $$
6415 North Mesa St.
(915) 584-2626
International Bakery and Deli is a no-nonsense place to get amazing, homemade sandwiches and baked goods. The sandwiches and baked goods here were previously served at the Lo Mart Delicatessen, which is now closed. The head pastry and sandwich chef at Lo Mart opened this International Bakery in a nearby location and the rest is history. International Bakery does not carry a large selection of imported packaged goods, but they do specialize in European foods and at the deli counter you can order a number of high quality food items from various parts of the world. Meats and cheeses are available, with Boar's Head being one of the featured brands.

Those that are fans of the deli style restaurant know that one of its draws is the fact that food can either be consumed on premises or taken home. Thus, no waiters are employed in this extremely casual atmosphere where offerings are served in basic baskets, and customers do not have to leave a tip. The staple menu item here is a selection of sandwiches, such as tuna salad, which are available from the counter and come hot or cold on a variety of breads. The sourdough bread here is particularly nice.

Most of the sandwiches come with a side of tasty housemade potato salad that is mustard based. Another wonderful option is the Wiener Plate, which can be served as either a sandwich or a lunch plate, and is a traditional German style lean wiener. The baked goods here are also a main attraction, with such a large variety of cakes and cookies available that you would have to come back every day for a month to sample them all! All in all, the International Deli and Bakery would make an excellent stop for a quick lunch or afternoon snack, or to pick up a selection of hard-to-find international meats and cheeses to take home.

Eastside

CORNER BAKERY CAFÉ $$
1350 George Dieter
(915) 855-1873
www.cornerbakerycafe.com

Scrumptious sandwiches, delicious muffins, hearty breads, and scrambled breakfasts grace the menu at this, El Paso's newest fast casual dining experience. This well-put-together cafe boasts a relaxing atmosphere that is clean and trendy where you can enjoy delicious, well-prepared foods and a host of taste tempting choices. Most of the menu items here focus on innovative seasonal offerings, such as pumpkin muffins in the fall and spring vegetable salads. And their decadent desserts are not to be missed. They offer a number of hot, made-to-order breakfasts incorporating traditional as well as Southwestern favorites, handcrafted salads made fresh when ordered, sandwiches, signature panini sandwiches, pastas, seasonal soups, specialty breads, freshly baked sweets, and a premium selection of hand-roasted coffees, espresso beverages, and gourmet teas. This is a great place to go for lunch, a late Sunday breakfast, or any morning that you have a hankering for a good cup of strong coffee and a reliably tasty muffin.

FINE DINING
Central/Downtown

2900 KITCHEN/LOUNGE $$$–$$$$
2900 North Mesa St.
(915) 544-1400
www.goto2900.com
This sleek wine bar and upscale restaurant serves a variety of cocktails and a few beers and has an extensive wine cellar that includes some rare and hard-to-find wines, both New and Old World. Open since February of 2008, 2900 represents a departure from the norm of the El Paso restaurant scene. Opened by third-generation El Paso restaurateur Mark Heins, whose ground-breaking Greenery Restaurant and Market changed the landscape of dining

and retail specialty food and wine in El Paso, 2900 continues to grow in popularity with outstanding service and new-American menus. Focusing on seasonally inspired, regional cuisine, 2900's creative menu is crafted by El Paso native, Chef Karina Ramirez.

Though the menu here is definitely a star, the bar is a great place to sip a bottle of wine and taste an artisanal cheese plate, or have dessert and a cocktail. Their cellar includes a world-class collection of fine wines and spirits, showcased in a temperature-controlled wine wall, the focal point of the lower level dining area. Separating the two downstairs dining areas is an 18-foot water wall that can be seen from every vantage point within the dining areas. Another cool feature of this restaurant is the kitchen, which is open to the dining area through a large window and houses in-kitchen Chef's Table. There is also an upper level dining area that can be booked for special events and features an outdoor patio perfect for late-night alfresco dining or drinks. 2900's interior space combines the warmth of an Asian-inspired dining room with urban industrial design in the factory-like concrete walls and exposed ventilation system. The bar is a simple, chic low plastic counter with ample liquor bottles displayed on a modern shelf that is lit in soft blues. Just up the street from the Cincinnati Avenue Entertainment District, 2900 is a sleek, upscale alternative to the madness of the college drinking crowd.

CAFÉ CENTRAL $$$–$$$$
109 North Oregon St.
(915) 545-2233
www.cafecentral.com
One of El Paso's most upscale restaurants, Café Central opened in 1918 in Juárez, Mexico, and quickly developed a clientele

of gamblers and cabaret-goers who grew to expect an excellent culinary experience in the region at this chic nightspot. After Prohibition ended, Café Central migrated closer to the border, and finally crossed into downtown El Paso, at which time it became known as Miguel's Central Café. Finally in 1991, V. Trae Apodaca III noticed the need for a chic bistro downtown and opened Café Central in its current location. With a chic black and cream interior that sets off Apodaca's collection of original art, this restaurant is truly elegant, its centerpiece an ornately gated New Orleans style courtyard.

Today's Café Central is famous for its menu, which features dishes that are a combination of decades-old traditions and bold, innovative flavors. Seasonal menus are on offer here, so you never know what types of delicious surprises you'll find and almost never have to eat the same thing twice. Many of the selections incorporate a Southwestern twist, with special attention to the inclusion of green chiles into the mix.

A *Wine Spectator* Award of Excellence winner twice and having received rave reviews from the *New York Times*, Café Central is definitely the place where high rollers go in El Paso. That said, the restaurant's air of quality is ever present but not off-putting, and their wine cellar is as good as one might expect from a *Wine Spectator* award recipient, with particular emphasis on vintages from California and, unexpectedly, South Africa.

DOME RESTAURANT $$$$
101 South El Paso St.
(915) 534-3000
www.crelpaso.com
Set in the grand Camino Real Hotel, the Dome Restaurant is both elegant and unique, named for the antique Tiffany glass dome that crowns the space in the historic hotel bar. The Dome is the place to go for formal, gourmet dining, as it is the area's only 4-Diamond restaurant. All of the traditional classic entrees are on offer here, from Escargot Bordelaise to the roast rack of lamb. If the food here could be overshadowed, it could only be outdone by the unbelievable turn-of-the-century setting, where you could imagine Pancho Villa taking in a gourmet meal. The Dome's menu is complemented by its selection of vintage wine.

The best way to enjoy the Dome is to make an evening of it. Plan to enjoy dinner in the restaurant first (be sure to make reservations, as it does fill up with locals and traveling businessmen), taking your time to enjoy the extremely elegant and classic flavors and textures of the food on offer. Once you've had your fill of the rich, delicious food, retire to the opulent Dome Bar next door, where you can enjoy the view of the vintage glass dome while sipping a whiskey or strong cocktail.

Westside

BILLY CREWS $$$–$$$$
1200 Country Club Rd.
Santa Teresa, NM
(505) 589-2071
www.billycrews.com
Wine and steak lovers looking for a great restaurant, look no further. Great steaks and great wines go hand-in-hand at Billy Crews, a *Wine Spectator* Magazine Grand Award winning restaurant for some 20 years. The menu at this classic, traditional restaurant runs the gamut of what you might expect from a wine-awarded establishment: custom-cut steaks, fresh seafood, prime rib, chicken,

(Q) Close-up

El Paso—A Foodie's Dictionary

For those of us raised in the Southwest, *enchiladas* and *rellenos* are quite simply a culinary way of life. But for visitors here, the type, style, and particularly the names of the dishes can be overwhelming. El Paso cooking draws influences from so many culinary traditions: Spanish, Mexican, Native American, and Anglo-American cooking have all bestowed their bits and pieces into the food of the Southwest. Many of the dishes, in fact most of them, have Spanish names, which can be difficult for visitors to pronounce. The ingredients, too, can be quite simply too much to take in.

Herein is a short guide to help you eat your way around El Paso. Included are some of the more popular dishes and cooking styles, including their names, how to pronounce them, and what they generally consist of. One thing is certain—each restaurant and chef add their own unique style to the dishes, so the dishes will look and taste different almost everywhere you go. This is one of the true joys of eating in the Southwest, and I hope this menu guide helps you on your way to discovering all that El Paso cuisine has to offer.

al pastor (all-pah-STORE)—literally "Shepherd style," refers to meat (mainly pork) that has been cooked on a Middle Eastern–style rotating spit.

arroz (ah-ROS)—rice.

barbacoa (bar-buh-KOH-uh)—barbecue, or meat slow-roasted over an open fire.

camarones (kah-mah-ROH-nes)—shrimp or prawns.

carne adobada (carnay-ad-oh-BAH-dah)—pork marinated in red chile, sometimes seen in its New Mexican form, *adovada*.

carne asada (carnay-ah-SAH-da)—thin cuts of roasted beef, often flank or skirt steak.

carnitas (car-NEE-tas)—braised or roasted meat, often pork.

chimichanga (chi-mee-CHAN-gah)—deep fried burrito.

empanada (em-pah-NA-da)—stuffed and baked bread pastry similar to an Italian calzone.

enchiladas (en-chee-LA-das)—rolled or flat sandwiched corn tortillas filled with cheese or meat and often topped with chile sauce.

flautas (FLAUW-tas)—small, rolled tacos. Also known as *taquitos* ("little tacos").

frijoles (free-HO-les)—beans.

gordita (gor-DEE-ta)—small stuffed sandwich similar to a taco, but with a thicker tortilla.

guacamole (gwa-ka-MOH-ley)—traditional dip made from avocados.

lamb, and veal. The prices, though, are surprisingly reasonable, and if you're not looking to spend a bundle, you can still enjoy a tasty pre-cut steak for a decent price.

The most impressive thing at Billy Crews, though, is undoubtedly the massive wine cellar, with more than 23,000 bottles. They also stock some 200 imported and specialty beers—a truly admirable amount—and a complete selection of liquors and spirits. They have an on-site lounge that is open every day and features live evening enter-

huevos (HWEY-vos)—eggs.

huevos rancheros (hweh-vos-ran-CHER os)—Classic breakfast dish consisting of fried corn tortillas, fried eggs with a tomato-chili sauce, refried beans, and potatoes.

menudo (meh-NOO-doh)—clear brothy soup made with hominy and tripe, usually with a red chile base.

mole poblano (MOH-ley-poh-BLAH-no)—sauce made of dried chili peppers, ground nuts, spices and Mexican chocolate, resulting in a thick, black spicy sauce.

papas (PA-pas)—potatoes.

pico de gallo (piko-deh-GUY-yo)—light, fresh salsa made from uncooked tomatoes, onions, and sometimes chiles. Literally, "rooster's beak."

pollo (POI-yo)—chicken.

posole (puh-SOL-eh)—hearty stew made with hominy (relative of corn) and pork. Also seen as *pozole*.

quesadillas (keh-sah-DEE-yas)—Snack food made primarily of cheese inside a folded tortilla and fried until the cheese melts.

queso (KEH-so)—cheese

refritos (re-FREE-tos)—refried pinto beans.

relleno (reh-YEH-no)—green chile pepper stuffed with cheese, battered and deep fried

tamale (tah-MA-leh)—corn meal stuffed with meat (usually pork) or vegetables, then wrapped in a husk and steamed. Also known as *tamal*.

tomatillo (toe-mah-TEE-yo)—small, savory green tomato, typically used in making *salsa verde*, a type of non-spicy green salsa.

sopapilla (so-pah-PEE-ya)—light, crispy Native American fry bread, often served with honey and sometimes stuffed and baked like a burrito.

torta (TOR-ta)—Mexican sandwich served on a crusty roll and filled with any number of ingredients, such as pork, steak, onion, pepper, and other vegetables or meats.

tostada (toe-STAH-da)—flat or bowl-shaped tortilla that is deep fried and covered in a number of toppings. Also known as *chalupa* (cha-LU-pah) or sometimes taco salad.

---

tainment from Wed to Sat. To add to the already massive stock of liquor here, Billy Crews also operates a package liquor store, which is open seven days a week and offers all wines from the cellar at excellent prices.

GERMAN
Eastside

GUNTHER'S EDELWEISS $$
11055 Gateway West
(915) 592-1084

For many years Fort Bliss has had a training facility for the German Air Force, and as a result there has been a large enough German population to support some very good German restaurants here. Gunther's Edelweiss Restaurant is both the oldest and the largest of these, still operating as many of its contemporaries have closed their doors through the years. The tasty German cuisine here is of the type and style that one might actually find in Germany. Like most good German restaurants, the food here tastes fresh, with very simple ingredients providing the flavors. Dinners start out with bread and soup, and if you go on a day when lentil soup is being served you are in for a real taste treat. The restaurant is also known for its German salad—a mixture of several simple but flavorful greens. Schnitzels, which are one of the specialties of the restaurant, come in several varieties, including the breaded Viennese Wienerschnitzel.

In addition to the hearty, authentic food served at Gunther's is its beloved Biergarten, where you can spend hours enjoying huge steins of German lager under the El Paso sunshine. They also often have live polka music being played. A trip to Gunther's is no light affair, though, quite literally. Expect to come away extremely full, if not tipsy. In fact, it may be best not to eat for an entire day before enjoying one of the massive bratwursts here.

INDIAN
Westside

CHUTNEY INDIAN RESTAURANT   **$$**
5435 North. Mesa St., Suite B
(915) 587-7788
www.chutneyelpaso.com

One of the most reasonably priced Indian restaurants in the city, Chutney Indian Restaurant offers a healthy selection of Indian favorites at prices that quite simply astound. Among their better dishes, the Chicken Tikka Masala is a delicious choice with excellent flavor but spices that don't overpower the food. The waitstaff are super friendly, as well. The interior of Chutney, too, is a delightful surprise. Unlike the heavy decor of many Indian restaurants, Chutney has employed a light, airy modern design with minimalist decor. A Hindi-themed print hangs on one wall, while the other is accented in a deep red to match the simple wooden tables scattered around the dining area. The feeling of dining here is casual and comfortable, to match the fantastic prices.

INDIA PALACE   **$$$**
5830 North Mesa St.
(915) 833-2245
www.indiapalaceelpaso.com
India Palace serves Northern Indian style cuisine, with flavorful but not-too-spicy dishes that are most popular in the United States. If you are a lover of spicy food, you may have to ask for your dishes to be spicy, or even extra spicy, here, but either way, you can always expect an extremely delicious meal with lovely flavors and spices.

An equal number of vegetarian and meat-lovers' options are on offer here, making it a great place to go in a group with mixed dietary needs. Meat-eaters and vegetarians alike will truly enjoy the Chana Masala, a chickpea dish with tomato sauce that is remarkably hearty and filling, despite its lack of meat. Regular naan bread here costs extra, but you may not need it, as the rice is plentiful and delicious. India Palace also offers a number of unusual beverages, from the popular Indian Tea, which is made with spices and herbs, to the truly unique yogurt shakes, which come both salted and sweetened. The restaurant is open for dinner seven days a week, with a lunch buffet every day.

ITALIAN
Central/Downtown

CAPPETTO'S $$-$$$
2716 Montana Ave.
(915) 566-9357
www.cappettos.com
Started in 1956 by Eddie and Alice Davis, this little family restaurant is just that. The simple dining room is exactly what you expect a family Italian-American restaurant to look like: a smattering of square tables with red and white checked tablecloths and a few simple paintings on the unremarkable walls. Stepping into Cappetto's dining area, you know the focus here is on the food. The menu consists of all your childhood favorites: pastas, house specials, pizza, and stromboli, as well as a few unique additions, such as the spinach frittata—an Italian omelet—and the Mediterranean hamburger steak—a ground sirloin patty seasoned with Mediterranean spices and cooked in a pizza oven. The old standards also make an appearance—veal Parmesan, chicken cacciatore, baked ziti, and lasagna, and Cappetto's gives you the option of ordering family style by taking your pick of five pastas and sauces to feed everyone.

Approaching Cappetto's original location on Montana Avenue, you can instantly see the 1950s influence in the unique awning that extends from the front door and the vintage neon sign above. And while

their newer location on the Eastside, 2285 Trawood Ave. (915-591-8907), lacks some of the charm from the outside, the food is still gloriously the same. Lunch and dinner are served here daily and they offer free wireless Internet access to customers.

Westside

IL POSTO ITALIANO $$$
7128 North Mesa St.
(915) 585-2221
www.ilpostoitaliano.com
Walking into Il Posto is like walking into an Italian villa. Bunches of red and green grapes hang idyllically out of ornate vases. Vines drape across open surfaces and stacks of old boxes line up against the Venetian plaster walls. On one side of the restaurant, Corinthian columns hold up a large wine wall with rows upon rows of Italian reds, and the dining area itself is spacious and airy, with plenty of tables dotted around but enough space between them to allow for a private eating experience.

The menu at Il Posto includes all of the traditional Italian favorites, such as spaghetti, lasagna, and ravioli, and they offer a number of unique specialties here, such as portobello mushroom ravioli, farfalle primavera (bowtie pasta with mixed vegetables in a light cream sauce), and veal marsala. They also offer quite a few chicken and pork dishes, with a smattering of veal and steak and one lone but tasty smoked duck offering. Their decent wine list includes plenty of Italian bottles, while the dessert menu consists mainly of those typically found on Italian-American menus: tiramisu, spumone, and chocolate cannoli. Il Posto is open for lunch and dinner seven days a week.

Eastside

MICHELINO'S ITALIAN
RESTAURANT $$-$$$
3615 Rutherglen St.
(915) 592-1700
www.michelinos.com
Michelino's has been in business for more than three decades. It is the classic fine Italian restaurant, but with such reasonable menu prices that it is perhaps one of the best value Italian restaurants in El Paso. In the past, Michelino's has been awarded the "Feast of the East" prize for best pasta, and the complete Italian menu here includes specialties like eggplant Parmigiana and chicken Jerusalem. Many of Michelino's pasta dinners are available in either a half or full order, and all come with complimentary house salad and garlic bread. Although the menu gives the option of upgrading to the classic salad for just $1, there is really no need, as the house salad is absolutely delectable and comes with their special dressing, made in-house. Furthermore, the wine list here consists of two dozen or so bottles of European wines, most of which go for little more than you would pay at the supermarket. Michelino's dining room is dimly lit and cozy, providing a dining experience typical of many Italian restaurants, but one that will bring you back for another meal. They are open for lunch on weekdays only, but serve dinner everyday.

MARKETS

Central/Downtown

PIKE STREET MARKET $-$$
207 East Mills Ave.
(915) 545-1010
www.pikestreetmarketep.com

Pike Street Market is not so much a market as a family deli and coffee shop, located right downtown. The menu here consists mainly of fresh sandwiches and salads, and also includes a few soups, cookies, pastries, and other delectables. The coffee menu consists of the usual fare: espressos, cappuccinos, lattes, and mochas, and they also do one of El Paso's only coffee happy hours, with espresso drinks going for half off for an hour each day. Pike Street also offers a breakfast menu, which actually just consists of either a bagel or croissant breakfast sandwich, which has been a favorite with downtown office workers and tourists looking for something besides the cold cereal in their hotels.

Inside, you can choose from a small selection of tables, or opt to sit at the counter, which is a great spot for people watching through the large windows. This downtown deli is nestled on the first floor of the Hotel Cortez, right next to the Post Office, and is open weekday mornings for breakfast and lunch.

Westside

GREENERY RESTAURANT &
MARKET $$-$$$
750 Sunland Park Dr.
(915) 584-6706
www.gotogreenery.com
You would never expect an upscale restaurant and international food market to be located in a mall, but Greenery is a foodie's dream. This classy restaurant and artisanal market is located inside the Sunland Park Mall on the Westside. While the restaurant was founded in 1982, the Greenery expanded its reach when it opened an upscale market next door in 2001. This food heaven quickly became one of the best places in town to find fine

wines, artisan breads, upscale cheeses, and finely crafted pastries and desserts. Greenery Market features a bakery, fresh seafood, hand-cut prime beef, along with an ever-increasing variety of specialty meat products, a deli, and an amazing array of imported, domestic, and artisanal cheeses from the United States, Europe, and Australia. Wine lovers will drool over the extensive selection of quality wines and international foodies will salivate when they browse through Greenery's many specialty food items from around the world. Plan to have lunch at the restaurant first and then browse the marketplace, and be sure to come with an empty stomach and deep pockets.

Regarded for its consistently high-quality, creative food and outstanding service, Greenery Restaurant offers over 150 freshly prepared menu items, along with a seasonally inspired featured entrée menu for dinner. Paired with the market's unparalleled specialty food and wine selection, Greenery is a truly unique dining and food shopping experience. On offer for brunch each Sunday is a Southwestern-inspired menu that includes Mexican and Tex-Mex favorites done with a gourmet twist.

RIPE EATERY & MARKET $$$
910 East Redd Rd.
(915) 584-7473
www.eatripe.com
Ripe Eatery is one of those truly hip yet completely friendly places to eat that only comes along once in a while. The vision behind Ripe was to "create a casual yet gourmet neighborhood eatery where everyone could get a creative and flavorful meal prepared by people who are genuinely excited about being in the kitchen." The food here is accessible, reasonably priced international cuisine—a kind of fusion between homespun delights

and global flavors, making Ripe one of a kind in El Paso.

The interior of Ripe is clean and cute. Mahogany tables are placed neatly around the bright dining area and overseen by colorful local paintings, a few twinkle lights and soft overhead fans. Fresh flowers decorate each table. Chalkboards are a common thread here, with the most impressive one a massive vertical board labled "What's Cooking?" that displays the daily specials for the entire month on sticky notes stuck under it each day. The food here is upscale, but the dining arrangement is about as casual as they come. Orders are made at the counter and the food is delivered to your table, and many patrons come here for the free Wi-Fi Internet access, the drinks, desserts, and appetizers.

Ripe is also set up as a market. All of the items on the menu are available for take-out, and the rest of the market offerings amount to specialty drinks, wine, desserts, and a few other items.

MEXICAN AND TEX-MEX
Central/Downtown

CASA JURADO $$
226 Cincinnati Ave.
(915) 532-6429
www.myspace.com/casajurado
With its original location situated right along the Cincinnati Avenue Entertainment District, this family-owned, family-style restaurant is an El Paso institution. Casa Jurado has been serving phenomenal Mexican food here for almost three decades and recently expanded to a second location on the Westside at 4772 Doniphan Dr. (915-833-1157). The original restaurant is sandwiched in between a café and a bar, making it easy to overlook, but make no mistake, the food here is no-frills deli-

cious. Casa Jurado's menu includes just about every type of traditional Mexican cuisine, from enchiladas to *pollo en mole* (mole chicken) and *pescado ala Veracruzana* (Veracruz fish). One particular menu highlight is the flauta plate—a beautiful concoction of four rolled tacos surrounded by fresh Spanish rice, beans and guacamole, and topped with *chile con queso*. The decor inside is minimal but bright, with festive colors that keep it in line with the convivial, party atmosphere of the rest of the street. Casa Jurado serves a nice variety of wines and beers and the Doniphan Drive location on the Westside has a full bar. If you're planning to go out drinking on Cincinnati Avenue, this is a great place to stock up on hearty food beforehand.

FORTI'S MEXICAN ELDER
RESTAURANT $$–$$$
321 Chelsea St.
(915) 772-0066

The ambiance at this sprawling hacienda style restaurant is only topped by the reliable food, which is of a unique El Paso style Mexican cuisine. The exterior of the building, which is designed in Territorial style architecture with brown stucco walls, brick edging, and tiled overhangs, is inviting. Black wrought-iron lamps hang above circle-topped windows, and everywhere you look are thoughtful, delicate garnishes of Mexican tile. Inside, three levels of seating areas maze through the home-like rooms and a large patio welcomes guests to dine in shaded comfort. Popular with locals and tourists alike, there are many dishes on the menu here that will appeal to just about every diet and tastebud. The salsa is particularly tasty, and other favorites include the Tampiqueña Steak, which is a grilled sirloin covered in fresh green chile salsa and accompanied by

a red chile smothered enchilada. The dishes here tend to be the mix of New Mexican and traditional Mexican cuisine that characterizes El Paso's local food.

You have to want to find Forti's, as it is situated on an out of the way street in a semi-industrialized area. The parking lot harkens to the size of the restaurant, a fact that makes Forti's a great place to go if you are starving and simply don't want to wait to be seated.

H & H CAR WASH AND
COFFEE SHOP $–$$
701 East Yandell Dr.
(915) 533-1144

It is easy to drive by this slightly out of the way little hole in the wall. In fact, you would scarcely know it was there if you didn't already know it was there. Attached to a car wash, this minuscule coffee shop exists in a time warp all its own and serves up some of the freshest, tastiest Mexican food that you'll find in El Paso. In recent years, the place has become a favorite of locals for breakfast and lunch (or breakfast at lunch, which they also serve here) and even garnered national recognition when it received the James Beard Foundation award. A number of dignitaries have dined at H & H, including former First Lady Laura Bush.

A tiny diner, inside H & H is hardly larger than an old gas station convenience store (which it probably was, at one time) and it gets completely packed during the lunch hour. Perhaps the best times to visit are mid-morning and mid-afternoon, or if you're truly fanatical, around 7 a.m. when they open for breakfast. A lot of locals will tell you that H & H is one of the best places to get Mexican food in town, a superlative not taken lightly around here. Of the more popular menu items, not to be missed are the chile rellenos (green chile peppers stuffed with cheese and then battered and fried), which are made fresh every Tuesday. This dish is so popular, in fact, that H & H often runs out by the end of the week, so if you want to give it a try, your best bet is to stop in on a Wednesday.

Eastside

CARNITAS QUÉRETARO $$
9077 Gateway West
(915) 633-9877
Originally opened in Ciudad Juárez in the 1980s, this restaurant's name comes from its original specialty dish, *carnitas*, or kettle-cooked pork. The restaurant has since expanded to three locations in El Paso—the massive cartoon pig on the sign makes them easily recognizable—each as good as the next, with a divine selection of Mexican dishes. The great thing about the menu at Carnitas Quéretaro is that there's a little something for everyone. Many families come here to indulge in Mexican comfort foods, but there are plenty of familiar items on the menu, such as tacos and burritos. However, if you want Mexican cuisine served in the traditional hearty style, including a lot of dishes that aren't typically found on Mexican-American menus, this is the place to go. *Lamb barbacoa* (barbecue), *mole*, and *buche* (stomach) are among the more adventurous offerings, and these are really the reason to eat at Carnitas Quéretaro, as opposed to the more typical Mexican-American items, which aren't as good here. The prices are truly divine, and despite the restaurant's expansion, it still tastes and costs similar to a hole in the wall joint. A second and third location are

at 10801 Pebble Hills Blvd. (915-644-6545) and on the Westside at 6516 North Mesa St. (915-584-9906).

JULIO'S CAFÉ CORONA $$$
8050 Gateway East
(915) 591-7676
www.julioscafecorona.com
When thinking of Mexican restaurants, images of fine dining under sweeping chandeliers don't usually come to mind, but such is the atmosphere at Julio's Café Corona, a family-run business that has been open since 1944. First started by Julio and Lupe Ramirez, who by themselves managed the restaurant and cooked the food, today Julio's is kept in the family by their daughter.

The atmosphere at Julio's is fancy, but the prices don't necessarily reflect that. Lush red carpeting and tableclothed dining tables are crowned by a row of vintage electric chandeliers that really take the ambiance up a notch. And seated in front of a heaping plate of red chile enchiladas, you can almost imagine that you're enjoying Sunday dinner at the home of a well-to-do Mexican family. Most of the recipes at Julio's reflect the fact that they have been passed down through the family in flavor and appearance. Once serving only Mexican food, today Julio's menu has been expanded to include Spanish, international, and seafood dishes, as well as charbroiled steaks. Some of the most popular items on the menu here are the Chicken Tampiqueña, a grilled breast served with pepper strips, guacamole, beans, and an enchilada, and the Salpicon, a dish of cold shredded beef that is combined with onions, tomatoes, cilantro, avocado, and cubed cheese to form a kind of delicious beef salad. Julio's is open every day and offers an extensive breakfast buffet on Sat and Sun.

LOS BANDIDOS DE CARLOS & MICKEY'S $$$
1310 Magruder St.
(915) 778-3323

This massive family restaurant has a gigantic menu with plenty of offerings and serves up just about every type of Mexican and Tex-Mex dish that you can think of. Almost all of the food at Carlos & Mickey's (as it is generally known locally) is good, though very few items on the menu are life-changing. This is the type of restaurant that is great to visit with the whole family or with a big group, as most everyone can usually find something to their tastes on the huge 70-plus item menu. So, whether you love the basic deliciousness of a cheese enchilada or yearn for something a bit more authentically south-of-the-border, such as Tacos al Pastor, stewed pork soft tacos garnished with green onion and pineapple, you'll probably be able to order it here.

Carlos & Mickey's is a family-run establishment that has been in business for several decades and enjoys a solid reputation among El Paso locals. They are well-known for hosting live Mexican and jazz music in the evenings between Thursday and Saturday, or conversely, you are likely to run into mariachi music here quite often. This combined with the fact that they serve excellent, strong margaritas, makes Carlos & Mickey's a great place for either a family night out or a fun evening among adults. The bar offers a happy hour from 4 to 7 p.m., and the restaurant is open every day for lunch and dinner.

PIZZA
Westside

HELLO PIZZA $–$$
1071 Country Club Rd.
(915) 581-5000

You might not expect El Paso to have a true blue New York style pizza joint, but that's just what Hello Pizza is. Owned and operated by an actual New Yorker, the pies here resemble the heaping cheesy monuments that you would find along any of Manhattan's back streets. The ambiance at Hello Pizza comes from the fact that there is no ambiance. A tiny unit in a strip mall along Country Club Road on the far Westside, inside you'll find little more than a few unadorned tables, a walk-up counter, and a classic overhead menu that boasts "Coke" in pure 1980s vintage.

The pies here are truly delicious. The owner makes sure to source his ingredients directly from New York, so the cheese, dough, and sauce all reflect the type of taste that you would find in the Big Apple. A deli as well, Hello Pizza boasts a large number of meat items, and as you walk in, your senses are almost overwhelmed by the delicious smell of baking pizza. Hello Pizza does not have a full Italian menu, but enough dishes are available to qualify it as a "sit down" restaurant, though the atmosphere is always informal and orders are taken at the counter. In addition to pizza, calzones are the specialty of the house. There is a small outdoor patio that is popular in summer and makes for a great spot to enjoy a heaping slice and a cold soda.

SUNSET BREWERY & PIZZERIA $$
4176 North Mesa St.
(915) 532-2700

Perhaps one of the greatest combinations in the history of food is the pairing of pizza and beer, and it is this combination in which Sunset Pizzeria specializes. A microbrewery and pizza joint, here you can enjoy a deluxe, wood-oven fired pizza and a cold, fresh house beer brewed on the premises. The addition

(Q) Close-up

Nighttime Would Find Me in Rosa's Cantina . . .

Out in the West Texas town of El Paso
I fell in love with a Mexican girl.
Nighttime would find me in Rosa's Cantina;
Music would play and Felina would whirl.

In 1959, cowboy crooner Marty Robbins released his fifth album, *Gunfighter Ballads and Trail Songs*. On it was a tune that would forever seal Robbins' name, and El Paso's, into American cowboy legend. That tune was *El Paso*, a narrative song told from the perspective of a cowboy living in the Wild West who falls in love with a Mexican maiden, Felina, one night at a bar. When another man makes a move on Felina, the narrator guns him down and then flees to the badlands of New Mexico. Poignant and beautifully arranged, *El Paso* reached number one on the pop charts in early 1960 and went on to win a Grammy Award for Best Country & Western Recording the following year. It is a song now instantly recognizable in most people's ears for its Mexican melodies and haunting Spanish guitar arrangements. It later became the fight song of the UTEP Miners and was covered by the Grateful Dead.

In the song, the narrator meets his lovely Felina at a bar named **Rosa's Cantina**, which many are surprised to learn is an actual place in El Paso that still exists. Rosa's Cantina captures the Wild West essence of the song and its story with its ancient stonemason walls and tiny, cavernous dining room. From the outside, it truly looks outlawish and you could almost picture the cowboy sipping a tequila and watching his Felina whirling around the small dance floor inside.

Nowadays, Rosa's Cantina has undergone a few improvements but none that compromise the ambiance of the beloved song. The walls are lined with gold records and photos of country music singers—an obvious nod to the little dive bar's claim to fame—and at a few funky tables you can order Mexican dishes and drink a cold beer whilst daydreaming about cowboys and outlaws and gunslingers, and of course, the beautiful Felina. Rosa's Cantina is an easy stop off of I-10 at the Sunland Park exit on the Westside, and serves a family friendly lunch on weekdays and operates as a bar on Saturdays and in the evenings.

Rosa's Cantina is located on the Westside at 3454 Doniphan Dr. (915-833-0402).

of an outdoor seating space completes the ultimate trifecta of pizza, beer, and patio.

The pizzas here are more Old World than New York style, with crispier crusts, lighter sauces, and the addition of fresh, unique toppings. The pizzas are 9 inches and tend to be a meal unto themselves for one person, or perhaps several pizzas could be split between a few people. There are a number of interesting topping combinations, from the regulars to the more unusual, such as spinach and artichoke hearts. On the beer front, they offer a small sampler flight of each of the microbrews in one-ounce glasses, giving you a chance to taste all of their house beers before ordering one in a pint.

While this may not be the place to go if you're looking for a truly gourmet dining experience, if what you're after is beer, pizza, and a relaxed atmosphere, you might not be able to do better than Sunset Pizzeria in El Paso.

SEAFOOD
Westside

PUERTO VALLARTA GRILL $$–$$$
7200 North Mesa St.
(915) 760-6612
Named for the port city on Mexico's west coast, this small El Paso seafood restaurant prepares fish the way that you would find it in coastal Central Mexico. Many of the popular Pacific favorites are on offer here, like fish tacos and shrimp cocktail, but the real stars here are the whole fish fillets, which are roasted and come smothered in any number of delicious toppings, like tomato and green chile salsa or fresh garlic. Also typically Mexican, when you order a *plato* here, it will come adorned with a scoop of yellow rice, mashed potatoes, and a small garden salad. The restaurant serves tacos and tortas, but otherwise the menu is strictly fish and shrimp. Not much can be said for the ambiance here. Like many of El Paso's best restaurants, it is located in a corner unit of an unassuming strip mall on the Westside, with a few simple tables. Don't come here for the atmosphere, come for the food. Puerto Vallarta Grill is open everyday except Sunday.

Eastside

LA ISLA MARISCOS $$–$$$
8140 North Loop Dr.
(915) 594-4672
www.laislamariscos.com
While El Paso is not necessarily the city to find traditional seafood, *mariscos*, or Mexican

seafood dishes, are abundant here, and La Isla is one of the better places to try them out. Traditional Mexican style fish and seafood is very different from American seafood cooking, with the focus on a number of different sauces and styles. The chefs at La Isla are masters at this, with some 14 different sauces from which to choose on either fish or shrimp, ranging from garlic to Pibil Maya Sauce, which is a chunky, spicy sauce made from *achiote* chile. Fish cooked in this manner is baked inside tin foil, causing it to retain the colors and aromas so abundant in the sauce naturally.

The interior of La Isla is a funky and fun collection of coastal decor that hearkens to a Mexican beach. In addition to the house specials and salads, they have a very short (and somewhat uninteresting) dessert menu and do offer a selection of Mexican and American beers, including the infamous Clamato cocktail—a mix of tomato juice and beer popular in Mexico and the Southwest. La Isla is definitely the real deal, but you should be aware before going in that the entire menu is in Spanish and most of the staff will approach you in Spanish, so brush up on your *palabras comidas* beforehand.

STEAK
Eastside

CATTLEMAN'S STEAKHOUSE AT
INDIAN CLIFFS RANCH $$$$
Far East Lower Valley
Fabens, TX
(915) 544-3200
www.cattlemanssteakhouse.com
This ranch-steakhouse-petting zoo is both an attraction and a restaurant, and a fine one at that. Where better, of course, to enjoy

a steak than on an actual ranch? Cattleman's Steakhouse consistently draws large crowds of both tourists and locals who want to partake of their big juicy slabs of beef, cooked just right. Beyond steak, the menu offerings here extend to mesquite-smoked barbecue, seafood, and no-nonsense poultry dishes. And the beautiful sunsets over the ranch also make the trip well worthwhile. Located on the grounds of Indian Cliffs Ranch in Fabens, Cattleman's offers hayrides and is a great place for a large group or a family to enjoy an afternoon outdoors. If you go early, you'll have some time before dinner to see the sights at the ranch, including recent movie sets. Little cowpokes will love Indian Cliffs Ranch, a place where they can live their dreams of becoming a real cowboy for a day. Let the kiddies run wild, check out the animals, and play in the hay as you work up a cowboy appetite.

The restaurant itself looks and feels like a large ranchhouse and inside the rustic ambiance is enhanced with uneven adobe walls and wooden vigas across the ceilings. Wagon wheel chandeliers and photos and memorabilia lining the walls complete the old west experience, which is only outdone here by the massive steaks.

DELANEY'S STEAKHOUSE   **$$$**
1545 North Lee Trevino Dr.
(915) 599-2600
www.delaneyssteakhouse.com
This upscale Eastside restaurant offers a fancy dining experience in a nonetheless casual atmosphere. The menu here includes aged hand-cut steaks, cooked at 1,200 degrees to sear in their natural juices, and fresh, never frozen seafood. A number of unique side dishes on offer include a delicious sweet potato and pecan casserole, as well as tempura (deep fried) green beans, which add to a hearty steak meal. Delaney's has a sizeable wine list and full bar, and they offer dining on a large patio. In the bar, happy hour is from 2 to 7 p.m. daily, with half-price appetizers. Though the dining area here leaves a little something to be desired, with basic bland carpeting and little in the way of unique decor, the beautiful marble-topped bar is a lovely place to cozy up with a glass of wine. Performances of live music happen on Tuesday and Saturday evenings.

Northeast Side

GREAT AMERICAN
LAND & CATTLE   **$$$**
7600 Alabama St.
(915) 751-5300
www.grtamerican.com
This El Paso destination restaurant has been around for a number of years serving steaks, including its signature seasoning that is used on all steaks and is available for sale to take home. It is the quality of the steaks here that makes this a "destination" restaurant, with several cuts available, including some small portions that most steakhouses don't offer. The New York strip steak is an extremely lean cut from USDA aged choice beef and comes in the smaller 10-ounce portion for those that wish to eat a steak without becoming too full. Another highlight of Great American is their Steakburger, such that a popular local nickname for the restaurant is Steakburger.

This concoction is a thick, juicy, ground steak turned into a burger and served with the usual hamburger fixings, like cheese, green chile, and garnishes, providing a more manageable meal for someone with a smaller appetite. All of the Great American restaurants offer the same side dishes, including pineapple flavored coleslaw, cabbage, ranch beans, baked potato, or steak fries.

Slightly confusingly, the Great American chain, which operates three restaurants in El Paso, has franchised out to several independent owners who operate basically the same restaurant under the same name. Most of the meals you will eat in any of these restaurants will be very similar, and the steaks are always the highlight, with the ambiance of the large, busy steakhouse dining rooms taking a backseat to the beefy flavors. A second and third location are at 9800 Gateway North on the Eastside (915-759-9314), and on the Westside at 701 South Mesa Hills Dr. (915-585-7873).

NIGHTLIFE

For years, people have overlooked the nightlife scene in El Paso, preferring the rowdier and more inclusive style across the border in Juárez. Indeed, many young people used to cross the border just to go drinking or clubbing, although that practice has waned in recent years as the violence in Juárez has gotten worse. What remains true, though, is that El Paso has a vibrant nightlife scene that is now being rediscovered as people opt to stay away from Mexico. There are literally hundreds of bars, clubs, discos and other nightlife options across the Sun City, even despite its reputation as a quiet town.

El Paso's nightlife options are quite spread out across the city, with options for drinking, dancing, and cinema-going from the Eastside to Downtown. The Cincinnati Avenue Entertainment District is located across from the University of Texas at El Paso and is one of the more concentrated areas of nightlife, with a number of bars and nightclubs packed into a small strip along Cincinnati Avenue. Downtown you'll find a burgeoning selection of chic cocktail bars and gourmet restaurants where DJs spin the hottest new electronica. You can more or less pick your poison, as well as your favorite ambiance. If you are interested in sampling local beers, El Paso has a number of celebrated microbreweries. Or, if you prefer to dance the night away, take your pick of themed nightclubs and DJ sets. Many bars and clubs also take advantage of El Paso's amazing weather with huge patios, where you can sit under the vast Texas sky and enjoy a tall cocktail or brimming-over pint.

OVERVIEW

This chapter presents a range of nightlife options, from bars and clubs to country and western dance halls and cinemas, listed by geographic area of the city. Of course, there are plenty of cultural outings to be discovered in El Paso, but those can be found listed in the Arts chapter of this book. Here, you'll find a wide range of bars and pubs, clubs, country and western dance halls, cinemas, casinos, and a selection of El Paso's finest in alternative, gay and lesbian entertainment.

The legal drinking age in Texas is 21, as in the rest of the United States. However, across the border in Mexico, the drinking age is 18, which has made Juárez a popular nightspot with many underage college students in the past. There are plenty of restaurants in El Paso that also serve alcohol, but for the purposes of this chapter, the listings are focused on any place that does not do food or where food is not the main draw of the venue. In some cases, restaurants have attached bars that I felt were worth mentioning here in the Nightlife chapter, and in that case you will find information about the bar in this chapter, as well as the food and menu in the Restaurants chapter. Be sure to check the Restaurants chapter for more information on where you can go for a great dinner and drinks in El Paso.

While most bars and pubs in El Paso don't charge a cover for entrance, if a live band is playing, you can expect to pay between $5 and $10. Similarly, nightclubs and dance clubs often charge a similar amount in cover fees, especially on weekend nights or if a famous DJ is playing. Most of the country and western dance clubs will impose a cover fee between $3 and $7 on weekends. It is worth noting that many bars and nightclubs around town offer free entrance or waive their cover charges for anyone with a military ID.

i Looking for listings? *El Paso Scene* is a monthly magazine that covers many of the gigs, performances, DJs, concerts, and cultural events going on around the city. You can pick it up for free on racks around town, or access it online at www.epscene.com.

El Paso's nightlife is extremely spread out and public transport options are limited late at night. If you plan to go out drinking, please be sure to use a designated driver or plan ahead by calling a taxi to get you to and from your bar of choice. If you are visiting El Paso for a short stay and are interested in nightlife, you may want to plan your hotel choice around one of the busier nightlife districts, such as Cincinnati Avenue, which is located in Central El Paso.

BARS AND PUBS
Central/Downtown

1914 LOUNGE
115 Durango, Suite A
(915) 544-4191
www.1914lounge.com

This downtown lounge is a self-proclaimed mix of "the at home feeling of a bar and the pound your ears and dance your feet feel of a club." Opened in 2005, this was the first place in town to offer real bottle service and semi-private VIP tables. It has won a number of "best of" awards, including Best Bar Atmosphere, Hottest Staff, and Best Place to Shake Your Booty. This is a place to see and be seen, to sip expensive cocktails, and to wear your best clothes for a night on the town. DJs here spin a mix of electronic and dance music that complements the chic decor, which is a mix of sleek dark wood, underlit bars, steel pillars, and modern lamps. Bottles of booze are lined up in various nooks behind the bar creating a very non-traditional format, which is complemented by the bar's long, maze-like layout. They often do weekend beer specials like $1 bottles of beer and cheap shots to coincide with DJ parties. If you love the moody, fashionable crowd but prefer not to have to shout over the music, you can retire to the patio for some quieter drinks.

2900
2900 North Mesa St.
(915) 544-1400
www.goto2900.com

A wonderfully atmospheric bar and restaurant, the cocktails and wine list are the stars at 2900, operated by Mark Heins, a well-known El Paso restaurateur. Located not far from the Cincinnati Avenue Entertainment District, 2900 represents a departure from the usual noisy college crowds that tend to bustle through the area on a weekend night. Instead, 2900 is a dimly lit, industrial-but-chic bar space for sipping strong cocktails in quiet corners. The decor here is modern and sleek, with the long, icy white bar the main feature when you first enter. 2900's interior space combines the warmth of an Asian-inspired dining room with urban industrial design in the concrete walls and exposed ventilation system. The bar is a simple plastic counter with ample liquor bottles displayed on modern shelves that are lit in soft blues. Separating the sleek bar from the cozier restaurant side toward the back is an 18-foot water wall, while a wine wall along one side of the bar showcases the bar's impressive selection of worldwide vintages, for which 2900 has garnered the impressive *Wine Spectator* "Best Award of Excellence" in 2009. Bottles range from an affordable but tasty Chilean Sauvignon Blanc to elegant French reds with price tags to match, all of which are best enjoyed accompanied by one of the restaurant's artisanal cheese plates. 2900's interesting selection of designer cocktails corresponds to the bar's avant-garde decor with offerings ranging from Nu-Fashion, a pomegranate and ginger ale concoction, to the downright decadent P.I.N.K.-tini, an unscrupulous mixture of P.I.N.K. vodka, X-Rated liqueur and cranberry juice.

BLACK MARKET
110 West Robinson Ave.
(915) 351-1515
Black Market is hidden a bar that is in the alley behind the corner of Mesa and Robinson, behind the Mesa Street Bar and Grill. An eclectic bar, Black Market has a little something for everybody: a range of music, a dance floor, and a patio with an outdoor bar. The staff is friendly, and they run great drink specials like $2 call drinks on Tuesday, and $2 rum on Wednesday. Smoking is allowed on the patio, and Black Market also has a pool table, a flat screen TV, live music, and DJs, depending on the day of the week. A unique selection of art is displayed all over the walls

inside, and the mishmash of faux artsy decor gives this place a comfy, cluttered vibe with a lot of color.

i The Cincinnati Avenue Entertainment District can get very lively with a college and younger drinking crowd, especially on weekend nights. This is a great place to go for cheap drink specials; just be careful crossing the road, as cars can go very fast through this area and visibility is low.

CINCINNATI BAR
207 Cincinnati Ave.
(915) 532-5592
www.cincinnatibar.biz
The Cincinnati Bar is located in the Cincinnati Avenue Entertainment District. Just a short walk from the Don Haskins Center, the Sun Bowl, and other UTEP venues, the bar caters to a college crowd, sports fans, and professionals. It is a popular pre- and post-game and concert destination, as well as a great place to relax and watch a game. During the day, the Cincinnati Bar has a friendly, pub-like ambience and is a neighborhood joint where professionals gather to discuss the events of the day, sports, and politics. Later in the evenings, the bar fills up with a younger crowd, the music is turned up, and the revelry is wild. Drinks here are reasonably priced and specials are abundant. They also boast a food menu that transcends regular bar food, from handmade meatballs and seafood stew to a tasty New York strip and beloved burgers. They also serve breakfast all day. If you want to avoid the crowds here, stop in for dinner and drinks on a weeknight, rather than weekends or game days.

DOME BAR
101 South El Paso St.
www.caminoreal.com

This classic, historic bar at the Camino Real Hotel is very popular with downtown office workers and business travelers during happy hour, when there's usually live entertainment in the form of jazz bands. The Dome Bar is named for the large Tiffany glass dome that is its crowning feature and allows a constant stream of colorful muted natural light into the space. Upon entering the bar, which is situated just off the hotel lobby, you might feel as though you're on the set of *Titanic*, as crystal chandeliers hang over the grand marble and brass staircase that leads up to the second-level Dome Restaurant. As you might expect, the ambiance of this bar is rather genteel, with a round wooden bar counter and antique furnishings that beckon to a bygone time. You'll find a slow but steady flow of alcohol is poured, but the bartenders and the drinkers both take their time, so this is more a place to sip a quiet scotch than to watch a rowdy football game or meet singles.

GARAGE TEQUILA BAR
4025 North Mesa St.
(915) 543-9530
www.myspace.com/garagetequilabar

As its name would suggest, the main event at this dive bar is definitely tequila. They have dozens of types of rare and unusual tequilas on offer, and they mix about 20 specialty margaritas in a variety of flavors, from fruity to downright strange. The interior is styled like a souped-up garage, with large roll up doors where there could be windows, lots of sports flags hanging from corrugated steel walls, and dim lighting that gives it a slightly fancier feeling. This is a great place to watch a game, have a quiet night with friends, or sample the finer art of tequila tasting. The quality of tequilas here ranges from high-quality sipping tequila to basic cheap tequila you can slam. If tequila just isn't your thing, you can also choose from an extensive list of Mexican beers, including Corona, Negra Modelo, and Bohemia. There's no cover charge here and drinks range from $3 to $5, with high-end tequila going for up to $30. They have one of the longest happy hours in El Paso, from 1 to 7 p.m. Thurs through Sun, as well as an all-day happy hour on Mon. There are themed nights all week, including karaoke night, live bands, an indie night, and a resident DJ on Sun. With eight flat screen TVs and an extra large projection TV this is an excellent place to catch NFL Sunday Ticket or Monday Night Football.

HEMMINGWAY'S
214 Cincinnati Ave.
(915) 532-7333

Hemmingway's is a down-home beer bar with a selection of 11 specialty beers on tap and 150 imported and microbrewed bottled beers. It has the feel of a college town bar with a fashionable crowd, and a house band plays live music often. The crowd is definitely infiltrated with the under-30 set, but it can be a nice place to sit over an afternoon brew or head with friends on a weeknight if you aren't into the packed-out college weekend scene. Despite the plethora of college kids, Hemmingway's still has one of the best beer selections in El Paso, and for that alone it is worth a visit. The bar occasionally hosts theme nights, including cigar evenings and mariachi nights.

JAXON'S
4799 North Mesa St.
(915) 544-1188
www.jaxons.com
Anyone that appreciates microbrews and craft beers must pay a visit to Jaxon's. This restaurant and microbrewery has a rotating selection of their own house-made beers. Though Jaxon's "King" margaritas and signature cocktails are regarded as some of the best in the region, the real star here is, of course, the beer. Jaxon's is the fourth oldest brew pub in the state of Texas and pours a variety of award-winning handcrafted ales and lagers. Regularly at Jaxon's, you'll find they offer an American-style lager, an amber ale, a brown ale, and one of the milkiest stouts you'll ever come across. Rosa's Raspberry Ale is a truly unique fruit beer with a truly El Paso name. The atmosphere at Jaxon's is all you would expect from a modern microbrewery— relaxed and friendly with a heavy emphasis on good beer and food (see the entry in the Restaurants chapter, p. 66). You may opt to sit in the dining areas or on stools at high tables in an attached bar, where a long bronze bar counter overlooks windows into the brewing vat rooms. A second and third location are located far Northwest at 4799 North Mesa St. (915-544-1188), and on the Westside at 7410 Remcon Circle (915-845-6557). All three locations have a bar and free wireless Internet access.

THE LOFT
2626 North Mesa St.
(915) 532-0589
www.myspace.com/loftbar915
This tiny upstairs bar is dominated by the wooden dance floor and a plethora of colored disco lights and strobes that make it feel even smaller. A quaint corner bar sits at one end of the room with a few barstools that quickly go unused as the night becomes more dance-oriented. The beers and cocktails are pricey, but people are mostly here to dance and be seen, or meet someone. If you're looking for a sit-down drink, this is not the place, but if you're ready to shake your booty in close quarters with glammed up strangers, hit the Loft. DJ Adrian mixes top 40, hip hop, dance, and old school music everyday. There are actually two full service bars at the Loft, one serving on the outdoor smoking balcony, and bottle service is available starting at $100 a bottle. A strict dress code is enforced, so dress to impress.

MARCO POLO DIVE BAR
2708 North Mesa St.
(915) 544-3483
Belly up to the tiled counter or perch on blue plastic bar chairs in this pool-themed place to see and be seen. In some ways, Marco Polo is anything *but* a dive bar, despite its name that suggests otherwise. It's mostly a place for overheated college students to let loose over an expensive bottle of beer or a Skyy vodka. Located in the Cincinnati Avenue Entertainment District, one great thing about Marco Polo is that you can go between it and O2 lounge at your leisure, giving you access to two bars in one. The DJs here play a decent selection of hip hop and house music, but the drinks are on the pricey side and it is a tiny place.

O2 LOUNGE
2700 North Mesa St.
(915) 532-0202
This place is where it's at if you're looking to shake your booty! DJs here spin old hip hop jams like Cypress Hill, Gangsta's Paradise,

Naughty By Nature, and plenty of other crowd pleasers that are great to dance to. Perhaps the best part about O2 Lounge is that the majority of people here spend their time dancing, leaving plenty of space to chill out outside on the patio (which is warmed with heat lamps during the winter). The overall atmosphere here is a fun, young vibe where a lot of people are welcomed. The narrow walkway that leads from the bar at the entrance to the outside patio sometimes gets crammed with people waiting for the restrooms, but anyone that loves a full bar and club atmosphere won't mind the squeeze of a little traffic jam now and again.

On any given night here, you're likely to meet locals, especially those of the good looking and fashionable crowd, so don't be surprised if you run into local sports stars (or maybe their cheerleaders). Without a real dance floor, the lounge gets packed with standers, dancers, and people generally milling around, and it is connected to Marco Polo Dive Bar through the backyard, so there will always be a place to escape if you find yourself tired of the scene inside.

Though the drinks here are on the pricey side, the bar itself has one of the best top-shelves in town, with a fine selection of scotch, bourbons, and a huge selection of flavored and infused vodkas. A lot of attention is paid to detail, all the way down to premium garnishes such as edible orchids, fresh muddled berries, and out-of-the-ordinary juices like white cranberry. On the beer front, only a very safe selection of domestic and imported bottles are on offer, so don't come expecting to drink cheap or cheerful. The DJs are top notch and are also part of the draw, as there is a heavy regular crowd here most of the time.

The main bar queues up four deep on weekends and getting a drink is easiest by occupying a table and waiting for a waitress, or hanging out on the patio on Friday, where the bars are just as full-service as the inside. Generally speaking, O2 is a hip place to beat the downtown crowds with creative bar offerings and a fashion-conscious crowd.

O'HAGAN'S IRISH PUB
2602 North Mesa St.
(915) 351-9775
www.ohagansip.com
This neighborhood pub is owned and operated by a real Irish man, Matt Hagan, but you almost wouldn't know it. Small, dark, and slightly dingy, at first glance, O'Hagan's appears more like a dive bar than a true Irish pub, but the spirit is alive here nonetheless. On the weekends, this UTEP-adjacent pub is stocked with fun, laid back, loyal patrons and a friendly bar staff. Inside, the featureless strip-mall style room has been converted with green walls and a sufficient enough supply of shamrocks, leprechauns, and green, orange, and white decor to make it look and feel Irish. They are open every day of the week with plenty of specials, including Wednesday evening, which is Ladies' Night. At happy hour here, which runs from 3 to 8 p.m. on weekdays, you can score extremely cheap food and drink: hot dogs for just $1 and pints for just $2 to $3. They also offer free popcorn all the time, which is a nice change from grubby bar peanuts.

SOHO
500 North Oregon St., Suite A
(915) 532-7646
www.sohococktaillounge.com
Soho is an upscale cocktail lounge with unique decor that will make you feel like

you're in a French movie. Richly upholstered couches and chairs, dark blue paint, lavish tapestries, antique furnishings, bejeweled lamps, and gold pillows abound in this fully furnished lounge. Candles flicker on tables, there's a choice of style magazines on the walls, and flare bartenders at the full bar pour plenty of strong cocktails, including 25 varieties of martinis, while table and bottle service is available. Their Bose surround sound system pumps a variety of music every night of the week, from live bands to DJs that crank out house, electronic, dance, top 40, industrial, and even goth music, which varies depending on the day. Be sure to wear your chicest outfits to fit in with the fashionistas that frequent Soho. There is a cover charge every other Sunday for "Sunday Mass."

TAP BAR & RESTAURANT
408 East San Antonio St.
(915) 532-1848
Tap is not for the faint of heart. A true dive bar through and through, you'll want to be prepared for the dingy when you enter. But Tap is welcoming of all, from downtown suits to border jumpers and everyone in between, and so long as you can speak some Spanish to the servers here and avoid looking like a tourist at all costs (that means putting the camera away), you can drink. You might get stares when you first walk in the door and you might be put off by the slightly rundown exterior of this ancient downtown joint, but don't let those factors stop you. Inside, you'll be a world away and you'll feel like you're somewhere in the heart of Mexico. You may also have to plug your nose from the slightly unfortunate aroma of mop water, but isn't that what dive bars are all about? Tap serves two things: cheap beer and fantastic Mexican food, most of which won't run more than about $5 a plate. Grab a pitcher and keep a low profile in one of the ancient booths at this, one of El Paso's true institutions.

YES SUMATRA HOOKAH LOUNGE
916 North Mesa St.
(915) 543-9900
www.myspace.com/sumatrahookahbar
The Middle Eastern tradition of hookah smoking is alive and well at the Sumatra Lounge. A hookah is a communal pipe (everyone gets his or her own sterile mouthpiece) used to smoke a variety of flavored tobaccos. The Sumatra does not serve alcohol, but patrons are invited to bring their own and must pay a small cover fee to do so. As such, this is a convenient place for the under-21 crowd to hang out, or for anyone that enjoys the laid back art of hookah smoking. Decor here is minimal—a few couches and chairs are scattered around low tables good for hookah stands, and the music ranges from Wu Tang to Lady GaGa, with a lot of chilled-out music on offer to enhance the relaxed vibe. On occasional nights, Sumatra shows movies at the bar with a $2 cover charge. Among the flavors of tobacco available, you can choose from fruity scents like apple and peach to chocolate and other more exotic flavors.

Sumatra also functions as a head shop where you can buy your own hookahs and accessories, as well as flavored tobaccos, shisha, coal, and flavored bases. If you buy a hookah here, you are welcome to smoke it on the premises. They are open most nights until midnight or 2 a.m.

ZEPPELIN'S UNDERGROUND
111 West Robinson Ave.
(512) 947-3066
www.myspace.com/zeppelinsep
This local music club is situated across from Black Market not far from UTEP. With its excellent selection of beer, it is a hangout that doubles as a live music venue. If you are at all interested in hearing some live music, be it a local indie rock band or a national touring hip hop group, you are likely to find something going on at Zeppelin's. The small patio often gets crowded with smokers on weekend nights and when there isn't a gig on, modern club music is blasted from within, which can be a turnoff to live rock music seekers and a draw for those who just want to dance. Inside, the space has a minimalist feel, with a few wrought iron patio tables and chairs scattered around the mostly concrete inner rooms. Cover charges here range from $3 to $10, depending on the act that's performing, and sometimes they open the bar to under 21 patrons during the early evening or for certain shows. If you love live and local music, Zeppelin's calendar is one to keep an eye on (or look for their posters around town).

Westside

ACEITUNAS BEER GARDEN
5200 Doniphan Dr.
(915) 581-3260
www.aceitunaselpaso.com
Voted El Paso's best singles' bar, Aceitunas Beer Garden on El Paso's Westside has been popular for its open patio and casual charm since it opened in 1985. It has always been a great pick-up joint for college fraternity boys and middle-aged men losing their hair—and, as it turns out, it's a great place for local bands to pick up new fans, too. Despite its somewhat questionable patronage, Aceitunas is actually just a really great place to go drinking. The name "beer garden" is entirely appropriate for this open-air lounge where trees decorated in twinkle lights grow up through the middle of the bar. The space is more like a massive porch where picnic tables and hanging potted plants are the decor of choice. Inside, the entire bar is made of wood and stone, giving it an indoor/outdoor ambiance. And the crowd is as relaxed as the furnishings. If you can overlook the meet-market crew, you'll love the cheap beers and extensive outdoor space, where you can sit all night and enjoy the fantastic El Paso weather. Thursdays through Saturdays, Aceitunas features live bands, and their specials include happy hours every day from 4 to 8 p.m., as well as daily offerings of cheap beers and well drinks.

BJ'S BREWHOUSE
11905 Gateway West
(915) 633-8300
www.bjsbrewhouse.com
Though a national chain, this brewhouse is worth mentioning for its fine beers and tasty Chicago style pizza. Boasting a full menu and a rotating supply of craft beers, BJ's is a good place for a meal or just a fresh pint. BJ's was started in 1978 as a deep dish pizzeria in Santa Ana, California. Since then, the restaurant has expanded throughout the western United States, and in 1996, the first BJ's brewery began production. The relaxed but high-energy environment here is fun and child-friendly, making it a great alternative to some of the seedier and rowdier bars you'll find near UTEP. The BJ's location in El Paso offers a full bar that includes their standard range of craft beers like Brewhouse Blonde, Harvest Hefeweizen, Jeremiah Red,

and Tatonka Stout, as well as a rolling selection of seasonal beers depending on the time of year. They have happy hour specials with cheap pints and are open every day until 11 p.m. or midnight.

KING'S X
4119 North Mesa St.
(915) 544-4795
www.thekingsx.com

The King's X is the quintessential local Texas bar. It has an extremely loyal customer base that, even after it closed for several months and reopened in 2009, returned and made the bar as homey and cozy as it was before. The basic atmosphere at King's X is that of a classic, ever-so-slightly grungy Texas honky tonk with vintage Budweiser signs lighting up the cheap wood paneling. This place is a local favorite where you can catch an NFL game, listen to a blues jam, sing karaoke, and drink a cheap bottle of America's favorite beer. Live music is provided every weekend by local blues, western, and classic rock bands, and the bar opens at 10 a.m. every day for those mornings when you need a little hair of the dog. They have happy hours from 4 to 7 p.m. every night of the week, and if you're hungry, you can grab a bite at I Love Lucy's, a Tex-Mex restaurant located inside the bar.

LLOYD'S PUB
6110 North Mesa St.
(915) 581-5793

Lloyd's is an El Paso institution that's tucked away in a strip mall on the Westside. Purportedly a favorite watering hole of UTEP basketball legend Don Haskins in his day, Lloyd's is just popular enough to attract an assortment of locals, but not so popular that you can't find a seat. Prices are reasonable and service is friendly, but there are no servers, so you'll have to place your drink orders at the bar. Sometimes you just don't want to pay $12 for a drink, and it is those nights for which Lloyd's Pub is perfect. While the drinks here may be cheaper, they're definitely not weaker, and there are literally people of all ages and backgrounds here, with a little something for everyone. The jukebox never stops and the music ranges from good old Zeppelin to the more modern rock that is current on the radio. If you are looking to let your hair down and meet some interesting people, then Lloyd's is your bar!

Eastside

BULLDOG ENGLISH PUB
1201 Bob Hope Dr.
(915) 859-9099
www.myspace.com/bulldogbar

Despite its name, there is very little about Bulldog that is British. It is, however, a comfy Eastside bar with a great beer selection and it is a good place to escape the madness of Cincinnati Avenue. They have over 50 different beers and malt liquors in stock and have a special every day, including Monday Night Football, Tecate Tuesday, and free Texas Hold 'em tournaments on Wednesday. They also host karaoke, live bands and NFL Sunday Ticket for sports fans. A generous happy hour goes 3 to 8 p.m. every day and there are drink specials every night of the week. The mahogany bar, red lighting, and small wooden pub tables give it a British flair, but it is mostly just a regular El Paso watering hole with a good international beer selection. Two pool tables, an Internet jukebox, and bar top games will keep you entertained, but don't come expecting a pint of Old Speckled Hen or Fullers ESB. If you don't care about authenticity, and just need a decent little bar in a strip mall, then it might do you just fine.

CLUB 101
1148 Airway Blvd.
(915) 544-2101
www.club101.com
This dark nightclub has been the center of El Paso's rock music scene for years, and was recently resurrected at a new location on Airway Boulevard. In addition to the Friday Top 40/Hip Hop and Saturday "Retro" themed nights, Club 101 still serves as a venue for touring musical acts, with regular performances by local and national alternative and rock bands. If you can overlook the swarms of scantily clad women, you'll probably enjoy taking in a gig in this no-frills place where it's all about the music. A collection of foosball tables and pool tables provides entertainment, while the standard Budweiser neon signs hang along the wooden slatted walls. A dark stage is set up in one corner of the room, from which bands project their tunes. Part pub, part music club, and part honky tonk, Club 101 lives up to its name as one of the most quintessential El Paso joints. They have an extra large smoking patio, DJs every night, three full bars, and a huge dance floor. Thursday is ladies night and ladies over 21 drink free.

POCKETS
1441 North Zaragoza Rd.
(915) 857-2807
This unassuming billiards club in the Plaza Las Misiones strip mall is all about the pool. There are 28 pool tables lined up on rich red carpeting and overseen by low green table lamps, making this the classic billiards club. Pool tables cost around $6 an hour for any size group, but often fill up fast, so get there early or put your name on the waiting list and have a drink. They have a smoking patio in the front and a VIP party room available for birthdays and events. The tables here are well kept and the place is clean and classy, rather than the dingy pool halls you often find. They also do absurd-looking 96-ounce beer towers for the thirsty, and good deals on beers, shots, and buckets. Their very reasonable food menu includes wings and other bar snacks should you get hungry.

Northeast Side

MULLIGAN'S NORTH BAR & GRILL
10710 Gateway North, Suite A-1
www.myspace.com/mulligans_north
Despite its Irish name, this bar is a quintessentially El Paso joint and one of the only decent watering holes on the Northeast side. If you live or happen to be on the Northeast side or are visiting Fort Bliss, this is a decent Texas-style bar with good specials and a funky interior. A mishmash of western, Southwestern, and uniquely Texas decor gives Mulligan's an eclectic vibe. The standout bar counter is covered by a corrugated steel "roof" on which hang several neon beer signs. In addition to its full bar, Mulligan's also boasts a large smoking patio, two pool tables and a foosball table, 11 TVs and a big screen, a jukebox, and darts, which makes it a great place for a quiet but entertaining night of drinking. This is also a great place to drop in for cheap lunch specials during the week, as they have a full menu on offer that mostly consists of pub grub and Southwestern favorites. On weekend nights, you might also catch live shows by long-haired aging rock bands, for which there is usually a minimal cover charge.

CLUBS

CLUB DEDO
204 East Rio Grande
(915) 533-4684
www.clubdedo.com

Whether you prefer to hang in the shadows or get on the dance floor, Dedo was one of the first nightclubs in El Paso to incorporate different styles of music and themed concept nights under one roof. Open three nights a week, you'll experience something different each night from Thurs to Sat, and you can also expect them to host themed parties at other times of the year, for instance Christmas and St. Patrick's Day. Generally speaking, Dedo is one of those no-frills dark nightclubs decorated only with red strip lighting across the ceiling and a few sparse stools and benches. Club Dedo's themed nights include the Liverpool Lounge on Thursday, where you'll hear a mix of Brit-pop and Motown; Synthetic Friday, which features EBM, Synth, Darkwave, Psytrance, and Electro; and Dedo Madness on Saturday where almost anything goes. Patrons here tend to be of the Goth and New Wave variety and you might stand out if you wear anything but black. Club Dedo also often opens its doors to the 18+ crowd, which makes it a good nightlife choice for those under 21.

EMPYRE
524 San Francisco St.
(915) 546-4000
www.myspace.com/empyreclub
Empyre is a massive split-level nightclub with a full bar, an extra large dance floor, and a large smoking patio, and this is the place to go for after-hours nightlife and lots of be-seen dancing action. Collections of uber-chic plastic and leather furniture in deep colors are set in groups, with small glass tables, mirrors, and rock walls, which you probably won't notice because of the dark lighting, strobes, and pounding music. The club itself is a large square, with the seating areas both upstairs and downstairs surrounding a huge

central dance floor. They generally impose a $5 cover charge for men, while ladies are welcomed free before 11 p.m. Empyre is only open on Saturday nights, which means that it is usually extremely crowded, most often with the super glammed up crowd. In addition to their beer tubs, specials here include extremely cheap beers and well drinks before 11 p.m., and even though the doors open at 8, the place doesn't get busy until midnight. A dress code is enforced, so make sure you put away the sneakers and look your best.

VANILLA
115 Durango
(915) 351-2000
www.myspace.com/vanillabar
The name of this super classy nightclub is taken from the reams of white curtains that drape from every open space and the rows of puffy white leather furniture open for sitting on. While this is definitely a dance club, there is plenty of space to sit, sip a cocktail, and look pretty or wait for that pretty someone-or-other to approach you. The overall atmosphere is sexy chic and very pretty, with a lot of red, blue, and purple lighting complementing the generally bleached decor. You can definitely expect to run into a lot of well-dressed (and sometimes underdressed) fashionistas here, and the dance floor usually gets so crowded that one can barely move. One nice perk is the table service, which makes it possible to avoid approaching the three deep bar and spilling your expensive cocktail. Thurs night here is College Night, so it is often packed with the under-21 crowd, but they offer drink specials all evening as a consolation. Fri and Sat, meanwhile, are 21 and over, with plenty of DJs spinning the latest in electronic, hip hop, and house beats.

COUNTRY AND WESTERN DANCING

BRONCOS
8750 Gateway Blvd. East
(915) 592-5600
www.myspace.com/broncosdiscoteque

Broncos, located where Margaritas used to be, has a reputation for keeping Tejano music fans *bailando* around the dance floor for hours. This hotbed of Latin tracks has been packing in El Paso fans with a steady fix of concerts, dance lessons, and simply great dance music. Inside, you'll find a country style decor surrounding a nice, spacious dance floor perfect for salsa'ing or chacha'ing the night away. There is also a great patio and several pool tables, as well as a snack bar and two beer bars. Though Broncos most definitely has a scene all its own, most people that come here are only interested in dancing. Even if you are not, it is perfectly acceptable to take up space at one of the no-frills tables that are dotted around the dance floor and just watch. Salsa dancing lessons are offered every Wednesday at 8 p.m. and the club is open to everyone 18 and over.

THE STORM
5500 Doniphan
(915) 833-8300

The Storm is a re-opened incarnation of the old honky-tonk mainstay, the Stampede, which closed in December 2006. Fortunately for boot-scooters, the bar didn't stay closed long. The rejuvenated superclub is still all about the dancing and draws a crowd of loyal patrons who come for one thing and one thing only: shaking their booties. The Storm is open Thurs to Sat, with various themes each night, including Latin dancing on Fri and country and western dancing on Sat. With a 40,000-watt sound system, the club can really blow your ears off with loud and proud music, while dancers whirl around the floor in two-stepping delight. As you might expect in a club that is geared toward dancers, there is not a huge selection of drinks here, but you can expect the standard range of bottled domestic beers and basic mixed drinks. Various cover charges apply; most are around $5 for a full night of dancing. The crowd is usually very relaxed, as is the dress code.

> **i** Fancy trying line dancing? You can enroll in beginner lessons through Michelle's Line Dance Floor, which meets on Wednesday and Friday nights at 7 p.m. For more information, check out Michelle's Web site, www.margaritas1.com.

GAY AND LESBIAN HOTSPOTS

THE OLD PLANTATION
301 South Ochoa St.
(915) 533-6055

Known locally as simply "the OP," this is the liveliest gay and lesbian hangout in El Paso, and is considered to be one of the city's premiere alternative lifestyle bars. The OP has been around for some 30 years and is the oldest and biggest gay nightclub in all of Texas. If you can think of something night-life related, it is probably going on at this pumping club. From karaoke to foam parties, comedy nights, drag shows, live music, and even strip nights, this place covers the entire spectrum of lifestyle choices. The OP is open Fri and Sat from 9 p.m. to 4 a.m., Sun 9 p.m. to 2 a.m., which makes it one of the latest bars in the city. The decor is unusual, located in an old warehouse, the Old Plantation, which was converted into a nightclub.

Signs around the place proudly announce that the OP is owned and operated by gays and lesbians, and many in El Paso consider it to be one of the best places in the city for dance music, which is always an up-to-date selection of electronic and top 40. The venue itself is massive but doesn't offer anything extra in the way of frills. Graffiti is splashed around the room to make it look hip and the dance floor is large with an area upstairs overlooking the scene. This is not the place to go if you're looking for a quiet drink or a more mature crowd, but it can be a lot of fun if you're in the mood to be outrageous. A number of specials are on offer, including no cover for anyone 21 and over on Fri before 10 p.m., and free entrance all night long on Sat. Cover charges here, when they are imposed, generally run between $3 and $5. Members of the military are welcomed for free with a valid ID.

CASINOS

SPEAKING ROCK ENTERTAINMENT CENTER
122 South Old Pueblo Dr.
(915) 860-7777
www.ysletadelsurpueblo.org

Speaking Rock Entertainment Center is operated by the Ysleta del Sur pueblo, a Native American tribe whose pueblo lands sit along the Mission Trail south of downtown El Paso. This large facility is hard to miss, with vivid neon signs that provide a bright greeting as you drive into the pueblo on Alameda Avenue. Since the El Paso smoking ban does not extend to Native American land, which is goverened separately by tribal law, the structure is a noisy smoker's haven that contains several themed restaurants and lounges, from a full service bar with drink specials to a buffet cafeteria. Big screen

TVs throughout the facility show local and national sporting events, and concerts are often held in an on-site live music venue. Games and prizes include a sweepstakes and video game rooms. Often referred to as a casino, there actually is little of interest here if you are looking for traditional gambling tables or slot machines. Regardless, it is still a popular spot with locals.

SUNLAND PARK RACETRACK & CASINO
1200 Futurity Dr.
Sunland Park, NM
(575) 874-5200
www.sunland-park.com

In nearby New Mexico, Sunland Park racetrack and casino features slot machine gaming, live horse racing, simulcast wagering, four dining options including a Las Vegas–style buffet, live entertainment, and concerts, as well as a convention space and meeting rooms. Without a full set of table games, Sunland Park is really more of a slot parlor than a true casino. Races at Sunland Park feature both thoroughbreds and quarter horses from Dec through late Apr and live racing is traditionally held here four days a week, on Tues, Fri, Sat, and Sun. Tickets for Grandstand seats are free, while seats in the posh Turf Club run $7.

CINEMAS

El Paso has a number of cinema options, from large chain theaters that show all the latest Hollywood releases, to small movie screenings for true film buffs. Cinemark operates three large theaters, including the Westside staple, **Cinemark El Paso** (7440 Remcon Circle; 915-587-5145), which has 16 screens; the massive, shiny new **Tinseltown** on the Eastside (11855 Gateway West;

915-590-4676), which has 14 screens; and the 14-screen **Cielo Vista Mall Cinema.** Other commercial theater options include the 12-screen **Starplex East Pointe** (8300 Gateway East; 915-590-0280), **Carmike 16** (9840 Gateway North; 915-751-6867), and the giant 18-screen megaplex **El Paso Premiere Cinema 18** (6101 Gateway West; 915-771-7900).

If it is indie film that you're after, the **El Paso Filmmakers Association** (www.epfilm .org) lists a number of options, including local film festivals and screenings being held throughout El Paso and the region every year. Additionally, the **Film Salon** (801 North Mesa St.; 915-533-2674; www.filmsalon.org) hosts a regular monthly ongoing film series that features classic and foreign films, and is where El Paso film buffs gather to appreciate and discuss the world's best movies. The salon is held on the first Saturday of each month at Trinity-First United Methodist Church on the corner of Mesa and Yandell Streets.

ATTRACTIONS

Wild West. Gunslingers. Outlaws and lawmen. Working cattle ranches with cowboys on horses. Orchards with lush lines of trees and fertile vineyards that produce delicious wines. Scenic mountain drives, a corn maze, and a spooky cemetery. Fascinating Native American culture, ancient churches, and sites where the very founding of American history took place. Though sometimes not thought of as a big tourism destination, there is so much rich heritage and culture to be found in the Sun City that you would need a lifetime explore everything. Here you can pay a visit to the grave of John Wesley Hardin, one of the baddest outlaws in the West. If military history piques your interest, take the time to see some of the first airplanes ever used in war combat. Or if you need a moment of repose, spend a few hours taking in the deep spiritual rituals of some of the oldest native cultures on earth. The city is a veritable playground of attractions just waiting to be uncovered, so get out there, because the sun is sure to be shining and it's a great day to explore.

This chapter presents a wide variety of El Paso's most interesting attractions and should give you a good starting place to begin your Southwestern sightseeing adventure in the Sun City, and will appeal to grown ups and kids alike. Instructions have been included at the end of the chapter for how to enjoy a scenic mountain drive overlooking the city. Meanwhile, several of the more specific types of listings can be found in other chapters. For instance, El Paso's many art museums have been included in the Arts chapter, while other museums relating to history, archaeology, and culture are listed here. Most outdoor spots, like Keystone Heritage Park and McKelligon Canyon, are covered in the Parks and Recreation chapter. Most of the city's family oriented activities, such as El Paso Zoo and Western Playland Amusement Park have, likewise, been covered in the Kidstuff chapter.

Price Code

The following price code has been included to give you a rough idea of what one regular adult ticket or entrance fee will cost at each of the following places. If the fees or costs associated with a particular activity or place are varied, no price has been given and you should use the contact information provided to find out details. More specific pricing and discount information is included in the listings, where available.

$	$1 to $5
$$	$6 to 10
$$$	$11 to $20
$$$$	$21 and up

MONUMENTS AND HISTORIC PLACES

CONCORDIA CEMETERY   FREE
3700 East Yandell Dr.
(915) 842-8200
www.concordiacemetery.org

Concordia Cemetery is so much more than a graveyard. Perhaps one of El Paso's most intriguing historical sites, buried here are some of the most captivating personas of the landscape of the American West, from Mormon pioneers to Buffalo Soldiers, famous outlaws and the lawmen that killed them. The cemetery began as a ranch founded by in 1853 by Hugh Stevenson. Stevenson's wife died after being gored by one of their pet deer, and so he buried her on the site of what would become the largest cemetery in the Southwest. Concordia is home to more than 60,000 historical personas of El Paso and Juárez, and this sprawling cemetery is filled to the brim with leaning crosses and crooked headstones. Among the most famous residents of Concordia are the infamous gunman John Wesley Hardin, his killer lawman John Selman, the Reverend Joseph Tayes, and others. There are two entrances to the cemetery; the east entrance is accessible from North Boone Street, while the west entrance is located on North Stevens Street. The cemetery is divided into several sections, which were used historically for different groups of people. A large swath of land on the east side of the cemetery was consecrated and reserved for the Catholic Diocese, while a green section just south, known as Mount Sinai, is the home of many deceased Jewish El Pasoans. Hardin's grave, easily the most visited site in Concordia, is located right in the center of the cemetery,

surrounded by a stone and wrought iron cage that is labeled with two pistols and the denomination "J.W.H."

The cemetery is open morning to evening every day of the year. Around Halloween, a local historical society dedicated to preserving the cemetery puts on guided ghost tours with guides dressed as Concordia residents.

EL PASO COUNTY HISTORICAL SOCIETY'S BURGES HOUSE   FREE
603 West Yandell St.
(915) 533-3606
www.elpasohistory.com

This mansionesque former home of Jane Burges Perrenot, daughter of a prominent El Paso family and collector of El Paso and Texas history, now belongs to the El Paso County Historical Society and is used as a research facility. Burges's historical collections provided the foundation for the society's collection of historic photos, postcards, and archives. Included are more than 9,000 photos that date from 1875 to present, including El Paso buildings, people, and many interesting photos of the Mexican Revolution. There are also family scrapbooks, old publications, historical documents and maps, and over 7,500 postcards from around the world. Occasionally, the society holds presentations and lectures at the Burges House, as well. The house is open Tues and Thurs from 9 a.m. to 4 p.m., and Fri from 9 a.m. to 3 p.m.

FIREFIGHTER'S MUSEUM   FREE
8600 Montana Ave.
(915) 771-1000

El Paso was one of the first towns west of the Mississippi River to form a municipal fire department. In this small museum, you can explore some interesting firefighting equipment, including two antique fire engines, as well as other equipment and historic artifacts related to firefighting. You will also learn about some of the more famous fires in El Paso, some with shocking photographs of houses or buildings on fire. Admission is free. Open Mon through Fri, 8 a.m. to 5 p.m.

HERITAGE HOUSE MUSEUM   FREE
UTEP Campus
Corner of Kerbey and Randolph
(915) 747-5700
www.utep.edu/heritage
This small white bungalow house is the main repository of historical documents and UTEP memorabilia, tracing the university's history from its founding in 1914 as the Texas College of Mines. The building was first commissioned as a home, built in 1921 by the first dean of the College, Stephen Worrell. Among the many changing exhibits throughout the year is an annual special exhibition, Golden Grads, around the time of Homecoming, which honors famous and notable graduates. One entire interior wall of the Heritage House is devoted to the timeline of various memorabilia items and photographs dating from 1913 to the current time. Open Wed to Fri 10 a.m. to noon.

MAGOFFIN HOME STATE
HISTORIC SITE $
1120 Magoffin Ave.
(915) 533-5147
www.visitmagoffinhome.com
Joseph Magoffin was one of El Paso's earliest civic leaders and he lived in a beautiful homestead near what is now downtown El Paso, built in 1875. Today, the Magoffin

Home is a museum that offers lots of insight into the early days of El Paso's township. Through a series of exhibits throughout the homesite, you learn about the stories and exploits of one of the area's first and most well-known multicultural pioneer families. Members of the Magoffin family actively participated in the westward U.S. expansion and settlement, traded on the Santa Fe–Chihuahua Trail, bore witness to Civil War turmoil, and served in the military, working toward better U.S.–Mexico relations. The house, built in 1875, is an excellent early example of the Territorial style of architecture that is so unique to the Southwest, with a flat roof, smooth stucco walls, wooden window lintels, and an open center courtyard and peaceful landscape. Exhibitions inside the home include authentic art and furnishings that reflect the daily lives of the historic El Paso family. Open Tues through Sun 9 a.m. to 5 p.m. Guided tours are given on the hour with the last tour beginning at 4 p.m.

MCCALL NEIGHBORHOOD
CENTER   FREE
3231 East Wyoming Ave.
(915) 566-2407
The McCall Center is dedicated to local and national African-American history. It is located in the historic home of Marshall and Olalee McCall, a notable black couple from El Paso. Marshall McCall was El Paso's first African-American postal worker, while his wife Olalee was principal of the all-black Douglass School. Their converted home is now a center for black culture in El Paso, boasting archives and a museum with a photographic collection on local and national black history, gift shop, and several rooms in which classes and meetings are held for fraternal,

civic, and cultural organizations. The McCall Center also plays host to the major African-American celebrations such as Kwanzaa and an annual Juneteenth Breakfast. Open Mon through Fri 10 a.m. to 3 p.m.

MEDICAL HERITAGE COLLECTIONS
   MUSEUM   FREE
1301 Montana Ave.
(915) 533-0940

El Paso has a long medical history that includes the notable Texas Tech Health Sciences Center medical school. If you're interested in medical history, you should pay a visit to this museum, which is located inside the Turner House. Among the collections here are some unusual medical equipment (some of which may make your stomach turn!), as well as old documents and books related to the practice of medicine in El Paso. Three of the rooms inside the house have been converted into 20th century period rooms, including a pharmacy, a doctor's office and an operating room. Housed inside the rooms is a collection of letters, photographs, medical books, journals, instruments, and medical equipment. Among them are an early 20th-century postcard collection, a complete set of stereoscopic anatomical cards, and a collection of prescription labels from many pharmacies that once existed in El Paso. Tours of the museum are given by appointment only from Nov through May and you must call to schedule an appointment if you wish to visit.

MOUNT CRISTO REY   FREE
McNutt Road
Sunland Park, NM

If you've driven around El Paso's west side at all, you've probably noticed the massive statue sitting upon a hill overlooking Sunland Park and the entire West Side. Located just off McNutt Road in Sunland Park, New Mexico, the huge crucifix sits atop a small 800-foot peak on the borders where Texas, New Mexico, and Mexico meet. Its location here is symbolic of good relations between the U.S. and Mexico. This 29-foot-high statue of Christ, sometimes referred to as the "Christ of the Rockies," was created by acclaimed Spanish sculptor Urbici Soler and serves as the site of an annual religious pilgrimage. The small mountain on which Cristo Rey sits was once a favorite place for the *conquistadores* exploring the area to water their mules and was also a good landmark for those who wanted to ford the Rio Grande. In recent years, primarily because of its proximity to Mexico, Mount Cristo Rey has received bad publicity as a hotspot for vandalism and bandits who lurk nearby and rob or assault visitors. As such, if you wish to visit the shrine, it's best to hike up the mountain in a group or opt to partake in one of the annual pilgrimages.

PIONEER PLAZA
Corner of El Paso and San Francisco Streets

Named for El Paso's two first pioneers, Fray García de San Francisco and Don Juan de Oñate, this plaza is a main feature and site downtown and was the hub of public activity in early El Paso. In those days, raids by Apache Indians were a constant danger, so a United States military guard was posted here in the late 1870s to defend citizens. Military bands often gave performances here, and an irrigation ditch flowed along the south side of the plaza, nourishing a line of trees that provided shade for the area. One such tree became known as the "Newspaper Tree" because public notices were often posted on it. Throughout history, the plaza was a crossroads for major roads and trails and saw some of the most activity and trade in the entire region. In October of 1909, U.S. President William H. Taft and Mexican President Porfirio Díaz each passed through the plaza en route to the Chamber of Commerce building for their historic meeting.

Today, the plaza is a lovely space that sits squarely among the tall buidings of downtown El Paso. Two bronze sculptures in the plaza depict the early settlers. The first is a 14-foot sculpture of Fray García himself, which honors this priest who founded the first mission in the area. The second sculpture in Pioneer Plaza, that of Juan de Oñate, a legendary name in Southwestern history, is the tallest equestrian bronze in the world. Sitting atop his rearing horse Helicon, Oñate surveys the plaza from high above. Both sculptures were created by John Houser, son of Ivan Houser who assisted in the carving of Mt. Rushmore.

PLAZA DE LOS LAGARTOS   FREE
San Jacinto Plaza
Downtown El Paso
San Jacinto Plaza is often called "Plaza de los Lagartos" or "Alligator Plaza" and if you visit the plaza, you'll see in the center its most distinctive feature: a colorful fiberglass sculpture of several alligators frolicking in a fountain. Had you been visiting in the 1950s, though, the gators would've been very real and very much the main attraction in San Jacinto Plaza. It was J. Fisher Satterwaite, city Parks and Streets Commissioner, who transformed San Jacinto Plaza from what was essentially a dirt lot into an attractive, leafy green space in the heart of downtown

El Paso. And it was J. Fisher Satterwaite who first introduced alligators into the park's pond. Several local legends have tried to surmise why exactly Satterwaite did such a thing, but the gators were instantly a favorite with local passersby, who would stop and linger over the walls to watch them. Though initially there were only three alligators in the pond, later on there were up to seven reptiles living in San Jacinto Plaza, most of them having names and being an integral part of El Paso culture. Sometimes the gators were moved to other locations as part of a practical joke, and one alligator named Sally was used in a guessing game, whereby the contest who could most closely guess her weight won $100 and a trip to Mexico. In the 1970s, it was finally decided that the plaza was a poor habitat for the gators, several of which had suffered assaults with sticks and stones, and so they were moved to El Paso Zoo. Today, Luis Jiménez's sculpture holds the place of the beloved reptiles that are still very much part of older *Paseños'* childhood memories. San Jacinto Plaza is located downtown and is squared in by Oregon, Main, Mills, and Mesa Streets.

PUEBLOS AND RESERVATIONS

TIGUA CULTURAL CENTER   FREE
305 Yaya Lane
(915) 859-7700
www.ysletadelsurpueblo.org
The Tigua Indians have lived in the El Paso area since long before Spanish *conquista-dores* arrived and settled here. Today, the local tribes, or *pueblos*, are located southeast of downtown along a string of reservations that make up the popular Mission Trail, where the area's first churches were established. Located at 305 Yaya Lane at Socorro

Road just east of the Ysleta Mission, the Tigua Indian Cultural Center is the best place to get a basic understanding of the rich 500-year history of the local tribal cultures. The center features a Tigua tribe museum, including exhibits about its relationship to the Tiwa people of Northern New Mexico, as well as examples of Tigua arts and crafts. Several family-operated gift shops are also located inside the center, with artists working at the shops. Traditional Native American social dances are often held in the plaza, which is an amazing opportunity to see a centuries-old performance and experience the sounds of ancient Tigua songs. You can also take home a decorative piece or souvenir from one of the gift shops, which offer an array of jewelry, artifacts, and timeless mementos, or taste the local fare, a type of hearty bread baked in *hornos* (outdoor ovens). Guided tours of the facility and pueblo are given by Tigua youth most days. Performances are held on the weekends at 11:30 a.m. and 1:30 p.m., and the shops are open from 10 a.m. to 3 p.m. Wed to Sun

SPEAKING ROCK ENTERTAINMENT CENTER   **FREE**
119 South Old Pueblo Rd.
(915) 870-7777
www.ysletadelsurpueblo.org
By contrast to the ancient cultural richness of the Tigua Cultural Center, Speaking Rock Entertainment Center gives insight into modern Native American industry. This large facility is hard to miss, with bright neon signs that provide a blinking greeting as you drive into the pueblo on Alameda Avenue. With a number of restaurants, lounges and betting areas, Speaking Rock is more an entertainment facility than an actual casino by definition, although it was formerly known

as such. There are plenty of video game rooms for interactive fun, while big screen TVs project major sporting events and offer opportunities for betting. A visit to Speaking Rock Entertainment Center is best done after exploring the Tigua Cultural Center and the Mission Trail, as it provides a fascinating contrast between ancient Native American culture and modern life. The center stands in brightly-colored contrast to the muted hues of ancient Native American crafts and architecture and nods to the evolution of Native American commerce today.

THE MISSION TRAIL

El Paso's most popular and important tourist attraction is the Mission Trail, a tourist track that follows the course of three very important and old missions. These were the first churches established in the area, built by early Spanish Catholic priests and friars who came seeking to convert the local Indian populations to Christianity. Today, the churches still stand, now on reservation land that belongs to the local Indian tribes for which they were originally built. A visit to the Mission Trail is worth a half-day drive, during which time you can explore the main missions themselves, as well as several related Native American sites including the Tigua Cultural Center and Los Portales Museum, as well as do some shopping for Native American goods, if that interests you. Plan this drive in the afternoon, if possible, so that you can take in dinner at the Cattleman's Steakhouse at Indian Cliffs Ranch (see the Kidstuff chapter), which is an attraction in and of itself. To get to the Mission Trail, follow I-10 to the Zaragosa Road exit and head south. Pass Alameda Avenue and turn left onto Socorro Road. Immediately on your left, you will see Ysleta Pueblo, the mission, and the

Speaking Rock Entertainment Center. There is ample parking behind Speaking Rock and the mission sits just a short walk north of the entertainment center.

Ysleta Mission

This first church on the tour was established in 1682 and later rebuilt in 1851 after several damaging floods. It is constructed of adobe mud bricks, straw, and Spanish vigas, and you will notice the beautiful Spanish silver dome, which combines interestingly with the Native American designs in this, the oldest continuously active parish in Texas. While you are here, you may luck into watching a traditional dance, which are often performed by members of the pueblo in front of the mission. Alternatively, venture into the Speaking Rock Entertainment Center for a taste of gambling and sports. Continuing south on Socorro Road from here, you will come to the Tigua Cultural Center, a museum where you can learn about the Tigua Indian tribe's history and unique heritage (see the listing in this chapter for further information).

Socorro Mission

About 2 miles further south on Socorro Road you will come to the next church on the Mission Trail, the Socorro Mission. Like Ysleta, the white-faced Socorro church was built in 1682 for the Piro Indians who had fled the Pueblo Revolt of 1680 in northern New Mexico and relocated to the outskirts of what is now El Paso. The vigas, or roof supports, of the church's interior ceiling, are original cypress decorated by the Piros when the church was first constructed. Continuing south on Socorro Road, you may choose to make a short detour right, down Glorietta

Road to the Licon Dairy to taste some locally produced cheese and let the kids enjoy their petting zoo (see the listing in the Kidstuff chapter for further information).

San Elizario

Continuing south on Socorro Road further yet, you will come to perhaps the most elaborate and stunning of the three missions, the San Elizario Mission. The stark whitewashed adobe structure, with its rounded parapets and traditional clock tower nook, is a prime example of Spanish mission architecture. This structure, like the Ysleta church, was damaged by flooding and civil unrest, and so the present-day chapel was completed in 1882. Anchoring the south side of the small plaza, the chapel is flanked to its left by Los Portales Museum, where you can learn about the local history of San Elizario, which was the first seat of El Paso County government. Take note of the museum's extended porch, or *portal* for which it was named, a distinct feature of early Spanish colonial architecture in the region. Dotted around the plaza are the remains of several original adobe buildings, which you can notice by their obvious mud bricks, many of which are in partial or total ruins.

To reach Cattleman's Steakhouse at Indian Cliffs Ranch for a prime steak dinner and an Old West experience, continue to follow Socorro Road south until it meets up with TX 20/Alameda Road. Here you'll enter the town of Fabens and eventually turn left (northeast) onto Fabens Street/Ranch Road 793, and follow this until you reach the entrance to the restaurant. To get back to El Paso from here, go further northeast on Ranch Road 793 to the intersection with I-10 and take the interstate west back to downtown El Paso.

(Q) Close-up

Los Murales

If you spend any time at all exploring the streets of downtown El Paso or wandering through one of the city's parks, you will eventually happen upon a colorful painted wall mural. El Paso has over a hundred documented murals, most of them painted by Hispanic artists looking to express themselves publicly about various political movements through the years. In fact, El Paso's murals have become such a part of the city's landscape that it has been said that the city could change its nickname from "Sun City" to "City of Mexican-American Murals."

Many of the murals are controversial, being an outdoor, public piece of artwork on a permanent space. They often depict historical and political themes and usually reflect some aspect of Hispanic cultural identity. The first murals were painted in El Paso in the 1930s as part of federal relief and reconstruction programs after the Great Depression. Murals were also an integral part of Hispanic artistic expression during the 1970s Chicano Movement, and were an integral part of protestations against the Vietnam War, as well as a colorful way of educating the larger public about the community and history of Mexican-Americans.

El Paso's murals often depict the city's historical figures, honoring people who have made contributions to the city or had significant impact on the area. In them, you may notice Pancho Villa, a Mexican revolutionary figure, or other important figures such as David Carrasco who founded the El Paso Job Corps. Other murals depict more controversial themes, such as images about gang pride, or religious and historical images like Aztec gods and Catholic imagery.

If you are interested in taking a mural tour of El Paso, there are a number of interesting murals that can be seen around the city. Though there are far too many murals around El Paso to describe them all, the following few are easily accessible in parks, on the sides of buildings, or even inside city spaces.

CHUCO TOWN (Lincoln Park)
Perhaps the most mural-saturated area of El Paso, the neighborhood known as Segundo Barrio, around Lincoln Park in the Lower Valley, is full of murals with themes that depict the Azteca, Chicano, and Mestizo heritage of the local residents.

Lincoln Park is located right under the Spaghetti Bowl, a massive overpass at the interchange of I-10 and US 54, where every open concrete space has been covered with murals, including beams, highway supports, and walls. The murals here mostly depict the long story of El Paso's history.

BOXER'S MURAL (De Soto Hotel, 309 East Mills Ave.)
Located on the side of a building at 309 East Mills Ave. downtown, the Boxer's Mural is supposedly one of the largest boxing murals on earth. Rows of boxers, many of which are actual members of the El Paso Boxing Hall of Fame, stand in defense stances, set against a backdrop of desert landscape. Among the more famous boxers depicted in this mural, which was completed in 2004, is Oscar De La Hoya.

AIDS (6th and Ochoa, behind La Fe Clinic).
The theme of this mural is the danger of AIDS. The disease is portrayed as a tornado ravaging the desert countryside, while people flee in fear. Several of the characters

shown in the mural are also meant to symbolize the different ways of transmitting AIDS; for instance, one woman kneels in anguish knowing her child will be born with the disease, while another man injects himself. The mural was sponsored by several local councils and coalitions, as well as the Texas Department of Health..

GUARDIAN ANGEL (9th Avenue at Tays)
This mural depicts a well-known scene where an angel watches over two young children who are walking across an unstable wooden bridge. The picture is meant to symbolize a sense of responsibility to the community and a general care and watchfulness that people of the community should have for one another.

EL CHUCO Y QUE (Virginia at Fr. Rahm Avenue)
This mural,the title of which is Spanish slang for "El Paso, so what?," is concerned with the unique local identity. The phrase "El Chuco y que?" expresses the idea that El Paso is what it is and is unique in its mix of people and cultures under pressure to carve out a unique identity in an area that is culturally tied to Texas, Mexico, and New Mexico.

NUESTRA HERENCIA (Chamizal National Memorial)
Located at the Chamizal National Memorial, Nuestra Herencia, or "Our Heritage," is a mural that depicts the important themes of the memorial itself: a scenes that reflect the diversity of culture within the Borderlands. Images within this mural include mariachis and fiesta dancers, Native American iconography, an Indian warrior juxtaposed against a Mexican flag, and even a portrait of President John F. Kennedy, who was key in helping resolve the border dispute in the 1960s.

HISTORY OF THE SANTA FE RAILROAD (Charles Road at Zikio Chalcon)
This mural depicts the important part that the railroad has played in the development and growth of the historic Chihuahuita (Little Chihuahua) district of El Paso. Since its arrival in 1881, the Santa Fe Railroad provided jobs and positive community support, and improved the dynamics of an area that was once riddled with gun violence, gang warfare, and drug abuse.

IXTLACCIHUATL AND POPOCATEPETL (Campbell near Fr. Rahm Avenue)
When a group of juvenile gang members contacted him about it, Felipe Adame directed this mural project as a part of a drug abuse prevention program. The gang members provided ideas of the images they wanted to become part of the mural. The overall scene of the mural depicts a native legend of the volcanos, and within the pictures are deeper images that portray themes of neighborhood, downtown and community.

OUR HISTORY (El Paso County Courthouse atrium)
Commissioned by El Paso County, "Our History" spans three walls beneath the glass ceiling of the modern building. The mural is the artist's interpretation of the historical experience of the local community and reflects historical and cultural concepts that encompass El Paso County in a blend of past, present, and future. Over 50 characters and scenes are depicted with vivid colors and dynamic movement in this almost overwhelming to look at mural.

MUSEUMS

CENTENNIAL MUSEUM AT UTEP　　　　FREE

UTEP Campus
Wiggins Road at University Avenue
(915) 747-5565
http://museum.utep.edu
Part of the University of Texas at El Paso, the Centennial Museum was established in 1936, while the Gardens were dedicated in 1999 and serve the binational community of the Chihuahuan Desert region. Permanent exhibits at the Centennial Museum focus on the natural and cultural history of the Chihuahuan Desert and include galleries themed around geology, paleontology, mammals, and birds and cultural history. In several temporary galleries, the Museum presents a wide range of rotating exhibits on themes related to border life and culture, the Americas, and UTEP activities. The museum's extensive stored collections are available for scholarly research while its past rotating exhibits have featured photographs of desertscapes, historic maps, pottery, and others themed around the local habitat. The galleries are open Tues through Sat 10 a.m. to 4:30 p.m. and the gardens are open every day from dawn to dusk.

EL PASO HOLOCAUST MUSEUM　FREE

715 North Oregon St.
(915) 351-0048
www.elpasoholocaustmuseum.org
Not unlike many other Holocaust museums in other cities, the El Paso Holocaust Museum & Study Center is a collection of images, stories, artifacts, and documents that trace the history of the Nazi Holocaust. The center, which was designed by artist and graphic designer Victor Mireles, houses tastefully depicted exhibits that intersperse graphic black and white photographs of Holocaust scenes with actual artifacts like prisoner uniforms displayed under soft lighting in glass cases. The maze of exhibits, which is decorated with large colored images and well-designed interior displays, guides visitors on an interactive journey through the establishment of the Third Reich, giving an all-too-real picture of what life was like in Nazi Europe. The museum was established to educate the public about the Nazi Holocaust, and to honor those who perished and those who survived this World War II tragedy. Open Tues through Fri 9 a.m. to 4 p.m., Sat and Sun 1 to 5 p.m.

EL PASO MUSEUM OF HISTORY　FREE

510 North Santa Fe St.
(915) 351-3588
www.elpasotexas.gov/history
The long history of the "Pass of the North" is chronicled here in the El Paso Museum of History, which opened in June of 2007. This broad-reaching and well laid out history museum should be a stop on the itinerary of any first-time visitor to El Paso. Both permanent exhibits and rotating exhibitions take guests on a journey through time, from the era when the earliest native inhabitants hunted and gathered here, to the intrigue of the Mexican Revolution and into modern day. El Paso A to Z is a three-dimensional, immersive, and encyclopedic look at El Paso's most colorful and varied stories, while The Changing Pass is an exhibit that carries visitors through an overlapping, 400-year chronology of regional history. The museum also features temporary exhibits related to the region's complex multicultural history, which usually require an extra ticket for a fee. The museum is open Tues through Sat 10 a.m. to 5 p.m., Sun 12 to 5 p.m.

EL PASO RAILROAD & TRANSPORTATION MUSEUM   FREE

400 West San Antonio Ave.
(915) 543-6747
www.elpasorails.org

The railroad first came to El Paso in the 1880s and for decades it was the lifeblood of the area, creating the first viable passage from east to west and nearly doubling the city's population within a few years. Although not the massive east-west transportation hub that it once was, the railroad's impact on the area can be understood at this small transport museum. Located just around the corner from the modern Amtrak train station and across from the Convention Center in downtown El Paso, the museum offers lots of information about the arrival and construction of the railways through El Paso, including what the lives of railroad workers might've been like. A restored locomotive provides the most interesting of the displays, and other exhibits offer insight into the evolution of railroad transportation through the years. Open Tues through Sun 11 a.m. to 5 p.m.

FORT BLISS MUSEUM AND STUDY CENTER   FREE

Fort Bliss
Marshall Road, Building 1735
(915) 568-3390
www.bliss.army.mil/museum/fort_bliss_museum.htm

This large complex on Fort Bliss is actually a series of three museums that portray the rich history of Fort Bliss, from its establishment as an army post in what is now downtown El Paso in 1848 with a regiment of mounted infantry to its present day status as America's Air and Missile Defense Center of Excellence. The Air Defense Artillery Gallery is devoted to the history of war planes, including the introduction of the airplane as an offensive weapon in World War I. The museum chronicles the general history of the army and its unique history along the U.S.–Mexico border. A number of fascinating pieces of machinery are on display, including a V-2 rocket, decommissioned missiles, tanks, and other military equipment, which greet you in the museum's parking lot. Inside, you'll find more vehicles, weapons, and photos dating to the early days of the base. To visit, you'll need to be granted access to Fort Bliss, so be prepared to show ID, vehicle insurance, and registration. You'll be given a day pass to the base for access to the museum.

FORT BLISS REPLICA MUSEUM   FREE

Fort Bliss
Corner of Pleasonton and Pershing Road
(915) 568-4518

The Old West days of the "Soldiers of the Pass" are relived through replicas of original adobe fort buildings and military artifacts here in another of the military history museums located on Fort Bliss. This unique museum first opened in 1955 and is a lifelike reproduction of the Magoffinsville Army Post, Fort Bliss's precursor that existed near what is now downtown El Paso from 1854 to 1868. Visitors here can experience what historic life at Fort Bliss was like through authentic period rooms, exhibits, and outdoor displays. As with the other attractions located on Fort Bliss, you will need to present your ID, vehicle insurance, and registration to gain a day pass for access onto the base.

INSIGHTS SCIENCE MUSEUM $$

505 North Santa Fe St.
(915) 534-0000
www.insightselpaso.org

This interactive science museum presents science in a fun and interesting way, with exhibits that play on the more intriguing sides of sciences that appeal to both kids and adults alike. The permanent exhibits here are designed to make learning an active, hands-on experience, and they are complemented by temporary exhibits that change on a regular basis. The permanent gallery showcases interactive displays about electricity, magnetism, light bending, illusions, and other science-cool stuff. Traveling exhibits in the past have ranged from unique explorations of holography and geology to in-depth looks at wildlife and the Earth. Although geared toward kids, both the young and the young at heart can enjoy the exhibits here, which make science accessible and interesting to all. Insights is open Tues to Sat from 10 a.m. to 5 p.m., and Sun from noon to 5 p.m.

LOS PORTALES MUSEUM & TOURIST INFO CENTER   FREE
1521 San Elizario Rd.
San Elizario
(915) 851-1682
Located right next door to the San Elizario church (one of the last stops on the Mission Trail) on the town plaza, this museum contains exhibits that focus on the history and legacies of San Elizario, which is in fact older than El Paso itself. Among them, visitors can learn about the "First Thanksgiving," when Spanish conquistadors arrived some 50 years before the British made it to Plymouth Rock. There is also an extensive amount of information about the San Elizario Salt War of 1877 during which local groups fought over the rights to nearby salt flats. More interesting than the exhibits, though, is the building itself, which is an authentic 1850s

Territorial style structure that was originally built as a governor's palace. Along the outside, you will notice a large *portal* (for which the museum is named), or extended porch, that runs along the front of the building, as well as gorgeous historic wooden doors. Inside, be sure to take note of the red tiled floors, uneven whitewashed adobe walls, and dark wooden *vigas* (beams), all of which are original elements of Spanish architecture in the region. If you are feeling adventurous, here you can also pick up a self-guided walking tour brochure of the little town area. The museum is open Tues through Sat from 10 a.m. to 2 p.m., and Sun from noon to 4 p.m.

MUSEO MAYACHEN   FREE
2101 Myrtle Ave.
(915) 533-9710
www.museomayachen.org
Run by La Mujer Obrera, an organization dedicated to creating economic opportunities for displaced, low income women workers, Museo Mayachen's mission is "to preserve and disseminate a historically equitable record of the unique experience for working class Mexican people on both sides of the border." Mayachen has worked tirelessly in collaboration with the local Hispanic communities to chronicle a "people's history," from early indigenous beginnings to the experiences of modern people, with a special focus on the experiences of immigrant women garment factory and farm workers. Inside, one finds a series of interactive exhibits and spaces that offer oral histories and audio-video presentations, which, along with the special events and workshops that are put on by the museum, educate the public about the Mexican culture and history that is so unique to this area of the world.

MUSEUM OF ARCHAEOLOGY
AND WILDERNESS PARK   FREE
4301 Transmountain Rd.
(915) 755-4332
www.elpasotexas.gov/arch_museum
The El Paso Museum of Archaeology tells the natural history of the first inhabitants of the El Paso area, the greater Southwest, and northern Mexico. Inside, visitors follow exhibits about the lives and material culture of the earliest inhabitants, from the Paleoindian Ice Age hunters to their modern Native American descendants. Outside, the museum's grounds include 15 acres of nature trails, outdoor exhibits, and a mile-long nature trail with signage about the more than 250 varieties of native plants in the area. As you explore the trail, you'll get amazing glimpses of the Franklin Mountains and, on a clear day, Mt. Sierra Blanca, hundreds of miles away in New Mexico. Along the trail, you'll also find a ring of tepee replicas and a replica of an Apache brush hut similar to one that Apaches would've inhabited hundrewds of years ago. There is also working a fire pit for roasting agave, a type of spiny desert plant, as well as a replica of a prehistoric pueblo that was found nearby. Walking the trail, you may also catch sight of local wildlife, such as snakes and other reptiles, rabbits, insects, and birds.

The museum and grounds are open Tues through Sat from 9 a.m. to 5 p.m., and Sun noon to 5 p.m.

NATIONAL BORDER PATROL
MUSEUM   FREE
4315 Transmountain Rd.
(915) 759-6060
www.borderpatrolmuseum.com
Weapons, badges, uniforms, vehicles, and a small selection of sculptures and paintings make up the collection in this unique, if not a bit nationalistic, museum dedicated to the U.S. Border Patrol. Exhibits here cover the history of the patrol, which is charged with guarding the front lines of America's land borders, from the Old West to current operations. Admission is free. The museum is open Tues through Sat from 9 a.m. to 5 p.m.

WAR EAGLES AIR MUSEUM $
Doña Ana County Airport
Santa Teresa, NM
(575) 589-2000
This spacious but out-of-the-way aviation museum is only a must-visit for airplane buffs and anyone interested in viewing period aircraft. Located about 20 miles from El Paso at the nearby Doña Ana County Airport in New Mexico, the War Eagles Museum houses a collection of some 30 military and civilian aircraft in an airy hangar-type display hall, most of which date to the World War II and Korean War eras. Many of the planes on display are flight-worthy; to be found among the collection are the P-51 Mustang, the P-38 Lightning, the P-40 Warhawk, the F-4U-4 Corsair, plus a twin engine Invader bomber, a DC-3 transport, and a German observation aircraft, the Fiesler-Storch. There are several jets built in the 1950s, including an F-86 Sabre, a T-33 Silver Star, and MIG-15s. In addition to this flight collection are a number of antique cars on display. The museum is open Tues through Sun from 10 a.m. to 4 p.m., with last admission at 3:30 p.m.

RANCHES, FARMS, AND ORCHARDS

BOWEN RANCH $$–$$$
8690 Edge of Texas Lane
(915) 821-1496
www.edgeoftexas.biz

The Bowen Ranch is one of the few historic working cattle ranches still in existence around El Paso. Owned by lifelong cowboy Jimmy Bowen, the massive 88,000-acre ranch has been transformed into a veritable amusement park of Old West fun. It's still a working cattle ranch where the Bowens raise both Hereford cattle and buffalo, both of which can be seen grazing along the mountain slopes and flatlands of the ranch, which sits along the Texas/New Mexico border near Fort Bliss north of El Paso. The Bowens have owned the ranch since the 1800s and more recently transformed it into the children's playground and western park that it is now, as well as opening the Edge of Texas Steakhouse some 5 miles away along US 54. A trip to the Bowen Ranch offers the chance to view real cowboys going about their daily work herding cattle, riding horses, and sometimes helping bring a new baby calf into the world. Children can get up close with the animals and ask questions about cowboy life. The ranch also has facilities for hayrides and stagecoach rides, western shows, and staged gunfight shows, as well as a number of different sporting facilities. The best way to plan your trip is to visit the ranch during the day and enjoy a steak dinner at the Edge of Texas Steakhouse on your way home.

LYLES FAMILY FARMS $$
3855 West Picacho
Las Cruces, NM
(505) 526-1919
www.mesillavalleymaze.com

Lyles Family Farms is a working farm located in the fertile Mesilla Valley of New Mexico northwest of downtown El Paso. The Lyles, who still run their farm as a family operation, create the Mesilla Valley Maze, a massive maze carved out of their acres of cornfields. In the past, the maze has taken on some amazing shapes, including a cartoon cow, a windmill, a tractor, and a map of the United States! While the maze, which opens in Sept and Oct each year, is the biggest attraction at Lyle Family Farms, it is by no means the only draw. The Lyles began farming in the Mesilla Valley in 1985 with 35 acres and now the farm has grown to over 1,000 acres, providing fresh produce to markets across the country. Other activities offered here include hayrides, a pumpkin patch, gem mining, school tours, a trike track, duck races, and more. During the autumnal harvest season, you can pick your own vegetables and fresh flowers in their U-Pick Garden. Lyle Family Farms provides a wonderful opportunity to explore agriculture and understand better the workings of a true local farm, which are becoming rare.

STAHMANN FARMS &
COUNTRY STORE   FREE
22505 NM Highway 28
La Mesa, NM
(575) 525-3470
www.stahmanns.com

It isn't difficult to know when you reach Stahmann Farms. This huge pecan grove sprawls on both sides of NM Highway 28 as you drive toward Las Cruces from El Paso. Here, rows upon rows of trees stretch out in perfectly straight lines as far as the eye can see. This massive, sprawling orchard is Stahmann Farms, the world's largest family-owned pecan grove. You can stop in to explore the groves and purchase a few tasty take-aways at Stahmann's Country Store, an on-site shop where you can sample and buy mouth-watering chocolates, pecan pie, and other pecan confections. If you have an hour or so to kill, sign up to take a tour of Stahmann's pecan shelling facility and candy factory, where you'll see firsthand the process of growing and producing pecans and pecan-related treats. The store is open to visitors every day from 10 a.m. to 5 p.m., with a late opening at 11 a.m. on Sun.

WINERIES

LA VIÑA WINERY $
4201 NM Highway 28
(915) 544-3200
www.lavinawinery.com
La Viña, New Mexico's oldest winery, is situated in the ripe, green Mesilla Valley northwest of El Paso. The vineyard produces New Mexico varietals of Italian and French style wines, including cabernet, zinfandel, syrah, chardonnay, and others. Many of the bottles on offer are mixed varietals, such as their unique Rojo Loco red, which is a fruity blend of ruby cabernet and zinfandel. The real treasure of La Viña, though, is definitely the winery's ambiance. Set in a newly built structure designed to conjure up a Tuscan villa with gentle slate walls and sweeping views, the tasting room and patio are open every day to accommodate wine drinkers. Inside the tasting room is painted with a dull taupe color and matched with hanging grapes, old bottles, and rustic trinkets to give it an Italian flair. Outside, the views from the open patio cascade down over rolling hills dotted with vines to far-off desert mountains. The tasting room and patio are open daily from noon to 5 p.m. in the summer, and tours of the vineyards and winemaking facilities are offered for a nominal fee that includes a tasting. For true wine lovers, the quality of New Mexico wines may disappoint. However, the experience of sitting on the open patio sipping a light, crisp wine and enjoying the pinking

view of the mountains as the sun sets is unparalleled.

STAR CANYON WINERY   FREE
2601 North Stanton
(915) 544-7000
www.starcanyonwinery.com
This boutique tasting room is a completely unique wine experience in El Paso, as it is both a store and a tasting room. With 26 different wines on offer in bottles and by the glass, Star Canyon Winery offers a variety of wines to sample, as well as wine flights, which are small samplings of five different wines for a reasonable price. Several wine specials here include a Star Canyon Winery Merlot, a Desert Bloom, which is a blush wine alternative to white zinfandel, and a Rio Grande Red, their sweet red table wine, all of which are stored and fermented in large oak barrels at Star Canyon Winery. You can also order a cheese plate, which comes with crackers, garlic stuffed olives, pecorinos, and dark chocolate to be paired properly with the wines. Also available are wine accessories such as wine keys and stoppers, and unique custom drawings on any bottle you purchase, which make for great gifts.

ZIN VALLE VINEYARDS   FREE
7315 NM Highway 28
Canutillo, TX
(915) 877-4544
www.zinvalle.com
One of the newest vineyards in Mesilla Valley, Zin Valle Vineyards was recently established in 2000 and has produced a few years of quality vintages so far. Starting with a bold red zinfandel grape varietal, the family-owned operation quickly expanded into a second vineyard for growing white wine grapes. Inside the luxurious stucco facil-

ity is a tasting room and the Barrel Room, where private parties can be booked to dine among the wines as they age in oak barrels. Guests are welcome to stroll through the actual vineyards and see the grape vines growing under the dry Texas sun, or to kick back with a glass of wine in the cool shade of several willow trees. The tasting room is open Fri through Mon from noon to 5 p.m. or by appointment.

SCENIC DRIVES

One truly beautiful way to see and experience the scenery of El Paso is to take a drive through the Franklin Mountains. A 1.82-mile loop, Scenic Drive is a continuous landmark carved into the Franklin Mountains reaching 4,222 feet above sea level. From a variety of pullouts along the route, you can take in views of the Rio Grande, El Paso, and Ciudad Juárez. Just below the top area of Scenic Drive is a place to take photos with loved ones or enjoy a bite to eat, so be sure to pack a picnic and take it slow.

To do the Scenic Drive loop, allow at least a couple of hours so that you can really take your time and enjoy the views, eat a picnic lunch, and take some photos. The loop starts at Richmond Avenue and Kentucky Street in northeast El Paso and winds its way up through the mountains, ending in a Y at Arroyo Park, where you can follow either Rim Road or East Robinson Avenue. There are few bathrooms or disabled facilities along the way and little in the way of wheelchair accessibility, but this should not prevent anyone from taking the drive, as most of the views are best experienced from the comfort of your vehicle.

THE ARTS

The Southwest has always been a virtual Mecca for artists. Even long ago, the first groups to reach the Borderlands area were compelled to draw it, carving petroglyphs into the rocks in the mountains above what is now El Paso. Something about the arid desert landscapes—the hues of brown, yellow, and red dirt contrasting against a vivid blue sky that stretches for miles—have since ancient times captured the hearts of artists and found their way onto canvases. So, it is no surprise that El Paso today has a thriving art scene that includes many visual artists who have migrated here from other places, often coming for a short stint and then finding themselves unable to leave. The dozens of art galleries dotted around the city and the handful of excellent museums speak to El Paso's commitment to the visual arts, and the willingness of the community to both support and participate in maintaining a vibrant local art scene.

Visual arts aren't the only thing one can find in El Paso, though certainly the Martian-like landscape provides special inspiration for them. Music, opera, film, and theater all thrive in the city, with organizations like the El Paso Symphony Orchestra, El Paso Opera, and El Paso Pro Musica holding excellent series of musical seasons each year. The existence of many beautiful, historic venues only furthers the city's capacity to host a wide variety of performances, from Shakespearean plays to rock concerts, and everything in between. So, whether you are interested in seeing a formal opera or a casual afternoon of children's theater with the kids, you are sure to find what you're looking for in El Paso.

OVERVIEW

This chapter is designed to give you a broad overview of the many arts-related activities and venues available in the El Paso region. Though not an entirely comprehensive list, those places and events catalogued here present the best of El Paso's arts community. The listings are presented in alphabetical order by heading and subheading.

It should be noted that the museums listed in this chapter are specifically arts museums only. To find out more about the many history, archaeology, nature, and other local museums in and around El Paso, refer to the Attractions chapter. Likewise, listings for bookstores have been kept to the Shop-

ping chapter. Also, since operating hours and entrance fees are always subject to change, they have been left out of these listings. However, every effort has been made to procure contact information for these venues and organizations, including Web addresses, so you should have no trouble finding out the current hours and prices. There are plenty of arts-related events and venues around El Paso that are geared specifically to children. These are not included here, but can be found in the Kidstuff chapter, along with plenty of other kiddie-related activities to keep your young ones occupied.

ARTS CENTERS

THE BRIDGE CENTER FOR CONTEMPORARY ART
1 Union Fashion Center, Suite B
(915) 532-6707
utminers.utep.edu

This modern art center aims to inform and educate the public about contemporary art issues by hosting numerous events, exhibitions, readings, and seminars on a variety of artistic aspects, from visual arts to music, poetry, and spoken word. In addition, their journal, the Bridge Review, provides arts reviews, essays, and interviews with artists, educators, and key members of the El Paso, Las Cruces, and Juárez arts communities. The Bridge is a great place to explore the avant-garde and edgy artistic communities of the El Paso area.

EL PASO'S CRAFTERS CORNER
5660 El Paso Dr.
(915) 541-8995
www.myspace.com/crafterscornerelp

Experience an era gone by in this centrally located, 1924 historic home. At this crafty little spot you will have access to an array of arts and crafts activities, including a host of arts and crafts classes, the chance to make your own wares, and even sell them through Crafters Corner. For those interested in all types of arts and crafts, Crafters Corner covers a huge list of activities, including painting, stained glass, Southwest art and antiques, ceramics, jewelry, soap and candle-making, scratch art, floral designing, silk screening, and woodworks.

THE FORUM ARTS AND CULTURE
705 Texas Ave.
(915) 351-6521
http://forumac.org

The Forum Arts and Culture is a contemporary art gallery that previously operated as Under the Sun Gallery. As one of El Paso's newest galleries of contemporary art, the Forum's reputation and collections are still growing, but they already enjoy a solid reputation within the El Paso art scene. The gallery's exhibitions change from month to month, with showings mostly by El Pasoan artists. Studio space is also available for rent here. Jeff Litchfield, who runs the gallery, says the space is devoted to showing a broad range of local, high-quality contemporary art.

STANLEE AND GERALD RUBIN CENTER FOR THE VISUAL ARTS
UTEP Campus
500 West University Ave.
(915) 747-6151
www.rubincenter.utep.edu

The three galleries at this gallery run by the University of Texas at El Paso (UTEP) Art Department, offer modern art exhibitions by recognized international artists and is one of the best places in El Paso to see upcoming local and international art for free. The Stanlee and Gerald Rubin Gallery is the largest of the three and shows mostly large-scale works and sculptures, while the smaller L Gallery handles smaller pieces and more intimate showings. The third gallery, Project Space, is an experimental space reserved for new artists or those changing their artistic directions. The Rubin Center is located on the UTEP campus, just south of Sun Bowl Stadium in an original campus building renovated in 2004.

UTEP ART DEPARTMENT
UTEP Campus
500 West University Ave.
(915) 747-5181
www.utep.edu/arts

There are two galleries at the massive UTEP Art Department, the Main and Glass Galleries, which host about a dozen exhibitions a year, most showing works by students of the department. The galleries are located on the third floor of the Fox Fine Arts Center on the UTEP campus and is overseen by a student. The UTEP art program fosters understanding of experimental and new visual arts and their relationship to positive social change. Prior exhibited artists have included Enrique Chagoya, Jean Lowe, Margo Sawyer, Willie Varela, and Eddie Dominguez. All events and exhibits are free and open to the public.

ART GALLERIES

ENCAUSTIC INTERNATIONAL ART STUDIO & GALLERY
7100 Westwind, Suite 120
(915) 833-0454
www.brigittevonahn.com

The specialty of this galler is encaustic artwork, which is an ancient form of beeswax painting. This unique, colorful form of art looks similar to heavy oil painting, and many of the pieces on offer are themed around El Paso motifs, including local flora and fauna and the surrounding desertscapes, which have obviously inspired many of the artists. In addition to the variety of local artists that are shown throughout the year, the gallery features ongoing showings by German artists Monika Romer and Brigitte von Ahn. An on-site studio offers group encaustic painting classes, private lessons, and special workshops.

ESCAMILLA ART STUDIO & GALLERY
1457 Amstater Circle
www.albertoescamilla.com
(915) 857-7789

This is the private gallery of El Paso Hall of Fame artist Alberto Escamilla. A native Texan, Escamilla is known for his landscape and garden scene paintings that incorporate broad color, and most admirers of his artwork will laud the extensive inspiration he draws from the El Paso surroundings. In addition to regular showings of his most recent oil and pastel works and zarzuela posters, Escamilla also holds oil, drawing, and pastel art lessons in his studio. The studio/gallery is open to the public by appointment for viewing and purchase of the artwork. Original oils and signed reproductions of original artwork are available.

GALLERIES AT THE MEMORIAL
800 South San Marcial St.
(915) 532-7273
www.home.nps.gov/cham

Chamizal National Memorial commemorates the amicable resolution of the U.S.–Mexico border dispute between El Paso and Ciudad Juárez. With three art galleries inside the Visitors' Center, the work exhibited at the Memorial Galleries usually reflects the local history and landscape of the border region and, particularly, the border dispute resolution. Los Paisanos Gallery is located in the west wing of the Chamizal National Memorial administrative building and houses a rotating selection of exhibitions that have included photos and artwork related to the Mexican Revolution. The Abrazos Gallery presents a broader range of subject matter, often focusing on culturally interpretive and natural themes. The smallest of the three exhibit areas at Chamizal, the Borderland Gallery generally showcases a small selection of photographs by a local artist. Viewing the works exhibited in the Galleries at Chamizal National Memorial can really give the visitor a truer sense of the themes, both historical and natural, that relate to the Borderlands region.

GOLDEN EAGLE GALLERY
1501A Main St.
San Elizario, TX
(915) 594-8424
www.goldeneaglegallery.com
Situated right along the Mission Trail in nearby San Elizario, the Golden Eagle Gallery, along with the Horseshoe Gallery and Main Street Gallery, showcases local area artists and utilizes educational opportunities and art-inspired events to promote the San Elizario Historical District. Here, you will find a variety of Southwestern artwork, much of which is directly inspired by or related to the historic Native American pueblos of the area. A stop in to these galleries, all of which are directly adjacent to one another on Socorro Road, is a nice addition to a day of sightseeing along the Mission Trail.

HAL MARCUS STUDIO AND GALLERY
800 North Mesa St.
(corner of Mesa and Yandell)
(915) 533-9090
www.halmarcus.com
Hal Marcus is a huge name on the El Paso art scene. A native born and bred El Pasoan, Marcus, who is an El Paso Hall of Fame artist, has been painting in and around the region for decades and has truly helped to shape regional fine arts in El Paso. The Hal Marcus Studio and Gallery thus specializes in local art, showing not only the work of Hal Marcus himself, but also the work of many other regional artists, who in the past have included Bill Sullivan, Teresa Fernandez, Friar Vincent Petersen, Francisco Romero, Mauricio Mora, and Mark Paulda. Full of color, the warm and inviting space, which was once

Marcus's grandmother's home, displays over 250 works of art in a changing exhibit gallery, an Early El Paso Art Salon dedicated solely to artwork and research materials on Early El Paso artists, and Hal's painting studio where you can catch him painting, as well as see his newest works. The rest of the gallery contains a wide selection of art from many popular regional artists. There is also a gift shop full of cards, prints, and calendars by the featured artists, so even if you can't afford to purchase a piece, you can take the artwork with you.

PIXY STUDIOS
305 East Franklin Ave.
(915) 203-1466
www.pixystudios.com
This photography studio turned print gallery is a wonderful place to experience some beautiful photography, as well as to commission commercial photography. The Two Thirds Print Gallery and Event Space features photographic prints from the community and can be rented out for private functions. Pixy Studios itself is a photography studio specializing in baby prints and sports photography, with a variety of photography services available to the El Paso area.

THE ROSE AND CROWN GALLERY
3616 McRae Blvd.
(915) 633-8870
This local fine arts gallery shows both developing and established artists, with works that encompass a panoply of artistic genres, from painting, drawing, and printmaking to photography, sculpture, architecture, and even video and performance art. Some of the Rose and Crown's original exhibitions travel domestically and abroad, and the gallery also hosts traveling exhibitions from

elsewhere, giving the El Paso community a space to understand artwork from other areas, usually showing some 60 works at a time. The Gallery Shop inside sells small work, prints, cards, and more. Each month, the Rose and Crown highlights a feature artist on the gallery's display towers, and also hosts talks and demonstrations on a variety of fine art subjects.

SUNLAND ART GALLERY
750 Sunland Park Dr.
(915) 584-3117
www.sunlandartgallery.com
This half gallery, half art shop located inside the Sunland Park Mall is a cooperative gallery sponsored by the El Paso Art Association, so it shows the original artwork of member artists. A broad range of artistic genres is represented here, from local Southwestern art to more traditional genres like Realism and Impressionism. Contemporary and abstract pieces are also sometimes shown, as well as a variety of other media like sculpture, ceramics, and even some jewelry. This is a great, down to earth place to go if you are interested in a lot of different genres or are looking to make a purchase but are afraid of the more traditional high-brow art vendors.

TOURIST DISTRACTIONS ART SHOPS
1125 Texas Ave.
(915) 691-0797
Truly living up to its name, the Tourist Distractions Art Shops is the place to go for a full day of art gazing, window-shopping, or just plain shopping! Here, an array of different artwork is collected together in one building within a variety of unique shops and art studios. You can spend hours browsing through the vendors, which include art workshops, photography studios, stained glass designs,

flower arrangements, metal and wood furniture, and an antiques shop.

TRANSMOUNTAIN GALLERY & STUDIO
6845 Second St.
Canutillo, TX
(915) 877-3741
www.capartonline.com
Transmountain Gallery is the personal studio of impressionist painter Carol Ann Parsons. Her work includes oil paintings, prints, and pastels, all in gently colorful El Paso themes. If Monet ever visited the Southwest, his paintings might have looked something like Carol Ann Parsons': lilacs draped down rich brown adobe walls, sunflowers bursting in yellow, and the Rio Grande reflecting the intense blue of El Paso's sky. The gallery's hours are by appointment only, but drop-ins are also welcome.

ART MUSEUMS

EL PASO MUSEUM OF ART
1 Arts Festival Plaza
(915) 532-1707
www.elpasoartmuseum.org
The El Paso Museum of Art is the city's main municipal art museum, located right downtown across from the Camino Real Hotel. The museum's permanent collection consists of some 5,000 works of art, including 13th- to 18th-century European art, modern American art, and Mexican folk art. Particularly special are the museum's collection of Southwestern *retablos* (folk paintings). In addition to these permanent collections, the museum also hosts rotating exhibitions that change every few months, and have in the past included Impressionist prints, documentary film series, Mexican mixed media art, and much more. Admission to the main collections is free, but you must purchase an

extra ticket to the special exhibitions for a small fee. The museum also often hosts lectures and other educational activities, such as summer camps and art classes, which enhance its commitment to providing an aesthetic environment and artistic resources for the community.

INTERNATIONAL MUSEUM OF ART
1211 Montana Ave.
(915) 543-6747
www.internationalmuseumofart.net
The International Museum of Art is located in the Turney Home, once the historic mansion of the Turneys, a wealthy El Paso family around the turn of the 20th century. The spacious museum now houses permanent collections of international artwork and is the best place in El Paso to find Asian and African art. The museum is also home to a Mexican Revolution collection, which includes a replica of Pancho Villa's death mask and a replica of a Mexican *casita* (little house) as it might have looked at the time of the revolution. The museum hosts several national and international exhibitions each year and offers art-related programs, activities, and special events.

TIGUA CULTURAL CENTER
305 Yaya Lane (at Socorro Road just east of the Ysleta Mission)
(915) 859-7700
www.ysletadelsurpueblo.org
The El Paso region is rich with Native American heritage, and the Tigua Indian Cultural Center offers a glimpse into 300 years of pueblo history. Centered around a museum housing ancient Tigua artifacts, the Cultural Center also offers guided tours of the pueblo, usually given by a local Tigua youth. Very often, weekend dances are performed in

front of the Ysleta Mission, Tigua Pueblo's historic church, which is the first of three along the Mission Trail. Several family-operated gift shops are nearby, with artists working at the shops. The museum houses a collection of Tigua artifacts and history, and documents the El Paso Tiguas' relationship to the New Mexican Tiwas. For anyone interested in the arts, crafts, and history of El Paso's Native American populations, a visit to the Tigua Cultural Center is a great starting point.

UTEP CENTENNIAL MUSEUM
UTEP Campus
Wiggins Road at University Avenue
(915) 747-5565
museum.utep.edu
The UTEP Centennial Museum, established in 1936, and Gardens, dedicated in 1999, are part of the University of Texas at El Paso, and also serve the binational community of the Chihuahuan Desert region. Permanent exhibits at the Centennial Museum focus on the natural and cultural history of the Chihuahuan Desert, and its extensive stored items are available for scholarly research. In several temporary galleries, the museum presents a wide range of rotating exhibits on themes related to border life and culture, the Americas, and UTEP activities.

EXHIBITIONS AND EVENTS

ARTS INTERNATIONAL
500 West Paisano Dr.
(915) 534-7377
www.artsinternat.com
Arts International is a juried open art exhibition for artists from Texas, New Mexico, and Mexico, and serves as El Paso Art Association's major annual fundraiser. The exhibition is the largest of its kind in West Texas and Southern New Mexico, and is typically held

in October each year at the Main Branch of El Paso Public Library. Several hundred entries are exhibited, including paintings, photographs, sculptures, and other media by artists from the entire Southwestern region. Arts International is open to all artists from Texas and New Mexico, as well as the five bordering Mexican states of Chihuahua, Tamaulipas, Nueva Leon, Sonora, and Coahuila.

FILM

FELLINI FILM CAFE
220 Cincinnati Ave.
(915) 544-5420
www.myspace.com/fellinicafe
A unique concept for lovers of fine coffee, food, and good movies, Fillini Film Cafe is both coffeehouse and video rental boutique. Located on trendy Cincinnati Avenue near UTEP, this is place where you can enjoy a true European–style cappuccino and a tasty meal, and choose from a large collection of foreign and alternative movies. Their fresh salads, sandwiches, and homemade desserts make for a delicious lunch, and you can spend hours perusing their massive selection of foreign and art-house films for rent.

PLAZA CLASSIC FILM FESTIVAL
(915) 533-4020
www.plaza-movies.com
If you absolutely adore Abbott and Costello, yearn to see *Breakfast at Tiffany's* on the big screen, or want to relive your childhood by watching *Star Wars* in the theater again, you absolutely must attend the Plaza Classic Film Festival, which features only the best oldies and goodies from the silver age of cinema. Easily one of El Paso's coolest annual events, the festival takes its name from its flagship venue, the Plaza Theatre in

downtown El Paso, which has several cinema and theater spaces for vintage movie viewing in a classy vintage environment, as well as a garden and the Oasis Lounge for enjoying a drink before or after the film. The festival is usually held for 10 days in early August, and features mostly family-friendly films, with a few movies that are marked for "adults only." Check out their Web site for ticket sales and info on the upcoming year's film lineup.

LITERARY ARTS

BORDER BOOK FESTIVAL
The Cultural Center de Mesilla
2231 A Calle de Parian
Mesilla, NM
(575) 523-3988
www.borderbookfestival.org
The Border Book Festival is an annual event that takes place in April each year in the nearby village of Mesilla, New Mexico. A variety of lectures, book signings, readings, art exhibitions, and sales booths featuring books and literature related to the Borderlands region are included in the festival, which is held over the course of one weekend. In addition to the annual festival, the Border Book Festival organization hosts events and workshops throughout the year. The newly opened Galería Tepín is an art gallery located inside the Cultural Center de Mesilla, home of the Book Festival, where artists and writers come together to partake in a multi-dimensional art space. Information about their upcoming events is available on their Web site.

EL PASO WRITERS' LEAGUE
Dorris Van Doren Library
551 Redd Rd.
www.elpasowritersleague.org

The El Paso Writers' League is an organization dedicated to encouraging, inspiring, and supporting El Paso writers. Founded in 1935, the group is comprised of both published and unpublished writers from a variety of genres, including fiction, non-fiction, and poetry. Members are given the chance to participate in an annual writing contest, critique groups, writing workshops, and lectures by guest speakers, and receive a regular newsletter. The league generally meets monthly on a weekend afternoon at the Doris Van Doren Library. Anyone interested in writing can join for an annual fee of around $25.

UTEP LIBRARY
UTEP Campus
Wiggins Rd.
(915) 747-6726
www.utep.edu/library

The UTEP Library is a huge, multi-functional academic research library open to students and faculty, as well as community users for an annual fee. Inside, you'll find more than a million books, hundreds of thousands of government documents, and about a million microforms. There are over 200 works of art on permanent display, including paintings by Tom Lea and over 100 original drawings by Jose Cisneros, and a small used bookstore located in the library atrium. Perhaps the best reason to visit the UTEP Library, though, is to get a glimpse of the world's largest published book. *Bhutan: A Visual Odyssey Across the Last Himalayan Kingdom* is on permanent display in the library. It weighs 133 pounds, measures 5 by 7 feet, and requires two people to turn a page. This exquisite Bhutanese treasure is both a work of art and a literary wonder that can only be found in El Paso.

MUSIC

ALFRESCO! FRIDAYS
Arts Festival Plaza
Downtown El Paso
(915) 541-4481
www.elpasoartsandculture.org

Alfresco Fridays provide a casual way to experience both well-established and upcoming El Paso bands as they strut their stuff on stage. Originally conceived as a way of keeping employees downtown at the start of the weekend, the concerts quickly became a draw for visitors to the area. Past seasons have featured bands from a variety of genres, like big band, jazz, reggae, classic rock, ska, blues, and more. Recent seasons have also featured an Artist Market, providing local artists and artisans a venue to connect with the community.

EL PASO PRO-MUSICA
6557 North Mesa St.
(915) 833-9400
www.elpasopromusica.org

El Paso Pro-Musica is a chamber music organization that puts on an annual concert season of chamber music and ensembles. Bringing world-class musicians to perform in El Paso, Pro-Musica hosts some of the best classical music in the city during its regular concert series, as well as during the Chamber Music Festival, which spans most of January each year. Free lunch concerts are often held at the El Paso Museum of Art, giving downtown employees and tourists a chance to reinvigorate their day with a burst of chamber music, and other events including many ensemble performances and several music film series round out Pro-Musica's season. Ticket prices are usually kept within an affordable range, with heavy discounts offered to students and military personnel, and some events are even presented for free. Ticket information, events schedules, and more are all available on Pro-Musica's Web site.

EL PASO SYMPHONY ORCHESTRA
1 Civic Center Plaza
(915) 532-3776
www.epso.org

The El Paso Symphony Orchestra (EPSO) was established in the 1930s and is the oldest performing arts organization in El Paso, as well as the longest continuously running symphony orchestra in Texas. In addition to its annual 12-concert series held downtown in the Plaza Theatre, the EPSO provides special events, educational activities, and outreach programs designed to entertain and educate El Paso's unique multicultural community. The symphony also targets the youth of El Paso through its annual Young People's Concerts, which feature exceptional young musicians from within the El Paso community. Patrons are invited to attend open dress rehearsals, while backstage tours are given for teachers, students, and other groups. Free tickets are available to low-income students and seniors. Comprised of local musicians, the EPSO fulfills an important educational function in El Paso, as its musicians also serve as instructors in the public and private schools, at the University of Texas at El Paso, and through private lessons. Information on the current and upcoming seasons is available through the EPSO's Web site.

JAZZ EL PASO
(915) 317-5503
www.jazzelpaso.org

If you like the subtle maze of notes that is jazz music, check out Jazz El Paso. Jazz El Paso Connection, a non-profit organization, specializes in bringing national jazz acts to El Paso, as well as putting on a variety of jazz-related events and projects throughout the year. Harlem Nights is, according to Jazz El Paso's Web site, a "speakeasy night of 1930s sophistication"—a fundraiser that brings together all the elements of a '30s nightclub: dancing, bar and food service, casino tables, and, of course, live jazz music! Jazz El Paso also puts together several festivals and concert series, is involved with a book project tracing the history of jazz music in the Borderlands, and works together with El Paso's public schools to provide jazz music education to local students. To find out where you can hear jazz around El Paso or when to catch the next jazz festival, check out their Web site.

MUSIC UNDER THE STARS
Chamizal National Memorial
Amphitheatre
800 South San Marcial St.
www.elpasotexas.gov/mcad

This festival enjoys the superlative title of El Paso's favorite concert series. Everything from jazz, blues, and Latin to garage band rock and zydeco is performed at this outdoor series held in the scenic Chamizal National Memorial Amphitheatre, just minutes from the Mexican border. The event is hosted each year by the El Paso Arts and Culture Department. Check local listings for schedule information.

OPERA

EL PASO OPERA
310 North Mesa St.
(915) 581-5534
www.epopera.org

The El Paso Opera has been performing in one form or another since 1992. Running from autumn to spring, the Opera's season features all sorts of performances, from classical operas like *La Bohème* to more modern pieces, such as Gershwin's *Porgy & Bess*. Unlike some of Europe's fancy opera houses, the El Paso Opera does not operate a dress code, although most patrons to the opera tend to don cocktail attire or formalwear. Tickets to most of the operas run from very reasonable for seats in the back topmost balcony, to around $80 for prime spots right in front. All of the operas put on by El Paso Opera are performed in the language in which they were originally written, but supertitled translations are provided on screens while you watch. Parking at the Abraham Chavez Theater can be tricky, so it is suggested you arrive at least 45 minutes before curtain time, lest you are late and have to wait to be seated. Tickets and seating information for the current season are available through El Paso Opera's Web site.

SERVICES

CULTURE CRUISE
Union Plaza Transit Terminal
400 West San Antonio Ave.
(915) 541-4481
Cruise around to the best of downtown El Paso's galleries, arts and crafts stores, museums, and libraries for a dose of all the culture on offer in the city aboard the once-a-year Culture Cruise. Put on by the municipal Museums and Cultural Affairs Department, the cruise usually features more than a dozen stops where patrons can partake in local flavor and color through artwork, as well as food, beverages, and special collections at each of the venues. Each year in May, the Culture Cruise implements a different theme, with past themes like "Spanish heritage" giving cruise-goers a greater

understanding of El Paso's unique cultural situation. In collaboration with Sun Metro, cruisers are carted around downtown on local city buses that depart from the Union Plaza Transit Terminal and loop through the entire area. Get-on, get-off is the name of the game, so you can feel free to spend as much, or as little time at each venue as you wish. Admission to all locations is free unless otherwise noted, and many of the locations offer refreshments and live music.

SUPPORT ORGANIZATIONS

EL PASO ART ASSOCIATION
500 West Paisano Dr.
(915) 534-7377
www.elpasoartassociation.com
The El Paso Art Association (EPAA) is the oldest art organization in El Paso, with more than 50 years of existence since its founding in 1949. The association promotes the visual arts in the El Paso region and sponsors art shows, classes, and workshops annually. Among their most well attended events is the Arts International exhibition held each October, which draws some 100 artists from across West Texas and Southern New Mexico. The EPAA also sponsors two local galleries: Sunland Art Gallery and Crossland Gallery located in the Art Junction building. Memberships are available in several categories for artists and art aficionados.

INTERNATIONAL HISPANIC CULTURAL INSTITUTE
123 West Mills St.
(915) 838-7374
Founded in 2002, the International Hispanic Cultural Institute (IHCI) applies creative expression and the arts to develop Hispanic cultural awareness and create opportunities for Hispanic youth. Formed in an effort to

minimize the dropout rate in El Paso schools, the IHCI uses the arts to motivate children to stay in school and go on to seek higher education. Each year, it hosts the International Latino Arts Fiesta, honoring the Latino cultural heritage of local residents. In addition to this celebration, the institute hosts many other events, performances, contests, and workshops each year.

SHOWTIME EL PASO
(915) 544-2022
www.showtimeelpaso.com
Formerly known as Community Concerts, Showtime El Paso is a volunteer organization that promotes a season of music concerts each year. Showtime is the city's second oldest performing arts organization and boasts the largest performing arts membership in El Paso. Shows promoted by Showtime El Paso are generally contemporary music acts that span a wide variety of genres, from jazz to bluegrass to instrumental and rock. Most of the Showtime concerts are held at the Abraham Chavez Theater downtown, and both individual and season tickets are available through a form on their Web site.

THEATER

BROADWAY IN EL PASO
The Plaza Theatre
125 Pioneer Plaza
(915) 231-1111
www.theplazatheatre.org
Broadway in El Paso brings popular Broadway shows and musicals to the historic Plaza Theatre downtown. The season typically runs from Oct to June and gives El Pasoans the chance to partake in some of Broadway's best without having to head for the Big Apple. Past seasons have included greats like *The Wedding Singer*, *Riverdance*,

and *The Wizard of Oz*. Tickets are available from the Plaza Theatre's box office, or online through its Web site. Season passes are also on offer, which grant you access to all of the season's shows.

UTEP DINNER THEATER
UTEP Campus
Union Ballroom, 207 Union West Wing
www.utep.edu/tickets
If you love musicals, you will want to take in a dinner theater show at UTEP Dinner Theater, which is a part of the UTEP Department of Theater, Dance and Film. Drawing from local talents and the hard work of students and faculty at UTEP, the Dinner Theater stages four musicals a year, as well as a holiday special. Presented in UTEP's beautiful Union Ballroom, guests enjoy a seated view of the stage and are served a delicious dinner cooked by Union catering. Tickets are available from University Ticketing and generally run around $40 for an adult ticket, with special discounts for students and those with a military ID. Fri and Sat dinner performances are the most expensive, while tickets for weeknights and Sunday matinees are slightly cheaper. Past performances have included *Cats*, *Joseph and the Amazing Technicolor Dreamcoat*, *Chicago*, and more.

VIVA! EL PASO
3 McKelligon Canyon Rd.
McKelligon Canyon Amphitheatre
(915) 231-1165
www.viva-ep.org
Colorful costumes, spectacular sets, and dazzling special effects bring the stage to life in this award-winning outdoor musical presented during the summer months. The play chronicles several centuries of struggles faced by the early Indian, Spanish, Mexican,

and Western American settlers in the El Paso area. This is delightful way to learn some local history in a truly entertaining way, and the outdoor setting at McKelligon Amphitheatre brings the audience vividly into the storyline.

VENUES

ABRAHAM CHAVEZ THEATER
1 Civic Center Plaza
(915) 534-0633
www.visitelpaso.com/abraham_chavez.sstg
The unusual sombrero shape of the Abraham Chavez Theater, known locally as the Chavez Theater, is a distinctive element in El Paso's downtown skyline. The Chavez is named for longtime conductor of the El Paso Symphony Orchestra, Maestro Abraham Chavez. Located adjacent to the El Paso Convention & Performing Arts Center, the theater has a three-story-high glass windowed entry and a four-tiered seating system including more than 1,000 seats in the Grand Tier, 395 seats in the balcony, and 1,053 seats in the Orchestra and Orchestra pit together, for a combined capacity of 2,500. Throughout the year, the theater hosts dozens of performances, from El Paso Opera to Showtime El Paso's concerts. Parking is available for all shows in an underground garage.

EL PASO PLAYHOUSE
2501 Montana Ave.
(915) 532-1317
www.elpasoplayhouse.org
This non-profit community theatre stages a new production almost every month. Supported by grants from the Texas Commission on the Arts and the El Paso Museum & Cultural Affairs Department, the El Paso Playhouse provides entertainment and educational experiences through plays and theatrical events. Over the years, the Playhouse has become a beloved venue of local artists, technicians, patrons, and community members, allowing all to participate in the arts through season productions, children's performances, holiday performances, theater classes, and post-show discussions with audiences. Open call auditions are held for most of the productions, allowing community members with a thespian flair to try their hands at community theater.

JUDSON F. WILLIAMS CONVENTION CENTER
1 Civic Center Plaza
(915) 534-0600
www.visitelpaso.com
The Judson F. Williams Convention Center, known simply as the Williams Convention Center, is maintained by the El Paso Convention and Visitors Bureau in downtown El Paso. Named for a former El Paso mayor, the Convention Center was remodeled and expanded in May 2002, and houses 17 meeting rooms with services for hosting meetings, conventions, and banquets, as well as three large halls and 80,000 square feet of unobstructed exhibition space. Events at the Williams Convention Center vary throughout the year, from arts and bridal fairs to sporting events and private conferences.

MCKELLIGON CANYON AMPHITHEATRE & PAVILION
1500 McKelligon Rd.
(915) 534-0682
This 1,500-seat amphitheatre is situated against the striking backdrop of McKelligon Canyon and provides a stunning venue for a variety of performances, concerts, and festivals throughout the year. Next door to

the amphitheatre is a similar, smaller venue, McKelligon Pavilion, which seats a maximum of 300. Most notably, each year McKelligon Canyon Amphitheatre hosts Viva! El Paso, a colorful dramatization of the area's multi-cultural heritage and rich history. There are three parking lots available at the amphithe-atre for events, and the on-site box office is open the day of events for ticket sales.

THE PLAZA THEATRE
125 Pioneer Plaza
(915) 231-1111
www.theplazatheatre.org
When you watch the floor-length red velvet curtains open for the first time in the Plaza Theatre, you know you are in a truly historic building. Opened in 1930, the Plaza was at one time the largest theater of its kind in the entire Southwest region. While the captivating exterior was designed in Span-ish Colonial Revival architecture and styled after a historic mission, the interior is truly opulent, with elaborately painted ceilings, mosaic tiled floors, and antique furnishings. The crown jewel of the Plaza Theatre is the majestic Wurlitzer organ, which rises out from the orchestra pit and is even played during certain annual events, such as the Classic Film Festival. This centerpiece of his-toric El Paso architecture is a must-visit and is most especially enjoyed by taking in a proper show or concert there.

PARKS AND RECREATION

There's no doubt about it, El Paso is an outdoor-lover's delight. Seeing some 320 days of sunshine a year, the Sun City's nickname is entirely appropriate and makes it an excellent place both to play and watch sports, or go picnicking, hiking, camping, and more. El Paso has hundreds of acres of parkland and open space, miles of hiking, walking, and biking trails, and dozens of recreational and sports facilities to cater to every interest. The Franklin Mountains offer a seemingly endless array of hiking trails and mountain recreation. Golf is a very popular sport and there are several courses around the city, both private clubs and municipal courses. A number of private country clubs offer a range of sports and spa facilities and there are plenty of municipal swimming and tennis facilities all around El Paso. Several sports teams, both collegiate and professional, are based in El Paso and provide great sporting entertainment in baseball, hockey, basketball, football, soccer, rugby, and more.

This chapter covers city and state parks and national monuments, as well as listings for recreational activities from hiking to skateboarding. Major sports, including golf, soccer, swimming, and tennis are also covered. You'll want to check out the Kidstuff chapter for more information on activities for kids such as the El Paso Zoo, bowling alleys, and family fun centers, and children's sports leagues in the city. El Paso's many spectator sports are also covered at the end of this chapter, including the El Paso Patriots soccer team and the Diablos, a South Division independent professional baseball team. El Paso also plays host to a number of exciting rodeo events throughout the year, and information about those can be found in the Annual Events chapter. A specific header for camping has not been included. Instead, check through the parks listings in this chapter, as well as the Day Trips and Getaways chapter, which will give you ample information about state parks, national forests, and recreational areas that provide opportunities for camping.

Price Code

The following price code has been included to give you a rough idea of what a regular ticket or entrance fee will cost for each of the following places. If the fees or costs associated with a particular activity or class are varied, no price has been given and you should use the contact information provided to find out details. More specific pricing and discount information is included in the listings, where available. Every effort has been made to include a variety of activities across a broad spectrum of prices to cater to every possible budget. For the Golf listings, no price code has been included because it proved impossible to cover the range of greens fees and membership fees for every golf club. Instead, check the individual golf club listings themselves for information about greens fees and membership options.

$.....................Less than $5
$$ ....$5 to $10
$$$ .... $11 to $20
$$$$............ More than $20

PARKS

**CHAMIZAL NATIONAL
  MEMORIAL   FREE
800 South San Marcial St.
(915) 532-7273
www.home.nps.gov/cham**
Chamizal National Memorial commemorates the amicable resolution of the U.S.–Mexico border dispute between El Paso and Ciudad Juárez. Large lawns sprawl across several acres here, and a sparse collection of trees make the park a nice place to enjoy a picnic, play a game of Frisbee, or have a soccer match. The Visitors' Center contains three galleries with exhibits relating to the resolution of the border dispute, as well as art exhibitions about the history and landscape of the border region. Though certainly not the largest park in the city, the Chamizal Memorial is popular because of its historic significance. There is plenty of free parking and, from the south lawn, you can get an interesting view of the Bridge of the Americas border crossing.

**FRANKLIN MOUNTAINS
  STATE PARK $
1331 McKelligon Canyon Rd.
(915) 566-6441
www.tpwd.state.tx.us/spdest/findadest/
parks/franklin**

The largest urban park in the United States is located right here in El Paso: the 24,000-acre Franklin Mountains State Park. The Franklin Mountains, which oversee the entire city from their northern vantage, are an impossible-to-ignore feature of the El Paso landscape and provide an endless supply of outdoor recreation to El Pasoans. From guided hikes to walking trails, hidden caves, canyons, performance spaces, and old mines, the Franklin Mountains are El Paso residents' easy getaway right in the city. If you're unsure where to start, try taking a guided ranger hike through the Tom Mays Recreation Area, where you'll learn about wildlife, vegetation, geology, and Native American usage of the area. Camping is also available here. Alternately, McKelligon Canyon is a beautiful canyon park with great hiking and picnicking, and is home to the McKelligon Canyon Amphitheatre performance space.

i The City of El Paso operates more than 200 municipal parks providing ample, free outdoor recreation to the entire metro area. Most of the parks have children's playgrounds and picnic areas, while others have tennis courts, soccer or baseball fields, rec centers, and more. The best way to find a park near you is to visit the Parks & Recreation's Web site, where they keep a listing of all city parks, their addresses, in which district they're located, and what types of facilities are available on site.

**HUECO TANKS STATE PARK $
6900 Hueco Tanks Rd., No. 1
(915) 857-1135
www.tpwd.state.tx.us/park/hueco**
This 860.3-acre park is named for the large natural rock basins or *huecos* that have fur-

nished a supply of trapped rainwater to dwellers and travelers in this arid region for millennia. Of the many unique aspects of Hueco Tanks, the most fascinating are the strange thousand-year-old Native American mythological designs, and human and animal pictographs that are painted and carved on the rocks in the area. The site's notable pictographs include more than 200 face designs or "masks" that were left by the prehistoric Jornada Mogollon culture. Other groups, like the Apaches, Kiowas, and earlier Indian groups, also camped at Hueco Tanks and left behind pictographs recounting their adventures. The tanks also served as watering places for the Butterfield Overland Mail Route in the 1850s. The possible activities at Hueco Tanks range from a guided tour of the pictographs to hiking, rock climbing, camping, or simply packing a picnic to enjoy the unusual geological surrounds of the park. Entrance fees: Adults (13 and above) $4; children (12 and under), seniors (77 years and older), and veterans with at least 60 percent disability, free. Opening hours are generally 7 or 8 a.m. to 6 or 7 p.m. seasonally.

i Texas residents 65 and over with valid ID receive a 50 percent discount on the entrance fee to Hueco Tanks State Park.

KEYSTONE HERITAGE PARK & BOTANIC GARDENS $
819 West Sunset Rd.
(915) 584-0563
www.keystoneheritagepark.org
Keystone is a unique natural attraction that incorporates an archaeological site, a wetland area and an arid botanical garden. The 52-acre park is home to Middle Archaic Native American ruins, some of which are more than 4,000 years old. Keystone Wetlands, one of the last remaining wetland areas along the Rio Grande, is visited by hundreds of migratory birds a year, including several dozen rare species, and is a hot spot for bird watching. Keystone Heritage Park also houses El Paso Botanical Garden, where you can discover the many types of cactus that grow in the area, stroll among butterflies, fill your nose with amazing smells in the Sensory and Culinary Garden, or find solace among the many plants with healing qualities in the Healing Garden. Visiting Keystone Heritage Park is a walking affair, but it is not a strenuous activity. A gentle stroll will take you through most of the site in an afternoon and give you a chance to explore all the beautiful natural areas on offer. If you are interested in bird watching, be sure to stop by during migratory times in spring and fall when birds are sure to be flying through. Entrance fees are $2 for adults, $1 for seniors, military, and children (2 to 12).

WYLER AERIAL TRAM $$
1700 McKinley Ave.
(915) 566-6622
www.tpwd.state.tx.us/spdest/findadest/ parks/wyler_aerial_tram
A ride on Wyler Aerial Tram is an exciting four-minute climb up to Ranger Peak in the Franklin Mountains for a feast for the eyes, seeing El Paso from high above. The tram takes a 946-foot vertical rise up to Wyler Observatory, which, at an altitude of more than 5,600 feet, affords amazing views of the Hueco Mountains, New Mexico's White Sands, and Mexico. The Wyler Tramway is Swiss-made aerial gondola that travels along a thick steel cable. The ride to the top includes a voiced descriptive tour of the local flora and fauna that you pass along the way. The station at the top provides

accessible ramps and paved grounds leading into an observation deck with a 360-degree view. Pay per view high power telescopes located along the observation deck enhance the viewing experience. Rides cost $7 per adult (13 and up) and $4 for each person 12 years and under.

RECREATION

Cycling

El Paso is truly a fantastic place for cycling, with its endless sunshine and arid weather. Whether you are an avid road-cyclist or prefer the challenge and scenery of mountain biking, there is a route to cater to every level and ability. The **El Paso Bicycle Club** (915-667-0202; www.elpasobicycleclub.com) is a great place to get a feel for the local trails, with resources such as bike trail maps, organized rides, and a forum on their Web site where you can connect with other El Paso cyclists and ask questions. Memberships start at $18 for an individual one-year subscription.

If you are a mountain biker, you'll find no shortage of great trails and rides in and among the Franklin Mountains. Transmountain Road, which cuts a slice through the eastern portion of the mountains, runs a 50-mile loop that provides on-road cycling through mountain scenery. The climb along Transmountain Road can be steep at points and it is not a ride for beginners or anyone unaccustomed to bicycling at higher altitudes. Access to Redd Road and Crazy Cat Mountain areas, which are rife with off-road trails, is also available via Transmountain Road. The trails here include paved roads, jeep roads, and single tracks, many of which provide access to some of the more amazing spots in the Franklin Mountains, with stunning views overlooking El Paso and Mexico.

Another popular El Paso bicycle circuit is the road to Old Mesilla, New Mexico, which runs along NM 28, a small state highway, and takes you through pecan farms, vineyards, and the lush and fertile Mesilla Valley. From El Paso, this route is approximately 70 miles round trip and is most frequented by cyclists on sunny weekend mornings.

ℹ For more information about the sights and stops available along NM 28, check out the section on Old Mesilla in the Day Trips and Getaways chapter.

With so much outdoor cycling available in El Paso, there are plenty of bike shops that cater to seasoned cyclists and beginners alike. Many of these shops rent bikes, as well as performing all types of bicycle repairs and selling gear. **Crazy Cat Cyclery** (915-585-9666; www.crazycatcyclery.com) is located on North Desert Boulevard in West El Paso, a few miles from the northwestern end of Transmountain Road. This popular bicycle shop sells and rents a large range of bikes, and performs services from basic tune ups to complete overhauls and flat tire repair. The **Bicycle Company** (915-544-2453; www.the-bicycle-company.com) on North Mesa Street, meanwhile, stocks everything from road bikes to cruisers and ladies-specific bicycles and offers a range of services and repairs.

If you're into BMX racing, the **Sun City BMX Track** (915-867-6906; www.suncitybmx.com) features dirt jumping trails, an automatic starting gate, and lights for night riding. The track is open for practice Tues from 5 to 7 p.m. Races are held on Sat from 3 to 5 p.m. and this is a great time to get in on the dirt-flying action of a real BMX racing team. Spectator admission to the races is free.

PARKS AND RECREATION

Hiking, Jogging, Walking

El Paso's warm, dry climate and plethora of year-round sunshine make it a wonderful place to explore the outdoors on foot. Whether you are an avid jogger, love to hike in the great outdoors, or just want to get out and take a stroll, there is literally a path and place for almost anyone to get on their feet around El Paso.

A number of walking and jogging trails maintained by the city are scattered around El Paso. The trails have varied distances and altitudes, so if you aren't yet acclimated to El Paso's altitude, you should stick to trails and areas closer to downtown and the Lower Valley at first, before venturing into the heights and the mountains. All of the walking paths are located within and/or around municipal parks, so the best way to find a good spot for walking is to head to your nearest park. If you're unsure where to start, you should make for **Ascarate Park** (see this chapter's Close-up), the largest recreational park in El Paso County, which is encircled by a 1.4-mile walking and jogging path.

Hiking in El Paso's surrounding areas is a joy. The Franklin Mountains, which rise to over 7,100 feet inside the city limits, are a stone's throw from downtown, providing acres upon acres of hiking trails and open parkland for nature lovers to enjoy. The scenery of the Franklin Mountains, unlike alpine hiking, is arid and open. Ridge hiking is a popular way to take in the surroundings, where trails lead along the highest ridges from peak to peak. Although the mountains are not lush and green, the plethora of small bushes and rocks dotting the Franklin Mountains allows you extremely wide vantage points that would otherwise be blocked by trees in an alpine environment.

Outside of the Franklin Mountains, other nearby parks, such as Hueco Tanks State Park, as well as places further afield like the Organ Mountains of New Mexico and Guadalupe State Park a few hours east of El Paso, provide hikers with an amazing variety of landscape and natural surroundings that beg to be explored. For weekend getaways, you can venture farther into New Mexico, where the Gila Wilderness and national forests in the north part of the state will keep you hiking for days on end. Closer to home, **El Paso Ridgewalkers** (www.elpasoridgewalkers .com) is a hiking group that organizes local area hikes and events for hiking enthusiasts. Getting involved with the Ridgewalkers can be a great way to make like-minded friends and get an introduction to some of the better local hikes on offer.

i El Paso's high and dry climate can pose challenges for outdoorsy types. If you aren't used to exercising at altitude, be sure to take it slow your first few days and weeks as you adjust. It is also very easy to become dehydrated in the local desert environment, so always carry a water bottle on your excursions, and protect yourself from the sun with sunscreen, a hat, and long sleeves.

Horseback Riding

EL PASO COUNTY 4H HORSE CLUB
Texas Agrilife Research Center
1380 A&M Circle
(915) 525-9858
http://elp.tamu.edu/4h
Youth aged 5 to 19 can join the local El Paso chapter of 4H, an agriculture and livestock club. Although the club is called the horse club, members actually participate in all

aspects of the 4-H experience including sewing, cooking, entomology, consumer decision making, public speaking, leadership, record keeping, photography, and many animal based projects. Annual enrollment costs just $2 and meetings are held at 7 p.m. on the second Monday of each month.

POKI RONI RANCH
782 Lomita Dr.
(915) 591-3074
www.pokironiranch.com
This most basic of horseback riding stables offers birthday packages, children's riding lessons, and pony rides. The multi-colored party pavilion, brightly painted train caboose, and open playgrounds that decorate the property seem to be more of the attraction here than any actual equestrian activity. On a recreational level, this would make a great place for an alternative birthday for your child or a weekend of ranch-style fun. However, for anyone interested in serious horsemanship, there are other places in El Paso that are geared toward more competitive aspects of the sport.

TRES MILAGROS STABLES
649 Bailey Rd.
(915) 494-3380
www.tresmilagrosstables.com
Tres Milagros Stables is located in the quiet Upper Valley of El Paso County, not far from Sunland Park Racetrack. The facility offers boarding for racehorses, team roping, rodeo, and riding lessons. A large lighted roping arena is located on the premises with cattle and roping outings scheduled on a regular basis for advanced ropers. Rodeo contestants are encouraged to practice their team roping and barrel racing here, and the arena is also available for hunter/jumpers and

other types of exercising and riding. They also offer a private riding lesson program, as well as goat roping for children. Call for more information about enrolling in private lessons.

REC CENTERS AND SPORTS PARKS

ACOSTA SPORTS CENTER
4321 Delta Dr.
(915) 534-0254
This large sports complex in South El Paso is home to a number of facilities, including the El Paso Baseball Fields, where several adult baseball and softball leagues practice and play their games.

SPORTSPLEX OF CHAMPIONS
1780 North Zaragosa Rd.
(915) 857-7676
Champions Sportsplex is a multifunctional sports facility that houses baseball fields, volleyball courts, and lighted T-ball fields. Several sporting leagues operate out of Champions, including sand volleyball co-ed leagues, women's, girls' and men's softball, and youth baseball for ages 5 to 14. The park can easily accommodate a 200-team tournament, with games played during the day and at night. A concession stand is also available for games, tournaments, and events.

SPORTS
Football

SUN CITY FLAG FOOTBALL LEAGUE
(915) 227-9947
www.elpasoflagfootball.com
This adult flag football league offers both four-man and eight-man non-contact football in a friendly, competitive environment

Rec Centers

El Paso has 15 recreation centers across the city that offer a variety of classes, leagues, and activities for both children and adults. To find out what is on offer at each rec center, you should contact them individually or visit the **El Paso Parks & Recreation** Web site at www.ci.el-paso.tx.us/parks.

Armijo
700 East 7th St.
(915) 544-5436

Carolina
563 North Carolina St.
(915) 594-8934

Chihuahuita
417 Charles St.
(915) 533-6909

Galatzan
650 Wallenberg
(915) 581-5182

Gary Del Palacio
3001 Parkwood St.
(915) 629-7312

Leona Ford Washington
3400 East Missouri St.
(915) 562-7071

Marty Robbins
11600 Vista Del Sol
(915) 855-4147

Multipurpose
9031 Viscount Blvd.
(915) 598-1155

Nolan Richardson
4435 Maxwell St.
(915) 755-7566

Pavo Real
9301 Alameda Ave.
(915) 858-1929

Rae Gilmore
8501 Diana Dr.
(915) 751-4945

San Juan
701 North Glenwood St.
(915) 779-2799

Seville
6700 Sambrano
(915) 778-6722

Veterans
5301 Salem Dr.
(915) 821-8909

Westside
7400 High Ridge
(915) 587-1623

for El Paso football lovers. Games are played in various city parks around El Paso. Up-to-date information about the next sign-up period, as well as fees, rules, and tournament schedules, is available from the Web site.

Golf

BUTTERFIELD TRAIL GOLF CLUB
1858 Cottonwoods
(915) 772-1038
www.butterfieldtrailgolf.com
Butterfield Trail Golf Club is an 18-hole, par 72, championship public golf course and club located among natural sand dunes and native flora and fauna. The course itself provides a challenging, yet amiable, unspoiled

golf adventure. Features include 55 feet of elevation changes, vertical transitions, and signature holes on Dominant Plus Bent grass. Greens fees range from $35 to $80 depending on day and time. They also offer golf instruction and several on-site restaurants.

CORONADO GOLF & COUNTRY CLUB
1044 Broadmoor Dr.
(915) 584-1171
www.coronadocountryclub.com
This members-only country club is located in the Franklin Mountains on the Westside. Established in 1957, the club features an 18-hole golf course, several tennis courts with lights for evening play, a gym and a

large swimming pool, banquet facilities, and a restaurant. The club's location at 4,700 feet up in the mountains affords stellar views of El Paso and the surrounding areas and the holes on the golf course range from elevated tees to finely groomed greens. Membership information is available through their Web site or over the phone.

EL PASO COUNTRY CLUB
5000 Country Club Place
(915) 584-1111
www.elpasocountryclub.com

The facilities at El Paso Country Club cater to many interests, from golfing to tennis, swimming, or simply relaxing. A beautiful swimming pool, eight tennis courts, a fitness room, and dining facilities encompass the amenities at this members-only club, while its main attraction is a 6,781-yard, par 71, golf course. Several extra facilities are available for free to members. These include a driving range, a practice putting green, and a chipping green, as well as electric carts, and caddies. The tennis facility is comprised of eight lit and shaded, plexi paved courts, all of which are surrounded by manicured lawns with an adjacent covered patio. The tennis program here includes both adult and junior memberships, private and group lessons, drills, and a number of USTA tournaments and teams.

The outdoor swimming pool has a depth up to 12 feet with a lap lane, a 1-meter diving board, and a water slide for the kids' enjoyment, and is fully staffed by trained lifeguards. They also have a competitive children's swim team.

The on-site pro shop here provides access to a range of clothing, as well as shoes, rackets, balls, accessories, and services, including racket stringing and demonstrations.

EMERALD SPRINGS GOLF & CONFERENCE CENTER
16000 Ashford
Horizon City, TX
(915) 852-9110
www.emeraldspringsgolf.com

Tucked away in the hills of the Eastside in nearby Horizon City, it was at Emerald Springs that still-undiscovered golfer Lee Trevino started his career when he upset the daunting PGA golfer, Raymond Floyd. Built on a natural spring in 1963, this leafy golf club was renovated in 2007, including an expansion of the clubhouse, which now houses a stately coral reef aquarium. The clubhouse restaurant overlooks the 18th green, while the 3,000-square-foot fitness center houses over 40 pieces of exercise equipment, including free weights, cardio stations, stationary bicycles, universals, and abdominal equipment. Each cardio station overlooks the pristine swimming pool and lush green front yard bordered with weeping willows. Memberships start at $40 per month with a one-year commitment, while greens fees range from $20 to $35 depending on day and time.

LONE STAR GOLF CLUB
1510 Hawkins
(915) 591-4927
www.whatsinyourcity.net/LONE_STAR

Touting itself as El Paso's most popular public golf course, the tree-lined fairways of this classic club were designed by Marvin Ferguson. The club opened in 1975 and is known for its friendly staff, well-groomed greens, and a fine restaurant. The clever design of the course challenges most golfers with understated breaks in the greens and strategically placed sand traps, and the scenic location provides beautiful views of the Franklin Mountains and El Paso's desert surrounds. A fully lit driving range and two lighted chipping and putting greens allow patrons to practice day or night. Greens fees range from $14 to $26 depending on day and time. Golfing lessons are also available.

PAINTED DUNES DESERT GOLF COURSE
12000 McCombs St.
(915) 821-2122
www.painteddunes.com
This 27-hole championship golf course has received accolades from a number of respected golf publications and local and regional newspapers. Designed by Ken Dye and Jeffrey Brauer, Painted Dunes opened in 1991, offering gently rolling greens and hills, which emphasizes the golfer's putting game and strategy play. Aggressive golfers might find this course challenging, as it forces the golfer to tackle each hole patiently. The clubhouse offers a standard array of food options and amenities, including a pro shop, and the course often hosts tournaments. For practice, there is also a green and a pitching field, as well as a driving range and PGA certified instructors.

UNDERWOOD GOLF COMPLEX
Fort Bliss
3200 Coe Ave., Building 3191
(915) 562-2066
www.blissmwr.com/golf
George V. Underwood Jr. Golf Complex is a golf center located on Fort Bliss, which features varied landscape on two golf courses: arid desert scenery on the Sunrise Golf Course and a lush, parkland style on the Sunset Course. The complex also houses a pro shop and restaurant. Other golfing facilities here include a lighted driving range,

two practice putting greens, golf carts, and a computerized handicapping service. The course is open to both military personnel and civilians, and greens fees range from $9 to $25, depending on the day, time, and your military or civilian status.

VISTA HILLS COUNTRY CLUB
2210 Trawood Dr.
(915) 592-3535
www.vistahillscc.com
Located in East El Paso, this private country club is home to an 18-hole championship golf course overseen by golf pro Terry Jennings. A driving range and several practice putting greens allow you to hone your game before heading out to the course. To complete its recreational offerings, the club also has a pro shop, a lounge, several dining areas, and a junior Olympic swimming pool. Club golf tournaments are often held here, and the club is home to a Women's Golf Association.

i Boxing and Open Gym are available at several of El Paso's Rec Centers. Armijo, Carolina, San Juan, and Pavo Real offer boxing times and classes. Open Gym hours, including some cardio training circuits and open basketball, are available at Armijo, Nolan Richardson, Veterans, and Marty Robbins.

Hockey

EL PASO HOCKEY ASSOCIATION
Sierra Providence Event Center
4100 East Paisano Dr.
(915) 479-7825
www.elpasohockey.org
The El Paso Hockey Association is a 501 C3 non-profit organization promoting ice sports

in El Paso. The hockey program has adult and youth hockey courses that range from those just starting out on the ice to competitive travel teams. These leagues emphasize team work, structure, fitness, and fun. The youth ice hockey programs are open to children at all skill levels ranging in age from 4 to 18, and other activities, such as "Learn to play hockey" classes, hockey schools and camps, and power skating are available for kids at different times throughout the year. Several competitive teams also compete within the North Texas Hockey League. Adults interested in hockey can participate in the Adult Leagues, which play on Tues and Wed nights. Alternatively, for those just looking to have some fun on the ice, Hockey at a Fun Pace (HAFP) is an adult skating program for beginners, intermediates, and other players that want to have fun, improve their games, and get a good workout.

Public skating is available at the Sierra Providence Event Center rink most weekends for $7. The rink is open Fri nights from 7 to 10 p.m., Sat from noon to 10 p.m., and Sun noon to 4 p.m., as well as all major holidays. Rental skates are available in both children's and adult's sizes for free.

Soccer

There are a number of soccer leagues in El Paso that cater to both children and adults. If you or your child is interested in joining a soccer league, consult the following listings to get an idea of the teams and leagues available.

ADULT INDOOR SOCCER LEAGUE
El Paso Parks & Recreation
(915) 757-2743
www.ci.el-paso.tx.us/parks/sports.asp
Visit the Web site for information on the league and how to register.

EL PASO YOUTH SOCCER LEAGUE
(915) 525-4696
www.elpasoyouthsoccer.com
El Paso's main youth soccer organization, El Paso Youth Soccer League consists of a number of sub-leagues that operate throughout the city. More information about this youth soccer league is available in the Kidstuff chapter.

EL PASO CLASSIC SOCCER
(915) 474-9575
www.epclassicsoccer.com
Serving the entire city, El Paso Classic Soccer League is a non-profit and educational soccer organization run by board members, officers, and support members. Games are typically held at the Westside Sports Complex.

Skateboarding

EL PASO SKATEPARK ASSOCIATION
www.elpasoskatepark.org
Formed in 2007 by a group of serious skateboarders, the El Paso Skatepark Association (EPSA) is dedicated to "the development and stewardship of safe, freely accessible public skateparks in El Paso." They seek to form collaborations and partnerships between skateboarders and area businesses, and work to bring the desires of the skating community to the attention of local officials. Each year, EPSA joins the art and skateboarding communities together for the Deck Art Show fundraiser. They have also facilitated a 3,000-square-foot bowl mural project at the Carolina Skatepark in an effort to deter offensive graffiti and tagging. From 2008–2009, they consulted on the design and building of the community's second custom concrete skating facility at Westside Community Park. Association membership is open to almost anyone via a simple form on their Web site.

i A list of the 10 skateparks operated by the City of El Paso is available on the El Paso Skatepark Association's Web site, as well as 5 skateparks in greater El Paso County and 3 in Doña Ana County, New Mexico. www.elpasoskatepark.org.

Softball

**EL PASO MEN'S INTERNATIONAL
SOFTBALL LEAGUE**
El Paso Sportspark
(915) 598-6922
www.epsportsparksoftball.com
If you're interested in softball, you can get involved with a team or start your own through this league. Men's competitive softball games are held on Sun mornings and Thurs evenings, while co-ed mixed games are held on Mon. You can opt to join an existing team or start and register your own team through the league. Information about which teams have spots open for new team members is available by calling the league director at the listed number. More information about league standings, as well as photos and schedules, is available on the Web site.

EL PASO SOFTBALL
4321 Delta Dr.
(915) 351-6266
www.elpasosoftball.com
This adult softball league is run by the City of El Paso's Parks & Recreation department. Starting in January of each year, there are several sessions of league and tournament play, including Men's, Mixed, and Women's leagues. Games are played at the Acosta Sports Center on Delta Drive in South El Paso, and participation requires a fairly hefty fee that includes enrollment in the US Specialty Sports Association.

Swimming

The City of El Paso's Parks & Recreation Department operates 14 aquatic facilities that include nine indoor heated pools that are open year-round, as well as five outdoor aquatic facilities, which are only open during the summer from May to August.

Each of these aquatic facilities offers swimming classes for people of all ages and abilities, as well as water aerobics classes, a summer swim league, recreational swimming, lap swimming with a 100-mile club for those who want an extra challenge, and master fitness classes. General admission to any of the pools is $2 for adults (18 to 55), $1 for youth (up to 17), and $1 for seniors (55 and older).

i If you plan to swim often, invest in a punch card or a family card, which costs $124 a month and allows unlimited entry to aquatic centers for recreation and lap swims to a family consisting of two adults and two youth.

Indoor Pools
- **Armijo:** 911 Ochoa St., (915) 543-9598
- **Delta Pool:** 4451 Delta Dr., (915) 542-0087
- **Hawkins:** 1500 Hawkins Blvd., (915) 594-8031
- **Leo Cancellare:** 650 Wallenberg, (915) 584-9848
- **Marty Robbins:** 11065 Vista del Sol Dr., (915) 855-7456
- **Memorial:** 3251 Copper Ave., (915) 565-4683
- **William W. Cowan:** 8100 Independence Dr., (915) 860-2349
- **T & I:** 9031 Viscount Blvd., (915) 598-1163
- **Veterans:** 5301 Salem Dr., (915) 821-0142

Outdoor Pools

- **Chelsea:** 819 Chelsea St., (915) 775-4629
- **Grandview:** 3100 Jefferson Ave., (915) 566-5586
- **Lionel Forti:** 1225 Giles Rd., (915) 595-2756
- **Nations:** 8831 Railroad Dr., (915) 759-8434
- **Pavo Real:** 110 Presa Place, (915) 858-6315

Tennis

Between the several private country clubs and tennis clubs and the many municipal tennis courts located in parks across the city, there are literally dozens of places to play a game of tennis, take a lesson, or hone your serve in El Paso. At the **El Paso Youth Tennis Center** (915-751-1181; www.epytc.org), kids and teens can play for free or take lessons, while **Tennis West Sports and Racquet Club** (915-581-5471; www.tennis-west.com) is a private sports club with 14 lighted tennis courts, a fitness room, and swimming facilities, and they offer rental equipment, lessons, and membership plans for individuals and families.

The following is a comprehensive list of tennis courts located in municipal parks across El Paso. These courts are free to play on and many are lighted, but you will need to bring your own equipment (racquet and tennis balls). The listings are arranged by area of the city and provided are the name and address of the park.

Central/Downtown

- **Grandview:** 3100 Jefferson Ave.
- **Loretto-Lincoln:** 4500 East Yandell Dr.
- **Memorial:** 1701 North Copia St.

Eastside

- **Cielo Vista:** 9030 Cosmos Dr.
- **Eastwood:** 3110 Parkwood Dr.
- **Lomaland:** 7115 Lomita Dr.
- **Pueblo Viejo:** Roseway Drive and Presa Place
- **Shawver:** 8100 Independence Dr.
- **Thomas Manor:** 7901 Knights Dr.

Northeast

- **Arlington:** 10350 Pasadena Circle
- **Dolphin:** 5900 Marlin Dr.
- **Franklin:** 6050 Quail Ave.
- **Skyline:** 5050 Yvette Ave.
- **Sunrise:** 3800 Sunrise Ave.

Westside

- **Mission Hills:** 3800 O'Keefe Dr.
- **Madeline:** 900 E. Baltimore Ave.
- **Milagro:** 5310 Annette Dr.
- **Paul Harvey:** 6220 Belton Rd.

SPECTATOR SPORTS

Baseball

EL PASO DIABLOS $–$$
Cohen Stadium
9700 Gateway Blvd. North
(915) 755-2000
www.diablos.com

The El Paso Diablos baseball team, which is now an affiliate of the American Association of Independent Professional Baseball, has been an El Paso institution for decades. The Diablos' season runs from Apr through Aug and home games are played in the comfortable 10,000-seat Cohen Stadium in Northeast El Paso. On home game nights, there is almost always a special promotion including fireworks on Fri and 25-cent hotdogs and ice cream sandwiches on Sun. Tickets can be purchased at the Cohen Stadium Box Office, online at their Web site, or over the phone.

Ascarate Park—Recreation in the Heart of El Paso

El Paso County's largest public-use recreational park, **Ascarate Park** (6900 Delta Ave., 915-772-5605; www.epcounty.com), covers 448 acres in the southeast part of the city. With a lake, several playgrounds, a multitude of sports facilities, a golf course, and jogging and bike trails, this is an amazing spot to relax with the family on a sunny El Paso afternoon. The 18-hole **Ascarate Golf Course** (915-772-7381) sits on 280 acres at the south end of the park and a 9-hole short course is available at the north end, both of which offer stunning views of the Franklin Mountains as you golf. One of the most reasonably priced courses in the city, greens fees here range from $15 on weekdays to $19 on weekends, including a golf cart, or you can play the short course on foot for just $10.

Ascarate Lake covers 48 acres of the park, offering boating, pontoon tours, canoes, and pedal boats. The lake is home to a number of fish including trout, catfish, bass, and carp, and makes an excellent urban spot for an afternoon of fishing. The park has several fishing events yearly that hundreds attend.

The **Ascarate Aquatic Center** (915-772-5605), meanwhile, features a 50-meter Olympic-size competition pool (one of the few in El Paso County), two diving boards, a children's pool, five water slides, two sand volleyball courts, and a picnic area. Located inside Ascarate Park, the Aquatic Center plays host to three swim meets each year and families just out for a swim take advantage of the pools here on a daily basis. The center is open Tues to Thurs from 3 to 9 p.m. and Fri to Sun from noon to 5 p.m. An individual swim costs $2 per person.

Ascarate Park also has five softball fields, two soccer fields, and one baseball field for practices or tournaments. Two basketball courts and two tennis courts are located at the north end of the park, as well as two handball courts on its east side. If you're out for a game of volleyball, there are two sand courts adjacent to the Aquatic Center near the park's main gate. Joggers and walkers can enjoy the pleasant 1.4-mile trail that encircles Ascarate Lake. The park is also a great place for picnicking, with more than 50 picnic shelters, plenty of tables and grills, and two children's playgrounds to keep the kids occupied.

College Sports

UTEP MINERS ATHLETICS
500 West University Dr.
(915) 747-5347
http://utepathletics.cstv.com
The University of Texas at El Paso has a huge Division 1-A athletics program, with many teams that are often very competitive across a range of college sports. Men's and women's basketball are played during the winter in the Don Haskins Center, a large indoor arena named after legendary former UTEP basketball coach. In the fall, you can catch Miners Football playing at the massive 51,000-seat Sun Bowl Stadium, scene of the nationally televised collegiate bowl game.

Horse Racing

SUNLAND PARK RACETRACK &
  CASINO   FREE–$$
1200 Futurity Dr.
Sunland Park, NM
(575) 874-5200
www.sunland-park.com

Sunland Park is a racetrack and casino featuring slot machine gaming, live horse racing, simulcast wagering, four dining options including a Las Vegas–style buffet, live entertainment, and concerts, as well as a convention space and meeting rooms. The track first opened in 1959 and operated for several decades as just a racetrack. In the 1990s, the decline of the horse racing industry around the nation pushed New Mexico to design legislation that allowed racetracks to incorporate slot machines and today, Sunland Park is one of several racetracks around New Mexico that operate these so-called "racinos." Without a full set of table games, Sunland Park is really more of a slot parlor than a true casino.

Races at Sunland Park feature both thoroughbreds and quarter horses from Dec through late Apr. Live racing is traditionally on offer four days a week, on Tues, Fri, Sat, and Sun, though the track occasionally races on Wed instead of Tues. The annual highlight race is the Sunland Derby, a 1⅛-mile thoroughbred race for three-year-olds, which is held in late Mar of each year. It is free to watch races from the grandstand, or you may purchase tickets to sit in the decked-out Turf Club for $7. Free guarded parking, free valet parking, and RV hookups are all available at the track, which is located 10 minutes west of downtown El Paso, off I-10 Exit 13.

Ice Hockey

EL PASO RHINOS $$–$$$$
El Paso County Collesium
4100 East Paisano St.
www.elpasorhinos.com

The Rhinos are a Junior "A" Tier III ice hockey team that compete as part of the Mid-West Conference of the Western States Hockey League. Home games are played at the Sierra Providence Event Center located inside El Paso County Collesium. A very popular team in El Paso, the Rhinos often support local charity organizations and wear special jerseys during the games to help raise funds for local causes. The Rhinos' season runs Sept through Mar and tickets can be purchased at local Ticketmaster outlets (including online) as well as at the Sierra Providence Event Center box office on game nights.

Indoor Football

EL PASO GENERALS
(915) 598-7277
www.elpasogenerals.com

The El Paso Generals are a professional indoor football team that plays as part of the Indoor Football League. This pro league was created in 2008 out of the merger between the Intense Football League and United Indoor Football. The El Paso Generals play all of their home games at the El Paso County Coliseum. Player tryouts are held in January of each year, and the Generals' season runs from Apr through Jul.

Rugby

EL PASO SCORPIONS
(915) 740-8340
www.elpasorugby.org

This semi-pro and collegiate level rugby team has been playing in El Paso since the mid-1970s, and since 1979, have won 12 Rio Grande Union Championships and sent multiple players to All Star teams. The El Paso Scorpions are a 1st division team of the United States Rugby Union. The Scorpions organization also oversees the administration of rugby athletic programs across several El Paso high schools, with a few of these teams becoming quite competitive.

Soccer

EL PASO PATRIOTS   **$$**
Patriot Stadium
(915) 771-6620
www.elpaso-patriots.com
The El Paso Patriots are a professional United Soccer Premier Development League team that plays in the Mid-South Division of the Southern Conference. Founded in 1989, they were the Open Cup Runners-Up in 1995, won the Mid-South Division title in 2004, and in 2005 took home the Southern Conference Championship. The Patriots' season runs all summer, from Apr through Labor Day. Home games, which usually begin at 8 p.m., are played at the small 3,000-seat Patriot Stadium, located just off of I-10 in East El Paso near the Cielo Vista Mall.

KIDSTUFF

El Paso is truly a family friendly town. There are lots of activities going on for the young and the young at heart throughout the city. El Paso's sunny climate lends itself well to year-round outdoor activities, like miniature golf and soccer, and there are plenty of fun but educational activities available, too. Artistic-minded kids will love At the Clayground, where they can try their hands at painting their own ceramic pieces, while more adventurous families will certainly enjoy a day at Wet 'N' Wild, El Paso's exciting water park.

Be sure to check the Attractions chapter and the Parks and Recreation chapter, which contain more listings that might be of interest to families and kids of all ages. There are plenty of outdoor activities, public parks and recreation areas, swimming pools, and professional sporting events in the El Paso area that are listed in those chapters. The following listings are child-specific activities to let your little ones blow off some steam, as well as places that your too-hip teens will probably want to check out. The price code below gives you an idea of what entrance fees (if any) and costs will be like to attend or visit any of these places.

Price Code

The following price code has been included to give you a rough idea of what a regular ticket or entrance fee will cost for each of the following places. If the fees or costs associated with a particular activity or class are varied, no price has been given and you should use the contact information provided to find out details. More specific pricing and discount information is included in the listings, where available. Every effort has been made to include a variety of activities across a broad spectrum of prices to cater to every possible budget.

$..........................$1 to $5
$$ ....$6 to 10
$$$ .... $11 to $19
$$$$ ....$20 and up

BE CREATIVE

AT THE CLAYGROUND
5860 North Mesa, Suite 127
(915) 533-2529
www.attheclayground.com
At the Clayground is a paint-your-own-pottery studio that offers fun and creative activities for kids and adults. The basic premise is fairly simple—kids get to choose from a selection of ceramic pieces and paint colors and then paint their piece in any way they choose. Once finished, At the Clayground will glaze and fire the piece and the finished product is ready to be picked up within a week. This is great spot for kids to flesh out some of their colorful desires without ruining your carpet or crayoning the walls at home! An all-inclusive package includes the price of the ceramic piece and the paints, as well

as use of the brushes and tools and the final glazing and firing. At the Clayground is also open to parties and private functions, so this might be a creatively alternative way to schedule your artistic child's birthday party. Opening hours: Mon to Thurs 10 a.m. to 7 p.m.; Fri and Sat 10 a.m. to 8 p.m.

i *El Paso Kids* **is a monthly magazine and family resource guide that can be picked up at some 900 locations around the city. Inside, you'll find listings for child-related services and shopping and an up-to-date family events calendar. Download a free PDF copy online at www.elpasokids.com.**

EL PASO KIDS-N-CO   **$–$$**
1301 Texas Ave.
(915) 351-1455
www.kidsnco.org
El Paso Kids-N-Co is a children's theater compaing that offers the children of El Paso the chance to participate in theatrical training, with a focus on a diverse selection of kids from all backgrouund. Kids-N-Co operates a successful theater school where children ages five and up can learn about all aspects of the theater industry, from acting to costume-making and set design. They also run several theater camps during school holidays. Each season, Kids-N-Co puts on four or five productions starring all-youth casts, with past productions including *Willy Wonka*, *Little Women*, and *The Brothers Grimm Spectaculathon*. There is no cost to the young thespians for participation in productions, but casts are chosen through traditional auditions held throughout the year. Scheduled performances are at 7:30 p.m. Fri and Sat and 2:30 p.m. Sun at the Kids-N-Co

Performance Center unless otherwise noted. Tickets are available at the door. Reservations are not accepted.

EL PASO SYMPHONY YOUTH ORCHESTRA
(915) 525-8978
www.epsyos.org
A subsidiary of the El Paso Symphony Orchestra Association, El Paso Symphony Youth Orchestra (EPSYO) offers the chance for the talented young musicians of El Paso to participate in a professional-style musical ensemble and to receive high quality musical instruction. The EPSYO maintains a strong commitment to fostering the type of supportive atmosphere that young musicians need to grow in their arts. Each year, the Symphony Youth Orchestra performs four classical music concerts. All students from second grade to college undergraduate are eligible to apply, so if your child is a budding musician, he or she can try performing with a classical group. A trip to hear the Symphony Youth Orchestra perform is, likewise, an excellent way to expose your children to classical music being performed by their own peers. EPSYO concerts are performed at varying locations in downtown El Paso. Call or visit their Web site for more information on the current season.

i **Got a teen driver? You can keep an eye on his or her driving habits and whereabouts using the Youth Driving Safe vehicle GPS tracking system. Instantly monitor your teen's driving habits and help keep them safe on El Paso's roads. Visit www.youthdrivingsafe.org or call (888) Youth-16.**

THE MAGIC BRUSH
255 Shadow Mountain G
(915) 867.4707
www.themagicbrushart.com

This kids' art school aims to provide a creative, artistic outlet to kids and teens through painting, drawing, sculpting, or computer graphics. They offer ongoing group and private classes to all ages, from toddlers to adults, and also often host art shows to exhibit some of the recent creations of students. At their summer camp, kids aged four and up can participate in learning about all types of artistic media for three hours each day. Walk-ins are welcome for individual classes, which start around $30 an hour, or you can register by the month. Get your toddler started on creative expression or send your arty teen in to learn the basics of painting—all are welcome at the Magic Brush! Classes and hours vary—call or visit the Web site to find out the current schedule.

GET SPORTY

EL PASO HOCKEY
Sierra Providence Events Center
4100 East Paisano Dr.
(915) 479-7825
www.elpasohockey.org

Got a little one with way too much energy? Enroll him or her in youth ice hockey! Unlike pro hockey, which can sometimes be aggressive, El Paso Youth Hockey focuses on the basics of ice skating, stick handling, shooting, and positional play with an emphasis on fun. The Mini Mites/Mites program is aimed at total beginners under the age of 8, while the Youth Recreational League handles the more experienced players between the ages of 8 and 18. An adult league is also open to parents who want to hit the ice. All players are required to wear full protective gear and

games and other fun activities are incorporated into the program to make sure that the kids keep a good, sportsmanlike perspective.

EL PASO ICE MONITOR
Sierra Providence Events Center
4100 East Paisano Dr.
(915) 479-7825
www.elpasoicemonitor.com

For all things related to ice skating in El Paso, the El Paso Ice Monitor has the scoop. The organization is based out of the Sierra Providence Events Center on the grounds of the El Paso County Coliseum, which houses a large ice rink and is the home of the Sun City Blades Figure Skating Club, El Paso's youth hockey league, and an ice skating school. They offer skating classes for all ages and skill levels, public skate times, hockey and figure skating events, tournaments, camps, and more. The rink is also available for private rentals for birthdays and parties, and offers basic skating-related services, such as skate fittings and sharpening.

i El Paso Parks & Recreation operates many youth sports leagues throughout the city, from indoor soccer to girls' fast pitch and volleyball to basketball, as well as classes, camps, and after-school programs. See the Web site for more details: www.ci.elpaso.tx.us/parks/default.asp.

EL PASO YOUTH SOCCER
www.elpasoyouthsoccer.com

If you have a child that loves to run, can't get enough kick time, and idolizes David Beckham, he or she will definitely want to join El Paso Youth Soccer, which offers a variety of programs and leagues to cater to just about every age group and ability level. The teams

🔍 Close-up

Ama Kids

Have you ever felt frustrated about where to take your kids for a haircut? Ama Kids, El Paso's first and exclusive children's hair salon, provides a beautiful, kid-friendly answer to this problem. Featuring Small Paul by Paul Frank and Original Sprouts organic baby skin care line, there is no reason your child can't indulge in a fancy day at the spa, just like you! Original Sprouts is a line of natural products for children: a paraben- and sulfate-free hair and skin care line that is "worry-free luxury for babies and up."

Sometimes, the worst part about taking the kids in for a haircut is keeping them still for the stylist, but Ama Kids solves this problem by making beauty treatments fun. Each styling chair features a flat screen TV where your child can choose from dozens of satellite TV channels or play a selection of video games while getting a haircut. As a kids-only salon, Ama Kids really understands how to work with children, and their stylists are specially trained as children's beauty professionals. They also understand completely the stresses of being a parent and are forgiving if you need to reschedule your appointments or if the kids get a little unruly. They also have a wonderful program designed to ease very young children into their first haircuts so that they will enjoy going to the stylist rather than dread it.

Ama Kids offers tons of great specials. On Tuesday, your daughter can get her nails prettied for just $15 with the Marvelous Mani and Pedi Package. Wednesday gets a break on the price, as all haircuts are only $10 from 3 to 5 p.m. On Thursday you can enjoy a 10 percent discount off full-priced merchandise and the Original Sprouts products line, while Friday is BFF Diva Day—your child can bring her best friend along and you'll pay $35 for two haircuts and best friend charm bracelets. Saturday is for the boys—your little man can get a free Spraylights washable highlight with his haircut.

You may also want to savor those fleeting moments of beauty just after the cut and before they spill chocolate on themselves again. In that case, Ama Kids will take a Polaroid picture of your child and put it in a personalized picture frame to keep for just $5.

Ama Kids is located at 9112 Alps Drive, Suite B, inside Ice Castles Too Learning Center (915-751-0262; www.amakids.biz). Hours are Tues to Fri 10 a.m. to 6 p.m.; Sat 10 a.m. to 4 p.m. Be sure to consult their Web site for printable coupons and monthly specials, and even schedule your appointment online.

play at a variety of parks in and around El Paso, and often travel all over the United States and abroad. Truly competitive soccer players can participate in the South Texas and national competitions and cups, as well as the Olympic Development Program. All of the players, coaches, and officials involved with El Paso Youth Soccer are covered by a secondary accident insurance, and every coach, administrator, and volunteer must clear a mandatory background check before assisting in the organization, so you can rest assured that your child is in safe hands. To participate, your child must be registered with a regional association.

EL PASO YOUTH TENNIS
CENTER   **$$–$$$**
4770 Woodrow Bean Transmountain Rd.
(915) 751-1181
www.epytc.org
Tennis is not only a fun game, it's also great exercise, so if your kids need to burn off some energy or they want to be the next Venus Williams, they can enroll in tennis lessons at El Paso Youth Tennis Center. The center aims to keep kids "on the courts, not in them" by promoting an active lifestyle and giving kids a healthy outlet for their interests. They offer reasonably priced beginner through advanced group and private tennis lessons for ages 4 to 18. Adult development lessons and court times are also available upon request. Scholarships are offered for disadvantaged youth, and the center hosts four tournaments a year as part of the United States Tennis Association and other local tennis associations. Lesson times are scheduled for after-school hours, from 4:30 to 7:30 p.m. on Tues, Wed, and Thurs, and on Sat afternoons.

GYMBOREE   **$$$$**
7410 North Mesa St. (Remcon Circle),
Suite C-3
(915) 581-6262
www.gymboreeclasses.com
Gymboree is a great way for parents to get in shape and spend time with their little ones. In a safe environment, take your baby to play and learn music, art, sports, and school skills in preschool classes for baby, infant, toddler,

and preschooler age groups. Gymboree Play & Music has been fostering creativity and confidence in children ages birth to five for more than 30 years. Their age-appropriate activities help develop children's mental and social skills and take a unique approach to parent involvement by encouraging total participation in and understanding of each child's development. If you have several children, bring everyone to the Family Play & Learn, Music, or Art Classes, which are open to children up to five years of age.

JUST FOR KIDS SPORTS LEAGUE
www.jfksportsleague.com
Just For Kids Sports League is a privately owned co-ed youth flag football league. They operate flag football seasons in spring, summer, and fall. Just For Kids takes a very equitable approach to the sport, allowing all children to shine and never forcing a child to sit out because of ability level. Registration for any of the three seasons usually occurs the month prior, and events schedules are available on their Web site.

PUTT-PUTT GOLF AND GAMES $–$$
8836 Montana Ave.
(915) 772-4794
www.puttputt.com
Miniature golf is a family pastime that never gets old, and Putt-Putt is one of the most well-known minigolf chains in the U.S. The El Paso Putt-Putt Golf and Games is a recreational family fun center that features 18 holes of classic minigolf, where you can try your hand at putting the ball over the clown and through the windmill! El Paso's Putt-Putt center also features bumper cars, an arcade, bumper boats, and a snack bar, so there is something to keep just about everyone occupied. The best thing about

Putt-Putt is the extremely reasonable prices, which means that you can keep your kids entertained and out of your hair for that much longer. Opening hours vary by season, but they are usually open from mid-day to around 9 p.m.

ROLLER BOMB $
12320 Lorenzo Ruiz, Suite A
(915) 855-2662
www.rollerbomb.us
Grab a glow stick, throw on your skates, and bomb around the rink at Roller Bomb. This classic kids' activity is not to be over-looked—it's back in vogue with sleek new inline skates or old-fashioned square skates available for rent or sale in the skate shop at Roller Bomb. The Roller Café snack bar inside serves pizza, popcorn, nachos, and other snacks that your kids will love. Party packages are available if you'd like to make your child's next birthday party into a skatef-est. Opening hours: Mon to Tues open for private functions; Wed to Thurs 2 to 8 p.m.; Fri 2 to 11 p.m.; Sat 11 a.m. to 11 p.m.; Sun noon to 9 p.m.

SOCORRO AQUATIC CENTER
Student Activities Complex
1257 Southview Dr.
(915) 937-0544
www.sisd.net/athletics
The Socorro Aquatic Center is part of Socorro Independent School District (SISD) but is open to the public for a variety of aquatic activities. In the summer months, the pool is open for recreational swimming, while year-round you can participate in lap swimming and water aerobics. The center also features a spa that is available for public use. "Learn to Swim" classes taught by Red Cross certified instructors are open to children ages 4 to 6

and 7 to 12, meeting for half an hour twice a week. Private one-on-one lessons can also be booked. A variety of combination passes can be purchased that get you entry to the pool for lap swimming, spa use, aerobics, and the many other activities on offer. Recre-ation swimming times are held from June to Aug, Mon to Fri 11 a.m. to 5 p.m. Call or visit their Web site for lap times and other hours.

SOUTHWEST BASEBALL LEAGUE
Irwin J. Lambka Park
6600 Cloudview Dr.
(915) 845-3223
www.fmanningbaseball.com
Getting your kids into Little League Baseball is getting them into a beloved American pastime. With fields at Irwin J. Lambka Park on the Westside, the Southwest Baseball League allows your little ones to learn to bat and run at the base of the Franklin Mountains. The league is operated by local citizens and family members of players in the league who volunteer their time. All teams are scheduled for at least one game a week, and game days are typically Mon through Sat, while fall games are scheduled on Sun only. The season begins on the last Mon in Mar with an Opening Day weekend event to kick it off. More information on registering your child with a team or volunteering your time is available online.

LET LOOSE

EL PASO SPEEDWAY PARK $$$
14900 Montana Ave.
(915) 857-6700
www.epspeedwaypark.com
Take the kids out for a dizzying evening of auto racing at El Paso Speedway Park, where a variety of vehicles, from super trucks to hobby cars and stock cars, race regularly on

Sat nights from Apr to Oct. The speedway is a 3/8-mile oval racetrack made of clay dirt. If your child or family is into cars, this is a great place to see some of the best racecar drivers in the Southwest pitted against each other in an exciting duel to the finish. The hum of the cars as they speed around the dirt track is exhilarating for both the young and the young at heart. Ages 10 and under are always free, and student discount rates are available with a valid student ID.

EL PASO ZOO $$–$$$
4001 East Paisano Dr. across from the
County Coliseum
(915) 521-1857
www.elpasozoo.org
If your little ones are climbing up the walls, take them for a day of animal mania at the El Paso Zoo. The 18-acre zoo is home to over 220 species of animals including mammals, reptiles, amphibians, fish, and invertebrates from around the world. The zoo's habitat exhibits include the South American Pavilion, the Americas Aviary, Cisneros Paraje, Birds of Prey, the Forest Atrium, Asia Grasslands, the Asian Endangered Species Walk, and the Elephant Complex. If your wildlife safari leaves you hungry, stop in to one of the zoo's two cafes, the Grassland Café or the Passport Café, and pick up a few goodies to bring home from the Safari Outfitters Gift Shop. Opening in phases beginning in early 2010 are the new Reptile House and the Passport to Africa exhibit, which will feature lions, zebras, giraffes, meerkats, and various African hoofed animals. There are also several special presentations in which you can take part at El Paso Zoo, including sea lion training and the Asian Elephant Encounter, where you can get up close with the gentle beasts. The zoo is open daily except Thanksgiving, Dec 25, and Jan 1. Opening hours: June to Sept, Mon to Fri from 9 a.m. to 4 p.m., and 9 a.m. to 5 p.m. on weekends; Oct to May from 9 a.m. to 4 p.m. every day. The grounds close 30 minutes after the ticket booth closes.

i Connect with other parents; browse listings, classifieds, and events; and keep up-to-date with parenting in El Paso on epParent, an online parenting Web site for El Paso moms and dads: www.epparent.com.

**FIESTA LANES AND FAMILY
  ENTERTAINMENT CENTER** $
5850 Onix Dr.
(915) 842-9696
www.fiestalanes.com
Fiesta Lanes and Family Entertainment Center is a shiny entertainment venue and the perfect place for a big birthday bash or a night of simple bowling. One of El Paso's largest bowling venues, Fiesta Lanes features 40 lanes, as well as a 2,300-square-foot video arcade to keep your kids busy when they get bored of bowling. Inside, you'll also find Frankie's Sports Grill, complete with billiards tables, a bar, and booths where you can grab a burger or play a round of pool. Bowling geeks will enjoy the range of equipment and bowling balls on sale in the pro shop, or you might want to join one of the many bowling leagues that play at Fiesta Lanes. If you're planning a to-do, they also have three party rooms to accommodate you, along with a larger conference room, or you can book the VIP section. Catering is available for events. Opening hours: Mon to Wed 4 p.m. to 12 a.m.; Thurs 12 p.m. to 12 a.m.; Fri 2 p.m. to 1 a.m.; Sat to Sun 12 p.m. to 1 a.m.

KIDSTUFF

INDIAN CLIFFS RANCH AT
CATTLEMAN'S STEAKHOUSE   FREE
3450 South Fabens Carlsbad Rd.
Fabens, TX
(915) 544-3200
www.cattlemanssteakhouse.com
Little cowpokes will love Indian Cliffs Ranch, a place where they can live their dreams of becoming a real cowboy for a day. Don't forget to bring your video camera to this all-in-one ranch, private zoo, aviary, lake, western old town movie set, maze, working stables and hayride, restaurant, and bar. Let the kiddies run wild, check out the animals, and play in the hay as you work up an appetite for one of El Paso's best steaks at Cattleman's Steakhouse. A trip to Indian Cliffs Ranch is like a journey back in time, where you can experience the Southwest as it was long ago through Old West memorabilia, antique wagons, walking trails, and dirt roads. Hayrides run once per hour on Sun from 1 to 7 p.m. and are free for customers who have eaten, or $2 for others.

LICON DAIRY   FREE
11951 Glorietta Rd.
San Elizario, TX
(915) 851-2705
www.licondairy.com
This is a good spot to take the whole family for a day of picnicking and exploration. Children will enjoy hand feeding animals in Licon's mini-zoo, which houses goats, bison, donkeys, ponies, and deer, and they can interact with talking parrots and big-beaked birds while mom and dad can enjoy a cheese tasting. Licon Dairy has become well known over the years as one of the best small dairies in the area, renowned for its asadero cheese, a thin six-inch disk of soft, mild, whitish Mexican cheese, which comes with

or without jalapeños. Licon Dairy is located a few minutes east of El Paso on the San Elizario Mission Trail and is open every day of the year, free of charge.

PAINTBALL AT RICKY'S $$$$
1773 Pali Dr.
(915) 855-7473
www.rickyspb.com
Master your skills with your friends at Ricky's Paintball on one of the largest paintball fields in the area. The fields at Ricky's are perfect for every level of paintball player, from beginner to advanced, with plenty of obstacles and open spaces for hiding out and running amok. In the past, they have even served as a training ground for military personnel. Located in the middle of the city, the unique setting at Ricky's provides an astonishingly large area for paintballers to have fun, and their pro shop can cater to all paintball equipment needs. A basic package includes an all day pass, unlimited compressed air, 500 paintballs, and a camouflage jacket for $25, and if you need equipment, a rental package including a paintball gun, safety mask, paintballs, compressed air, and jacket runs $35. Additional sets of paintballs are also available. Opening hours: Mon closed, Tues to Sun 10 a.m. to 8 p.m.

WESTERN PLAYLAND
AMUSEMENT PARK $$$
1249 Futurity Dr.
Sunland Park, NM
(915) 772-3914
www.westernplayland.com
Western Playland is El Paso's answer to an amusement park. Located in nearby Sunland Park, New Mexico, Western Playland covers more than 25 acres with the standard small-market amusement park fare of rides,

arcades, games, snacks, and other amusements. The most popular rides at Western Playland include the steel Bandido Roller Coaster, the Drop Zone, which is a 90-foot tall ride where you drop at 3G force with your legs dangling in mid-air, and the slightly ill-named Tsunami, where roller coaster meets water ride. Less adventurous kiddies might enjoy some tamer entertainments, such as the Yo-Yo, a spinning swing, and the Sky Glider, a chairlift that boasts scenic views of the nearby mountains. Western Playland offers a range of pricing options to accommodate just about every situation, including regular unlimited riding tickets, non-rider discounted tickets, and pay-per-ride tickets at $2 each. Ages two and under are admitted free but are not allowed on the rides. Opening hours vary considerably depending on time of year and day of the week, but generally the park opens around 2 or 3 p.m. and closes between 7 and 10 p.m.

WET 'N' WILD
WATERWORLD   **$$$-$$$$**
8804 South Desert Blvd.
Anthony, TX
(915) 886-2222
www.wetwild.com
The wonderful El Paso weather makes attending this waterpark a real pleasure. Wet 'N' Wild is an aquatic amusement park designed in a volcanic garden theme, with huge fiberglass water slides, shady picnic areas, a restaurant, and a snack bar. The more than 200 mature trees provide all kinds of shade from the intense Southwest sun, and visitors are invited to bring in their own food and drink for a summertime picnic in between slides. The longest slide at the park is the Amazon, a 50-foot-high slide that cascades through water curtains and twists and

turns around dark corners before splashing into the Wild Island Wave Pool. During the summer, Wet 'N' Wild is the site of numerous music festivals, as well as the Balloonfest over Memorial Day weekend. Kids under one year are admitted free of charge. Wet 'N' Wild is open from May to Sept. Opening hours: Mon to Fri 11 a.m. to 6 p.m.; Sat to Sun 10 a.m. to 7 p.m.

El Paso Public Library

Each year, the El Paso Public Library sponsors a poetry contest for children in grades 1 through 12. Children may write the poems in either English or Spanish and awards are given to each grade level and for each language. For more information, call (915) 543-5470 or e-mail indaleciol@elpaso texas.gov.

Most branches of the El Paso Public Library also operate craft and storytime hours, many of them bilingual in English and Spanish. Usually, storytime hours are one morning a week. To find out when a storytime hour is happening at your local library, look online at www.elpasotexas.gov/library/kidszone.

WINKEYDOODLES PAINTBALL
ADVENTURES   **$$$$**
401 Anthony Rd.
Canutillo, TX
(915) 877-2110
www.winkeydoodles.com
This large paintball facility on El Paso's West-

side has five fields, a 5,000-square-foot covered staging area, and over 45 available rental guns. The playing field is changed often, so you'll never have the same experience twice, and there are large bunkers for the bigger/older players. In addition to a fully stocked pro shop, they have lockers (bring your own locks) and full bathrooms. If you or your child like to play paintball but don't wish to be total cannon fodder, then the huge playing fields make this a great place to go. All players must use paint purchased on-site. Opening hours: Sat 10 a.m. to 6 p.m.; Sun 12 to 6 p.m.; weekdays open by reservation for groups or parties of 15 or more.

PARTY IT UP

ADVENTURE ZONE $$–$$$
251 East Redd Rd.
(915) 585-9663
www.adventurezoneelpaso.com
Adventure Zone is an all-in-one arcade fun center where kids can go wild playing with a number of arcade games, virtual reality experiences, shooting galleries, go karts, and bumper boats. Game Zone is an arcade experience with cutting edge virtual reality, full motion simulator games, and a western-themed eight-player shooting gallery. Speed Zone is a go-karting course with more than

800 feet of twists and turns spread out on one acre, and Bumper Zone lets you collide boats with your friends in 100,000 gallons of water, while averting a small tropical island. Other activities include miniature golf and a kid-safe extreme trampoline. Grab a snack in the Food Zone or host a birthday bash in the Party Zone, which has a large function room. Specials include two-for-one prices on Tues and $1 tacos on Thurs. Opening hours vary, but are generally from 11 a.m. to 9 p.m. every day.

BOB O'S FAMILY FUN $–$$$
3851 Constitution Dr. off Sunland Park
(915) 587-6070
www.bobosfun.com
Bob O's is a family fun center with a huge variety of kid-friendly activities under one roof, including laser tag, go-karts, an 18-hole miniature golf course, miniature go-karts, bumper boats, a miniature train, batting cages, and a full service arcade. This bright, clean, friendly activity center is a great option for a day of kid craziness on the Westside. Their snack bar offers all the standard kid fare: pizza, hot dogs, nachos, and sodas, and they are also available for birthdays and other special events. Opening hours vary by season, but are generally mid-morning to 10 or 11 p.m.

SHOPPING

Whether you are interested in art and antiques, want to find a good used book to curl up with, or want to get in the Texas spirit in a pair of cowboy boots, there is an endless array of things to be bought here. The city's location along the U.S.–Mexico border has long made it a hotbed of cheap retail stores and outlet markets where locally produced goods are sold. The North American Free Trade Agreement of 1994 opened up a world of possibilities for trade between the U.S. and Mexico and allowed many businesses to begin freely importing and exporting between El Paso and Juárez. As a result, you'll find a large number of Southwestern and Mexican-inspired goods for sale here, particularly furniture and home decor, as well as affordable clothing manufactured locally.

Often referred to as the Boot Capital of the World, El Paso has one of the largest concentrations of boot manufactures and retailers in the world, providing plenty of opportunities to find a pair. Among your choices is the Cowtown Boot Company, which claims to be the world's largest boot factory outlet store, and the world-famous Tony Lama Factory Store.

There are plenty of unique and upscale clothing and gifts available in the area's sweet little boutiques, and if it's books that you're after, El Paso is home to some of the best small presses and bookstores in the Southwest. The Book Gallery offers new, used, scarce, and rare books, while Cinco Puntos Press is a nationally known literary publishing house that specializes in printing the literature of the Borderlands, Mexico, and the American Southwest.

Antiques stores also abound in El Paso. In fact, there are so many antiques stores you might have trouble getting to them all! A number of flea markets and swap meets are also held regularly across the city, so if you have a hankering to peruse the used and unusual, you'll find no shortage of great spots. The city is also dotted with malls, national chains, outlets and shopping centers.

OVERVIEW

In these pages you will find listings for a variety of shopping opportunities across the Sun City. Of course, it would be impossible to list everything (that's what phone books are for!), but instead I have tried to give you examples of the best, most unique, and unusual stores in El Paso—places that stand out from the rest and where you will hopefully find what you're looking for at good prices with great customer service. There are many, many more national chain stores, which are not listed here but can often cater

SHOPPING

to the day-to-day shopping needs of many. These include Wal-Mart, Target, K-Mart, and of course the dozens of chain stores you'll find inside El Paso's malls.

There are *a lot* of places to buy cowboy boots in El Paso. Aside from Southwestern home decor, the cowboy boot is perhaps the most unique and sought-after item produced in the city. I have, therefore, included a large number of listings for where to buy cowboy boots, from the cheapest outlet stores to extremely high-end boutique crafters that cater to celebrities. I've also given you a bit of history about cowboy boots and their production in El Paso in one of the Close-up boxes.

ANTIQUES

ANTIQUE TRADERS
5034 Doniphan Dr.
(915) 833-9929
Antique Traders is a large antiques mall on El Paso's Westside. Inside the market, you'll find 10 different rooms filled to the nines with traditional antiques, like period furnishings, jewelry, collectibles, furniture, and much more. This is a great place to go once or many times to check for whatever is newly acquired. Antique Traders is generally open Tues through Sun and closed Mon.

THE TIME CAPSULE
6501-D North Mesa St.
(915) 845-2415
You could spend hours perusing the hundreds of trinkets, action figures, comic books, records, and antique toys at this unusual collectibles shop. From Star Wars action figures to The Doors on vinyl, the Time Capsule helps you relive your golden years one shopping spree at a time. The Time Capsule is

Golden Horseshoe District

This colorful downtown shopping district is composed of many Mexican-style shops that sell clothes, shoes, and trinkets and draw visitors from both the U.S. and Mexico for the plethora of goods at cheap prices. The Golden Horseshoe District consists of several downtown streets including San Antonio Street, Overland Street, El Paso Street, Mesa Street, and Stanton Street, which are lined with some 300 shops that boast prices as low as 60 to 80 percent off. The area is named for the two streets that comprise its outer rim, El Paso Street and Stanton Street, which are shaped like a horseshoe. Walking around the Golden Horseshoe district you are bound to see a lot of electronics, clothes, and shoes spilling out onto the street from busy, packed-in shops and hear the sounds of loud Tejano and Mexican pop music bursting from sidewalk speakers.

a must-visit for anyone that is into vintage vinyl and music memorabilia, as they carry thousands of albums and 45s that span genres from rock and roll, country, rhythm and blues, and jazz to techno and hip hop. The store also carries pop culture items, movie and TV memorabilia, and hundreds of unique items, and unlike a lot of other stores, the Time Capsule also buys and trades, so if you have a collectible comic book or vintage action figure you'd like to get rid of, this is place to come. Most of their new products are stocked from wholesale distributors around the U.S. While a lot of the collectible merchandise sold by The Time Capsule can be found on eBay, going to the store allows you the chance to look at items closely before you purchase them, which means you always get exactly what you want. You also save on shipping costs by buying locally, and the Time Capsule claims that their prices are comparable to, if not better than, prices for the same goods online.

WESTSIDE ANTIQUE MALL
5024 Doniphan Dr.
(915) 845-4441
Located in the Placita Santa Fe shopping center, the Westside Antique Mall & Consignment Shop is one of the best of its kind in the region, providing visitors with a wide selection of goods and merchandise. Inside, you'll find myriad period furnishings, such as wooden chests, dressers, tables, chairs, and sofas, as well as smaller collectible antiques like watches, jewelry, hats, and clothing. The merchandise is constantly being renewed, so if you are a true collector, you may want to check back here often to see what's been added since your last visit.

WHOOPEE BOWL ANTIQUE MALL
9010 North Desert Blvd.
Canutillo, TX
(915) 886-2855
Get lost in this seven-acre property as you wander through wonderful antiques and some of the most obscure treasures imaginable. Located just north of El Paso, Whoopee Bowl is one of the largest antique dealers in the area with a convenient location on the northwest side, between the Vinton and Anthony exits off I-10. All kinds of treasures are packed onto more than 11,000

square feet and seven acres at this massive antiquing paradise. This is a large mall where spaces are leased to a variety of antique dealers, resulting a wonderful and varied selection that can keep you there all day. Antique potbelly stoves, stained glass windows, furniture, wagon wheels, photographs, and rare books are among the many types of loot to be found inside. Also on offer are new items, such as cast aluminum lighting, furniture, and accessories.

BOOKS

BARNES & NOBLE BOOKSELLERS
Westside
705 Sunland Park Dr.
(915) 581-5353
www.barnesandnoble.com
This well-known chain has two branches in El Paso, one near Sunland Park Mall on the Westside and the other in Viscount Village along I-10 on the Eastside at 9521 Viscount (915-590-1932). They stock a typical range of best selling titles and offer one of the better selections of different genres in the city. If you are interested in El Paso history, check out the local sections of both stores, which tend to stock a decent range of locally written and published books on El Paso topics.

BOOK GALLERY
2706 East Yandell
(915) 562-7818
Serving El Paso since 1963, the Book Gallery offers new, used, scarce, and rare books. With a selection of more than half a million books, in both hardback and paperback, the books at Book Gallery cover more than 2,000 different subjects. The store covers 12,000 square feet on two levels, making it one of the largest bookstores in the state of Texas.

The store's specialty is in local, Southwestern, and military history. They also offer book repair for those tattered old books you just can't bear to part with, and free book search services are also available.

THE BOOK RACK
10780 Pebble Hills
(915) 598-2279
www.epbookrack.com

This local bookstore has been in business for more than two decades and has around 1,000 new and used books for sale. They offer sales on either a pay or trade basis, so if you have old books you'd like to get rid of, you can bring them in for trades. Among their stock are a wonderful selection of rare books, including out of prints, first editions, used and new books, audio editions, and more. They also have a great collection of kids' and young adult books for the young bookworm in your family, and if you've got the kids in tow, let them explore the Book Rack's kids' area stocked with toys, and of course books, for your kids to play while you shop. You can also bring your kids in to the shop every second Sat of the month, when Book Rack hosts storytime readings for children.

CACTUS CAFE & BOOKSHOP
7500 North Mesa St.
(915) 833-2233

The locally owned and operated Cactus Cafe & Bookshop is a wonderful place to escape for a morning of reading and coffee in the trendy Kern Place neighborhood. In the coffee shop, they offer tasty organic, fair trade coffee grown in a shady bird-friendly environment, which you can drink while you read! In addition to a great cup of coffee, this shop provides readers with an eclectic stock of new and used books for all ages, including a wide selection of Spanish-language books on hand. One great thing about the Cactus Cafe & Bookshop is that they are committed to stocking a variety of books, many of which come from local and/or independent publishers, so the selection here is sometimes more unique than what you might find in a larger chain bookstore.

CINCO PUNTOS PRESS
701 Texas Ave.
(915) 838-1625
www.cincopuntos.com

Cinco Puntos Press was created in 1985 by two writers, Bobby and Lee Byrd, who were hoping to have more time to write. The name, which means "five points," comes from the original location of their office, which had an address in El Paso's Five Points neighborhood. The publishing house has since grown into a nationally known, independent literary press, now owned by Perseus, that specializes in publishing the literature (fiction, non-fiction, poetry, and books for kids) of the U.S.–Mexico border area, as well as Mexico and the American Southwest. The location of Cinco Puntos not 3 miles away from the U.S.–Mexico border makes it ideally situated to gather together writers that can truly capture the essence of the Borderland through the written word, and most of the books they have on offer do just that. You can buy Cinco Puntos's books by browsing their Web site or going to the bookshop, which is located at the publisher's offices.

GEM'S GEMS
7744 North Loop 375
(915) 845-5437
www.gemsgems.org

This bookshop is run by a non-profit agency dedicated to supporting children's literacy in the El Paso area. The organization was started in 2002 by the Madriles family after their 16-year-old daughter Grace Elizabeth died in a car accident. Grace's mother, Paula, was a teacher at a school in a low-income area of South El Paso and wanted to use money donated in Grace's honor to buy used books and other educational materials for local teachers. Out of this, the idea for Gem's Gems was born and In 2004, the organization moved into their location in the Placita Santa Shopping Center. Here, thousands of children's books are shelved and prepared for distribution throughout the El Paso area. The books are available for free to area teachers, daycare workers, social service agencies, and other children's organizations, with the goal of arming children with books.

MESILLA BOOK CENTER
2360 Calle Principal
Mesilla, NM
(505) 526-6220
www.borderbookfestival.org
This full service bookstore in nearby Mesilla, New Mexico, houses a large selection of books, specializing in Southwestern American literature and a large selection of children's and general titles. The store also sells plenty of interesting gifts and decor items, such as Indian arts and crafts, maps, and blankets, and they have a notable selection of Navajo rugs. The building itself is an interesting place to visit, as well. The bookstore is housed in an historic mercantile building in Old Mesilla's plaza that dates to 1856. The shop also plays host to the Border Book Festival each April, where book nerds can come to enjoy lectures, signings, and readings and a trade fair.

BOOTS AND WESTERN GEAR

ARDITTI
1010 Cedar Dr.
(915) 474-9465
www.ardittionline.com
This designer couture boot brand is famous for their unique and diverse collection of boots, particularly those made from alligator skin, as well as crocodile, ostrich, lizard, and stingray. Many of their boots have been featured in specialty boutiques across the country, from Gorsuch Ltd. in Vail, Colorado, to Back at the Ranch in Santa Fe, New Mexico, as well as La Jolla and New York. Arditti also makes belts and buckles, designer wallets, briefcases, and what they term "executive accessories," which include leather-bound desk sets, humidors and cigarette cases, finger cases, DVD cases, and even pistol covers. For ladies, their leather slides and mules come in a variety of colors and styles, many of which are similar to the men's boot lines in ostrich and lizard skin, while others have a smoother style with stitched patterns. Don't come expecting to save money—a pair of mules here runs upwards of $475, and their signature handmade boot lines can go for a steep $4,000 or more.

BLACK JACK BOOTS
10787 Gateway Blvd. West
(915) 598-2668
www.blackjackboots.net
Black Jack Boots have been made in El Paso since 1996, with a commitment to produce fine all-leather handmade boots, belts, and accessories. The bootmaking process begins with the selection of the best leathers and findings around the world available to ensure fit, comfort, and durability. Then, Black Jack's Master bootmakers, who have

over 200 years of collective experience, use exotic and smooth leathers for vamps and heel foxing. Their boots feature Shenandoah calf and cream cow linings, and only leather side-seams and piping, and the soles of the boots are made with a durable 10-iron out-sole, 4-iron welt, and 9-iron insole. Among the leathers that they utilize in making their boots are alligator, caiman, elephant, ostrich, and stingray. The Black Jack bootmaking process includes 100 different steps and takes about four weeks total to finish one pair of boots. Black Jack's boots have a sig-nature look that is less about trendy colors and more about natural browns and blacks, often featuring a star design on the front of the boot, or a floral pattern that snakes up the leg.

CHAMPION ATTITUDE BOOTS
2100 Wyoming
(888) 547-7266
www.caboots.com
This family owned and operated boot com-pany makes beautiful cowboy boots of high quality that sell for quite a bit less than other handcraft bootmakers. The tradition of mak-ing all leather, handmade custom boots is a family tradition that they have passed down for four generations, from the time of Ilde-fonso Sanchez, who came to America seek-ing the American dream. Ildefonso settled in El Paso, and using his skills as a boot crafts-man, he worked alongside the famous boot-maker, Tony Lama, at Fort Bliss. He passed on the tradition to his children and each generation added to the knowledge and reputation of the family brand. Many of their boots feature traditional family patterns, but you can find plenty of boots with newer

and more modern designs, as well. CA Boots pride themselves on an authentic, old world style of craftsmanship, but allow you to customize your boots by choosing heel and toe style, color, scallop, and a vast array of options to make the pair of boots you buy completely unique. More down-to-earth than many other high fashion bootmakers, CA Boots makes the process of buying cus-tom cowboy boots seem less intimidating.

COWTOWN BOOTS FACTORY OUTLET
11401 Gateway Blvd. West
(915) 593-2929
www.cowtownboots.com
Claiming to be the largest cowboy boot factory store in the world, Cowtown Boots operates a 100,000-square-foot manufac-turing facility and factory store at their cor-porate headquarters right here in El Paso. Sold under the labels Acme, Dan Post, and Dingo, this company focuses on design-ing boots for comfort, and some of their famous customers have included the Dal-las Cowboys Cheerleaders and Texas House Speaker Pete Laney. Upon entering the mas-sive 50,000-square-foot retail showroom, you will be mesmerized by rows up on rows of cowboy boots in all shapes, sizes, and colors. They also carry a large selection of famous-brand clothing and accessories. The prices here are lower than you'd expect to find even at an outlet store, so you can walk away with a pair of boots for around $200. The selection here, as well, makes shopping a pleasure, and if you're in the market for your first pair of boots, you will feel more comfort-able in the try-it-yourself atmosphere of this huge store.

EL PASO SADDLEBLANKET CO.
6926 Gateway East
(915) 544-1000
www.elpasosaddleblanket.com
El Paso Saddleblanket is a massive collection of rooms, patios, hallways, and floor space that houses just about every Southwestern, Mexican, Native American, and cowboy-style item you could possibly want. They manufacture and import rugs, blankets, leather goods, saddles, pottery, and oh-so-much more, and show them all in a sprawling, maze-like one-acre showroom. In addition to housing massive amounts of decor here—rawhide lamps, lamp shades, skulls, furniture, rugs, and the like—they also have a huge selection of western gear, such as saddles, saddle blankets, bridles, and other actually utilitarian equestrian items. Whether you are in the market for something to put in your home or a a unique El Paso-style souvenir, or you just have a couple of hours to kill and want to do some window shopping, El Paso Saddleblanket Co. is worth a stop.

JB HILL BOOT COMPANY
335 North Clark Dr.
(915) 599-1551
www.jbhilltexas.com
This high-end boot company specializes in exotic and flat leather boots that are handmade. Some of their famous customers have included Robert Redford, whose JB Hill boots were featured in the movie *The Horse Whisperer*, as well as the likes of Marlon Brando and Harrison Ford. On a visit to the factory, you can observe the entire bootmaking process and see how the boots are designed and put together. You can also select the leather for your boots, along with receiving a personal fitting. During the fitting, you will try on several styles of boots and they may take custom measurements of your feet and legs, if necessary. You will then have the chance to select the leather personally for your boots. Their factory and showroom are open weekdays and by appointment only on weekends.

ⓘ If you're buying your first pair of cowboy boots, it's important to have your foot properly measured. Unlike regular shoes, cowboy boots differ in design and fit, so the wrong size or style could end up being painful down the road.

JUSTIN BOOTS FACTORY OUTLET
7100 Gateway Blvd. East
(915) 779-5465
www.JustInboots.com
Justin is one of the most well known cowboy boot brand names in the world. In 1879, H. J. Justin, the company's founder, relocated from Indiana to Spanish Fort, Texas, where he worked as a boot repairman. Initially, and eventually expanded to making his own line of boots from his home. Still a family-run company, Justin Boots bought out their rival, the Tony Lama Boot Company, in the 1990s. There are three Justin outlets in El Paso, the only Justin factory outlets in the country, and here you will find great Justin products at outlet prices. The store carries a huge selection of men's and women's western boots, ropers, and work boots, along with kids' boots and casual shoes. Justin also stocks a large selection of cowboy hats, belts, shirts, jackets, and gift items. Whether you are a true grit cowboy or a fashionista at heart,

SHOPPING

this is a great place to pick up western wear while in El Paso. Other locations are at 12151 Gateway Blvd. West (800-548-6138 ext. 03), 5040 North Desert (800-548-6138 ext. 02), and 7156 Gateway Blvd. East (800-548-6138 ext. 01).

LUCCHESE BOOT CO.
6601 Montana Ave., Suite L
(915) 778-8060
www.lucchese.com
The Lucchese Boot Company was founded ce 18830 when Sam Lucchese Sr. and his brothertoarrived to America. As a young man, Lucchese had a keen knack for boot-making and, at the tender age of 20, estab-lished the Lucchese Boot Company in San Antonio, Texas. Sam Lucchese's grandson eventually took over the family business in the 1960s and brought to Lucchese his own innovative style of bootmakingt.Lucchese boots have always been known as extraordi-narily comfortable boots, primarily because of the company's novel approach to fit and design. Lucchese's store in El Paso carries slightly irregular and discontinued boots at up to 60 percent off retail prices, along with offering great deals on belts, shirts, and accessories. Even if you aren't on the market for a pair of boots, the store makes for a fun visit just to see the photographs, boot casts, and other memorabilia of famous people who have worn Luccheses.

T.O. STALLION BOOT & BELT COMPANY
100 North Cotton St.
(915) 532-6268
www.stallionboots.com
This custom boot company produces high-end cowboy boots for wholesale and indi-vidual customers. Stallion's master craftsmen practice the artful and rare craft that has been passed on to them for generations, and it is one of the last remaining companies to make boots and belts in the painstaking old method—by hand. This quality craftsman-ship is paired with a choice of the highest quality leathers, precious metals, and stones from around the world to create stunning, well-crafted fashion boots. With a unique sense of style, Stallion owner and designer Pedro Muñoz has caught the attention of the high-end fashion world in Europe and the U.S. Some of the most recognized names in the fashion industry like Dior, Dolce & Gabbana, Ralph Lauren, and Tommy Hilfiger have requested special Stallion boots for their collections, and their boots have been shown on runways in Milan, Paris, and New York. Some of their famous customers have included Edge (U2 guitarist), Brooke Shields, Madonna, and Larry Hagman, and Bob Dylan said of Stallion, simply, "Man, I love your boots."

TIM'S BOOTS
15460 Ryan Wesley
(575) 824-0354
www.timsboots.com
Tim's Boots is a retail store based in El Paso, and was founded by Tim Urling in 2002. Tim runs the store himself and has good connec-tions with a number of top cowboy boot-makers, so the shop is always full of a variety of boot brands, many of which are made in El Paso. Their featured brands are Black Jack, Sedona West, and Cowtown Boots. They also carry a number of other leather goods, such as western belts and leather biker wear, but their true specialty lies in exotic cowboy boots, which come in a variety of designs

🔍 Close-up

All the Colors of Rocketbusters

Rocketbuster (915-541-1300; www.rocketbuster.com) is a small, but extremely fashionable bootmaker that creates unique boots that are more like works of art than utilitarian footwear. Colorful inlays and vintage styles that remind you of Roy Rogers make up their sets of custom designs, of which only 500 are made every year. Each one of their pairs of boots is lavishly decorated in a style that reflects the owner's unique personality. Many celebrities have bought Rocketbusters, including Billy Bob Thornton, Tom Cruise, Mel Gibson, Brooks & Dunn, Oprah, and Arnold Schwarzenegger, among many, many others. Rocketbusters range from $650 to $5,000 a pair and they will do custom logos, individual designs, ranch brands, and almost anything else you want on the boot. They also create several collectors' editions, including a Dia de los Muertos design and a vineyard boot covered in grape vines. Their "Museum Line" features boots with autographed linings by Roy Rogers and Gene Autry, who were both avid wearers of the boots. Located in a historic building downtown, the factory is filled with "West Texas Eye Candy"—boots in every color, shape, size, and age on numerous shelves. A massive neon sign with the Rocketbuster logo (a cowboy riding a rocket) flashes brightly along one brick wall over a variety of vintage knickknacks—autographed photos, old toys, a plastic saddle, and other cowboyish collectibles are everywhere. Touch samples are laid out so that guests can get a feel for the different leathers that are used. Tours of the factory include a foot measuring for custom handmade boots and give you a chance to get an up-close look at the bootmakers as they cut, stitch, and last new pairs of boots by hand. Visits to the Rocketbusters factory at 115 Anthony St. are available by appointment only.

and colors. Leathers available here include the more popular alligator, ostrich, stingray, lizard, and snakeskin, as well as much rarer leathers like shark, caiman, hippo, elephant, and frog. You can also pick up boots in the more traditional smooth leathers, and all of the boots are available in men's and ladies styles and sizes, including the exact color, toe, and heel shapes that you want.

TONY LAMA OUTLET STORES
7156 Gateway Blvd. East
(915) 772-4327
www.tonylama.com
Tony Lama, (now under the umbrella of Justin Boots), one of the most well known cowboy boot brands on earth, specializes in making high-end boots that are produced in a standardized fashion, which also means that their boots are generally more affordable than some of the more high-fashion bootmakers' offerings. With more than 80 years of bootcrafting experience, Famous customers of Tony Lama have included Travis Tritt, the Texas Tornadoes, Jay Novacek, and ZZ Top. Tony Lama's western boots are one of the most recognized brands in the world. Tony Lama operates three factory outlet stores in El Paso, which sell thousands of discontinued and imperfect boots at affordable prices, as well as belts and other leather goods, and some west-

ern clothing. Other locations are at 12151 Gateway Blvd. West (800-548-6138 ext. 03), 5040 North Desert (800-548-6138 ext. 02), and 7156 Gateway Blvd. East (800-548-6138 ext. 01).

BOUTIQUES
Children's

DUCK DUCK GOOSE
5860 North Mesa St.
(915) 833-6221
www.ddgoose.com
Stylish moms will love Duck Duck Goose's selection of original and specialty toys, clothes, and infant gear for their super chic babies. With its sweet and posh baby clothes, this quaint, locally owned store on El Paso's Westside is the type of place in which mamas and grandparents could spend hours. Need a stylish but utilitarian diaper bag, a souped up stroller, or a couture nursing sash? This is the place. They have a large selection of unique clothes and accessories for babies and toddlers and it is the ideal store to go shopping for a present for a baby shower, newborn, or toddler, or for moms to pick up a few stylish baby-related items.

Women's

DELIA'S BOUTIQUE
2623 North Stanton St.
(915) 544-2165
If you need to find the perfect outfit for a fancy function or fabulous party, head to Delia's Boutique, a cute and locally owned store located in the Kern Place district near UTEP. Inside the small, packed store you'll uncover some fantastic, unique clothing, like an unrivaled party dress, a super-trendy outfit, or a chic purse. They stock a wide variety

of ladies' apparel, from daywear to evening dresses and a host of unique accessories that you will simply love. While the clothing here is a bit pricey, you can rest assured that you won't find yourself staring at someone else wearing the same department store-bought dress at a party.

NONO'S
5857 North Mesa St., # 17
(915) 584-2081
www.nonosfashions.com
Nono's is an upscale modern clothing boutique where trendy women and their well-dressed children can feel at home. The store carries a number of different boutique and well-known labels, such as Nicole Miller, Nougat, and Bejeweled, and offers modern options for bridal parties, sophisticated evening gowns, and chic prom dresses. But Nono's isn't just for party clothes. They also carry a full line of contemporary womenswear that ranges from trendy casual wear and accessories for women to super stylish couture for children. Girlswear here ranges from newborn to age 16, and they also have a few options for special and stylish baby boys through 2 years of age. They also carry a line of home decor, including classy bedding, hand painted furniture, wall hangings, specialty lighting, and chandeliers, many of which are designed for cute and trendy children's rooms.

RUBY LOLA
5860 North Mesa St., Suite 111
(915) 833-5480
Ruby Lola is an uber-chic trendy clothing and gift shop that carries unique gifts, clothes, handbags, and jewelry. Among many of their items are those from designer labels, so you can either find something you know and love or a unique, small brand that no one

else will have. Stylish trinkets and glittering accessories are displayed on uneven block shelves around the store, while clothes hang in a rainbow of colors along one wall and white paper lanterns dangle above, giving the whole store a very clean and stylish feel.

TRES MARIPOSAS
5857 North Mesa St., #A
(915) 584-4444
www.tresmariposas.com
For four decades, Tres Mariposas has been known as a fashion oasis for sophisticated women of El Paso. The store carefully selects fashions from top designers and is known for its prompt, friendly customer service. From drapey, stylish summer dresses to fitted dark wash jeans, a myriad of colorful scarves, and useable accessories, Tres Mariposas stocks clothing that people actually want to wear. The store itself is spacious and boldly sophisticated, with beautifully dressed mannequins standing around the store sporting brightly colored, shiny outfits. The store's high ceilings and arched windows let in a lot of light, while jewelry is displayed in well-placed glass boxes around the floor. A set of red leather chairs gives fashionistas and their shopping-weary companions a welcome chance to take a load off. Tres Mariposas, whose name means "three butterflies," employs fashion consultants who are available after hours, for private fashion consultations that are given either at the showroom or at clients' homes.

VERSAILLES
6415 North Mesa St.
(915) 581-1810
www.versaillesfashion.com

This store offers high fashion women's apparel at below wholesale prices. Versailles stocks brand names at reasonable prices, with reliable quality and service backed by years' experience in the fashion business. The owner, Henri, takes care to collect and offer exclusive items so as to ensure that his customers can maintain an air of individuality in what they wear. He tends to only offer one or two similar pieces and concentrates mostly on one-of-a-kind designer clothing to protect upwardly mobile women from being seen wearing the same items. Versailles has dressed several famous people, including former First Lady Laura Bush.

GIFTS AND SOUVENIRS

COLLECTIBLES
4700 North Mesa St.
(915) 534-4243
www.ep-collectibles.com
If you're looking for a unique gift or just want to spend an hour browsing, head to Collectibles, a cozy little gift shop on the northwest side of El Paso. Established in 1979, at Collectibles you can find great gifts for almost everyone on your list, even if they are hard to shop for. If you aren't sure what to buy, Collectibles will probably have something to inspire you, from gourmet food baskets to luxury bath lines like Crabtree & Evelyn, accessories, candles, home decor, and more. They also sell a variety of flavors of whole bean coffee sold by the quarter pound, half pound, and pound, and they will grind the beans for you in store. Another nice touch is the scoop candy, which you can buy and put into fancy bags. Even more convenient is their custom gift basket service. So if you're

not in the mood to leave the house or just don't have time, give them a ring and let them whip up a custom basket to fit your tastes, occasion, and budget.

FEDORA'S
800 North Mesa St.
(915) 533-9090
www.halmarcus.com
Set on the top floor of the Hal Marcus Gallery not far from UTEP, Fedora's is a little boutique that is famous for its large selection of silk flowers, beautiful custom arrangements, ladies' and men's hats, handmade clothing, prints, cards, and more. Many of the items sold in the shop include the artwork of Hal Marcus and his favorite local artists, so this is a great place to get a unique card, print, or calendar for yourself or an art savvy friend. Among the more unique items in the store are the glass "good luck" charms.

THE GAZING BALL
4798 Doniphan Dr.
(915) 584-6711
Nestled in an historic adobe building along the Camino Real, the Gazing Ball is a delightful experience for all who enter. Each room of this quaint house is filled with unique gifts and home decor at surprisingly affordable prices. This is an extraordinary shopping experience with delightful gifts and decor for the home and garden, as well as unique gift ideas for teens. Among the items in their eclectic selection are bedding, bath products, jewelry, decor, and more in a relaxing and cozy atmosphere. Some of their items specifically geared for teens include the Ty Girlz line and the Webkinz accessory line, including all of their lip glosses. Gifts for older teens include bath creams, hand-made jewelry, and scarves, many of which are handmade by local artists.

THE TEXAS STORE
6966 Gateway Blvd. East
(915) 532-5688
If you're looking for a Texas-themed souvenir, look no further than this Texas-sized gift shop, filled to the brim with all things Texas. One of the largest souvenir stores in the state, the Texas Store has all the cheap and cheerful knickknacks and traditional tourist souvenirs, from magnets to postcards, Texas T-shirts, and more. They also stock collectible items by Coca Cola, Peanuts, Betty Boop, Cows on Parade, and Trail of Painted Ponies, among others.

JEWELRY

AZIZ JEWELERS
420 Montana Ave.
(915) 544-5263
Aziz Jewelers is a one-of-a-kind El Paso treasure. This store is a local secret that has built a strong reputation specializing in the sale of gold, silver, and platinum jewelry as well as diamonds. Aziz can source the same quality jewelry found at El Paso's most exclusive jewelers, at a fraction of the cost, a discount that is passed along to the buyer. If you're in the market for an engagement ring, a certified diamond, or perhaps just a good deal on loose stones, Aziz Jewelers can often provide just what you're looking for.

LACY & CO.
7040 North Mesa St.
(915) 584-4700
www.lacyandco.com
Lacy & Co. is an El Paso staple that was founded in 1946 and has a strong community reputation among locals. Among their timeless selection are all types of jewelry, diamonds, timepieces, and other luxury gifts,

many by extremely exclusive brand names such as Mikimoto, David Yurman, and more. They also have a notable watch collection. Lacy & Co. is a member of the American Gem Society, an organization dedicated to the highest standards of ethics, quality, and customer service in the industry. If you have older jewelry that is in need of repair, Lacy & Co. is a good option. The store employs the services of two Certified Gemologist Appraisers, four Registered Jewelers, and two Certified Sales Associates, as well as a full-time factory-trained watch repairman and a skilled jewelry repairman.

SUSAN EISEN FINE JEWELRY & WATCHES
Century Plaza
5857 North Mesa, #19
(915) 584-0022
www.susaneisen.com
This elegant jewelry store constantly makes El Paso "best of" lists and has been featured in national publications such as Town & Country magazine. The store has the type of elegant ambiance that you hope for when you're shopping for fine jewelry. Among the most special pieces in their collection are both sterling silver and 18-karat gold jewelry, including designers like Scott Kay and Steven Lagos. Rolex and Lacroix crown their large selection of watches, and among their other famous-name watches are Patek Philippe, Piaget, and Zodiac. If you are looking for something a little more vintage, they also carry a full line of estate and period jewelry and watches, and continually purchase fine jewelry in single pieces or entire estates. A fine art gallery on the premises shows works by artists from El Paso, New Mexico, and Mexico monthly to complement colorful hand-blown glass, American

crafts, and the Heartbeat of El Paso collection. A beautiful display of Southwestern and contemporary art and artistic jewelry from America's greatest designers are shown throughout the store.

VANITIES JEWELRY & GIFTS
Crossroads Village Shopping Center
7933 North Mesa St.
(915) 584-1183
If you're thinking about a gift but aren't totally sure you want to buy jewelry, stop by Vanities. This jewelry and gift store stocks a large selection of sterling silver jewelry, turquoise, and one-of-a-kind handmade, designer pieces, many of which have a local El Paso and Southwest flavor that is absent from the larger chain jewelry shops. They also carry a variety of unique gifts that range from Brighton purses and accessories to whimsical baby gifts, as well as a wide array of popular bath and body products and fragrant candles.

MALLS AND OUTLETS

BASSETT PLACE MALL
I-10 and Geronimo
(915) 772-7479
Bassett Place is a fairly average shopping mall that is located very conveniently off of I-10, right in the center of El Paso. While this mall's popularity (and, admittedly, business) has dwindled in recent years as most of the larger chains have migrated to newer shopping centers on the outskirts of the city, the draw of Bassett Place is its location. The mall, like most built in the 1980s, is an indoor strip of around 80 outlets that range from popular clothing stores like Target to food outlets in a moderately sized food court, which include a PretzelMaker, YogoBerry, and a

SHOPPING

Nestle Toll House cookie store. One of the mall's main draws is the Premiere Cinema 18, a fairly large and modern movie theater that shows a regular selection of first-run Hollywood films. There are also several restaurants located outside around the perimeter of Bassett Place, including a Steak and Ale, and there is a Costco wholesale store nearby. The mall hosts wide variety community events, arts and crafts fairs, and entertainment venues monthly and often extends its opening hours during the holiday season to accommodate late shopping.

CIELO VISTA MALL
8401 Gateway Blvd. West
(915) 779-7070
www.simon.com

Built in 1974, the Simon-owned Cielo Vista Mall is one of El Paso's longest enduring shopping malls and is still a local favorite today. Through the years, it has traveled the ranges of fashion through hip-hugging bell-bottoms, red vinyl jackets with too many zippers, grungy flannel in strange colors, and whatever those crazy kids are wearing these days. Cielo Vista is one of the larger malls in the area with some 150 outlets, making it easy to find what you're looking for. Located on the Eastside of El Paso, Cielo Vista is anchored by a range of large department stores, including two Dillard's, JCPenney, Sears, and Macy's. Some of the specialty shops include Abercrombie & Fitch, Ann Taylor, Build-A-Bear Workshop, Brighton Collectibles, and Pier 1, as well as a variety of shoe stores, such as Skechers. The Kidgits Play Area located in the lower level near Sears allows parents a few minutes of solace from the busy mall while their kids are entertained.

DUTY FREE AMERICAS
805 South Stanton St.
(915) 532-5996
www.dutyfreeamericas.com

El Paso's advantageous location near the U.S.–Mexico border makes it a prime spot for several Duty Free shops. These stores offer a wide variety of items tax free, in a similar selection to the duty free stores you might find in an international airport terminal. Among the goods available in Duty Free America's shops are fragrances and cosmetics, fine and casual watches, gifts, jewelry, travel-related merchandise, sunglasses, liquor, and tobacco, all from high-quality and fairly well known brand names. Duty Free operates more than 30 stores along the borders of Texas, Arizona, and California, with four outlets in El Paso alone. Three of the locations are at 919 South Stanton St. (915-544-2500), 780 South Zaragosa Rd. (915-858-4424) and 719 South El Paso St. (915-543-5226).

i If you're traveling from abroad, make sure to keep your tax-free receipts from duty free shops. With them, you can collect a refund on the tax you paid in the airport before you depart the United States.

EL PASEO MARKETPLACE
1886 Joe Battle at Montwood

If you live or are staying on the Eastside, take note. El Paseo Marketplace is a large outdoor shopping center located on the Eastside at Loop 375 and Montwood. Anchored by a SuperTarget, El Paseo Marketplace is home to a variety of stores that have allowed far Eastsiders to shop a little closer to home. You'll find a wealth of nationally recognized retailers here, such as Best Buy, Office Depot, and Marshalls, and on the other side of Loop 375 are a convenient Hobby Lobby and a Wal-Mart Supercenter, as well as several fast food restaurants.

LAS PALMAS MARKETPLACE
1310 George Dieter Dr.
(915) 633-1741
Surrounded by a row of towering palm trees for which it is named, Las Palmas Marketplace is one of El Paso's most popular shopping centers. Located right along I-10 on the far Eastside, this large, modern strip mall covers about 750,000 square feet of retail space with a collection of national chain stores. If you're out for a hardcore session of shopping, this can be an extremely convenient place to pick up a wide variety of different day-to-day items, from clothing to home improvement items. Among the stores is the economically priced Kohl's department store, a Lowe's home improvement store, a Bed Bath & Beyond bath and kitchen store, and a number of restaurants, such as the Bar-B-Q Company and Logan's Roadhouse. The 20-screen Cinemark Tinseltown USA megaplex theater anchors the shopping center and provides an escape for the weary after several long hours of shopping.

THE OUTLET SHOPPES AT EL PASO
7051 South Desert Blvd.
(915) 877-3208
www.theoutletshoppesatelpaso.com
For great name brands at totally bargain prices, head to the Outlet Shoppes at El Paso on the northwest side. If you've ever visited an outlet mall in another city, you will know just what to expect at this sprawling 385,000-square-foot shopping center. More

than 90 famous name-brand stores sell discontinued items and seconds at bargain prices between 20 and 70 percent less than department stores. The shops you'll find here include Nike, Coach, Brooks Brothers, Kenneth Cole, Banana Republic, BCBG, Jones of New York, Johnston and Murphy, and Hurley to name just a few. Strolling through the shaded outdoor aisles of this large complex, you can find some incredible gifts or save on the everyday stuff like jeans, socks, and shoes. And because it is an open-air shopping center, customers have an opportunity to enjoy El Paso's wonderful weather—a much more pleasant shopping experience than the traditional indoor mall. The outlet center provides plenty of accessibility services, from wheelchairs to strollers, as well as a children's play area, interactive fountains, and free Wi-Fi. If you're from out of town, ask retail staff about the Melek Tax Rebate. And of course, you'll no doubt get hungry after all that bargain hunting, so there is a food court where you can recharge your batteries with a meal. The outlet mall is extremely easy to find: the bright yellow, pink, and blue complex lights up I-10 as you head northwest out of downtown.

SUNLAND PARK MALL
750 Sunland Park Dr.
(915) 833-5595
Built in the late 1980s, this two-level regional mall is one of the Westside's largest shopping centers. Sunland Park Mall features a distinctive local architectural style and is anchored by several large department stores, including Dillard's, Macy's, Sears, Mervyn's, Gap, The Limited, and Victoria's Secret. Among the

130 other retailers are Aeropostale, American Eagle Outfitters, Bath & Body Works, and the standard selection of national chain stores found in most malls across the U.S. Among the more interesting outlets in Sunland Park Mall is the Greenery Restaurant and Market, one of El Paso's finest restaurants and specialty food markets. Located in the lower level near the mall's main entrance, the Greenery is renowned for the store's fresh artisan breads, delectable desserts, and an impressive wine list. P. F. Chang's China Bistro is another full-service dining option at Sunland Park Mall, or you can take advantage of a quick meal in the food court, where many fast food options await.

MUSIC

ALL THAT MUSIC!
1506-D North Lee Trevino Dr.
(915) 594-9900
www.allthatmusic.com
If you're searching for that hard-to-find LP or rare live show, or just want to find some great new music, browse the rows upon rows of music and movies in this packed record store. All That Music is one of the few major independently owned stores for music, video, and video games in El Paso. Having been open for several decades, over the course of time this store has come to be known as an El Paso institution when it comes to finding rare and collectible music, and selling and buying CDs, DVDs, and video games. In addition to their wide selection of CDs and DVDs, they also have a variety of pop culture and music-related memorabilia like T-shirts, buttons, patches, and posters. The owners and managers of the shop spend a lot of time searching for rare titles, taking special orders, and mounting popular

and hard-to-find posters, so if you're looking for an independent artist or a movie no one has heard of, this is probably the place you'll find it. Additionally, their previously owned CDs, DVDs, and video games are guaranteed to be good as new and come repackaged in brand new cases, and they pay fair market prices for pre-owned CDs and offer a 20 percent discount on any pre-owned items if you sell something to them. This is also the place to come for tickets to local gigs, or if you just want the in on the local music scene.

HEADSTAND
4409 Dyer St.
(915) 566-1561
This funky little shop on the northeast side doesn't look like much from the outside. But inside, you'll find a tiny music haven, with posters of The Smiths and The Cure lining the well-worn walls. As its name would suggest, Headstand is a head shop that also sells CDs and music. A haven for rock music junkies, tobacco lovers, and hookah smokers, this is the place to come for old school and unusual music T-shirts, retro discs, and tobacco supplies. Most people that have known and loved Headstand will tell you it is the place that you go to find something specific and come out with 50 more items you didn't know you wanted.

SOUTHWEST STYLE AND MERCADOS

CHARLOTTE'S
5411 North Mesa St.
(915) 581-1111
www.charlottesfurniture.com
Charlotte's is an upscale home furnishing store located right in Central El Paso on Mesa Street. In addition to selling a variety

of home decor and furnishings, Charlotte's operates a very successful interior design service, and they have consulted on a number of private homes and have decorated country clubs, boardrooms, and professional office spaces. Among Charlotte's classic collections are furniture, decorations, carpets and rugs, and antiques. Many of the items you'll find have a Southwestern or import feel, including Persian rugs, porcelain collectibles, fine linens, antique armoires, and one-of-a-kind poster beds. Imagine an upscale collection of your grandmother's most cherished sofas and sitting room furniture, and that is what you'll find among Charlotte's antiques. The gift shop houses plenty of knickknacks and upscale kitchen items, such as colorful glass vases and painted ceramic bowls. The store offers a wedding registry for your special day.

EL PASO CONNECTION
14301 Gateway Blvd. West
(915) 852-0898
El Paso Connection is a massive Southwestern store with 12 showrooms that are packed from floor to ceiling with rustic wood furnishings, pottery, blankets, and outdoor decor. Items spill over into the aisles and onto the floor, making it sometimes difficult to move inside and often impossible to see everything in one day. If you are looking for a specific type of wooden furniture, you can make a special trip here. Otherwise, its best just to spend a couple of hours browsing the entire store for gifts or trinkets. A number of fountains, cast iron and aluminum patio furniture, wind chimes, wagon wheels, wagon wheel benches, and other large-scale decorations comprise their humongous selection of outdoor and patio furniture. El Paso Connection buys their stock by the truckload

and passes the savings on to you, and it is a good place to go if you're looking for Mexican furniture, Southwestern style decor, and other items to give your home a unique El Paso feel.

EL PASO IMPORT COMPANY
311 Montana Ave.
(915) 542-4241
www.elpasoimportco.com
Even before you walk into their showroom just north of downtown, you can see that El Paso Import Co. is overflowing with colorful, weathered colonial and ranchero furniture. Despite its name, El Paso Import Co. was not born in the Sun City, but in Santa Fe, New Mexico when, in 1987, the owners began selling merchandise out of a pickup truck to local stores. Eventually, they opened their own retail outlet in Santa Fe and, over the years, have expanded to a number of locations across the Southwest and Texas. Today, the store sells a wide variety of antiques, vintage furniture, and reproductions to restaurant chains, designers, and people in the film industry. The main draw of El Paso Import Co. is their massive selection of Mexican antiques and reproductions, but they also stock a large number of handpicked Oriental imports from Eastern Europe, India, and China. If you're shopping for rustic furniture, you'll love the rows of wooden hutches, benches, and tables, many with charming imperfections, interesting color stains, and unique painted patterns.

GALERIA SAN YSIDRO
801 Texas Ave.
(915) 544-4444
Fancy an oversized 19th-century beer pot? You can most likely find it here. Often described as a treasure trove of decora-

tive arts and designer furnishings, this 62,000-square-foot, three-story warehouse store features antiques, art, unusual collectors' items, custom furnishings, beautiful lamps and hand-forged wrought iron, and western-styled pieces. An eclectic downtown gallery, Galeria San Ysidro is also home to one of the largest collections of Mexican primitive art in the area, as well as a wide array of treasures from around the world, such as antiques and folk art from Mexico, Morocco, and other African countries. On the three floors of this large warehouse building, you'll find kitsch, exotic, and rustic home accents. While Galeria San Ysidro is a popular spot for tourists from out of town, in recent times, it has also become popular among savvy El Pasoans, who come here when they wish to spruce up their space with dramatic and alluring pieces.

SOUTHWESTERN FURNISHINGS
11450 Rojas Dr., #D5
(915) 599-1455
www.southwesternfurniture.com
The name of this Eastside furniture store says it all: cabinets and chairs, dining tables and end tables, bed frames, lamp shades, and even office furniture, all crafted in the decorative, wooden style that is so unique to the Southwest. Unlike many of the other import stores around town, Southwestern Furniture actually handcrafts most of the items new and also creates custom designs for home and office. They also claim to craft their furniture with an "ecological conscience," which is refreshing in a world of mass produced goods. All of Southwestern Furniture's handcrafted pieces are made using old wood, creating an antique look but with the dependability of newly made furniture. They specialize in wardrobes, cabinets,

tables, chairs, benches, bedroom sets (complete or separate), and decorator accessories.

TRADICIONE'S
6990 Gateway Blvd. East
(866) 373-9292
www.southwesternfurniturerustic.com
Tradicione's is a colorful 20,000-square-foot store housing handcrafted furniture and accessories. In addition to Mexican and Spanish Colonial furniture, they have a good selection of wrought iron decor, Southwest and western style chairs, benches, and rocking chairs. If you're on the market for an entertainment center to match the Southwest feel of your home, they also feature custom made armoires, TV cabinets, and entertainment centers styled with a rustic touch of the Southwest. If you want your living room to complement a cowboy style, take home a western sofa set with Southwest designs or rustic wooden entertainment center. Tradicione's can also custom design western, rustic, Southwestern, or Mexican-style bars and bar stools, as well as complete Southwest bedroom sets or western bedroom accessories. Most of their items can be modified to your specifications to suit the decor style of your choice. Tradicione's is also a wholesale company, so they can crate and ship all of their furnishings at reasonable prices in case you'd like to take a large piece home with you.

WILD WEST FURNITURE
10910 Montana Ave.
(915) 629-9878
www.wildwestfurniture-riomfg.com
Large leather sofas, hided lamps, brass stars, wooden crosses, and myriad couches swathed in zigzagged Southwestern

designs litter the showroom of this funky El Paso–style Southwest furniture and decor store. Wild West Furniture is a division of Rio Furniture Manufacturing, so all of their unique pieces are made right here in El Paso. They offer a wide range of western and Southwestern upholstered furniture, as well as a variety of home accessories and artwork to complement the furniture. Among the many locally styled items you'll find here are chunky leather couches padded with cow-print pillows, rawhide lamps, unpainted oak nightstands, and even a set of steer horns or two thrown in for good, Texas measure.

XICALI IMPORTS
7824 North Loop 375
(915) 598-4427

Anyone that has ever visited a *mercado* in Mexico will already know and appreciate the festive yet functional experience of shopping at Xicali Imports. Whether looking for a practical piece of furniture or searching for the perfect unique gift, you can find just about any type of home furnishing or piece of Southwestern decor here. The family owned store has a variety of bedroom, dining room, and living room furniture and offers seasonal gifts and decorations for weddings, birthdays, and company parties, including silk flowers and invitations. There is also a selection of decorative items with a native flair, like oil paintings of Southwestern scenes, wooden clocks, and a few sports memorabilia. Perhaps their most unique offering is a collection of piñatas that resemble popular cartoon characters, like SpongeBob SquarePants, Lighting McQueen, and Batman, which make great unique favors for kids' birthday parties.

SPECIALTY FOODS

ARDOVINO'S FARMER'S MARKET
1 Ardovino Dr.
(575) 589-0653
www.ardovinos.com/farmersmarket
.html

Local farmers and artisans sell their fresh organic produce, cheese, herbs, and fine handmade wares on Sat mornings at this small farmers market in Sunland Park, about 15 minutes from downtown. In a series of tent rows, you can explore tall piles of green peppers that spill out of boxes and admire long strings of bright red chile ristras that hang invitingly from the draping tent covers. The produce here is so fresh and colorful that you will want to take it all home to cook a delicious meal. Even if you're not a cook, you can just relax, walk around under the El Paso sun, and maybe enjoy a coffee, pastry, or breakfast burrito from the CoffeeStream trailer. Breakfast and lunch are served on a lovely patio, often accompanied by musical entertainment and among the yummy snacks to tempt you are freshly made pastries, coffee cake, biscotti, and a variety of coffees, cappuccinos, and lattes. You can also partake in a morning yoga class to stretch and get healthy before taking home organic goodies for lunch or listen to a lecture on farming and other topics at one of the morning Garden Talks. Got kids? It's not a problem. Simply drop them off at the Kids Corral where they can spend the morning doing fun activities and crafts while you browse. Ardovino's Desert Crossing is open every Sat from early morning until noon beginning in early June and ending in the middle of Oct.

CHOCOLAT'
5860. North Mesa St.
(915) 581-7290

This store specializes in tasty treats, particularly of the chocolate variety, including hand-made chocolate truffles, chocolate-covered pretzels, chocolate cookies, and brownies made from Belgian imported chocolate. Chocolat's custom-made chocolates come in several styles, including some that are imported directly from Belgium, while many others are made on premises. If you're looking for a special party offering or gift, the delectable hand-dipped truffles, caramels, and delicate citrus ganaches here are great for any occasion. If you can't make it to their location or want to take some home with you, they also offer same-day delivery and nationwide shipping.

EL PASO CHILE COMPANY
909 Texas Ave.
(915) 544-3434
www.elpasochile.com

There is perhaps no more famous export from the Sun City than the delicious products made by El Paso Chile Company. The company's bright pink bag and logo are a sure sign that something scrumptious is coming your way. From salsas and bean dip to quick margarita mixes, El Paso Chile Co. is known for great gifts that say "El Paso" at a *buen precio*. The company produces many packaged and dried foods with interesting, original flavors and incredibly creative labels. Park Kerr, one of the main contributors to the El Paso Chile Co. recipe line, has been called everything from "the Drew Carey of Salsa" to "the Martha Stewart of the Border." All of the 93 products they make are from natural ingredients with big bold flavors and open-and-eat convenience. Family members still oversee the production of every batch of their hand-made salsas and artisan foods. The company's Chile Shop is housed in a rustic factory building full of unique treasures—useful and fanciful items, as well as lots of salsa, drink mixes, and cookbooks, most of which come from the Chile Company's own "three food groups": salsa, snacks, and margaritas.

GREENERY
750 Sunland Park Dr., Suite F5
(915) 584-6706
www.gotogreenery.com

Greenery is a foodie's dream. This upscale restaurant and artisanal market is located inside the Sunland Park Mall on the Westside. While the restaurant was founded in 1982, the Greenery expanded its reach when it opened an upscale market next door in 2001. This food heaven quickly became one of the best places in town to find fine wines, artisan breads, upscale cheeses, and finely crafted pastries and desserts. Greenery Market features a bakery, fresh seafood, and hand-cut prime beef, along with an ever-increasing variety of specialty meat products, a deli, and an amazing array of imported, domestic, and artisanal cheeses from the United States, Europe, and Australia. Wine lovers will drool over the extensive selection of quality wines and international foodies will salivate when they browse through Greenery's many specialty food items from around the world. Plan to have lunch at the restaurant first and then browse the marketplace, and be sure to come with an empty stomach and deep pockets.

SAN ELI FARMER'S MARKET
1521 San Elizario Rd.
(915) 487-5966

A trip down the Mission Trail would not be complete without a stop at the San Eli

Farmer's Market. Organized by the El Paso Mission Trail Association, the San Eli Farmer's Market is a weekend summer market where local farmers bring their produce and arts and crafts for sale right on the plaza. This is an amazing chance to support the surrounding community by partaking in some of the delicious things that are grown and produced right in the lush Lower Valley. The market opens in the late summer months and runs each Sat, from early morning until about 1 p.m., until early Nov.

STAR CANYON WINERY
2601 North Stanton St.
(915) 544-7000
www.starcanyonwinery.com
This small but elegant wine boutique is the only one of its kind in El Paso. In a cozy, Tuscan-inspired tasting room, visitors have the opportunity to learn about wines through taste-testing a wine flight, where you are presented with a small sampling of several wines to compare. With 26 different wines offered, Star Canyon's vintages range from the luxurious Texas Merlot to drinkable blush Desert Bloom varietal. Star Canyon is more than just a tasting room, though. The walls and shelves here are stocked with trinkets and goodies that any wine lover would be interested in, from wine keys, stoppers and other useful wine accessories to tasty gourmet treats. For a really unique gift, you can opt to have custom-drawn labels for any wine bottle that you purchase. The wines range from $9 to $40 a bottle and glasses range from $5 to $7.

SUN HARVEST
6100 North Mesa St.
(915) 833-3380
www.sun-harvest.com

Large piles of fresh broccoli crowns stand in front of freshly baked artisanal breads and bright, plump oranges in this Texas-based organic and natural foods store. Since the first store opened in San Antonio in 1979, Sun Harvest has been a favorite with healthy minded El Pasoans because it is committed to selling quality groceries at competitive prices. Unlike a lot of the larger health food chains, Sun Harvest doesn't kill you with the price and often they have sales and specials that make buying healthy food reasonable. They offer a wide selection of organic and natural foods and products for many different tastes and diets, and one of the nicest aspects of shopping at Sun Harvest is that you can be sure their foods and products do not come from morally questionable sources. Inside, you'll find a bakery, organic deli and fish counters, tons of super fresh produce, and a wide variety of vitamins and supplements. They also have weekly wine and cheese specials, where you can choose from a healthy selection of artisanal cheeses and local and international wines.

SPORTING GOODS

5 STAR DIVERS
6513 North Mesa St.
(915) 581-3329
www.5stardivers.com
You might not expect a great scuba diving shop to be located in the desert of El Paso, but 5 Star Divers is a PADI certified full service dive center that specializes in diving instruction, equipment, and travel. This small but well-stocked diving and snorkeling store is chock full of wet and dry suits, bathing suits, and diving gear, including gauges, fins, masks, regulators, and plenty of accessories. Instructors at 5 Star Divers also offer diving lessons, which take place in local pools. A

number of different certifications are available for both those who are new to diving and scuba pros who wish to become instructors themselves. They also specialize in dive travel with a travel agency that arranges scuba trips to popular diving spots around the world.

THE CHOKE OUT STORE
3233 North Mesa St.
(915) 532-8383
www.thechokeoutstore.com
Fans and practitioners of mixed martial arts will enjoy this well-stocked store, which offers fighters a choice in fight shorts and gives fans a selection in MMA fanwear. The Choke Out Store carries many favorite brands including American Fighter, Contract Killer, Full Contact Fighter, Kimura Wear, Premier Fighter, Punishment Athletics, and Xtreme Couture, among others, and they are constantly adding to their list of MMA products. Their stock is not limited to apparel, either. They also carry fighting gloves, training equipment, and fight wear, both in store and by special order from a number of name brands.

CRAZY CAT CYCLERY
2625 North Mesa St.
(915) 577-9666
www.crazycatonline.com
Bikes dangle from the ceiling amid a clean selection of gear and accessories at Crazy Cat Cyclery. This local chain is one of El Paso's favorite bicycle shops. A full service store, Crazy Cat offers bicycles and bike-related gear for sale and also operates a fully qualified repair department at each of their stores. They stock Cannondale, Electra, Giant, and Scott bicycles and do full fittings to make sure that every bike they sell is perfectly fit

to its new owner. Avid cyclists will appreciate that Crazy Cat's three locations are aptly situated near popular biking routes in case of a pesky flat tire or chain break. The second and third locations are at 5650 North Desert Blvd. (915-585-9666), and 6625 Montana Ave.(915-772-9666)

CROOKS SKATESHOP
5640 Montana Ave., Suite J
(915) 775-0493
www.crookselpaso.com
Crooks is a skate shop that is owned and operated by skateboarders. Dozens of skateboards line the colorful walls of this clean, well-appointed skate shop, while accessories and gear are located in counter cases around the shop. They have a good selection of skater-specific shoes and apparel, but are still obviously a skater-run local shop rather than a big corporate store. Jesse and Marcello Perez first had the idea to open a skate shop in 2004; but it wasn't until mid-2005 that the two actually opened their dream business. Avid skaters know that the skateboarding world is a tight-knit community, and Crooks sits at the center of El Paso's, with a focus on building and strengthening the local skateboard community.

HITCHKICK DANCEWEAR
6529 North Mesa St.
(915) 581-4848
Dancers of all kinds, from prim ballerinas to funky hip-hop stylists, can find all the various accessories, outfits, and shoes they need at Hitchkick, a dance apparel and shoe store in central El Paso. Operating in the same location since 1976, Hitchkick has been serving the dance communities of El Paso, Las Cruces, and Juárez for years. They specialize in individual customer care, with expert

pointe shoe fitting provided for dancers of all levels. Hitchkick also offers a good selection of gymnastics wear, competition swimwear, costumes, and more.

INTERNATIONAL SOCCER STORE
5460 Montana Ave.
(915) 564-3732
www.internationalsoccer.org
For all things soccer, from uniforms to shoes, head to International Soccer Store. This football-only house of soccer offers in-house graphics and designs for your team uniforms, as well as a wide range of replicas and official jerseys of professional soccer teams around the world. So if you can't get enough of Man United or want to show your true yellow, green, and blue colors by sporting a Brazilian jersey, you're bound to find one here. Along the walls and shelves are also a wide range of soccer balls, gym bags, socks, goalie gloves, and all the other types of soccer accessories for which you might be looking.

PETE JOSEPH'S PROSHOP
8951 Dyer St.
(915) 751-4551
Bowlers take note: Pete Joseph's is a bowling supply store with everything from balls, shoes, and bags to any incidental supplies

that you might need to make your game perfect. If they don't have your specific shoe size or ball weight in stock, they will special order it, and if you need to have your ball sized, you can make an appointment to bring it in. Pete, the knowledgeable owner, is very helpful in assisting you to get the correctly sized ball, and for new bowlers, he can also explain some of the more intricate technical details about bowling, such as how the ball's weight can influence curve balls. Best of all, Pete Joseph's is conveniently located just a few doors down from Bolero Lanes in northeast El Paso near Fort Bliss.

SAHARA SPORTSWEAR
11460 Pellicano
(915) 833-1145
Golf enthusiasts will especially like this upscale outdoor shop and outlet store, which showcases a variety of men's and women's clothing on a natural bent. Their featured collections include the Nature Tech EZ CARE/EZ WEAR line of moisture management sportswear products and the Sahara Gold Collection. Other products include golf shirts, polos, crewnecks, shorts, pants, jackets, caps, hats, and accessories. Be sure to visit their closeout and overrun section at the back of the store for discounts and good deals.

ANNUAL EVENTS AND FESTIVITIES

From exciting autumn rodeos to summer evening concerts and dizzying college football games, there is almost always something to do in El Paso for just about any interest and age group. The scenic Franklin Mountains provide a stunning natural venue for such events as the Poppies Celebration each March, while many arts festivals and holiday happenings take the stage right downtown. There are plenty of sporting events going on at the UTEP campus, including men's and women's basketball games during the winter and the nationally known Sun Bowl in December.

Several of these events span the course of more than one month, in which case they are listed in the month in which they begin. There are far too many entertaining goings-on in El Paso to be mentioned here in one chapter, so this is a roundup of some of the most popular and oldest traditions that the city has to offer. Not included in this list are the scores of fine and performing arts events, as well as many university and professional sporting events that go on in El Paso throughout the year. Be sure to check out the Arts chapter and the Parks and Recreation chapter for more information on those events. As well, admission prices for these events vary from year to year, so call ahead or check the Web sites listed for current pricing information.

JANUARY

EL PASO PUZZLER MOUNTAIN BIKE RACE
Bowen Ranch
(915) 845-1097
http://bmba.wordpress.com
El Paso's only endurance mountain bike race is hosted by the Border Mountain Bike Association. It runs along a 50-mile single-track with several climbs and descents, and a shorter 35-mile route is also offered. Food and prizes are distributed during the event.

PROVOST GUN SHOW
El Maida Shrine Temple
6331 Alabama Ave.
(915) 241-1761

This gun, small antiques, and Southwest art show includes new, used, and antique firearms and accessories, knives, coins, Southwest jewelry, military surplus, and other outlawish collectibles. Food concessions are available and parking is usually free. Anyone age 18 and younger must be accompanied by a parent or legal guardian.

FEBRUARY

RACE FOR THE CURE
Cohen Stadium
9700 Gateway North
(915) 566-9745
www.elpasokomen.org

The Susan G. Komen Race for the Cure Series, the largest series of 5K runs/fitness walks in the world, raises significant funds and awareness for the fight against breast cancer, celebrates breast cancer survivorship, and honors those who have lost their battle with the disease. As well as being a road race for runners, the Komen Race for the Cure is an opportunity for thousands of women, men, and their families, running or walking, to spread the breast cancer message within El Paso. Up to 75 percent of the funds raised in El Paso go toward providing breast health research, diagnostics, screening, treatment, services, and education for uninsured or underinsured women.

i For more information about what is going on in El Paso, pick up a copy of the *El Paso Scene*, a monthly entertainment and events guide, which is available at many local businesses, or check it out online at www.epscene .com.

SPRING HOME SHOW
El Paso County Coliseum
(800) 756-4788
www.homeshowelpaso.com
The El Paso Association of Builders presents this show, which features booths providing exhibits, demonstrations, and seminars aimed at the needs of homeowners, whether building a home or remodeling. One of El Paso's largest home improvement events, this home show attracts homeowners each year with events, attractions, and contests for incomplete home remodels, making homes more energy efficient, and buying or building a brand new house.

ASTC MARDI GRAS
New Mexico State University
Golf Course Banquet Room
Las Cruces, NM
(575) 646-4515
http://theatre.nmsu.edu/astc
Get into the Cajun spirit at the American Southwest Theatre Company (ATSC)'s annual "little bit naughty, little bit nice" Mardi Gras gala featuring live music, dancing, food, a cash bar, and a king and queen contest. The ASTC is a non-profit organization that works in conjunction with New Mexico State University's Department of Theatre Arts. All gala proceeds will benefit ASTC's programs, which include guest artists and community outreach events.

BOURBON STREET ON
CINCINNATI AVENUE
Cincinnati Avenue
(915) 534-0600
www.visitelpaso.com
Every year in El Paso on Fat Tuesday, Cincinnati Avenue, El Paso's popular nightlife district in the UTEP area, comes alive with beads and booze for the Mardi Gras celebration. Each year, 7,000 to 10,000 revelers flood in on the lively party district to experience the exciting street festival. Many of the local bars and restaurants offer heavy drink discounts and unique Mardi Gras drink specials.

TEXAS VS. THE NATION
Sun Bowl at University of Texas at El Paso
2701 Sun Bowl Dr.
(972)934-2211
www.texasvsthenation.com
Texas vs. The Nation is a post-season Division I-A Collegiate Senior All-Star Bowl football

game, which pits top Texas college players against top players from around the United States. Related events go on throughout the week including a "Legends of the Game" golf tournament and a dinner headlined by Hall of Fame pro football players.

MARCH

EL PASO MARATHON
300 West San Antonio St.
(915) 487-6775
www.elpasomarathon.org
Shed your layers at the start and pack dry clothes and your favorite post-race snack for the finish, or grab a jacket and stand alongside to cheer on the runners! The Michelob Ultra El Paso Marathon spans a full 26.2 miles, while the Good Time Stores Half Marathon is 13.1 miles long. Both races start early and go through Kern Place, the UTEP campus, and on through the scenic Upper Valley. The full marathon continues toward Sunland Park Casino into New Mexico before heading back to El Paso, finishing at the same location as the start. Proceeds from the marathon benefit several local charities and organizations.

FRANKLIN MOUNTAINS POPPIES
  CELEBRATION
Castner Range
Transmountain Road
www.franklinmountains.org
This all-natural event includes nature talks, wildlife displays, educational exhibits, demonstrations, crafts, music, and refreshments. The celebration runs all day and includes great local music and entertainment. Be sure to wear your strong boots for the tequila tasting in the afternoon.

GENERATION 2000
El Paso Convention Center
One Civic Center Plaza
(915) 880-5777
www.generation2000.net
Generation 2000 is a two-day fair that promotes children and parents working together. Dozens of special events, booths, games, and interactive exhibits are aimed at entertaining and educating children of all ages. In the past, these have included miniature golf, giant bubbles, a science area, clowns, mural painting, huge sand tables, and a beading area.

SIGLO DE ORO DRAMA FESTIVAL
Chamizal National Memorial Park
800 South San Marcial St.
(915) 532-7273
www.nps.gov/cham/planyourvisit/
chamizal-theatre.htm
This festival celebrates the "Golden Age" of Spanish dramatic arts, during which visionaries like Lope de Vega, Miguel de Cervantes, and Calderón de la Barca left a beautiful and passionate heritage of classical drama that has enriched the world. The Chamizal's Student Outreach Program gives hundreds of students every year the chance to examine the modern world through the relevant eyes of the past and to understand the ways that people and emotions have remained the same through the centuries. Over the past three decades, the Siglo de Oro Drama Festival has hosted more than 250 productions from 15 countries, involving more than 150 directors and 3,000 cast members, playing before a combined audience of 125,000.

SUNLAND DERBY
Sunland Park Race Track and Casino
1200 Futurity Dr.
Sunland Park, NM
(575) 874-5200
www.sunland-park.com
Horse racing has always been a popular pastime in the El Paso area, with tracks like Sunland Park and Ruidoso hosting some of the most prized races in the world. The Sunland Derby is considered Sunland Park's signature horse racing event of the year. A field of three-year-old thoroughbreds runs a course over 1 1/8 miles long to an exciting finish. The track offers a $100,000 bonus on any three-year-old winner with any other previous graded earnings, for a winner's share of $500,000.

GERMAN SPRING BAZAAR
German Community Center
(Soldatenstube)
Fort Bliss
(915) 568-0259
www.betreuung-in-el-paso.com
Every March, the German Catholic Church of Fort Bliss hosts this annual bazaar where hobby craftspeople display and sell their various goods, and German food and drink specialties are offered. This is an excellent chance to sample some authentic German fare or pick up a few crafty souvenirs or knickknacks. All proceeds from the bazaar are donated to the charity organizations "Aid for the Needy" and "Helping Hands" to benefit the poor on both sides of the border.

APRIL

DÍA DE LOS NIÑOS, DÍA DE LOS LIBROS
Washington Park
4201 East Paisano Dr.
(915) 543-5468
www.elpasotexas.gov/library

In 1997, at the request of renowned children's author Pat Mora, the El Paso Public Library and the Parks and Recreation Department began the tradition of holding an annual festival to celebrate the youth of El Paso. Since the festival's inception, organizers have given away more than 50,000 books and goodie bags filled with fruit, toys, and educational materials to the children who have attended. This effort helps bring the love of books and reading to children who might not otherwise have that opportunity. Festivities usually include fun-filled activities like game booths, jumping balloons, free books and goodie bags, an entertainment stage, and a parade. Food and drink vendors are also on hand passing out tasty treats for everyone.

FEATHERFEST
Keystone Heritage Park
4220 Doniphan Dr.
(915) 584-0563
www.keystoneheritagepark.org
Featherfest is a nature celebration that leads visitors on a trip through the local surrounds and gives an up-close taste of the history of the area. Take a tour, listen to presentations by local experts, find fun with lots of family activities, and get a good look at the developments at El Paso Desert Botanical Garden and the Chihuahuan Desert Experience at this event, held in Keystone Heritage Park, which has 189 species of migratory and local birds and a 4,500 year old archaeological site.

FIRST THANKSGIVING CELEBRATION
San Elizario Plaza
(915) 851-1682
Nearly 30 years before the first pilgrims set foot on Plymouth Rock, Spanish explor-

ANNUAL EVENTS AND FESTIVITIES

ers were celebrating the "first Thanksgiving" along the shores of the Rio Grande at what is now El Paso. "La Toma," as the event has come to be known, is regarded as one of the most significant historical events in the hemisphere and the first of its kind in America. Organized by the Mission Trail Association, "La Toma" is a reenactment of the first Thanksgiving at the Chamizal National Memorial held the last Sun of Apr.

FLORAFEST
UTEP Centennial Museum
Corner of Wiggins Road and
University Avenue
(915) 747-8994, (915) 747-5565
www.museum.utep.edu
If you enjoy plants or want to green up your thumb, you should definitely check out Florafest. Held at the University of Texas El Paso's Centennial Museum, Florafest is an annual native plant event. Listen in on one of the lectures about flora native to the El Paso region in the area's gardens, or purchase a few local seedlings to bring up in your own backyard.

MAY

ARMED FORCES DAY
Noel Field at Fort Bliss
(915) 568-4601
www.bliss.army.mil
Established in 1949 by the Secretary of Defense, this day allows Fort Bliss to showcase itself to the public. Fort Bliss activities include a 5K fun run, opening ceremonies honoring the armed services, a demonstration by the Military Police Working Dogs, all-day entertainment, and a health fair. Military equipment is put on static display for visitors to marvel at, and there are opportunities to try your hand at rappelling. Take a historical tour of Fort Bliss, taste test the best of El Paso

spice in a chili cook-off, and generally enjoy the food and drink and various other displays from numerous organizations.

KLAQ INTERNATIONAL BALLOONFEST
Grace Gardens
6702 Westside Dr.
(915) 886-2222
www.klaq.com
Hot air balloons of all shapes and sizes fill up the El Paso sky over Memorial Day weekend each year, as some 5,000 to 8,000 people come out to watch the early-morning launching of more than 75 colorful hot air balloons and get the opportunity to enjoy water rides and live concerts at Wet 'N' Wild Waterworld in nearby Anthony, Texas. In previous years, the event, which is sponsored by local radio station KLAQ, was held entirely at Wet 'N' Wild Waterworld, but a new launch site was recently opened at Grace Gardens in El Paso. Balloon pilots travel from around the world to fly at Balloonfest, making it a truly international event.

VICTORIAN SPRING TEA
Magoffin Home State Historic Site
1120 Magoffin Ave.
(915) 533-5147
www.visitmagoffinhome.com
Enjoy a traditional Victorian tea each May on the grounds of this 1875 Territorial style home, which features a center courtyard and peaceful landscape. The Magoffin family played an important role in El Paso's history and participated in the early U.S. settlement and expansion along the Santa Fe–Chihuahua Trail. In addition to enjoying delicious English tea, you can explore the home's authentic Victorian art and furnishings, which reflect the daily lives of this prominent El Paso family.

JUNE

ALFRESCO! FRIDAYS

Arts Festival Plaza
downtown El Paso
(915) 541-4481
www.elpasoartsandculture.org

Alfresco! Fridays is an arts and culture festival held in downtown El Paso every June. The festival was originally envisioned as a way to entice downtown workers to stick around and liven the area up a bit in the evenings. Most of the programs are musical in nature, offering a casual way to experience both well-established and up-and-coming El Paso bands performing on stage. Past seasons have featured bands from a variety of genres, like big band, jazz, reggae, classic rock, ska, blues, and more; while the recent seasons have also featured an Artist Market. This unique concept market helps to provide local artists and artisans a way to connect directly with the community.

LA QUE BUENA GORDITA FESTIVAL

Ascarate Park
6900 Delta Dr.
(915) 544-9797

This festival celebrates Mexican food, namely *gorditas*, which are a traditional Mexican dish in which various types of fillings are stuffed into a small, thick corn tortilla, creating a delightful sandwich. If you're interested in authentic Mexican food, beverages, and arts and crafts, this festival is a great way to sample some traditional fare and pick up a few home accents. The kids will be entertained in a children's zone with carnival rides, while you enjoy live entertainment that includes both national and local performers of Mexican and Tejano varieties.

VIVA! EL PASO

3 McKelligon Canyon Rd.
McKelligon Canyon Amphitheatre
(915) 231-1165
www.viva-ep.org

Viva! El Paso is a wonderfully colorful outdoor musical presented at McKelligon Canyon Amphitheatre during the summer months. The play chronicles the story of El Paso's history, with particular emphasis on the centuries of struggles that early settlers and Native Americans faced here. The play is renowned for its brightly colored costumes, spectacular sets, and dazzling special effects, and offers a delightful way to not only learn, but vividly experience some local El Paso history.

MUSIC UNDER THE STARS

Chamizal National Memorial
Amphitheatre
800 S. San Marcial St.
(915) 532-7273
www.ci.el-paso.tx.us/mcad/summer programs.asp

El Paso's favorite concert series, Music Under the Stars is exactly what it sounds like: a charming evening concert series held outdoors under the stars. Music Under the Stars presents everything from jazz, blues, and Latin tunes to garage band rock and zydeco performances on stage in the scenic Chamizal National Memorial Amphitheatre just minutes from the Mexican border. Hosted by the El Paso Arts and Culture Department, listings for the Music Under the Stars festival change from year to year, with surprising and wonderful new musical stylings with each go round.

EL PASO SUN CITY PRIDE PARADE & STREET FESTIVAL

Starting from Houston Park
Corner of Montana Avenue and
St. Vrain Street
(915) 474-3403
www.elppride.org

El Paso's LGBT communities get their pride on during this, the city's annual Gay Pride event. The parade, held in honor of National Gay Pride Month, starts at the corner of Montana Avenue and St. Vrain Street, and concludes at Pride Square (East Missouri and North Stanton) for the Gay Pride Street Festival, where you can expect to bar hop the night away alongside exuberant Pride-goers and attendees.

JULY

DOWNTOWN STREET FESTIVAL

Downtown El Paso
(915) 544-8864

A non-stop party throughout the downtown area, this street festival is a fantastic way to spend the 4th of July weekend in El Paso. Three different outdoor stages host rock, Latin, and kids' music, and vendors line the streets selling delicious treats, refreshments, ice cream, and beer. For kids, the best part of the street festival can be found inside the El Paso Convention Center where a variety of fun rides, games, and live entertainment take place.

YSLETA MISSION FESTIVAL

Our Lady of Mt. Carmel Church
131 South Zaragoza St.
(at Alameda Ave.)
(915) 859-9848
www.ysletamission.org

El Paso's culture, history, and traditions come alive through live music, food, games, and entertainment over the festival weekend. Adults and children of all ages gather on Ysleta Mission, one of El Paso's historic Catholic missions, for continuous entertainment by top local Tejano bands that showcase current emerging talent in West Texas. This festival is a great time to come to a better understanding of the unique El Paso music scene and the enjoyable local Tejano genre.

SOLDIER SHOW

Plaza Theatre
125 Pioneer Plaza
(915) 568-7506
www.theplazatheatre.org

Every year, this variety show is performed by soldiers, for other soldiers as well as the wider El Paso and Fort Bliss communities. During this live music review, you'll take in the talents of active duty soldiers selected by audition from throughout the Army. This unique Fort Bliss event is a rare opportunity to support the troops through the stylings of amateur artists with a passion for music, dance, and performing.

BAT FLIGHT BREAKFAST

Carlsbad Caverns National Park
Carlsbad, NM
(575) 785-2232
www.nps.gov/cave

Carlsbad Caverns in nearby Carlsbad, New Mexico, is home to one of the largest domestic bat colonies in the United States. At this annual breakfast, you will get the rare chance to watch these remarkable nocturnal animals as they dive into the cave entrance after a night outside feeding on insects. Park rangers also present programs about the bats' return flight in the early light of dawn, a sight that is very different from their out-flight in the evening. Admission to watch the bats is free, but seats for the breakfast must be reserved in advance and costs vary.

AUGUST

BUGFEST!
The El Paso Zoo
4001 East Paisano Dr.
(915) 532-8156
www.elpasozoo.org
Get ready for all things creepy crawly, as the young and the young-at-heart are sure to enjoy this bug-tastic event at El Paso Zoo. An annual "back to school" weekend expo, the event offers kids and adults alike the chance to get up close with all sorts of amazing insects, and there are plenty of games and activities for the whole family on offer to keep you amazed.

PLAZA CLASSIC FILM FESTIVAL
Plaza Theatre
125 Pioneer Plaza
(915) 533-4020
www.plaza-movies.com
There is perhaps no better way to see old movies than on the big screen. The El Paso Community Foundation gives you the chance to watch all your favorites from the Golden Age on the silver screen, as they were meant to be seen. Movies of all genres are shown in the Plaza's Main Theatre and the Philanthropy Theatre for 10 days each August.

FIESTA DE SAN LORENZO
San Lorenzo Catholic Church
611 Avenida De San Lorenzo St.
Clint, TX
(915) 851-2255
A traditionally Catholic festival, this event commemorates San Lorenzo, or Saint Lawrence in English. The annual celebration, which has origins in early Spain, is held one weekend each August at San Lorenzo Catholic Church in nearby Clint, Texas, with plenty of live music and food booths offering traditional foods. You will be dazzled by the colorful procession of the *matachines*, or Mexican mummer dancers wearing spectacular native costumes. A traditional procession goes from San Elizario Parish to the church grounds in the early morning hours, accompanied by the recitation of the rosary, hymns, and dancing. The procession is followed by a traditional Catholic Mass service at the San Lorenzo Catholic Church.

SEPTEMBER

SHAKESPEARE ON THE ROCKS FESTIVAL
Ysleta Fine Arts Amphitheater
8455 Alameda Ave.
(915) 227-2397
www.shakespeareontherocks.com
Shakespeare on the Rocks is a special production where performances take place in an intimate outdoor setting, feature scripts edited for modern audiences, integrate music and dance into the play, and feature the best local thespian talent. Both young and old are sure to enjoy the modern takes on the Bard's most famous works at these delightful summer outings!

SOUTHWESTERN INTERNATIONAL PRCA RODEO
Cohen Stadium
9700 Gateway North
(915) 755-2000
www.elprodeo.com
Rodeo is a staple in West Texas, and the Southwestern International PRCA Rodeo is one of El Paso's finest rodeo events all year. Cowboy up with tickets to watch the macho bull riders take on the world's fiercest animals, and razz on the exciting barrel racers as

they speed around the arena. You'll want to make sure to get your tickets early because they will sell out, as this is the best chance to see some of the top cowboys and cowgirls in the world wrangle it up!

KERMEZAAR
International Museum of Art
1211 Montana Ave.
www.internationalmuseumofart.net
Kermezaar is a weekend arts and crafts festival that presents both local and national artists' works. More than 70 artists are featured at this, El Paso's largest art show, which is held for two weeks each August. From oil paintings to pottery to handcrafted handbags to fine jewelry, Kermezaar features some of the most unique handmade items available anywhere in El Paso. This event also serves as the International Museum of Art's largest annual fundraiser, and the proceeds are used to keep the museum open free to the public, as well as helping to provide educational programming.

CELEBRATION OF OUR MOUNTAINS
(915) 542-1422
www.celebrationofourmountains.org
Celebration of Our Mountains is a six-week-long festival of events designed to encourage appreciation of the region's environment. Dozens of hikes, field trips, driving tours, nature walks, and other activities are offered to the public, most of which are free. This binational event highlights the natural and cultural history of the regional mountains—the Franklins in West Texas, the Sierra de Juárez in Northern Chihuahua, and the Cerro de Cristo Rey and the Organ Mountains in Southern New Mexico.

CHIHUAHUAN DESERT FIESTA
Tom Mays Park
(915) 521-1881
www.chihuahuandesert.org
One of the sub-events of Celebration of Our Mountains, the Chihuahuan Desert Fiesta will appeal to nature lovers and anyone interested in the unique El Paso surrounds. Held at Tom Mays Park, the event, which includes free entry to Franklin Mountains State Park, celebrates all things Chihuahuan Desert with a day-long program that highlights the unusual plant and animal life of the Southwest desert and the Rio Grande region. Activities include presentations by state park staff on topics such as helping protect threatened wildlife, the numerous bird species of the area, the restoration of vegetation along the Rio Grande, and more. Adventurous types won't want to miss the free rock climbing tutorials, and a chili cook-off feeds the famished.

MEXICAN INDEPENDENCE DAY
Chamizal National Memorial
800 South San Marcial St.
(915) 533-6311
As El Paso is inextricably linked with its Mexican sister city, Ciudad Juárez, so Mexican Independence Day is a huge celebration in El Paso every year. Honoring the day that Mexico began its rebellion against Spain, this festival includes a celebration at the Mexican Consul General with live music, dances by ballet *folklóricos*, and a fireworks display. Other events, such as theatrical performances, are held all over Chamizal National Memorial, an aptly symbolic location for the celebration along the U.S.–Mexico border.

FIESTA DE LAS FLORES
El Paso County Coliseum
4100 Paisano Dr.
(915) 532-3415
www.lulacelpaso.org

Developed by the League of United Latin American Citizens (LULAC), this fiesta celebrates El Paso's Hispanic culture and communities, and promotes Hispanic heritage and traditions in the region. Started in 1953, Fiesta de Las Flores now draws around 55,000 to 70,000 visitors a year, with more than 100 local businesses participating. Events include food and game booths, arts and crafts, a car show, the Fiesta de Las Flores Pageant, World Championship Huacha (washer throwing) Tournament, and evening concerts.

OCTOBER

AMIGO AIRSHO
Fort Bliss
Biggs Army Airfield
(915) 562-6446
www.amigoairsho.org

With zooming jets and floating gliders, the Amigo Airsho is El Paso's premier air show and an event that is sure to dazzle and entertain the whole family. This fun-filled day is chock full of innovative, safe, and exciting aerial performances, as well as other fun family activities. The Amigo Airsho organization is dedicated to raising awareness about the importance of aviation and the military in the El Paso region through this event, as well as providing exciting entertainment that El Pasoans of all ages are sure to enjoy.

BOO AT THE ZOO
El Paso Zoo
4001 East Paisano Dr.
(915) 521-1881
www.elpasozoo.org

Celebrate Halloween with the kids at El Paso's largest spooky outdoor festival. The event is aimed at providing a safe trick-or-treating environment and gives kids the chance to get up close with lots of different animals while they're at it. Vendors and booths provide plenty of entertainment, including pumpkin bowling, kiddie mazes, treat stations that are sponsored by local businesses, and, of course, costumes galore!

CONCORDIA WALK THROUGH HISTORY
Concordia Cemetery
3700 East Yandell St.
(915) 842-8200

Get into the spooky October spirit by visiting the ghosts of some of El Paso's most notorious historical figures. Each year in October the volunteers of Concordia Cemetery invite the public to take a walk through Concordia Cemetery and visit the leading citizens, Buffalo Soldiers, ex-Mexican presidents, Jesuit priests, and gunfighters that are buried there. Wild West characters like John Wesley Hardin seem to come back to life as volunteers dressed in period costumes share dramatic recreations of their past lives. Even if you aren't a history buff, this event is a great way to understand more about El Paso's past in a family friendly environment.

HUECO TANKS INTERPRETIVE FAIR
Hueco Tanks Historic Site
6900 Hueco Tanks Rd. #1
(915) 857-1135
www.tpwd.state.tx.us

Held in and around the amazing natural "basins" that comprise Hueco Tanks Historic Site, the annual Interpretive Fair is an event in which anyone from the public can enter the park and participate in the weekend festivities. There are many cultural exhibits and booths to explore, which give great insight to the park's history. Typically, activities include traditional Native American drumming and dance, pictograph and birding tours, cowboy skills demonstrations, climbing demonstrations, and booths with lots of information about the local environment and culture. Past fairs have also included a wonderful evening campfire storytelling program. This is a great chance to explore the historic petroglyphs left by ancient civilizations and to see history and culture come alive at one of El Paso's most unique natural areas.

NOVEMBER

SUN BOWL PARADE
Parade begins at the corner of Montana Avenue and Ochoa Street
Held since 1935, this annual Thanksgiving Day parade attracts some 250,000 spectators and features more than 100 entrants, including floats, marching bands, and mariachis. Dancers, clowns, horses, and balloons also make appearances. The parade, which begins at Montana Avenue and Ochoa Street and travels east to Copia Street, is held in conjunction with the Brut Sun Bowl, one of the nation's largest college football bowl games.

DÍA DE LOS MUERTOS FESTIVAL
Concordia Cemetery
3700 East Yandell St.
(915) 373-1513
www.ghosts915.com
El Día de los Muertos, or the Day of the Dead, is an important ancient holiday among many Hispanic cultures, and is widely celebrated across the Southwest. Though the subject matter is sometimes considered morbid from the perspective of other cultures, celebrants approach El Día de los Muertos joyfully. The traditional mood is much brighter than that of Halloween or All Soul's Day, with emphasis being placed more on honoring the lives of the deceased and the continuation of life, rather than on death. El Paso's Día de los Muertos festival is a series of events that bring together families from both sides of the border. The celebration, which typically occurs over three days at various locations in El Paso and Juárez, consists of live entertainment, lectures, children's theater, and an arts and crafts market. A mock funeral procession with professional actors, outrageous costumes, themed floats, and colorful displays depicting skeletons and deceased saints is usually the highlight of the celebration.

GERMAN ADVENTS-BAZAAR
German Community Center
(Soldatenstube)
Robert E. Lee Road
Fort Bliss
(915) 568-0259
Get into the Christmas spirit German–style at the Advents-Bazaar, a traditional German "Christkindlmarket," or Christmas market, held each year on Fort Bliss by the German Catholic Church. Here, beautiful Germanic arts and crafts meet bratwursts and beers in a festival that will fill your tummy and decorate your Christmas tree!

LUMINARIAS BY THE LAKE
Keystone Heritage Park
4220 Doniphan Dr.
(915) 584-0563
www.keystoneheritagepark.org
There is perhaps no more beautiful a sight than glowing luminarias during the holidays. These traditional holiday lights, paper sacks

filled with sand and lit from within by a small candle, can be found throughout the Southwest at Christmastime and offer a warming flicker of lights on cold winter evenings. Stroll the wetlands at Keystone Heritage Park as they are illuminated by hundreds of luminarias, their bright reflections twinkling softly off the water.

SEASON OF LIGHTS
UTEP Campus
(915) 747-8600

This annual holiday lighting ceremony held on the University of Texas, El Paso campus dates back to 1992. Join in with thousands of other spectators to watch the magical lights illuminate for the first time while you sip a hot chocolate and enjoy carol singing.

DECEMBER

BRUT SUN BOWL AND FAN FIESTA
Sun Bowl Stadium at the University of Texas at El Paso
2701 Sun Bowl Dr.
(915) 533-4416
www.sunbowl.org

One of the biggest tourism draws to El Paso, the Sun Bowl is an annual collegiate football game. The first Sun Bowl game was played between two El Paso high school football teams on January 1, 1935, as a fundraising event for the El Paso Kiwanis Club. The success of that first game resulted in the founding of the Sun Bowl Association, whose purpose was to present an annual football attraction of national importance, to promote El Paso, and to generate tourist income for the area. In 1963, the game was moved to the Sun Bowl Stadium, which seats more than 50,000 spectators. Accompanying the Sun Bowl is a weeklong carnival of festivities including the Fan Fiesta, a free kids event held at the El Paso Convention Center, as well as the Sun Bowl 5K Run and Walk.

SAN JACINTO PLAZA CHRISTMAS TREE LIGHTING
San Jacinto Plaza
111 East Mills Ave.
(915) 533-3311

El Paso's official city Christmas tree is displayed in San Jacinto Plaza right downtown, and its lighting ceremony has been a holiday tradition since the 1930s. In 1998, a 50-foot live Afghan pine tree was donated by Mrs. Corrine Boyce of El Paso in memory of her late husband Charles Boyce, and each year is adorned with thousands of amber, blue, green, and red lightbulbs, as well as hundreds of oversized ornaments. Dozens of other trees inside the plaza and along the nearby sidewalks are also lit, lit decals of Christmas characters are positioned around the square, and Christmas decorations are hung from every available surface, making the whole area burst with true shimmering holiday cheer.

DAY TRIPS AND GETAWAYS

El Paso is situated in an extremely convenient location at the border of two states and one international boundary. Although the city is packed with plenty to see and do, the possibilities for local day trips and nearby weekend getaways are virtually endless. Whether you are interested in history and culture, beautiful scenery, good shopping, or the outdoors, there is a sprinkling of everything within a half-day drive of El Paso. From downtown, you can be across the border into El Paso's Mexican sister-city, Ciudad Juárez, on foot, while further afield, natural wonders like Carlsbad Caverns and Kilbourne Hole are just a few hours' drive. For hiking, skiing, and outdoor exploration, head to the Guadalupe Mountains or Big Bend on the Texas side of the border, or Ruidoso, Gila National Park, and Truth or Consequences in New Mexico. The area is also bursting with historical sites where outlaws like Billy the Kid and famous revolutionaries such as Pancho Villa once engaged their Wild West enemies in shootouts.

OVERVIEW

If you are relocating to El Paso, you will certainly have plenty of time to explore all the surrounding areas; however, if you're just passing through, you may have to pick and choose some of the nearer sites. This chapter covers most of the best spots that are within a few hours' drive from El Paso, and the majority of these sites are fairly remote Southwestern areas that offer little in the way of public transportation. Generally speaking, you will require a car if you wish to visit the places covered in this chapter.

Included here are brief overviews of each site, accompanied by driving directions and distance, and entrance fees, if any. I have also done my best to include a suggestion on accommodation, where possible, but bear in mind that there will be many more options for accommodation than those listed here, so definitely check around to find the one that suits you best.

Price Code

The following price code has been included to give you a rough idea of what a regular adult ticket, entrance fee, or basic meal for two (excluding drinks) will cost at each of the following places. If the fees or costs associated with a particular activity or meal are varied, no price has been given and you should use the contact information provided to find out details. More specific pricing and discount information is included in the listings, where available.

$........................$1 to $5
$$ ....$6 to 10
$$$ .... $11 to $20
$$$$ ....$21 and up

CIUDAD JUÁREZ

Located just across the border from downtown El Paso, Ciudad Juárez is its rogue, rough and ready Mexican brother city and one of the largest cities in the Republic of Mexico. El Paso and Juárez have always been inextricably linked, at many times in their collective pasts being completely indistinguishable from one another. For most of history, the town on the American side of the border was known as El Paso, while its Mexican counterpart was called El Paso del Norte. Only in 1888 was El Paso del Norte renamed Ciudad Juárez in honor of former Mexican President Benito Juárez, finally differentiating between the two.

El Paso and Juárez share a lot in common: a border, an interlinked economy, outpost identities that are sometimes disregarded by their respective governments. They also have a lot of differences. And while El Paso has risen firmly into the 21st century as a thriving American metropolis, its renegade *hermano,* Juárez, has sunk deeper into a pit of depression, driven largely by out-of-control drug trade and violence that plagues the city on a daily, if not hourly, basis.

All of this is not to say that there isn't something to recommend Juárez as a tourist destination. In fact, the sole reason that many visitors find themselves in El Paso is to explore the outlawish history of the area and to cross the border into colorful Mexico. Tourists mostly come and go through the downtown areas of Juárez with few problems; however, if you choose to visit Juárez, be sure to check out the safety tips Close-up following for a few reminders about the very real situation of violence in the city and how to keep yourself safe while you're there.

Getting Across

Jumping the border into Juárez is fairly painless, but there are a few pieces of paperwork you must have before you set out. Citizens of all countries are now required to show either a valid passport from their country of origin or a U.S. passport card when crossing the international boundary. Coming into the U.S. from Mexico, visitors who require a U.S. visa must be in possession of and present their passport with a multiple entry visa, issued by U.S. authorities, together with the entry card received upon first entry into the U.S.

Four bridges in El Paso make it easy to cross into Mexico. Many tourists park in downtown El Paso and simply walk across the border, but it is also possible to drive between the two cities. From downtown, the Stanton Bridge provides car access into Mexico, while the Santa Fe Bridge connects Avenida Juárez to El Paso from the Mexican side. Pedestrians may cross both bridges going either way and must pay a toll to cross. Vehicles also pay a nominal fee each way. The Bridge of the Americas provides free access to cars from I-10, and further south, the Zaragosa Street Bridge near Ysleta meets Federal Mexico Hwy 2 on the other side. Both the Bridge of the Americas and the Zaragosa Bridge are off the tourist path and you should avoid using those bridges unless you know your way around Juárez or are going to a part of town specifically served by those bridges. For most tourists, it's best to use the two downtown bridges, Stanton and Santa Fe.

If you are driving across the border, you can check the wait times at the international bridges online at www.ci.el-paso .tx.us/international_bridges before you go.

Once every 31 days, U.S. residents may bring back duty free articles for personal or household use up to $400 in value, one quart of liquor per person over 21, and either one carton of cigarettes or 100 cigars (non-Cuban). It is prohibited to bring back live animals or birds, potted plants, lemons,

El Paso/Juárez International Bridge Tolls

On Foot:

Stanton Bridge (to Juárez)	50 cents	Downtown
Santa Fe Bridge (to El Paso)	50 cents (Mex $7)	Downtown

By Car:

Stanton Bridge (to Juárez)	$2.50	Downtown
Santa Fe Bridge (to El Paso)	$2.50 (Mex $35)	Downtown
Bridge of the Americas	Free	5 mi. to Downtown
Zaragosa Bridge (to Mexico)	$2.50	18 mi. to Downtown
Zaragosa Bridge (to El Paso)	$2.50 (Mex $35)	18 mi. to Downtown

apples, mangos, some herb teas, pork, ham, uncooked chicken, eggs, or products made from endangered species.

i If you have a question about which agricultural products you may bring back from Mexico, you can request information by calling (915) 633-7300 within El Paso.

Attractions

MISIÓN NUESTRA SEÑORA DE GUADALUPE   FREE
Plaza de Armas
(no phone)
Located right downtown, on the west side of the Plaza de Armas, this small mission is dwarfed by the much larger Cathedral of Juárez next door. Although the cathedral is rather disappointing for its lack of preservation, the mission is a historical treasure. Founded in 1660s by Fray García de San Francisco, the Guadalupe Mission is considered the mother of the El Paso Valley missions and it once provided sanctuary and food to the tired travelers along the Camino Real. It is now the oldest standing building in Juárez, a fact made evident by the building's humble whitewashed walls.

The mission is constructed solely of adobe, with a simple portico and Spanish colonial oval windows. If you stand at the main and side doors, you can appreciate the thickness of the building's original walls. One of the most stellar aspects of the mission is its ceiling, which is anchored by hand-carved original *vigas* (round wooden beams), as well as the wooden choir mezzanine toward the back of the church. Indian elements of the architecture are evident in the rectangular decorations, braiding, circular stairs, and the serpent pallets carved into every ceiling rafter. The church's stone altar, which was installed in the late 1960s, stands over the remains of the area's first settlers. If you look closely at the head of the altar, you will notice a finely carved wood and glass panel that displays the image of the Virgin of Guadalupe herself.

The Guadalupe Mission is open most days from 9 a.m. to 5 p.m. To reach the Plaza de Armas on foot from El Paso, walk due south from the Santa Fe Bridge crossing, down Avenida Juárez until you reach Avenida 16 de Septiembre. Turn right (west) and the plaza is located about two blocks down.

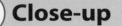 **Close-up**

Safety Across the Border

At the time of writing, Ciudad Juárez was being touted as the most dangerous city in the world, with some 2,000 murders occurring there every year, most of them related to the rampant drug cartel violence that has been slowly escalating for nearly a decade. Many people who grew up crossing the border between El Paso and Juárez and enjoying the cheap delights of the Mexican side have ceased to visit, fearing to be accidentally caught in a shootout or to become a victim of crime. Juárez police and even local military cannot be trusted, as they are generally bought off by one cartel or another. As the writer of this book, I cannot in good conscience recommend that you currently go across the border, as I dare not do so myself anymore. Of course, things can and hopefully will change in Juárez in the coming years. Juárez has been included in this chapter as a day trip on the sheer weight of its proximity and historic connection to El Paso, and on the true hope that the current situation will quell and tourism will open up in Juárez once again. If you do choose to go across the border, you will not necessarily be a victim of violence. In fact, you probably will not. There are a few things you can do to keep yourself extra safe during a day in Juárez.

- Check with El Paso police and border control about the current conditions in Juárez before crossing. Make sure to ask about any restrictions on what you can and cannot bring with you.

- Arrange with a local tour operator for a van or bus to take you over the bridge to various nightclubs and/or restaurants and back to El Paso. Check with your hotel for options.

- Use either the Santa Fe Bridge or the Stanton Bridge, both of which drop you into the main tourist areas of Juárez.

- Do not, under any circumstances, wander into alleys or off main roads. If possible, stay on Avenida Juárez and Avenida 16 de Septiembre, the main tourist drags.

- If you want to go to Ajuua! or someplace located further afield, take a taxi. Specify where you want to go and ask the price in advance.

- Don't drive your own vehicle into Juárez. To do so, you would require extra international insurance coverage and risk having your car broken into, stolen, or de-tired. You would also run into heavy drug searches on the way back.

- Women travelers should not go across the border alone. Mass female graves have been uncovered in the desert outside of Juárez and the city has been the site of murders of both local and tourist women. Stay in a group and don't go anywhere with a stranger alone.

- Never, ever carry drugs, weapons, or other contraband across the border.

- Avoid standing in one place to check your map or guidebook. Keep moving and be watchful of your surroundings. If you sense that something is amiss, it probably is.

MUSEO DE ARTE E HISTORIA
DEL INBA   FREE
Avenida Lincoln (at Coyoacán)
(656) 616-7414
The Juárez Museum of Art features a mix of artwork from different periods by local and internationally known artists in three galleries. Located in the former PRONAF center, perhaps the most interesting thing about this museum is its exterior, which has an unusual cone shape and is surrounded by a moat. Small outdoor bridges connect the main central gallery to the others. The rotating exhibits presented here throughout the year are a good place to get an understanding of local contemporary art, and you will often see unusual plastic pieces being shown. The museum is open Tues through Sun 10 a.m. to 6 p.m. The best way to reach the museum is by crossing at the Bridge of the Americas, walking through the Parque Chamizal, and heading south on Avenida Lincoln until you reach the Zona Pronaf.

MUSEO HISTÓRICO   FREE
Avenida 16 de Septiembre
www.juarez.gob.mx/juarez/museo-
exaduana.php
Housed in the city's former customs building, it is the building, rather than the exhibits at the Juárez History Museum that will wow you. The exhibits, which are labeled in Spanish, are a fairly run-of-the-mill mix of historic pieces from the surrounding region, as well as a few more interesting old photographs. The central hall hosts rotating exhibitions on archaeology, history, and anthropology, and the surrounding chambers are home to the permanent collections, which range from Chihuahuan prehistoric artifacts to the Mexican Revolution. The building itself, though, is a delightful old customs house with historic French architectural design, and it was here that the treaties ending the Mexican Revolution were signed. The museum is open Tues through Sun from 10 a.m. to 6 p.m.

PARQUE CHAMIZAL   FREE
East of the Stanton Street Bridge
Crossing
www.juarez.gob.mx/juarez/
parque-chamizal.php
The Juárez Parque Chamizal is the twin park of El Paso's Chamizal Memorial, erected to commemorate the Chamizal Convention of 1963, which resulted in the peaceful settlement of the century-long international boundary dispute between Juárez and El Paso. In contrast to the rather sparse open lawns of the El Paso memorial, the Juárez Chamizal is a richly forested park shaded by numerous palm trees, where many locals spend weekend afternoons picnicking and playing soccer. Several gardens contain replicas of some of the most famous sites in Mexico: Uxmal, Chichen Itza, and Teotihuacán. The park consists of approximately 800 acres of land that, at one point or another through history, have been both part of Mexico and the United States.

Inside the park, you'll find the tiny archeology museum, Museo de Arqueología de El Chamizal (www.museodelchamizal.com), which consists of two rooms: the Cultures of the North room is stocked with authentic Mexican pots and artifacts from pre-Columbian Casas Grandes, while the art gallery shows paintings and sculptures from well-known local and international artists.

Juárez Chamizal is located near the Bridge of the Americas northeast of the Plaza de Armas.

Restaurants

Juárez has a great selection of restaurants and it is not difficult to find great food here, from Mexican specialties to excellent steaks, seafood, and even Chinese food. The cuisine in Juárez is much different from El Paso's Tex-Mex fare, incorporating fresh ingredients, some seafood, and different styles of cooking. And one of the luxuries of eating in Juárez is the price, which is often half of the cost of a similar meal Stateside.

In addition to the city's many opulent steakhouses, Juárez is known for its burritos and taco stands, where take-away meals are made with fresh tortillas, vegetables, and a choice of several meats like beef, chicken, pork, and chorizo (a spicy Mexican sausage). Tacos are a super cheap meal, made to order, and you should not expect to pay more than 30 pesos or $2 to $3 for an order of four.

The restaurants listed here represent a cross-section of what you are likely to find around the tourist-friendly areas of Juárez, but that does not mean that they are necessarily tourist-geared establishments. Unless otherwise noted, restaurants listed here accept Visa and Mastercard.

AJUUAI FIESTA MEXICANA $–$$$
Norte Efren Ornelas No. 162

As its name would seem to suggest, Ajuua! is a colorful, party-hearty joint that is big on atmosphere and even bigger on tequila. With over 200 varieties available, this place will put most tequila selections to shame. Instead of the humdrum Jose Cuervo, why not sample a mango or celery tequila? Ajuua!'s colorful decor is a mix of bright multi-colored lights shining through stained glass windows onto a variety of large murals that splash across the walls in themes of folkloric dance, bull-fights, and equestrian scenes, while the central restaurant is designed in the fashion of a Mexican village plaza. The menu ranges from a full-service buffet at breakfast and lunch to a range of traditional Mexican fare at night, with selections of familiar beef, chicken, and seafood dishes. Nightly entertainment during dinner, and live bands on weekend nights, make this a popular party spot for locals and border hoppers alike.

BARRIGAS $$
Av. Paseo Triunfo de la República No. 4630
(656) 611-4840
www.barrigasrestaurant.com

This traditional Mexican restaurant has become a local institution, expanding to several locations across Juárez, El Paso, and Chihuahua. The interior is typically Mexican with high ceilings and wooden decor. The specialty of the house is Pachuga Barrigas, a plate of thin broiled and seasoned chicken breasts topped with green chiles and a whole avocado and covered in their house seasoning. The menu at Barrigas is extremely diverse, ranging from tacos to pasta to burgers. This is an excellent place to go with a group or if you're wary of trying the more colorful side of Juárez's cuisine but still want a tasty, reasonably priced meal.

EL HERRADERO $$
Av. Paseo Triunfo de la República No. 5535
(656) 251-0952

This high-class steak joint will serve up just about any type of beef your heart desires for a fraction of the price on the other side of the border. El Herradero bucks the traditional Mexican starters and offers, instead, a generous portion of chips, pork skins, a spicy red salsa, and fresh pico de gallo, made with tomatoes, chile peppers, and spices. The New York steak, a house favorite, won't run more than 120 pesos (around $10). Located one block east of the Hotel Villa Manport.

LOS ARCOS $$-$$$
Av. Paseo Triunfo de la República No. 2220
(656) 616-8608
www.restaurantlosarcos.com.mx
If you are keen to try Mexican-style seafood, head to Los Arcos, a national chain that has been around for more than 25 years. The dishes served at Los Arcos reflect the regional Baja cuisine of Mazatlan, a city on Mexico's west coast, incorporating fresh fish and seafood prepared in regional styles. If you are unsure where to begin, try one of the house specialties, such as the grilled octopus or tequila shrimp.

NUEVO MARTINO $$$-$$$$
Avenida Juárez Norte No. 643
This is perhaps the most famous and highly recommended restaurant in Juárez, built in the 1920s. Its truly antique atmosphere is anchored by red booths and white-gloved waiters, and it is because these traditional elements exist as if in a time warp that Nuevo Martino remains popular with locals and visitors alike. The menu is a solid but historic mix of haute-Continental fare that ranges from oysters Rockefeller to steak tartare, and Mexican favorites like *tampiqueño* (a cut of tender beef covered in chiles and Jack cheese, served with an enchilada). Mains here run between $15 and $25. The restaurant is only a short walk from the border on Avenida Juárez North.

Nightlife

KENTUCKY CLUB $-$$
Avenida Juárez Norte No. 629
If you have a hankering to visit a truly classy Mexican cantina, wander into the inimitable Kentucky Club, one of the few really old bars left in Juárez, and purportedly the place where the margarita was invented in 1946. Local legend states that when a Mexican bullfighter came in to down shots of tequila, his girlfriend asked for a more "ladylike" drink and the bartender came up with a mix of tequila, lime juice, and orange liqueur and named it after her. The Kentucky Club is classic. A long, wooden bar is backed by a huge mirrored oak façade and flanked with a series of tattered Mexican barstools. The high ceilings are banded with ancient wooden rafters and you can imagine the likes of John Wayne and Jack Dempsey drinking tequila in the row of antique half-moon booths along the facing wall. Indeed, some of the world's biggest personalities have attended the Kentucky Club, from Steve McQueen to Elizabeth Taylor, and Marilyn Monroe supposedly celebrated her divorce from Arthur Miller with a round here. The Kentucky Club is located along Avenida Juárez just a few blocks down from the Santa Fe Bridge and is a great place to take in a few afternoon margaritas and listen to the barman tell stories of the good ole days.

SALON MEXICO $-$$
Avenida 16 de Septiembre
If you are looking for more of a party atmosphere than quiet afternoon drinks, then Salon Mexico is the place. Located directly across the street from the Rio Grande Mall,

this large nightclub features a dance floor and weekend entertainment that usually includes a 6- to 10-piece Mexican studio band. It is frequented primarily by local couples who come to dance, eat, and have a good time. A painting in the foyer dating to 1989 depicts Señor Baca, the owner, and Maria Bonita of the well-known Maria Bonita restaurant, strolling across the street in front of Salon Mexico.

i If you read a little Spanish, you might try your hand at exploring the entertainment Web site, www .enfiestate.com, which contains listings for Juárez events, bars and nightclubs, parties, and more.

Shopping

MERCADO JUÁREZ
Avenida 16 de Septiembre
This bright pink two-story building near downtown Juárez is open from sunup to sundown. Here, one can browse a seemingly endless array of classic Mexican kitsch and cheap but cheerful knickknacks like velvet paintings, plaster of Paris sculptures, *zarapes*, and every other variety of typical Mexican souvenir you might want. Along one side the building, you'll find a string of cozy open-air cafes, food stalls, restaurants, and ice cream parlors where you can take a load off and grab a cheap bite to eat.

TONY'S CURIOS
Avenida Juárez No. 383
Tucked away on Avenida Juárez not far from the Santa Fe Bridge crossing, Tony's Curios has been in business for years and is stocked full of Mexican delights, from silver jewelry to chess sets, painted cow skulls, and cowboy

boots. What the tiny store lacks in ambiance, it makes up in selection. The carved leather purses and wallets are particularly charming, or if you're on the market for a new leather belt or even an authentic cowboy hat, Tony's probably has it. If you're not looking to buy but don't mind window-shopping, distract yourself with the interesting collections of carved western saddles and silver spurs.

NEW MEXICO TRIPS

New Mexico's nickname is "The Land of Enchantment" and it is a state of such beauty that it certainly lives up to the title. Because El Paso was part of New Mexico historically, the city has many ties to the state—arguably, it has more in common with New Mexico than Texas. New Mexico provides a wealth of sightseeing opportunities, outdoorsy fun and sheer natural beauty In its beautiful sunsets, wide-open wilderness and exotic landscapes. From El Paso, it is only a few minutes' drive to the New Mexico border and, from there, you can easily reach the entire state. Santa Fe, the state's illustrious, charming capital city, is only five hours from El Paso, while laid-back metropolis Albuquerque is a mere four hours. Closer still are the delightful hot springs at Truth or Consequences and the fantastic caves at Carlsbad Caverns.

Carlsbad Caverns

Located 120 miles northeast of El Paso (three to four hours' drive on US 62/180), **Carlsbad Caverns** (Carlsbad, NM, 575-785-2232, www .nps.gov/cave) is a series of several hundred massive caves, the largest of which, the Big Room, is the third biggest cave in the Americas and seventh largest in the world. This limestone chamber plummets more than a mile underground, and visitors can choose from either self-guided or ranger-led tours of the cave, which is the primary attraction at Carlsbad. Most of the caves are handicapped accessible, with a well-maintained series of lighted walkways that bring visitors along the 1¼-mile walk through the caverns. If you don't wish to hike back up, an elevator is available to carry visitors in and out.

Walking into the caves for the first time, you are struck by the sheer size and mass of darkness, as well as the cool temperatures. Especially if you are visiting during summer, the chilly, crisp temperatures inside the caves, which linger at 56°F year-round, can be a shocking contrast to the hot, dry weather outside. So, be sure to bring a light jacket or sweater with you to explore the caves. Inside, you will discover a delightful array of strange sculptures—a mix of stalactites and stalagmites formed by thousands of years of water erosion. Many of the formations are uplit with colorful light installations that bring the caves to life.

A designated UNESCO World Heritage Site, Carlsbad Caverns is also home to dozens of interesting flora and fauna; most notably, 17 species of bats including the Mexican free-tailed bat. From April through October, you can experience the awe-inspiring sight of thousands of bats emerging in dense, corkscrew flight out the caves around sunset. Early evenings from Memorial Day weekend to mid-October, visitors can partake in a presentation that includes a ranger talk and bat flight viewing.

Carlsbad Caverns is located inside Lincoln National Forest, which is an amazing ecosystem in and of itself. If you would like to see more than just caves, three hiking trails and an unpaved drive provide access to the desert scenery and local natural surroundings. Rattlesnake Springs Picnic Area, a detached part of the park, is a natural oasis with landscaping, picnic tables, and wildlife habitats and makes a good spot for a picnic lunch after a morning of exploring the caves.

Most visitors to Carlsbad Caverns stay in Carlsbad, New Mexico, which is about 20 miles drive north from the park along US 180/62. Camping is not allowed in the park, but there are ample campsites in the surrounding mountains, as well as in the towns of Whites City and Carlsbad. In Carlsbad, you'll find a variety of cozy, suitable accommodations, such as the **Best Western Stevens Inn** (575-887-2851; www .bestwesternnewmexico.com), which offers a complimentary breakfast, cable TV, and high-speed Internet. Although there is very little of interest in Carlsbad itself, the nearby **Brantley Lake State Park** (575-457-2384; www.emnrd.state.nm.us/prd/parkspages/ brantley.htm), 12 miles north, is the largest lake in Southern New Mexico and offers a plethora of recreational water sports, fishing, and camping. Likewise, the **Living Desert Zoo and Gardens State Park** (575-887-5516; www.emnrd.state.nm.us/prd/living desert.htm), perched on a hill overlooking Carlsbad, is a Chihuahuan Desert botanical park and zoo that offers visitors a chance to see numerous animals and desert plants, including a pack of Mexican grey wolves, a black bear, deer, elk, bison, rattlesnakes, and numerous types of cactus.

For more information on other things to do in the nearby surroundings, see the section on Guadalupe Mountains National Park under "Texas Trips" later in this chapter.

Kilbourne Hole

If you are interested in prehistoric volcanoes or geology or just want to explore a piece of desert landscape, head to **Kilbourne Hole** (575-525-4300, www.blm.gov/nm/st/en/ prog/recreation/las_cruces/kilbourne_hole .html), a maar volcanic crater located 30 miles west of the Franklin Mountains in the Potrillo Volcanic Field of Doña Ana County, New Mexico. A quick day trip from El Paso, Kilbourne Hole is a rare example of volcanic action without a mountainous rim. The crater is thought to be 80,000 years old, spans a width more than a mile long, and is over 300 feet deep. Two basalt cliffs with characteristic reddish purple columns, both about 40 feet high, stand inside the crater along its northeast and southeast sides. Sand dunes rising about 100 feet above the desert floor have collected on the east side, and a dry lakebed lies on the floor of the crater. On the south rim of the crater, layers of ashfall and crumbling sediment also rise about 40 feet, creating very soft mountainous footing that will not support your weight and can be dangerous to walk on. When exploring Kilbourne Hole, it is safer to stay on the basalt cliffs and the sand dunes rather than attempting to climb around the south rim. Anyone interested in gems and minerals can pick up green olivine, a rare gemstone that is available at only a handful of places on earth, including the Red Sea and Burma. Interestingly, the Apollo astronauts used Kilbourne Hole as a training site for extraterrestrial landings in 1969. You should allot about two hours driving (round trip) and a least a couple of hours for hiking and exploring the crater.

Arriving at Kilbourne Hole can be complicated. From El Paso, drive north on I-25 and take Exit 155 (Vado), following NM 227 west for 3 miles to NM 28. Go south (left) on NM 28 for 2 miles to Doña Ana County Road (CR) B008. Go west (right) 11 miles to CR B004 and turn south (left). Drive 6.5 miles until you reach railroad tracks, turning left across the tracks. From there, turn west (right) onto CR A017 and drive for 7 miles to CR A011. Turn west (right) and proceed 8 miles to Kilbourne Hole. Kilbourne Hole is on the right, past the big tan dirt bank. It is worth noting that many of the smaller county roads here are unpaved, grated dirt roads. It is best to take a four-wheel-drive vehicle and beware of inclement weather, such as summer monsoon storms, which may cause muddy conditions. Do not drive off the roads and make sure you have plenty of gas before setting off from the I-25 exit.

There are absolutely no facilities at Kilbourne Hole, and that includes bathrooms, drinking water, and shade. Be sure to bring plenty of water and food; wear long-sleeved shirts, long pants, and sturdy walking shoes; bring a hat and sunglasses; and put on ample sunscreen. As with any outdoor exploration in the El Paso area, when hiking around Kilbourne Hole, be extra watchful of rattlesnakes and scorpions—do not wander into any small holes or caves, stay away from tall brush, and watch your footing.

Las Cruces

Las Cruces (meaning "the crosses") is the largest city in Southern New Mexico and is only about 45 miles, or 30 minutes' drive, from El Paso. Las Cruces is more of an overgrown ranching town than a hip tourist destination, but there are a few interesting historic sites around town, which all together can make for an interesting day or afternoon getaway from El Paso. Las Cruces is home to New Mexico State University, the second largest college in the state. Due to its proximity to El Paso, there is no need to stay overnight in Las Cruces, which is a good thing, as there are few upscale or boutique hotels—most are run-of-the-mill highway-side motels found along any major American interstate. To get to Las Cruces, follow I-10 north/west from downtown El Paso until you reach Las Cruces.

For a more scenic drive, follow NM 28 from Canutillo in West El Paso through the fertile, historic Mesilla Valley. About 7 miles south of Las Cruces, you'll happen upon rows and rows of perfectly spaced trees and you'll know you're getting close to **Stahmann Farms** (575-525-3470; www .stahmanns.com), a family owned and oper-ated pecan farm that has been in operation for more than 75 years. The orchard consists of 128,000 trees and in the country store you can purchase chocolates, sweets, baked goods, and, of course, fresh pecans. Tours of the orchard are given May through August.

One of the most interesting stops along this route from El Paso to Las Cruces is the town of **Old Mesilla** (www.oldmesilla.org), which played a significant role in the area's history and has a very well-preserved old town plaza. Before the Gadsden Purchase of 1846, Old Mesilla was part of Mexico and a major stop on the Chihuahua Trail. Today, the town's delightful plaza consists of very old adobe buildings that are home to art gal-leries, boutiques, and restaurants. The town's church, the **Basilica of San Albino** (575-526-9349; www.sanalbino.org), founded in 1851, sits at the north end of the plaza and is one of only two designated basilicas in the state of New Mexico (the other being St. Francis Cathedral in Santa Fe).

To get a real taste of the work ethic, culture, and way of life of Southern New Mexico, visit the **New Mexico Farm and Ranch Heritage Museum** on Dripping Springs Road (575-522-4100; www.nmfarm

andranchmuseum.org), where exhibits teach visitors about the life of early cowboys in the area, the local dairy industry, and agri-cultural heritage. Las Cruces also has a small collection of decent museums operated by the **Las Cruces Museum System** (www .las-cruces.org/museums) that include the Branigan Cultural Center, which presents exhibits about the history and cultural arts of the region, the Museum of Art, the Museum of Natural History, and the Railroad Museum, all of which are free.

If you like wine, you might want to visit the country's oldest winemaking region here. The first wines were produced in the area in 1629 when the earliest settlers arrived from Spain, and today eight wineries oper-ate vineyards and tasting rooms in and around Las Cruces, most of them located along NM 28 in the Mesilla Valley, south of the city. **La Viña Winery** (4201 South Hwy 28; 575-882-7632; www.lavinawinery.com) is the oldest winery in the area, while **Amaro Winery** (402 South Melendres St.; 575-527-5310; www.amarowinerynm.com) is one of the few wineries located in downtown Las Cruces and hosts affordable wine tastings most afternoons.

Pancho Villa State Park

About 60 miles and about two hours from El Paso sits the tiny village of Columbus, New Mexico, just along the Mexican border. There isn't a whole lot in Columbus, but for history buffs and anyone interested in early military exploits, there is a wealth of intrigue and excitement to be found. On March 9, 1916, the famous Mexican revolutionary, Francisco "Pancho" Villa, attacked the tiny border town, then home to a small military outpost, Camp Furlong. Eighteen Americans were killed in the attack, which marked the one and only ground invasion of the United States between 1812 and 1916 and prompted a follow-up punitive raid into Mexico led by General John J. Pershing. Pershing chased Pancho Villa some 500 miles into Mexico for a year afterwards, never finding him.

Pancho Villa State Park sits on the location of the original grounds of Camp Furlong and houses several buildings listed on the National Register of Historic Places that remain from the 1916 raid. These include a 1902 former U.S. Customs House, two adobe structures dating from the Camp Furlong era, and the Camp Furlong Recreation Hall. The old Customs House now houses a museum that tells the entire story, beginning with the 1910 Mexican Revolution and ending with Pershing's command of the Allied Forces when the U.S. entered World War I. Expedition-era examples of the vehicles and technology employed by Pershing and his men are scattered around the site and the Main Exhibit Hall contains a full-size replica Curtiss JN-3 "Jenny" airplane, the first plane ever to be used in a U.S. military expedition. Other antique machinery housed at the park includes a 1916 Dodge touring car, historic artifacts, military weapons and ribbons, and an armored tank.

Several buildings from the time of Pancho Villa still stand in the dusty village of Columbus, including the Hoover Hotel and a restored railroad depot.

It costs $5 per vehicle to enter Pancho Villa State Park. The Exhibit Hall is open year-round, every day 8 a.m. to 5 p.m. An adjacent campground offers picnicking, 62 electrical hookups, and numerous tenting sites, and an extensive botanical garden covering much of the site offers walking tours and houses some 30 different species of cactus. To reach the village of Columbus from El Paso, take I-10 to Artcraft Road (which turns into NM 136) until it meets NM 9. Drive west on NM 9 for about 60 miles.

For more information, call (575) 531-2711 or visit www.emnrd.state.nm.us/prd/panchovilla.htm.

Ruidoso and Cloudcroft

Outdoorsy types should consider a weekend getaway to the Ruidoso/Cloudcroft area of New Mexico. Situated about 140 miles, or 3.5 hours, north of El Paso in the Sierra Blanca mountain range of the southern Rockies, the Ruidoso area is an outdoor delight, with a plethora of mountainous activities, from skiing in the winter to hiking and mountain biking in the summer. Over the years, Ruidoso has become a kind of miniature resort town, attracting weekenders from nearby West Texas and other parts of the state. Thus have sprung up a wide variety of entertainments in the area to supplement the traditional outdoorsy stuff, from horseback riding treks to performing arts, dinner theaters, and museums.

The **Ruidoso Downs** track (575-378-4431; www.ruidownsracing.com) is a major regional horse-racing center and hosts both thoroughbred and quarter horse races, including the All American Futurity, the richest quarter horse race on earth. Gamblers can also hit the slots or bet on races at the downs' in-house casino, the **Billy the Kid Casino.**

Skiers and snowboarders can hit the slopes at **Ski Apache** (575-464-3600; www.skiapache.com), a downhill skiing and snowboarding facility located in the mountains northwest of the town of Ruidoso. Ski Apache offers 750 acres of skiable terrain, with 11 chairlifts, 55 runs, a bowl, and a terrain park. Their Snow Sports Learning

Center provides group and private lessons for beginner skiers and snowboarders, while two pro shops offer rental gear and sell high-end equipment. Several restaurants, a coffeeshop, and a bar keep two-plankers and knuckle-draggers alike full and energized for a day on the mountain.

During the summer months, the mountains around Ruidoso draw visitors for camping, hiking, mountain biking, and fishing. An online tourism guide, **Go Ruidoso** (www .goruidoso.com), provides some information about the many outdoor areas to explore around the region.

i For info about the local mountain biking trails, drop in to High Altitude (575-682-1229; www.highaltitude .org), a bike shop in nearby Cloudcroft, where you can procure among other things a free map and friendly advice about the local trails.

A variety of hotels, motels, cabins, and guesthouses are available around Ruidoso and Cloudcroft for an overnight or weekend stay, from the posh **Escape Resort at Ruidoso** (575-258-1234; www.escape ruidoso.com), which invites visitors into the lap of luxury in private, lavish casitas, to the cheap and cheerful **Comfort Inn** (575-257-2770; www.comfortinnruidoso.com), where the kids will love to play in the indoor heated pool.

To get to Ruidoso, take US 54 out of El Paso. About 15 miles past Alamogordo, go north/west on US 70 and then turn off on NM 48 to Ruidoso.

Silver City and the Gila National Forest

About three hours and 180 miles northwest of El Paso in western New Mexico lies the quaint town of Silver City and the sprawling Gila National Forest beyond. Silver City, which takes its name from its mining and prospecting heritage, is, in some ways, a little town that time forgot. The main strip of buildings in the historic downtown district appears eerily similar to what one might expect an Old West town to look like. But Silver City is no ghost town. It is home to several interesting museums, a huge art community with dozens of galleries, and a rich Native American culture with both modern Indians and the remains of ancient native cultures found among nearby ruins and petroglyph sites, as well as plenty of places to camp, hike, and fish in the Gila Wilderness. The **Silver City Museum** at 312 West Broadway just west of NM 90 (575-538-5921; www.silvercitymuseum .org) is a cozy little place to get your bearings on the local history and culture, with exhibits about the early settlement of the area and the town's mining heritage. Silver City has plenty of accommodation for visitors, including hotels, motels, B&Bs, and RV parks. The **Inn on Broadway** (866-207-7075; www.innonbroadwayweb.com) is a reconverted Queen Ann style brick-and-stucco mansion with four individually decorated period guest rooms, a library, and a big veranda that overlooks a lovely garden. The historic **Palace Hotel** (575-288-1811; www.zianet.com/palacehotel), a more reasonably priced option, was opened in 1900 and boasts opulent red carpeting, hanging chandeliers, and antique furnishings.

If the outdoors is what you're after, take several days to explore the **Gila** (pronounced "hee-la") **National Forest** (575-388-8201; www.fs.usda.gov/gila)—3.3 million acres of rugged, undeveloped terrain that contains high mountain peaks, lush valleys, cascading waterfalls, hidden hot springs, ancient cliff dwellings, deep canyons and challenging trails, three lakes, miles of streams and rivers, and, best of all, unmatched high desert scenery that can only be found in the Southwest.

Chihenne Ranch (575-743-1602; www .zianet.com/4jranch) is a working dude ranch located in the beautiful foothills of the Black Range near the Gila National Forest. Grassy open and tree-covered slopes overlook deep rocky canyons with the Cuchillo Negro creek running through the middle of the ranch. The lodge and ranch house can accommodate guests in several rooms and make for a great base from which to explore the surrounding forest, try your hand at horseback riding and other ranching activities, or just get away from it all for a few days.

The many hot springs in the Gila Wilderness are located about 40 miles north of Silver City on NM 15, not far from the Gila Cliff Dwellings Center. Several lodges have sprung up to cater to those interested in soaking, including the **Wilderness Lodge** (575-536-9749; www.gilahot.com) and **Gila Hot Springs Ranch** (575-536-9314; www .gilahotspringsranch.com), both of which offer accommodation and camping sites, as well as private spring-fed pools and jacuzzis.

To reach Silver City, follow I-10 west from El Paso to Deming, then drive north on US 180 about 50 miles to Silver City. For more information, contact the Silver City Chamber of Commerce (201 North Hudson Ave., 800-548-9378, www.silvercity.org).

Truth or Consequences

If you are looking for a place to chill out and relax under a perfect New Mexico sky while relaxing in a natural hot springs pool, or spend a day boating across blue waters, just zip up I-25 two hours north from El Paso to Truth or Consequences (www.ci.truth-or-consequences.nm.us), a sleepy little town named after a 1950s game show. T or C, as the town is commonly referred to, would have very little to recommend it if it weren't for **Elephant Butte Lake** (www.elephantbuttelake.com), a man-made reservoir that provides a wealth of water recreation for residents and annual holiday-goers. During high season, the more than 24,000 water acres of this, New Mexico's largest and most popular lake, can warm up to 70°–80°F and accommodate water craft of all types, from Jet Skis to houseboats. With full facilities, it is possible to camp on the sandy beaches at Elephant Butte or utilize the RV hookups available around the lake's shores. Other recreational facilities, including picnic areas, playgrounds, hiking trails, and a marina, are also available. A number of species of fish can be caught in the lake, including bass, carp, catfish, and walleye.

The real hidden gem of T or C, though, lies within the town itself. Once named Hot Springs, New Mexico, T or C's mineral springs are the best kept secret in the region. A number of resorts have sprung up in T or C over the past few decades catering to soakers, most of them with private, indoor jacuzzis or pools that are fed from the natural springs. For a truly fantastic soaking experience, though, check in to the **Riverbend Hot Springs Resort and Spa** (575-894-7625; www.riverbendhotsprings.com). This reconverted hostel boasts the only outdoor soaking pools in town, tucked away at the end of Austin Street in the historic downtown district. Five pools are open to guests and the public, while private hidden pools can be booked for an extra fee. The two main pools sit on a lower level overlooking the Rio Grande as it arcs southeast (from which the resort takes its name) and offer stellar views of the night sky. The rooms, which are situated in a series of one-level adobe buildings and colorfully reconverted out-buildings, are bright, cheerful, comfortable, and clean, and guests have free access to the pools throughout their stay.

Just south of Truth or Consequences is the development site for **Spaceport America** (www.spaceportamerica.com), the world's first purpose-built commercial spaceport. Although still only in the early development stages at the time of writing, it is possible to visit the Spaceport America site through a rather costly "hardhat tour," which covers some history of the area as well as a guided tour of the construction site. Tours depart from the Sierra Grande Hotel in T or C and tickets cost a whopping $59 per person (including online discount).

White Sands National Monument

Just two hours (95 miles) north of El Paso in central New Mexico lies the exotic alien landscape of **White Sands National Monument** (575-679-2599, www.nps.gov/whsa). Here, tiny granules of white gypsum powder have accumulated over millennia to form mountains of snowy sand dunes as far as the eye can see. Here and there, a lone yucca plant prickles up from the surface, providing a dot of green amid the serene, lunar landscape and overhead, the intensely blue New Mexico sky is almost as blinding as the white dunes themselves. This 275-square-mile natural wonder is the largest gypsum dune field on earth, and easily one of the most exotic and strangely beautiful spots in the Southwest.

Whether you are the outdoorsy type interested in camping and hiking amid the lunar landscape, or wish to cruise the amazing scene from the comfort of your car, there

is a way for just about anyone to enjoy White Sands. A driving loop takes passenger cars on a scenic tour of the sands, with plenty of pull-out points and picnic areas where you can get out and explore on foot. **Sand-sledding** is also a popular pastime here, where kids and families bring (or buy on-site) plastic sleds to enjoy zooming down the dunes. Plenty of hiking trails wind in and among the dunes, giving you the chance to investigate the local flora and fauna that make White Sands their home. Local guided tours are also offered, as well as nature talks, stargazing, moonlit bicycle rides, and much more.

Making the exotic landscape of White Sands National Monument even more unusual is the fact that it is situated smack dab in the middle of one of the largest military missile ranges in the United States. From time to time, roads in and out of the White Sands area are closed due to testing, and for only two days a year (first Saturdays of April and October), the White Sands Missile Range opens its doors to the public for visitation of the Trinity Site, where the first atomic bomb was tested in 1945.

i During inclement weather and during missile testing periods, portions of US 70 may be closed to the public, making it impossible to reach White Sands National Monument. Call (575) 678-1178 to find out about closures before you embark.

To reach White Sands, take I-25 north from El Paso and then head west on US 70 until you reach the entrance to the site. The park's visitor center is open 9 a.m. to 5 p.m. in the winter and until 6 p.m. in the summer, while the Dunes Drive is generally open to cars between 7 a.m. and sunset everyday.

The nearest accommodation (aside from camping) to White Sands National Monument is in the sleepy town of Alamogordo, which offers little of interest to tourists other than the **New Mexico Museum of Space History** (575-437-2840; www.nmspacemuseum.org), where visitors can learn about the history and development of outer space travel. Other accommodation can be found by retracing your steps back to Las Cruces. White Sands makes a fairly easy day trip from El Paso, however, so no accommodation should be needed.

TEXAS TRIPS

El Paso opens onto the great state of Texas like a river mouth onto an ocean. Texas is so large that it is nearly impossible to drive across it in one day, and exploring all of its nooks and crannies would take a lifetime. Nonetheless, the wild, flat landscape of dusty West Texas offers some truly unique opportunities to explore the true American West. Here, oil rigs bob up and down with comforting regularity and cows chew absent mindedly on spittly grass. From El Paso, Guadalupe Mountains National Park is only a few hours' drive, while it is possible to reach the expansive Big Bend National Park in a weekend.

Big Bend National Park

Although a bit further afield than a typical day trip, Big Bend National Park (www.nps.gov/bibe, www.visitbigbend.org) is a true Texas treasure and is within a few hours driving from El Paso. It could easily be planned for a long weekend trip over three or four days, which would allow plenty of time to see and experience all of the natural wonders unique to Big Bend.

Comprising more than 800,000 acres, Big Bend is the largest protected area of the Chihuahua Desert in the U.S. It also contains 118 miles of international boundary with Mexico along the Rio Grande, which flows through the southern part of the park. There are countless corners of this vast desert wilderness to explore, from mountain peaks to sand dunes and colorful canyons. Camping, river rafting, horseback riding, boating, hiking, scenic drives, nature walks, off roading, mountain biking, bird-watching, fossil-hunting, and exploration of prehistoric Native American settlements are just some of the activities and treasures to be found inside Big Bend. There are even two golf courses situated very near to the park, and a real ghost town is just a few miles away.

In addition to a variety of campsites around the park, there are also several lodging options, both within the park itself and outside its borders in the nearby communities. **Chisos Mountain Lodge** (877-386-4383; www.chisosmountainslodge.com) is the only accommodation located inside Big Bend National Park. Set high in the scenic Chisos Mountains, the lodge offers comfortable overnight lodging all year in 72 non-smoking rooms, food service, a convenience store, gift shop, trail heads, and other guest services. They have a variety of different types of rooms, from luxury stone cottages to basic and affordable motel-style accommodation. The lodge is also home to the only full-service dining room inside Big Bend.

Big Bend is relatively quiet for much of the year. Visitation is highest in March and April and the park can be very crowded during spring break, which is usually the second or third week in March. Holiday weekends, such as Easter, Thanksgiving, Christmas, and New Year's, are also very busy. The best time of year to visit is in August and September when there are relatively few visitors and you'll have the park mostly to yourself, as well as your pick of campsites and rooms. The park is open 24 hours a day all year. The Panther Junction Visitor Center is open 8 a.m. to 6 p.m. every day except Christmas Day. The entrance stations and other visitor centers have variable seasons and hours.

To get to Big Bend from El Paso, drive southeast on I-10 to Fort Stockton and then follow US 385 south to the park. There is absolutely no public transportation to or in Big Bend National Park, so you will either need your own car or a rental vehicle to get there. Always be sure to keep your gas tank full, as the park is in a very remote area and the distances between towns and gas stations can sometimes be surprising.

i The U.S. National Parks Service offers several types of annual passes that permit entry into every national park in the United States. The pass admits the holder and any passengers in a non-commercial vehicle at per-vehicle fee areas, or the holder along with up to three other adults, at per-person fee areas. Passes can be obtained for any park by calling (888) ASK-USGS, ext. 1, or online at: http://store.usgs.gov/pass.

Guadalupe Mountains National Park

Guadalupe Mountains National Park, which is about 3.5 hours (100 miles) east of El Paso, is a must-visit spot for nature lovers and anyone looking to escape the city heat of El Paso for a long weekend. This trip should ideally be planned in conjunction with a visit to Carlsbad Caverns, New Mexico, which is only about 40 miles north in the Lincoln National Forest in New Mexico. There is no lodging available in Guadalupe Mountains National Park aside from several designated camping areas, so if you don't want to tent down for the night, you should plan to stay in Whites City, New Mexico, or Carlsbad, New Mexico, near the Caverns.

The Guadalupe Mountains are a treasure trove of beautiful flora and interesting animal life, as well as scenic canyons and breathtaking views. The park is a great place to get away and unwind from the stresses of work or school, to go hiking, fishing, camping, and backpacking. Thousands of visitors take advantage of the solace and beauty on offer in the Guadalupe Mountains each year. The best time to visit is in the fall—September or October—when the leaves begin to change and autumnal colors splash across the canyon walls, bringing the forest to life with blazing oranges, reds, and yellows.

There are several areas of the Guadalupe Mountains open for visitors to explore. **Campgrounds at Dog Canyon and Pine Springs** (near the Headquarters Visitor Center) provide tent sites and RV hookups. Over 80 miles of backpacking and 10 backcountry campgrounds exist within the park, catering to both serious hikers and those just out for a few hours of sunshine. Most of the trails, which can be rocky, steep, and rugged, eventually lead up to **Guadalupe Peak,** the base of El Capitan, up into the high country, and into **McKittrick Canyon.** Self-guided nature trails are located at McKittrick Canyon (McKittrick Canyon Nature Trail), at the **Headquarters Visitor Center** (Pinery Trail), and at **Dog Canyon** (Indian Meadow Trail). Visitors can also bring in their own horses or livestock for riding and packing within the park, and stock corrals are available at both Dog Canyon and Frijole Ranch.

The Headquarters Visitor Center at Pine Springs is accessed via US 62/180 between El Paso and Carlsbad, New Mexico. Here, you can pick up trail maps, find out the latest conditions, pay entrance fees, and obtain any backcountry permits. Dog Canyon, on the park's north side, is accessed via NM 137. The park is open year-round. The Headquarters Visitor Center hours are 8 a.m. to 4:30 p.m. daily (slightly longer during the summer) and it is closed on Christmas Day. McKittrick Canyon is a day-use area; the gate at the highway is open from 8 a.m. to 4:30 p.m., and until 6 p.m. during daylight savings time.

Appendix

LIVING HERE

In this section we feature specific information for residents or those planning to
relocate here. Topics include real estate,
education, health care, and much more.

RELOCATION

Congratulations on your decision to move to El Paso. It is a beautiful, urban metro area with all the delights of city living surrounded by the vast and incomprehensible beauty of the Southwest. Open desert meets mountains that provide the backdrop to El Paso's unique skyline, creating an ambiance unlike anywhere else in Texas. The history of the area, too, is a mix of revolutionary intrigue, outlaws, and cowboys that dates back to decades before the first pilgrims arrived on the East Coast.

Beyond its physical beauty, El Paso is both an entertaining city and an easy place to live. The sun shines for more than 300 days a year and outdoor activities abound. Taxes here are lower than in much of the rest of the country, as residents of Texas pay no state personal income tax and the local sales tax lingers at a gentle 8.25 percent. El Paso is also consistently ranked as one of the safest cities in the United States. The school systems in El Paso are excellent, with many magnet programs attracting high school students to specialized programs of study. The University of Texas at El Paso provides the crux of higher education to the region.

It is also a growing city with a low cost of living. The Eastside and Westside accounted for the majority of the city's growth over the past decade. Most of the city's expensive and newer homes are located on the Westside, going for $190,000 and up, while the Eastside is the next most expensive area and the part of El Paso that is seeing the most expansion in new homes and suburban sprawl. The most affordable and historic homes are located in the Central, Lower Valley, and Northeast areas of El Paso, with particularly inexpensive homes available in and around Fort Bliss.

Much of the relocation to El Paso is thanks to the Fort Bliss Military Reservation, which is a huge swath of land in the northeast part of the city. Hundreds of military personnel and their families are stationed at Fort Bliss each year and a significant number of posts also come from abroad, factors which, combined with El Paso's significant Hispanic population (more then 50 percent), make the city an extremely diverse place. Retirees are also drawn to El Paso. Whatever your reason for moving to El Paso, you will find life here to be easy and comfortable. Welcome to the Sun City!

OVERVIEW

This chapter is divided into several sections designed to orient you when you first arrive in El Paso, as well as help you begin your search for a home, whether it be a cozy downtown apartment or a comfy suburban house. Listings for the Chamber of Commerce and the El Paso Convention and Visitor's Bureau will give you a basic set of information about the city, while contact information about the local association of realtors can start you on the way to buying a home, should you so desire. Also included are the phone numbers and Web sites for utilities hookups, including water, gas, and electric, so that once you do move into your new abode, you will be able to get connected with ease. Descriptions are also included of El Paso's main neighborhoods to help you decipher which part of the city you want to call home. Here you'll also find information about getting your vehicle inspected and registered and applying for a local driver's license, as well as registering to vote and going to the library.

INFO FOR NEWCOMERS
Chambers of Commerce and Visitor's Bureaus

Both the Greater El Paso Chamber of Commerce and the El Paso Convention and Visitor's Bureau (CVB) can provide useful information about visiting the city and doing business here, but both are aimed primarily at attracting conventions and businesses to the city, rather than providing useful day-to-day information to newly relocated people. The El Paso CVB puts out a glossy magazine mentioning some of the main attractions and places to eat around the city, many of which are covered in this book. It is useful to keep in mind that, in most CVB and Chamber publications, ad space is purchased, so the listings provided are more like advertisements than recommendations. By visiting the El Paso CVB's Web site or their offices downtown, you can obtain a copy of their visitor's packet, which contains the glossy magazine, as well as some basic information about coming and going from El Paso and setting up conventions and businesses here.

EL PASO CONVENTION AND VISITOR'S BUREAU
1 Civic Center Plaza
(915) 534-0600
www.elpasocvb.com

EL PASO HISPANIC CHAMBER OF COMMERCE
2401 East Missouri
(915) 566-4066
www.ephcc.org

GREATER EL PASO CHAMBER OF COMMERCE
10 Civic Center Plaza
(915) 534-0500
www.elpaso.org

Metro Government

CITY OF EL PASO
2 Civic Center Plaza
(915) 541-4000
www.ci.el-paso.tx.us
The city of El Paso maintains a huge, though sometimes difficult-to-navigate, Web site with just about every bit of information you could want to find. If you are newly relocated, you might find yourself in a tizzy about where on the Web site to find the information that you're looking for and it may be more useful simply to call their information line than waste time perusing the site. That said, there is plenty of up-front information to be had on the Web site, including bus timetables and schedules, live traffic information, a city calendar, and public notices. You can also find a handy taxpayer's guide, as well as information about health and social services, should you need them.

Department of Motor Vehicles

Driver's License

Drivers are required to obtain a Texas driver's license within 90 days of arrival in the state. If you've never had a driver's license before and would like to get one, you will need to pass both a written and road test, and a vision test, and present two proofs of ID (including one proof of Social Security Number) in person at an El Paso Driver's License Office. If you are new to Texas and have a driver's license from another state, you can simply go to a driver's license office and present your out-of-state license, along with another proof of ID and proof of address, and you will be issued a Texas license. If you have a vehicle, you will also need to show proof of vehicle registration and insurance.

Driver's between the ages of 16 and 18 who have an out-of-state license can exchange it for a Texas license, but must show the aforementioned proofs of address, plus proof of a driver's education course. Young drivers who have never been licensed in Texas may apply for a "Hardship License," otherwise known as a Minor's Restricted Driver's License. This applies to teen drivers between the ages of 15 and 18 and is essentially the same as a regular driver's license, but requires a parental or guardian signature on the form.

The good news is that fees for driver's licenses in the state of Texas are relatively cheap: $24 for a new or renewal license lasting six years and $5 for a Minor/Hardship license. You can also renew your license online if you have a clean driving record and a credit card.

Vehicle Registration and Inspection
EL PASO COUNTY TAX OFFICE
500 East Overland Ave., Suite 101
(915) 546-2140
www.txdmv.gov

El Paso Driver's License Offices

All of El Paso's driver's license offices operate extended hours on Thursday from 7 a.m. to 6 p.m., and the Gateway office uses these hours Monday through Friday. For more information, check out www.txdmv.gov.

Gateway
7300 Gateway East
(915) 598-3487

Hondo Pass
4505 Hondo Pass
(915) 751-6455

Scott Simpson
11612 Scott Simpson Dr.
(915) 849-4100

Northwest
1854 Northwestern
(915) 877-1647

Within 30 days of arriving in Texas, new residents are required to have their vehicles inspected, as well as registering their vehicles in Texas. Vehicle inspection is a process of emissions and road safety checks on your car, motorcycle, or trailer, and is performed at any number of licensed inspection stations. These include auto repair shops and tire stores and there are literally dozens of locations across El Paso where you can take care of this simple process.

After your vehicle has been inspected, take the certificate of inspection, along with your proof of liability insurance and either your out-of-state registration or title to the El Paso County Tax Office to register it. There are a number of different fees associated with this process, including a registration fee, new resident tax, and title application fee, which together can add up to $150 or more.

ℹ To find the vehicle inspection station nearest you, visit the following Web site: www.txdps.state.tx.us/vi/inspection/new_locator.asp and enter your home zip code.

Voter Registration

It is a good idea for new residents to register to vote when they arrive in Texas. Even if you are registered in your previous state or city, re-registering in El Paso will allow you to participate in not only national elections, but local elections which can affect issues related to your neighborhood, school district, parks, and more.

Registering to vote in Texas is a relatively simple process. You can pick up a voter registration form from any post office in El Paso, or conversely fill one out online (www.sos .state.tx.us/elections/voter), print it, and mail it in. Your voter registration card will arrive in the mail a few weeks later and you should carry it with you as proof of registration to any election in which you plan to vote. To be eligible to register, you must be a U.S. citizen, 18 years of age, a resident of El Paso County, not a convicted felon (unless the sentence is complete), and not declared mentally incapacitated by law. Minors may submit their forms at 17 years and 10 months of age to be legally ready for voting by the time they reach 18. If you are already registered to vote in the state of Texas, you may submit a change of address online by visiting the Web site www.sos.state.tx.us/elections/voter and clicking "Change your name or address online."

Quick Utility Contacts

Electricity
El Paso Electric
(915) 543-5970
www.epelectric.com

Water
El Paso Water Utilities
(915) 594-5500
www.epwu.org

Natural Gas
Texas Gas Service
(915) 562-8411
www.texasgasservice.com

Cable and Internet
Time Warner Communications
(915) 772-4422
www.timewarnercable.com

Phone
Southwestern Bell/AT&T
(800) 464-7928
www.att.com

Trash Collection
Environmental Services
(915) 621-6700
www.ci.el-paso.tx.us/
environmental_services

Libraries

El Paso has an excellent library system that not only is home to thousands of books and research materials, but also plays host to a wide array of services and events, from children's story hours to art and literature festivals, lectures, exhibitions, and much more. There are 14 branches of the El Paso Public Library (EPPL) across the city, including three on the Westside, four in the Downtown and

Central areas, a handful on the Eastside, and one in the far Northeast, so you are sure to find a library nearby when you need one.

It isn't difficult to get a lending card. You will need to bring a picture ID and a proof of residence, such as a utility bill or bank statement showing your home address, to any branch and fill out an application form. Library cards are free of charge to all local residents and allow you to check out as many books as you would like for up to three weeks, as well as an assortment of CDs, DVDs, pamphlets, and kits. Most of El Paso's libraries also have research materials that may be used on-site but not checked out, so check with the local librarian if you are unsure about checking out the materials you need.

If you are only living in El Paso for a short time, you may apply for a temporary three-month library card by presenting an ID card including picture and permanent address, as well as proof of your local address, such as a bank statement or utility bill.

i Adults who wish to apply for an El Paso Public Library card but cannot present in person to the library should contact the Dial-A-Book Coordinator at (915) 543-5433 for assistance on obtaining a card.

RENTING AND APARTMENTS

These days, the best way to go about finding a rental apartment or home is to get online. There are plenty of Web sites with information about apartments and houses for rent around El Paso, from corporate apartment complexes to privately rented houses. **Apartment Guide** (www.apartmentguide.com) and **Apartment Finder** (www.apartmentfinder.com) are two

good Web sites to start with, especially if you are looking for an apartment in a large complex with plenty of amenities. If you are interested in a privately rented or more unique apartment or house, your best bet is to try **El Paso Craigslist** (http://elpaso.craigslist.org), but be aware that Craigslist is a known haven of scammers, so never divulge your personal information unless you are absolutely sure that the recipient is legitimate. The best bet is to make an appointment for a viewing via e-mail and be sure that you are given the address or general area upfront.

The newspaper is another good source for individual rentals. The *El Paso Times* usually has classifieds listings for apartments and houses for rent, often with the address included so you can do a preliminary drive-by to decide if you're interested. Another good source of rental listings is the UTEP paper, **The Prospector,** which can be picked up around the UTEP campus or viewed online at www.utepprospector.com. Most of these properties are geared toward students and are located in and around the UTEP area.

RENT NOW
www.elpasorentnow.com
This 100-plus-page glossy booklet contains listings for various apartment complexes around El Paso. The listings are organized by area of the city, which can help if you know more or less where you'd like to live but aren't sure what is available in that area. Most of the listings in *Rent Now* are large apartment complexes with multiple units, swimming pools, fitness facilities, and more. The advantage to using *Rent Now* is that it shows photos for every complex, lists starting rental costs for most units, and also gives you a list of amenities for each complex. If you are looking for a more unique or stand-

El Paso Public Library Branches

Central
Armijo
620 East 7th
(915) 533-1333

Clardy Fox
5515 Roberta Alva
(915) 772-0501

Main (Downtown)
501 North Oregon
(915) 543-5401

Memorial Park
3200 Copper
(915) 566-1034

Eastside
Cielo Vista
Under construction at the time of this
books' printing
Hawkins Blvd. at Vista del Valle Park
(915) 591-5812

Esperanza Acosta Moreno
12480 Pebble Hills
(915) 921-7001

Irving Schwartu
1865 Dean Martin
(915) 857-0594

Judge Marquez
610 North Yarbrough
(915) 591-3391

Ysleta
9321 Alameda
(915) 858-0905

Northeast
Richard Burges
9600 Dyer
(915) 759-2400

Westside
Doris Van Dor3en
551 Redd Rd.
(915) 875-0700

Jenna Welch & Laura Bush
Community Library
El Paso Community College NW Campus
6701 South Desert Blvd.
(915) 831 8840

Westside
125 Belvidere
(915) 581-2024

alone apartment or house, or a loft, then you probably won't find *Rent Now* to be that useful. However, it is a good starting place to get an idea of what's for rent in El Paso and it is available for free all over the place—a good place to find it is on small racks in gas stations.

i Renting-to-own can be a great way to get a head start on owning your own home. The Web site www .elpaso.irenttoown.com can help you do this, with listings by price, number of bedrooms, and area.

Realtors

GREATER EL PASO ASSOCIATION OF REALTORS
6400 Gateway East
(915) 779-3521
www.elpasorealtor.com
Buying a home in a new area can be exhausting and stressful work, especially if you are unfamiliar with the local market and surroundings. There are dozens of respectable, licensed Realtors in El Paso, so the best place to start in finding the one that fits your needs is through the Greater El

Paso Association of Realtors (GEPAR). This locally elected member board is part of the National Association of Realtors and only licensed member Realtors with the highest standards of business conduct are allowed to join. These are not just real estate agents, but top-notch, certified Realtors that really know El Paso and can guide you on your search for a home. GEPAR's Web site offers a wonderful selection of tools to help El Paso homebuyers commence their searches, including a home search tool and a search function for finding a Realtor. Here, you can browse through listings of realtors by name and keyword, see their photos, visit their Web sites, and read their bios. The property search tool allows you to find residential, commercial, and land/farm properties based on price, locale, year built, and a variety of building features (such as number of bedrooms, bathrooms, etc).

RETIREMENT

Over the past several decades, El Paso has grown in popularity as a retirement destination and is a popular place to live for the over-50 set. For reasons similar to Florida, Arizona, and New Mexico, retirees and seniors flock to El Paso for its sunny weather, abundance of outdoor activities such as golf and tennis, and the many resources for seniors that the city has to offer.

There are a number of services and organizations that offer help and organize activities for seniors and retirees. The City of El Paso's host of programs on that front include the Senior Library Web page and activities at the public libraries, the Foster Grandparent Program, and the Retired and Senior Volunteer Program. There are countless housing and care options around the city, as well, from independent living communities to homecare and full assisted living centers and nursing homes. The incredible healthcare network in El Paso, too, is a valuable resource for seniors who may be concerned about health care or hospital facilities.

This chapter is a good starting point for seniors thinking of moving to El Paso or those who will be spending a significant period of time holidaying here. Listed below is the contact information for a number of services and organizations geared toward seniors, a sampling of retirement communities on offer in El Paso, opportunities for volunteering in the Sun City, and information on El Paso's senior meal program.

SERVICES AND ORGANIZATIONS

AARP INFORMATION CENTER
8900 Viscount Blvd.
(915) 595-9841
www.aarp.org
AARP provides information on health, money, work, personal growth, and more. Members qualify for a variety of special discounts at participating companies. See the Web site for details and how to become a member.

AREA AGENCY ON AGING
1100 North Stanton St., # 610
www.riocog.org/AAA/AAA.htm
(915) 533-0998
The Rio Grande Council of Governments/ Area Agency on Aging (AAA) is one of 28 in the State of Texas. It acts as an advocate for systems integration and access, to consolidate regional planning of aging issues, and for quality of life issues in nursing facilities and in the community.

i The *Golden Pages Senior Services Directory* has a comprehensive listing of businesses and services of interest to El Paso seniors. The electronic version is available online at www.riocog.org/goldpages.html.

EL PASO LIBRARY SENIORS
www.ci.el-paso.tx.us/library/seniors.asp
El Paso Public Library operates many activities and events for seniors across the city. On its

Seniors Web site you can find information on the services the library offers, travel and leisure tips and links, retirement planners, health, and consumer information. Inside any El Paso library, access the "Golden Years" pathfinder for a list of senior-related topics and books.

JUST 4 SENIORS
2 Civic Center Plaza
(915) 541-4000
www.ci.el-paso.tx.us/seniors.asp
Just 4 Seniors is the City of El Paso's guide to senior services within the Sun City. Find information on everything from city transportation, public libraries, and volunteering to disabled discounts, peer counseling, and the local buddy system.

RED HAT SOCIETY
(866) 386-2850
www.redhatsociety.org
This fun-loving yet secretive women's group operates some 20 branches in the El Paso area. They believe silliness is the comic relief of life and proudly claim that members share a bond of affection, forged by common life experiences and a genuine enthusiasm for whatever life has in store. To find or join a local chapter, you must call or go online.

HOUSING

COMFORT KEEPERS
5927 Gateway Blvd. West
(915) 842-8195
www.comfortkeepers.com
This in-home senior care service provides assistance to seniors who could benefit from a regular caregiver but desire to continue living at home. Comfort Keepers services include individual treatment, medication reminders, cooking and meal prep, transpor-

tation, and housekeeping, and all nurses and staff provide the further comfort of chat and friendship to theirsekeeping.

EMERITUS AT DESERT SPRINGS
5901 Bandolero Dr.
(915) 842-0900
www.emeritus.com
This retirement facility is situated in a scenic rural area on the edge of the Franklin Mountains and specializes in assisted living and Alzheimer's care. They offer everything from in-depth dementia-related care to casual day programs for active seniors. Thirty apartment suites are available to individuals who need regular assistance but don't wish to give up a private residence.

THE MONTEVISA AT CORONADO
1575 Belvidere
(915) 833-2229
www.themontevistaseniorliving.com
This is an elegant retirement community with trained nursing and rehabilitation services, located in a charming setting near the Franklin Mountains, offering both independent living and skilled health care options.

MOUNTAIN VIEW HEALTHCARE CENTER
1600 Murchison Rd.
(915) 544-2002
www.mountainviewhcc.com
The dedicated and highly trained staff of this 182-bed skilled nursing and long-term care facility provides specialized short-term rehabilitation and skilled nursing care in a compassionate, patient-centered environment. They offer everything from basic medication administration to recreational outings, a barber and beauty shop, and religious services to cater to the needs of residents.

RIO NORTE
1941 Saul Kleinfeld Dr.
(915) 613-3714
www.holidaytouch.com/rio-norte
Touting itself as a "holiday retirement community," Rio Norte is part of the Holiday Touch Retirement network. They offer a unique approach to retirement services, emphasizing an active lifestyle for retired seniors that includes many activities such as Tai Chi, bean bag baseball, and even video games. Their extensive travel network allows residents with the travel bug to stay for free in dozens of locations and their award-winning chefs go above and beyond in preparing healthy and tasty meals. Studios and one- and two-bedroom apartments are available.

i Senior Transitions is a Texas referral service that connects seniors with appropriate housing communities, whether assisted living centers or independent retirement communities. Call (866) 353-5337 or visit www.senior community.net.

NUTRITION

BATEMAN SENIOR MEALS
2215 Murchison Dr.
(915) 351-1174
From basic day meals and lunches to event catering, Bateman Senior Meals covers a wide spectrum of nutrional offerings for seniors and senior-related activities in El Paso. All of Bateman's meals are prepared according to exact specifications and dietary needs under strict sanitary conditions. They offer a customizable delivery system and a huge database of meal options with all types of recipes. A second and third location are at 600 South Ochoa St. (915-351-0646), and 840 Hawkins Blvd., #A15 (915-778-4393).

Health Associations and Foundations

Alzheimer's Association
(STAR Chapter, El Paso)
4687 North Mesa, Suite 200
(915) 544-1799

American Diabetes Association
(800) 342-2383

Arthritis Foundation
(Greater Southwest Chapter)
(800) 477-7679

El Paso Parkinson
Sierra Medical Center
(915) 592-9568

HOPE Parkinson Support Group
Highland Regional Rehabilitation
(915) 851-4054

Lupus Foundation of America
(El Paso Branch)
(800) 458-7870

Texas Health Care Association
(512) 458-1257

SENIOR CENTERS

The nine senior centers around El Paso are operated by the City of El Paso Parks & Recreation department. These senior centers offer a variety of activities, classes, and groups in which active seniors can partake for a small monthly fee. Many are also free. Father Martinez Senior Center offers dance classes and a gem and mineral society is active at the Memorial Senior Center, while Eastside and Hilos de Plata Senior Centers have active choirs. Other activities on offer range from ceramics classes to bridge groups and painting workshops. The best way to find out about what is currently on offer is to contact

LIVING HERE

the senior center nearest you individually or visit www.elpasotexas.gov/parks.

EASTSIDE
3200 Fierro
(915) 591-4292

FATHER MARTINEZ
9311 Alameda
(915) 860-9131

GRANDVIEW PARK
3134 Jefferson St.
(915) 566-1217

HILOS DE PLATA
4451 Delta St.
(915) 591-4292

MEMORIAL PARK
1800 Byron St.
(915) 562-4260

POLLY HARRIS
650 Wallenberg St.
(915) 581-9525

SAN JUAN
5701 Tamburo Court
(915) 772-8365

i The *El Paso Times* Senior Fund Program provides once-a-year monetary assistance for El Paso County residents 60 years of age and older to obtain a variety of services, including dental, vision, and hearing care, a medication supplement, minor home repairs, and some transportation. For more information call (915) 533-0998.

SOUTH EL PASO
600 South Ochoa St.
(915) 577-9870

WELLINGTON CHEW
4430 Maxwell St.
(915) 757-2523

VOLUNTEERING

Seniors who are interested in volunteering in El Paso can find help from the organizations listed below. They can place seniors in active volunteering roles, whether working with children or sharing their lifetime of experience through community service.

i Want to read up-to-date news about senior topics in El Paso? Pick up a copy of *Southwest Senior,* the area's seniors-only newspaper aimed at the Baby Boomer generation and older. You can find copies at local El Paso Public Libraries and many local businesses, as well as online at www.southwest senior.com.

FOSTER GRANDPARENT PROGRAM
(915) 541-4379
www.elpasotexas.gov/commdev/fgp.asp

RETIRED AND SENIOR VOLUNTEER PROGRAM (RSVP)
(915) 541-4374
www.elpasotexas.gov/commdev/rsvp.asp

SENIOR CORPS
(800) 424-8867
www.seniorcorps.gov

EDUCATION AND CHILD CARE

Education arrived in El Paso fairly late in its history. For decades after the area was founded, it was simply an outpost, an army base, the Wild West. Although a basic school system was instituted in 1803, when El Paso was still part of Mexico, the public school system as it exists today was not founded until 1883, exactly 80 years later. The coming of the railroad in 1881 brought with it a huge population surge and a connection between El Paso and the outside world to Texas and beyond. It was at that time that a school board was elected and, a year later in 1884, Central School, El Paso's first educational institution, was finally opened in a small adobe building at the corner of Myrtle and Campbell streets. Interestingly, El Paso school district was the first in Texas to desegregate unconditionally, and the University of Texas at El Paso (UTEP), then called Texas Western, admitted Thema White, its first black student, in 1955.

Today, El Paso has a string of excellent public schools and many options for higher education. The city has one of the most highly educated Hispanic populations in the United States, with UTEP being nearly 75 percent Hispanic and the only major doctoral research university in the U.S. with a predominantly Hispanic student body. In El Paso's elementary and public schools, bilingual education is common and there are many opportunities for El Paso students to study and learn about the Borderlands' unique cultural heritage. A wealth of private schools, many of them religious schools or strong scholastic institutions, support the excellent public school system, in case you would like to incorporate an element of faith or academic rigor into your child's education. There is no shortage of higher education options in El Paso, either, from excellent four-year degree-granting universities to short-term training institutes where students can increase their computer and technical skills quickly. In this chapter, you will find information about all of these options to help you make the best choice about which school your child should attend. If you have young children, the end of the chapter presents a short sampling of the hundreds of daycare options available for busy parents in the Sun City.

HIGHER EDUCATION

Four major institutions of higher learning are located in the El Paso region offering undergraduate and graduate degrees in engineering, business, science, education, health sciences, and liberal arts; and associate degrees and certificate programs in technology. The University of Texas at El Paso (UTEP) prides itself on its status as the only major research university in the country with the majority of its students being predominately Hispanic. Established in 1969, El Paso Community College (EPCC) has five campuses throughout El Paso and educates around 28,000 students each semester. Other regional educational institutions include Howard Payne University's extension campus and Texas Tech University's College of Architecture and its Health Sciences Center at El Paso, which confers degrees in medicine, nursing, pharmacy, and biomedical and allied health sciences. A handful of other technical institutes educate El Pasoans in vocational and technological fields. The result is a highly educated El Paso population, most of which are of Hispanic descent, creating a truly unique educational atmosphere for the border region.

Colleges and Universities

DOÑA ANA COMMUNITY COLLEGE
www.dabcc.nmsu.edu
Doña Ana Community College (DACC), part of the New Mexico State University system, operates two colleges in the southern portion of Doña Ana County, New Mexico, near El Paso: Gadsden Center (1700 East O'Hara Rd., 505-882-3939) in Anthony and Sunland Park Center (3365 McNutt Rd., 505-874-7780) in Sunland Park. Both offer freshman- and sophomore-level coursework in vocational, technical, developmental, and general education, as well as associate's degrees in Arts, Criminal Justice, and Pre-Business. The centers also provide concurrent enrollment programming for the Gadsden School District and Customized Training and Community Education courses. ESL, GED, and citizenship classes for the border area are available through the Adult Basic Education program. Classes are scheduled in the afternoon and the evening to meet the needs of the local community.

EL PASO COMMUNITY COLLEGE
(915) 831-3722
www.epcc.edu
With 130 academic programs and 350 enrichment and continuing education courses, El Paso Community College (EPCC) is the fastest growing community college in the state of Texas. On five modern campuses, students can enroll in technology training programs or earn two-year associate's degrees in a variety of course subjects, from sciences to liberal arts. All of EPCC's campuses feature cutting-edge technology, modern training facilities, and innovative learning options. The Early College High School program gives returning or advanced secondary school students the unique chance to earn an associate's degree at the same time they are earning a high school diploma. More than 24,000 credit students and 8,000 non-credit students attend EPCC, many of them taking advantage of the Continuing Education and Workforce Development program, which offers alternative non-credit classes, vocational training, business programs, career development courses, health occupation certification courses, kid and teen interest classes, business service resources, personal enrichment, and online education.

HOWARD PAYNE UNIVERSITY—
EL PASO CENTER
1201 Hawkins Blvd.
(915) 778-4815
www.hputx.edu
Howard Payne University (HPU) is a Baptist liberal arts college that awards pre-professional and professional degrees in a Christian context. The El Paso campus is one of HPU's Extension Centers, open since 1991,

which meet the needs of non-traditional students who desire further educational experiences but are unable to attend classes at the main campus in Brownwood, Texas. The El Paso Center began as an extension of the School of Christian Studies to offer academic coursework and training for those preparing for vocational ministry. HPU's El Paso Center has since broadened its course offerings to include majors in Business Management and Criminal Justice. The El Paso Center holds three academic sessions per year with around 30 different course offerings. Fall and spring semesters are 16 weeks in length with each class meeting once a week. Classes are offered weekday evenings and Saturday mornings. The summer session is about eight weeks long with each class meeting twice per week. The very small campus is located across from the Cielo Vista Mall in northeast El Paso.

PARK UNIVERSITY: FORT BLISS
CAMPUS
639 Merritt Rd.
(915) 562-0450
www.park.edu/ftbl
Park University on Fort Bliss is a military college that specializes in high-quality educational services that allow working adults and military service personnel to earn a college degree. Park University is open to both military members and their dependents assigned to Fort Bliss, as well as all civilians from El Paso. Park University's goal is to make earning a degree easy and inexpensive, even while working full-time and juggling family responsibilities. Park therefore offers more choices of class times and plenty of online study options. An accelerated semester schedule allows students in a hurry to complete their degrees quickly, and financial aid is also available to help shoulder

the cost of higher education. Over 21,000 students annually take advantage of Park's undergraduate and graduate programs across the country. Their extensive distance learning program consists of two schools—the School for Extended Learning, which offers a combination of on-site and classroom studies, and the School for Online Learning.

TEXAS TECH COLLEGE OF
ARCHITECTURE AT EL PASO
(806) 742-3136
www.arch.ttu.edu
The College of Architecture (CoA) at Texas Tech University in Lubbock has partnered with El Paso Community College (EPCC) to offer third- and fourth-year classes in El Paso to students who have completed their associate's degree in architecture, resulting in a pre-professional bachelor of science degree. The classes are taught in facilities on the El Paso Community College campus. The CoA's expansion in El Paso reinforces the desire for community-engaged architecture, culturally sensitive urban design, and culturally responsive planning, which demands sophisticated professionals that represent all the cultures that make up the community. El Paso's largely Hispanic population aids the program in promoting a multicultural education for future architects in Texas. Those interested in attending the program should contact Texas Tech University in Lubbock.

TEXAS TECH UNIVERSITY HEALTH
SCIENCES CENTER
Paul L. Foster School of Medicine
4800 Alberta Ave.
(915) 545-6703
www.ttuhsc.edu/elpaso

Texas Tech University Health Sciences Center (TTUHSC) at El Paso offers students and residents a rich learning environment. Since 1973, TTUHSC students have gained experience in infectious disease, diabetes, migrant health, and community-oriented primary care. Through community partnerships, TTUHSC at El Paso faculty also lend their skills to underserved areas lacking adequate health care. Third- and fourth-year medical students currently train at the El Paso campus, along with residents in eight accredited programs. Texas Tech El Paso has played a vital role in El Paso's health care history. It has been the academic home to many outstanding medical students, residents, and faculty. In 1969, the 61st Texas Legislature gave approval for a School of Medicine in West Texas and in 1973, the Regional Academic Health Center in El Paso, now known as TTUHSC, officially opened with a teaching affiliation with R. E. Thomason General Hospital, accepting the entire medical school class for the first five years. Today, Texas Tech El Paso has close to 1,000 faculty and staff members and is a flourishing health sciences center and medical center with clinics located in east, west, central, and northeast El Paso.

**THE UNIVERSITY OF TEXAS
AT EL PASO (UTEP)**
500 West University Ave.
(915) 747-5000
www.utep.edu
The University of Texas at El Paso (UTEP) is a public university and a recognized affiliate of the University of Texas system, with an enrollment of more than 21,000 students. UTEP celebrated its 90th birthday in 2004, from humble beginnings in 1914 as Texas's first mining school. Student life at UTEP is dynamic, with more than 170 organizations ranging from academic and professional to social and service groups. The sprawling campus sits on 366 acres in central El Paso and boasts a unique Bhutanese architectural style that creates an academic, scholarly feel about the campus.

UTEP ranks second in the nation of schools awarding undergraduate degrees to Hispanics and combines academic research with innovative programs and services and an outstanding faculty. UTEP has been an important part of the El Paso community since it was founded as the Texas School of Mines and Metallurgy in 1914. The school opened with 27 students and a handful of faculty and staff. Now, more than 75 percent of UTEP's student population is of Hispanic descent, and it is also well known for its science, computer science, engineering, and mathematics programs. UTEP ranks among the top 7 percent of all U.S. universities in the Carnegie Foundation's Doctoral/Research University-Intensive category. In addition to the 81 undergraduate degrees and 65 master's degrees on offer, UTEP boasts 16 doctoral degree programs and much of the faculty research that goes on at UTEP focuses on areas such as environmental science and engineering, Borderlands history, and manufacturing engineering. Because of the university's strategic location, UTEP students also have many opportunities to participate in binational research programs between UTEP and higher education institutions in Mexico. 'Binational' is a word used quite often around El Paso and refers to both U.S. and Mexican joint programs or events that occur in both countries simultaneously.

UTEP has a beloved local athletic program that includes football at the massive

Sun Bowl Stadium, as well as basketball in the Don Haskins Center arena. The university's mascot is the Miners, a nod to its early history, and the school colors are orange, white, and blue.

Technical and Vocational Schools

In the early 2000s, a downturn in El Paso's local economy, combined with the flourishing of international trade and outsourcing because of the North American Free Trade Agreement, caused the closure of many garment factories and manufacturing plants that were once the lifeblood of the area. Many workers found themselves jobless and sorely lacking in technological skills coming into the new millennium. Thus were founded several technical and vocational schools around El Paso to help out-of-work citizens cope with a shortcoming in modern skills and the lagging local industries.

ANAMARC EDUCATIONAL INSTITUTE
3210 Dyer St.
(915) 351-8100
www.anamarc.edu

Anamarc Educational Institute is a mid-level vocational school that prepares learners for the diverse competitive workforce in the Upper Rio Grande Region. The school's key training programs are: Childcare, Office Technology Assisting, Medical Assisting, Medical Billing and Coding, Nurse Assisting, Phlebotomy Technician, Dialysis Technician, and Vocational Nursing. Anamarc also offers an Associate's Degree in Nursing (RN). To meet the needs of non–English speaking students, programs that include ESL training and GED preparation are offered as needed.

AXIS BUSINESS ACADEMY
1528 Goodyear Dr., Suite B
(915) 595-8840
www.axisbusinessacademy.com

Axis Business Academy is a small workforce training academy that specializes in technical and computer programs. Axis has an "Open Entry" admissions policy, which means that students are admitted once they enroll in a program and pay tuition. Axis offers a variety of career-focused programs including: Office Technology Specialist, Medical Assistant, Medical Billing and Coding, Phlebotomy Technician, Pharmacy Technician, and Professional Truck Driver.

CAREER CENTERS OF TEXAS—EL PASO
8360 Burnham Rd., Suite 100
(915) 595-1935
www.el-paso.careercenters.edu

Career Centers of Texas offers an education oriented for working adults, with classes scheduled during the day or in the evening, and a focus on small, intimate classroom sizes. Many students at Career Centers of Texas attend classes while also working. Programs include Allied Health, such as Medical and Dental Assisting, Information Technology, and Electrical Trades. As the school's name suggests, it offers services to help students develop their professional careers, including development training and career planning resources. The school occupies a 20,000-square-foot building built specifically for Career Centers of Texas. In addition to spacious classrooms and administrative offices, it offers a student lounge, faculty lounge, reception area, and a learning resource center with numerous periodicals, texts, reference materials, and videos.

INTERNATIONAL BUSINESS COLLEGE
www.ibcelpaso.edu

International Business College (IBC) is a small technical and business education college that operates on two campuses. Founded in 1898, IBC is one of El Paso's oldest colleges of business education. IBC aims to provide students with useful skills in technology to better their chances of succeeding in the job market. International Business College voluntarily participates in many community activities and has memberships in many service-oriented organizations. Programs include associate's degrees in Applied Science in Business Management, Administrative Assistant, Financial Records Manager, Pharmacy Technician, Computer Support Specialist, Medical Records and Health Information Technician, Office Support Specialist, Medical Assistant, Nurse Aide, and Customer Service Representative. The East Campus is located at 1155 North Zaragosa, Suite 100 (915-859-0422). The West Campus is located at 5700 Cromo Dr. (915-842-0422).

VISTA COLLEGE/COMPUTER CAREER CENTER
6101 Montana Ave.
(915) 779-8031
www.vistacollege.edu

Operating as Computer Career Center (CCC) in El Paso, Vista College offers programs of study leading to certification in a field of study or an associate's degree that helps students begin professional careers. CCC prepares students with knowledge in concepts and procedures that will immediately apply to their work environment. The college's programs cater to students interested in fixing computers, designing Web sites, doing administrative work in an office or hospital, or becoming a specialist in a field, and CCC has courses of study that any student can find applicable to a career. Programs include Allied Health, Business, and Technical Trades.

WESTERN TECHNICAL COLLEGE
Main Campus
9624 Plaza Circle
(888) 201-9232
www.westerntech.edu

Western Technical College is a small technical training institute that provides up-to-date technology and training for jobs that are in high demand. With a variety of programs split between two campuses, students at Western Tech are trained in a few months' time for diverse technical careers like welding, fiber optics, and massage therapy. Programs at the Main Campus include Automotive, ASE Testing, Diesel, Refrigeration HVAC, Performance Tuner, Welding, and Medical Assisting, while the Branch Campus (9451 Diana Dr.) offers Computer, Electronics, IT, Fiber Optics, Communications, A+, CISCO, Microsoft, Medical Assisting, Health Information, Massage Therapy, and Physical Therapist Assistant Program.

PUBLIC SCHOOLS

The El Paso city public school system is divided into four independent school districts (ISDs): El Paso Independent School District, Ysleta Independent School District, Socorro Independent School District, and Canutillo Independent School District. Generally, students are enrolled based on the geographic locale of their home address, but in El Paso's six magnet programs, students attend based on academic themes. Students who wish to attend a magnet school must go through an application process and be admitted based on scholastic record and vacancies within the school.

i If you're relocating to El Paso, you can check which school your child will attend by visiting www.episd .org/_schools and utilizing the Attendance Zones box by inputting your street address.

EL PASO ISD
www.episd.org

The El Paso Independent School District (EPISD) is the city's largest, with some 62,000 students attending school in 88 buildings. EPISD's schools include 13 high schools, 17 middle schools, 59 elementary schools, 6 magnet schools, and a handful of specialty and auxiliary schools. The six magnet programs include Capt. John L. Chapin High School, an engineering and science magnet school; Silva Health Magnet, which has a curriculum focused on health and the sciences; the Sandra Day O'Connor Criminal Justice/Public Service Academy at Austin High School; Connecting Worlds/Mundos Unidos at El Paso High School, which is a dual language program focusing on bicultural studies; the Academy for International Business and Public Affairs at Bowie High School in South El Paso, which focuses on international business and public affairs education; and the International Baccalaureate Diploma at Coronado High, which offers the chance for students to participate in a rigorous program that guarantees entry into some of the finest universities around the world.

SOCORRO ISD
www.sisd.net

Socorro Independent School District educates more than 40,000 students in southeastern El Paso County, serving Socorro, Horizon City, and the southeastern portion of the city of El Paso. Within the district are 5 high schools, 8 middle schools, 20 elementary schools, 6 combined elementary and middle schools, and 2 alternative programs. Montwood High School is one of El Paso's largest secondary schools. Socorro ISD operates a Student Activities Complex, which includes an 11,000-seat stadium and an Aquatic Center, open throughout the year, which has indoor and outdoor pools for student and community use.

YSLETA ISD
www.yisd.net

Ysleta Independent School District (YISD) is the second largest school district in El Paso and covers a wide swath of east El Paso, with around 45,000 students in 58 buildings. It is the third largest employer in El Paso. Ysleta ISD incorporates 7 high schools, 11 middle schools, 38 elementary schools (including two pre-kindergarten schools), and 6 special campuses, including Ysleta Community Learning Center for adults.

PRIVATE SCHOOLS

A large number of private and parochial schools exist in El Paso. El Paso Catholic Diocese (www.dioceseofelpasocatholicschools .org) operates 12 parochial schools, including 9 elementary schools, 1 high school and 2 combined elementary/high schools. Beyond that, you will discover a range of private schools, from those operated by churches and religious organizations to day schools and private academies. Making the

(🔍) **Close-up**

Supreme Court Justice Beginnings

Sandra Day O'Connor, U.S. Supreme Court Justice, was born in El Paso on August 26, 1930. Her parents owned a cattle ranch in southeastern Arizona called the Lazy B. In the early years, the ranch did not have electricity or running water, so Sandra grew up branding cattle, learning to fix whatever was broken, and enjoying rustic ranch life. Her experiences at the Lazy B shaped O'Connor's character and developed her belief in hard work, but her parents also wanted her to gain an education outside of ranch life. They decided to send her to El Paso to live with her grandmother and attend school. There, she attended Radford School, as well as Austin High School, from which she graduated sixth in her class in 1946. She later went on to earn a law degree from Stanford University and become an Arizona senator.

In 1981, then newly elected President Ronald Reagan appointed O'Connor to become the first female justice of the United States Supreme Court, where she served for more than 30 years before her retirement in 2005. Her memoir, *Lazy B: Growing up on a Cattle Ranch in the American Southwest,* chronicles how her young life in El Paso and Arizona shaped who she is. O'Connor attended her 50th high school reunion at Austin High in 1996, and her former classmates described her as fun-loving and unassuming, as well as being a good dancer. Today, Austin High School operates the Sandra Day O'Connor Criminal Justice/Public Service Academy in honor of its most famous alumnus.

choice to send your child to a private school can have the benefit of incorporating a religious faith into your child's schooling or enhancing his or her academic credentials. When shopping for a private school, be sure to have a list of important criteria and visit potential schools, once together with your child and at least once on your own. Be sure to ask questions about what type of curriculum the school uses, what (if any) religious material might be covered, what sports opportunities will be open to your child, and what the classroom sizes are like. You should also check the credentials of the school, including its accreditation. One difficult aspect of private schooling to cover is the cost, which can vary considerably from school to school. You should be aware,

though, that private schools do have the luxury of deciding their own tuition prices, which are considerably more expensive than utilizing the public school system.

Since such a large number of private schools operate around El Paso, it would be impossible to list them all here. Instead, I have provided a short rundown of several schools that encompass the vast variety of school types, from religious to academic.

EL PASO COUNTRY DAY SCHOOL
www.epcds.org

This secular, pre-kindergarten through 12th grade educational institution provides a targeted, individualized system of learning for children, which focuses on academic performance. Founded in 1980, the school boasts small class settings and a culturally and socially diverse student body, which, in previous years, has included students from 22 different countries and all socio-economic backgrounds. The average classroom size at El Paso Country Day School is eight students per teacher, and over 70 percent of its faculty members have advanced degrees. Many EPCDS graduates have been National Merit Scholars, and its seniors graduate with an average of 24 college credits already earned in dual-credit courses. The school prides itself on a 100 percent graduation rate, with all graduates attending university. Previous graduates were admitted to universities such as Northwestern, Georgia Tech, University of Washington, Austin College, and others. The school also incorporates a physical education program, as well as extracurricular athletics, depending on the interests of students from year to year. There are two locations, the Upper School at 109 Argonaut Dr. (915-533-4099), and the Lower School at 220 Cliff St. (915-533-4492).

EL PASO JEWISH ACADEMY
805 Cherry Hill Lane
(915) 833-0808
www.elpasojewishacademy.com
This community elementary and middle school (grades 1 to 8) provides an integrated Jewish and secular curriculum and welcomes children and their families from all the varied backgrounds of Jewish life. The school teaches Judaic concepts and traditions in a manner that acknowledges, respects, and celebrates the diversity of the Jewish people. Approximately 25 percent of the students' day is dedicated to Judaic studies, and various secular and Jewish subjects in the curriculum are carefully interwoven so

that many secular academic skills are taught or reinforced while students are learning Judaics. New students must go through an admissions process that includes past school records, standardized test scores, and a classroom visit.

FAITH CHRISTIAN ACADEMY
8960 Escobar Dr.
(915) 594-3305
www.fcaelpaso.com
Faith Christian Academy (FCA) is a fully accredited private Christian school that was established in 1980. It is a ministry of Abundant Living Faith Center and is home to more than 500 students. Faith Christian Academy offers students ages K–3 through 12th grade a diverse opportunity for quality education and enrichment in a supportive and challenging environment. FCA is known for excellent academic programs that utilize an accelerated, faith-based ABEKA curriculum, and a wide variety of extracurricular activities that include a large athletics program, fine arts, and a number of clubs and student organizations. FCA's 50,000-square-foot facility includes 22 classrooms, a gymnasium, and an auditorium. Bible classes and chapel services are a regular part of student life, and FCA incorporates a physical education program, computer classes, and Spanish into its curriculum.

LORETTO ACADEMY
1300 Hardaway
(915) 566-8400
www.loretto.org
Loretto Academy is an independent Catholic school that serves a diverse multicultural student population from pre-kindergarten through 5th grade in a co-ed environment,

(Q) Close-up

Education at Fort Bliss

Each year, thousands of military personnel from the U.S. and abroad come to Fort Bliss for a variety of reasons, whether to be stationed or to participate in one of the base's many international programs. If you are relocating to Fort Bliss, you will find plenty of help and services in getting your family settled into a regular education program. Three elementary schools and one high school are located on Fort Bliss grounds, all of which are part of the El Paso ISD. Bus transportation to off post schools, such as Chapin High School near the base, is provided. A variety of daycare options are also provided for military personnel and their families. The U.S. Army's division of **Family and Morale Welfare and Recreation** (MWR) at Fort Bliss (www.blissmwr.com) helps families readjust to relocation and offers a large number of events and services on base. Among them, **School Transition Services** (www .blissmwr.com/sts) assists school-age youth of military families in getting settled into local schools, as well as offering a host of extra services, tutoring, and other useful information for newly arrived personnel to Fort Bliss.

and from 6th to 12th grade in an all-girls setting. Every potential new student must undergo an admission evaluation process based on prior scholastic records, parent and student interviews, standardized test scores, attendance/tardy records, teacher recommendations, and a personal essay. Loretto's pre-kindergarten program (ages four to eight) focuses on the principles and stages of child development, fostering individual interests, social learning, and cultural and linguistic diversity through a curriculum of music, art, physical education, and Spanish. In the Middle School (grades six to eight), the focus is on addressing the unique needs of girls during a time of rapid development and physical and emotional changes. Middle School elective courses and enrichment programs include art, computer science, dance, music, Spanish, physical education, and reading. In the High School, interaction with each young woman is designed to help her experience academic success, build self-confidence, and develop

spiritually, physically, emotionally, intellectually, and socially. The average student/teacher ratio at Loretto High School is one teacher per 18 students. Loretto Academy also offers a variety of sports for elementary through high school, including basketball, cross country, golf, soccer, softball, swimming, tennis, track, and volleyball.

PALM TREE ACADEMY
143 Paragon Lane
(915) 581-7729
www.ptacademy.org
This small, non-profit Islamic academy offers full academics and Islamic studies to young students from pre-kindergarten through first grade. Combining Islamic principles and academic excellence, the school strives to create a learning process that is challenging, rewarding, and meaningful. The school offers full day programs, as well as an optional half-day program for pre-kindergarten children. The curriculum includes Qur'anic Studies,

Arabic, and regular academic subjects, and limited scholarships are available for students with financial need that are in good academic standing.

CHILD CARE AND PRESCHOOLS

With more than 700 licensed child-care centers in El Paso, you are certain to find the perfect place for your young one to spend the day. Of course, choosing a child-care provider or daycare center is a very personal decision and one that you will have to spend some time researching on your own. It is a good idea to make a list of priorities for what you want in a child-care provider before you start your search. It can also be helpful to consult other parents or neighbors for recommendations on the best place for your child. You will need to contact the daycare centers individually to find out about their availability and current openings for new children. Rest assured, though, that the hundreds of child-care options available in El Paso include many varieties, from religious organizations to children's play groups and home care providers, so you are sure to find just what you're looking for. While it would be impossible to list every child-care provider in the city, the following short list of daycare centers will give you a broad idea of what to expect.

ALL ABOUT ME CHILDCARE CENTER
10017 Montana Ave.
(915) 593-2100
www.allaboutmeelpaso.com
Providing curriculum for all ages by licensed child-care providers with CPR and First Aid certifications. Hours: 6 a.m. to 6:30 p.m. Mon to Fri.

GIMME A BREAK!
7108 North Mesa St.
(915) 587-5555
www.gimmeabreakelpaso.com
This hourly drop-in child-care center provides a unique approach to daycare with flexible drop-in services and no enrollment necessary. This is a great option if you don't wish to send your child to full-time daycare, but need to catch up on a few errands or take in a movie sans the kiddies. They serve children between 18 months and 12 years. No advance reservations are necessary for children over two years during the week, and you may also schedule weekend service for groups of five children or more with a reservation. Their program consists of day and evening child sitting, educational classes, and weekend parties. Hours: 8 a.m. to 8 p.m. Mon to Fri, weekends by appointment.

GRAMMIES DAYCARE AND
** LEARNING CENTER**
Main Office
634 Sunland Park Dr.
(915) 833-0776
www.grammiesdaycare.com
Their specialized curriculum, Learning About My World, is based on the Child Observation Record and encourages parent and family involvement to maintain consistency between the home and daycare. An after school program is offered at the newly opened Upper Valley location at 8030 Artcraft Rd. (915-587-0500), and the Spanish Enrichment Program helps begin and/or enhance children's understanding of the Spanish language.

JUST FOR YOU DAYCARE
11920 Vista Del Sol Dr.
(915) 857-5798
www.justforyou-daycare.com

This local chain daycare center serves newborn babies to children age 13 and have both a preschool and an after school program. Bilingual teachers supervise children in daily activities, games and play in the entertainment center and on the playground, and computer classes. Each center offers home-cooked hot meals and before and after school transportation. Hours: 5:30 a.m. to 6:30 p.m. Mon to Fri. The day care has three additional locations serving El Paso and nearby Horizon City at 2857 Saul Kleinfeld Dr. (915-856-1616), 13900 Montana Ave, (915-921-5000), 108 Biglow Place (Horizon City; 915-852-8181).

TEACHER'S APPLE/ANGEL'S WINGS
2812 Lee Trevino Dr.
(915) 592-2306

6501 Boeing Dr., Suite A-1
(915) 779-0888
www.teachersappledaycare.com

This daycare and preschool with two locations serves infants to age 12 in El Paso and Fort Bliss. They offer infant/toddler activities, arts and crafts, a preschool curriculum, learning through play, flexible hours, before and after school care, summer child care, and more. Their program provides opportunities for social, emotional, mental, physical, and language growth in a relaxed and positive atmosphere with exciting educational activities. Hours: 5:30 a.m. to 6 p.m. Mon to Fri.

HEALTH AND WELLNESS

El Paso has a unique public health situation because of its desert climate and its immediate geographical proximity to Ciudad Juárez. Because so many people cross the border between the U.S. and Mexico on a daily basis, local health departments such as the municipal Department of Public Health and the U.S.–Mexico Border Health Commission work tirelessly to promote better standards of living and decrease the incidents of tuberculosis and other infectious diseases transmitted between the two countries. Dehydration, sun and heat stroke, rattlesnakes, and scorpions are just some of the health risks present in the El Paso area, but luckily the city has an excellent health care system to tend to the needs of all residents. El Paso's hospitals are widely considered to be excellent both in terms of facilities and service. The sole general hospital in the city is University Medical Center, which boasts the only Level I trauma center in El Paso, while one of the foremost medical institutions in the area is the Texas Tech University–Paul Foster School of Medicine.

Despite these great facilities, El Paso's health situation is not without fault. In 2007, El Paso County had more than twice the national rate of individuals living below the federal poverty level and it consistently rates well below the national average of uninsured citizens. Still, El Paso County remains one of the lowest Texas counties in terms of cancer mortality rates and has better immunization rates than both the Texas and national averages. Interestingly, El Pasoans smoke nearly 7 percent less than most Americans and likewise the incidence of lung cancer in the county is far lower than the national average. All in all, El Paso is a healthy place and the year-round sunshine leads to many health benefits, as the city is full of outdoor sports and healthy activities.

OVERVIEW

This chapter presents a broad overview of the health and medical facilities available in El Paso. The area's main health departments are listed, as well as the city's hospitals and a sampling of the available urgent care/walk-in clinics, which provide basic medical service to just about anyone. If you traveling through El Paso and have a minor health condition like heat exhaustion or a broken bone, you can simply go to any of the listed urgent care/walk-in clinics to be treated.

Many of them do not require you to make an appointment or have a comprehensive insurance plan, and some offer discounts to uninsured patients. For more serious health conditions, such as a stroke or heart attack, you should go to a hospital emergency room immediately. Remember that there are many more doctors' offices and urgent care centers in El Paso, so trust the advice of local friends or check a phonebook for the nearest clinic to you.

In general, you're unlikely to have any major health concerns during your stay in El Paso. Be sure to carry plenty of bottled water with you if you plan to be out hiking or walking under the Southwest sun, and wear a high-SPF sunscreen, a hat, sunglasses, and other protective clothing.

HEALTH DEPARTMENTS

CITY OF EL PASO DEPARTMENT OF PUBLIC HEALTH

5515 El Paso Dr.
(915) 771-5712
www.elpasotexas.gov/health

El Paso's Department of Public Health (DPH) promotes, ensures, and improves the health and well being of citizens through a variety of programs, from immunizations to inspections of food establishments and animal services. It provides health information to the general public in the event of a public health threat or disaster, and presents community information initiatives related to bioterrorism, preparedness issues such as shelter-in-place, smallpox awareness, bioterrorism agents, and emergency kits. Each year, the DPH coordinates health fairs, conferences, training opportunities, and workshops to promote public health awareness on preparedness issues and emergency response and it is the lead agency in the Smallpox Vaccination Program.

i The Department of Public Health runs a children's dental clinic for El Pasoans 1 to 21 years of age. Fees can be paid on a sliding scale based on family income. Contact Rawlins Dental Clinic at 3301 Pera Ave., Mon to Fri 8 a.m. to 5 p.m. Mobile units also visit El Paso's public schools to provide dental care to students.

Immunization Locations

The city's immunization program provides immunizations to uninsured and underinsured children and adults of all ages at five health centers across the city. Centers are open 7 to 11:15 a.m. and 12:30 to 4:15 p.m. Tues through Fri with alternating Saturdays. Contact the Program Office at 5115 El Paso Dr.; (915) 771-5740. Clinic locations include:

- **Henderson,** 721 South Mesa St.
- **Northeast,** 5587 Transmountain Rd.
- **Tigua,** 7826 San Jose Rd.
- **Westside,** 5195 Mace St.
- **Ysleta,** 110 Candelaria St.

UNITED STATES–MEXICO BORDER HEALTH COMMISSION

www.borderhealth.org

The mission of the United States–Mexico Border Health Commission (BHC) is to provide international leadership to optimize health and quality of life along the U.S.–Mexico border. The commission, which is comprised of federal health secretaries, prominent community health professionals from Mexico and the U.S., and the chief health officers of the 10 borders states, provides the necessary leadership to develop coordinated binational actions to improve health and quality of life along the border in both countries. The BHC was created as a binational health commission in July 2000, with the signing of an agreement by the

Secretary of Health and Human Services of the United States and the Secretary of Health of Mexico.

The BHC serves all the people who reside within 100 kilometers, or 62 miles, on either side of the international boundary line, including six Mexican states and four states in the U.S. (Texas, New Mexico, Arizona, and California). The commission is comprised of 26 members in two sections, one for each country, which have 13 members each.

HOSPITALS

DEL SOL MEDICAL CENTER
10301 Gateway Blvd West
(915) 595-9000
www.delsolmedicalcenter.com
This full service Eastside hospital strives to deliver high-quality, cost-effective health care in the El Paso community. Del Sol Medical Center is a campus of Las Palmas Del Sol Healthcare and has a sister hospital, Las Palmas Medical Center in West El Paso. Open since 1974, this is the only full-service, acute-care facility in East El Paso, with specializations in Emergency Medicine, Maternal/Child, Women's Health, Rehabilitation Services, Outpatient Test and Treatment, Bariatric Surgery, Cardiovascular Services, and Oncology.

EAST EL PASO PHYSICIAN'S MEDICAL CENTER
1416 George Dieter Dr.
(915) 598-4240
www.physiciansmedcenter.com
East El Paso Physicians Medical Center (EEPPMC) is a general acute care hospital that offers both inpatient and outpatient surgery. They have a large medical staff of more than 312 physicians. Patients at EEPPMC stay in entirely private suite rooms that are modern and comfortable. In the Pre-Op area, family members are allowed to remain with patients in their rooms until surgery. Open seven days a week, EEPPMC has an emergency room; outpatient diagnostic services; inpatient surgery with a wide range of cardiac, orthopedic, gynecological and general surgery; a heart and vascular center; chronic pain management; MRI services; radiology; ultrasound testing, CT scanning; and a wound center.

LAS PALMAS MEDICAL CENTER
1801 North Oregon St.
(915) 521-1200
www.laspalmashealth.com
The sister hospital of Del Sol Medical Center, Las Palmas Medical Center is the main campus of Las Palmas Del Sol Healthcare and employs 845 individuals and houses 317 beds. The hospital is an acute-care facility that specializes in Cardiology, Women's Services, Labor & Delivery, Polly's Pediatric Place, Oncology Services, and Emergency Medicine. Las Palmas now also offers weight loss surgery through a comprehensive Bariatric Program that is led by an elite team of health care professionals. Las Palmas Rehabilitation Hospital is a 40-bed inpatient rehabilitation center that specializes in treating medically stable patients with orthopedic problems, strokes and other neurological diagnoses, multiple trauma, brain and spinal cord injuries, arthritis, and amputation.

PROVIDENCE MEMORIAL HOSPITAL
2001 North Oregon St.
(915) 577-6011
www.sphn.com
Since it opened in 1952, Providence Memorial Hospital (part of the Sierra Providence

Healthcare Network) has been providing generations of El Pasoans with a broad spectrum of advanced health care programs and clinical services in general medicine, surgery, pediatrics, and obstetrics. It has designated the only pediatric hospital in El Paso, the Children's Hospital at Providence, which offers pediatric intensive care, a pediatric transport team, pediatric cancer care, and Kidsville, Jungleville, Oceanville, and Teensville—the colorfully decorated inpatient units. The Border Children's Health Clinic is an outpatient clinic that provides care for children with chronic illnesses.

Providence Memorial has 508 beds and is an accredited Primary Stroke Center.

The hospital's specialties include a Sleep Disorders Center to diagnose and treat problems like sleep apnea; obstetric services, including a High-Risk Pregnancy program, a Mother-Baby Nursing program, as well as Labor, Delivery & Recovery Plus rooms and a neonatal intensive care unit; and a Digestive Disease Center for the diagnosis and treatment of digestive disorders. Providence also offers advanced health care services in the following areas: Cardiac Rehabilitation, Day Surgery Center, Diagnostic Lab & Imaging, Hospice Services, Hyperbaric Oxygen Chamber, Neurodiagnostics, Respiratory Care, and Women's Services.

SIERRA MEDICAL CENTER
1625 Medical Center Dr.
(915) 747-4000
www.sphn.com
Sierra Medical Center provides families with quality health care in an advanced acute care setting with more than 300 beds and a full range of advanced medical and surgical services. Sierra Medical Center's specialties include advanced cardiac care, neonatal

intensive care nursery services for critically ill or premature babies, and advanced neurological care including MinOp System-Endoscopic Neurosurgery, Deep Brain Stimulation and Stereotactic Radiosurgery, and Gamma Knife Radiosurgery. Sierra is accredited as a Chest Pain Center and is also the only hospital in El Paso ranked in the top 5 percent of hospitals nationally for overall orthopedic services. Sierra Medical Center also offers advanced health care services in Autologous Blood Storage, Diagnostic Lab & Imaging, HDR Brachytherapy, Neurosciences, Obstetrics Services, Orthopaedics, and Stereotactic Breast Biopsy.

SIERRA PROVIDENCE EASTSIDE
 HOSPITAL
3280 Joe Battle Blvd.
(915) 832-2000
www.sphn.com
A member of the Sierra Providence Health Network, Providence East Medical Center opened in May 2008 to serve the needs of East El Paso's growing community. This 110-bed hospital has 12 Intensive Care Unit beds, 6 Neonatal Intensive Care beds and a 20-bed Emergency Department. At the Birthing Center, families have access to a Level III Neonatal Intensive Care Unit, a 10-bed Labor and Delivery Unit, C-section rooms, and a Parents' Sleep Room. Surgical Services feature six operating rooms, four endoscopy rooms, and a Pre-Operative Testing Center. Other hospital services include: Emergency Services, Diagnostic Imaging, Cardiology, Medical/Surgical Unit, Post Partum/GYN, Respiratory Care, and a Telemetry Unit.

SOUTHWEST URGENT CARE CENTER
2030 North Mesa Street
(915) 532-7100
www.southwesturgentcarecenter.com

⊙ Close-up

El Paso Health Concerns

HEAT

During the summer months, temperatures nearly always stay around 90° to 100°F. The biggest dangers facing visitors at this time are dehydration and heat stroke/exhaustion. El Paso is in a desert and many people fail to take the heat seriously because the dry heat can actually feel less "hot" than it really is. Be sure to drink plenty of water and remember this cowboy word of wisdom: If you're thirsty, you're already dehydrated.

SUN

El Paso's intense, high desert sun can be extremely dangerous because of UV rays, which are much stronger at El Paso's altitude than at sea level. Wear a hat, sunglasses, and sunscreen.

WIND AND DUST

From January to April, El Paso experiences a windy season. During this time, high winds and blowing dust can make breathing difficult, especially for asthma sufferers. Blowing dust and sand can also reduce visibility on roads, especially in rural and outlying areas. Local highways sometimes close during high winds.

MOSQUITOES

It may seem surprising given El Paso's dry climate, but the area gets quite a few mosquitoes during the rainy season from June to September. Backyard pools and water gardens can be breeding grounds for mosquitoes, and the riverside along the Rio Grande also has mosquito problems. West Nile Virus has been recorded in El Paso, so the best advice is to wear insect repellent if you plan to be outdoors, especially in the evening when mosquitos are most active.

CREEPY CRAWLIES

There are plenty of critters on the loose in El Paso's dry, desert surroundings. Most common are rattlesnakes, black widow spiders, and scorpions, all of which can be dangerous to someone that is bit or stung. If you plan to go hiking or camping in the Franklin Mountains or in the rural areas near El Paso, stay on designated trails and check the ground for snakes as you hike. Also be sure to check tents, shoes, and sleeping bags for spiders and scorpions before use. Nonetheless, most of these creatures won't harm you unless provoked. If you come upon a rattlesnake, back away from it slowly and do not make any fast movements. If you are bitten or stung, call 911 and go to the nearest emergency room immediately.

This urgent care clinic specializes in minor emergencies and urgent care, general adult and geriatric care, and infant and pediatric services, as well as sports, school, and pre-employment physicals. Services are provided at a fraction of the cost of a regular ER visit and they guarantee no long waits, with most patients being seen within one hour. Walk-ins are welcome and no appointment is necessary. The regular clinic is open seven days a week and the emergency room is open 24/7. Most insurance plans are accepted and they offer a six-month payment plan to qualified patients with low or no insurance coverage.

SOUTHWESTERN GENERAL HOSPITAL
1221 North Cotton St.
(915) 496-9600
This beautiful hospital has stunning architecture, an intriguing history, and good medical services. With 102 beds, they offer short-term general medical and surgical services. In 1925, the Southwestern General Hospital was opened as a sanatorium for tubercular patients, and was then known as the Albert Baldwin Heath Resort. In 1936, it became a hospital and in 1937 was renamed to Southwestern General Hospital. In the 1990s, a group of local investors bought the hospital and made several renovations in the levels of services and equipment of Southwestern General. Today, the hospital's services include pediatric, laboratory, general medical/surgical, a 24-hour emergency department, inpatient and outpatient surgery, an intensive care unit, obstetrics, and physical therapy. It also offers radiology and cardio-pulmonary services equipped with the latest equipment to provide and guarantee high technology diagnoses and treatments.

UNIVERSITY MEDICAL CENTER
4815 Alameda Ave.
(915) 521-7755
www.umcelpaso.org
Formerly known as Thomason Hospital, University Medical Center (UMC) is the city's general hospital, the only Level I trauma center in the area, and is the designated facility to receive the President of the United States should he require medical attention while traveling in the area. It is also El Paso's only not-for-profit, community-owned hospital and health care system and is a regional referral center for patients in need of specialty care.

With 327 beds, UMC sees nearly 5,000 births a year and admits more than 22,000 patients annually. The history of UMC began in 1915 in a two-story, adobe building located in the area where Asarco is today. The move to 4815 Alameda happened just a year later when residents of the area raised the money to build a new hospital, which was named El Paso General. UMC was built in the 1950s, when locals voted to create the El Paso County Hospital District by taxing themselves to ensure the existence of a public health care system for the city. Today, UMC's Emergency Department is one of El Paso's busiest and the hospital is also home to some of the city's most unique health care services, such as El Paso CAREs for Kids After-Hours Pediatrics, a nighttime children's health care practice. The Mother/Baby Division includes complete labor and delivery services, and one third of all babies born in El Paso each year are delivered at University Medical Center. Other UMC specializations include the Pediatrics Unit, Medical Unit, Surgical Unit, Critical Care Unit, Telemetry Unit, and operating rooms, as well as a fully accredited regional laboratory, radiology department, and pharmacy.

WILLIAM BEAUMONT ARMY MEDICAL CENTER
5005 North Piedras St.
(915) 569-2121
www.wbamc.amedd.army.mil

This large Department of Defense medical facility has provided care for military personnel and their eligible family members since 1921. It specializes in complete medical care, hosts a medical education program, and serves as a trauma center for the surrounding community. All active duty military personnel, including family members and retirees, are eligible for comprehensive medical care here. William Beaumont Army Medical Center is also charged with ensuring the medical readiness of soldiers assigned and deployed at Fort Bliss and delivering skilled Warrior Medics to the armed forces. The hospital is located in the Central/Northeastern part of El Paso and contains a rather sizable Veterans Affairs Office for former military members who are in need of medical treatment.

URGENT CARE AND WALK-IN CLINICS

THE DOCTOR'S IN WALK-IN CLINIC
10965 Ben Crenshaw Dr.
(915) 594-4000
www.elpasomed.com

This family-run walk-in clinic is staffed by three competent medical professionals and serves patients with basic everyday injuries and illnesses. The clinic features separate reception and waiting areas for the family practice and worker's injury clinics to better meet the specific needs of each practice. The clinic is equipped with an on-site lab and x-ray facilities, 10 patient exam rooms, an orthopedic casting room, two fast-track minor surgical bays, and a specialized women's health exam room. Open Mon through Fri, 8 a.m. to 6 p.m. and Sat 8 a.m. to noon.

UNITED MEDICAL WALK-IN CLINIC
3130 North Lee Trevino, Suite 114
(915) 595-8815
www.umwic.com

A patient-centered, family-oriented, primary care facility with walk-in care at two branches. United Medical offers comprehensive health care for men, women, and children from newborn through geriatrics, including preventive care, employment exams, sport physicals, well child care, immunizations, newborn care, and minor surgical procedures. They also offer pulmonary and EKG services and have an on-site laboratory. The second location is at 1550 Hawkins, Suite 16 (915-317-6033). Both clinics are open Mon to Fri, 8:30 a.m. to 5 p.m.

UPPER VALLEY URGENT CARE CENTER
21 East Redd Rd.
(915) 584-8882
www.uvucc.com

A clean, new, well-lit, modern, family-oriented facility with state of the art computerized medical operations, Upper Valley has 10 exam rooms and an open-air clinical work area similar to a hospital emergency department to serve as many patients as possible quickly. Specializing in minor medical problems like cuts, scrapes, colds, and the flu, they offer x-rays and pregnancy testing and are equipped for EKGs. No appointment is necessary and Upper Valley prides itself on its short waiting time, but the prices for care here are higher than at a normal doctor's office. Open every day including most holidays: Mon to Fri, 9 a.m. to 9 p.m.; Sat to Sun, noon to 8 pm.

ALTERNATIVE MEDICINE
Chiropractors

CHIROPRACTIC EAST
2267 Trawood Dr. Suite G-3
(915) 593-1330
www.weislowchiropractic.com
This private chiropractic office has a "No Wait Policy"—all patients are seen immediately in large private treatment rooms. Practitioners have extensive knowledge of auto and work-related injuries and they accept both auto and workers' compensation insurance, as well as regular medical insurance policies.

i Chiropractic East offers a free consultation, exam, and x-rays to first-time patients. Simply visit their Web site and download the printable coupon at www.weislowchiropractic .com.

DESERT SUN CHIROPRACTIC
3800 North Mesa, Suite C1
(915) 838-1500
www.chirodesert.com
As a doctor of chiropractic medicine, Dr. Michael A. Ontiveros believes in natural healing, including chiropractic treatments, rehabilitation, therapy, and nutrition. He is board certified by the National Board of Chiropractic Examiners.

SOUTHWEST CHIROPRACTIC
1030 North Zaragoza Rd., Eastside
(915) 860-2233
www.southwestchiropractic.com
This chiropractic clinic specializes in the treatment and management of work-related injuries and auto injuries, offering the latest in quality physical therapy and rehab, including theraputic massage, x-rays, and special spinal traction. They have three locations on the Eastside and Westside and in Las Cruces, New Mexico. See the Web site for details.

Oriental Medicine and Acupuncture

BOUCHARD WELLNESS
3138 Aurora Ave.
(915) 238-3540
www.bouchardwellness.com
Bouchard Wellness offers acupuncture and Oriental medicine in a warm inspired atmosphere with the patient's comfort in mind. They treat pain, discomfort, and other acute and chronic conditions through acupuncture services, herbs, and whole food nutrition. They also offer Non-Needle Facial Rejuvenation, a non-invasive method of toning facial muscles for improved skin tone and wrinkle reduction.

ORIENTAL ACUPUNCTURE THERAPY
4026 North Mesa, Suite E
(915) 351-9444
www.orientalacupuncturetx.com
This small clinic offers a variety of acupuncture and Oriental medicine services that range from basic pain relief acupuncture, to treatment of cold and flu, as well as more serious conditions like addiction, immune disorders and joint and muscle problems. Oriental Acupuncture Therapy also offers weight control services utilizing Oriental medical practices.

Fitness Centers and Spas

CURVES
1201 Airway Blvd., Suite A2
(915) 779-6380

7230 North Mesa St.
(915) 875-0200

1188 North Yarbrough Dr., Suite H
(915) 595-1221
www.curves.com

Dedicated to women's fitness, Curves offers a 30-minute workout that combines strength training and sustained cardiovascular activity through safe and effective hydraulic resistance. Curves also has a commonsense weight management program that ends the need for perpetual dieting. In addition to the three listed here, Curves operates nine locations across El Paso, so there is sure to be a location that is convenient to you. Travelers with a Curves membership card may work out at any of their worldwide locations. See Curves' Web site for more details on all of their locations.

EFS TRAINING CENTER
120 Paragon Lane, Suite 201
(915) 833-3200
www.efstrainingcenter.com

EFS Training Center is a large fitness center with a wide array of equipment and fitness classes, from cardio equipment to free weights, and personal training to fitness classes. Hours: Mon to Thurs 5 a.m. to 9 p.m., Fri 5 a.m. to 7 p.m., Sat 8 a.m. to 1 p.m., Sun 9:30 a.m. to 12:30 p.m.

EP (EXTREME PERFORMANCE) FITNESS
145 Paragon Lane
(915) 833-4653

EP Women's Fitness—West
1035 Belvedere, Suite 160
(915) 842-0909

EP Women's Fitness—East
11705 Montwood Dr.
(915) 856-9550
www.epfitness.com

Extreme Performance Fitness is a local chain fitness company with eight locations across El Paso, including two specialty women's fitness facilities. Their motto is "affordable fitness for everyone" and they strive to offer a range of membership options to cater to all budgets. Membership with one Extreme Performance Fitness center grants you access to all of their locations across El Paso, each offering a good selection of cardio and strength-training equipment, group fitness classes, and personal training options. Several of their locations also boast indoor basketball courts, and child care is available at every EP Fitness location in El Paso. Visit their Web site for more information about hours and offerings at all eight of their locations.

i For just about any type of medical referral, from affordable child care to mental health assistance and counseling services, dial 211, a free phone number connected to nearly every service in Texas, available 24/7. Callers are referred to the best place in their community to get the help they need. If you have a life-threatening medical, police, or fire emergency, call 911 instead.

PLANET FITNESS
5700 North Mesa St.
(915) 585-7867
www.planetfitness.com

Planet Fitness is known for its low prices, its late-night hours, and its "Judgment Free Zone" philosophy, which means that members can relax, get in shape, and have fun without being subjected to the hard-core, look-at-me attitude that exists in many gyms. Hours: From midnight Mon until Fri at 9 p.m.; weekends 7 a.m. to 7 p.m. A second and third location are at 11160 Rojas Dr. (915-590-7867), and 1505 North Zaragoza Rd. (915-856-7867).

YMCA OF EL PASO
Fred and Maria Loya Family Branch
2044 Trawood Dr.
(915) 591-3321
www.elpasoymca.org
El Paso's YMCA branches offer a family-friendly workout environment with state-of-the-art fitness equipment, as well as wellness classes, group exercise classes, swimming facilities, saunas, ball courts and clean locker rooms. Exercise rooms are equipped with weights, treadmills, ellipticals, steppers and other typical exercise machines, while dedicated aerobics and spinning rooms are also open, with free classes for members of the YMCA. The atmosphere at the YMCA makes it a great place for those with children, as kids can participate in plenty of children's exercise classes and sports leagues. Meanwhile, the excellent childcare services make it possible for busy parents to stay in shape. A second and third location are at 7145 North Mesa St. on the Westside (915-584-9622), and 5509 Will Ruth Ave. (915-755-5685) in the Northeast.

MEDIA

With dozens of local media outlets around El Paso, you are sure never to be far from the latest headlines or newest pop songs. El Paso has an expanding media market that includes print news, local and regional television, dozens of radio stations, magazines, and more. The *El Paso Times* and *El Diario de El Paso* keep El Pasoans in-the-know in both English and Spanish, while TV stations such as KVIA and KTSM cover local and national news and air regular national TV. Local cable television can be connected through Time Warner Cable, and satellite TV options are open to El Pasoans through Direct TV and Dish Network. Several free entertainment publications keep locals updated on all the happenings around town, from gallery openings to rock concerts.

DAILIES

EL DIARO DE EL PASO
1801 Texas Ave.
(656) 629-1900
www.diariousa.com
El Diario de El Paso is the city's primary Spanish-language newspaper. The paper was founded on May 16, 2005 by *El Diario de Juárez* and it originally started out as a Mexican newspaper that was circulated throughout Ciudad Juárez under the name *Diario de Juárez*. In 1982, *Diario de Juárez* entered into the El Paso business community by opening a small sales and circulation office and the company eventually became incorporated in Texas as Editora Paso del Norte, Inc.

El Diario de El Paso competes with the larger, notoriously anti-Hispanic, English-language newspaper the *El Paso Times*, and it often openly criticizes the English daily through news stories and editorials.

The newspaper has a daily circulation of more than 20,000 copies and is intended to reach young, active adults (target audience 18 to 35) of Hispanic descent in El Paso. *El Diario de El Paso*'s sister paper, *Diario de Juárez*, was founded in February 1976 and has grown from a 1,000-copy-per-day newspaper in Ciudad Juárez to now more than 100,000 copies daily throughout the state of Chihuahua. It is now the fourth largest newspaper in Mexico. Each Friday, *El Diario de El Paso* publishes *Looking at El Paso*, a weekly, colorful lifestyle and entertainment newspaper included in the paper's circulation.

EL PASO TIMES
300 North Campbell St.
(915) 546-6119
www.elpasotimes.com
The *El Paso Times* is the primary English-language newspaper for El Paso, founded in 1881 by Marcellus Washington Carrico. It originally started out as a weekly but within only a year's time, it became the daily newspaper for the frontier town. The newspaper has a current daily circulation of

around 73,000 and 88,400 on Sun and is currently the only English-language daily in El Paso, but often competes with the Spanish-language *El Diario de El Paso*.

The *El Paso Times* prints a morning edition daily, which is delivered to subscribers by 6 a.m. Mon through Fri, 7 a.m. Sat, and 7:30 a.m. Sun. The *El Paso Times* prints news in several sections that include coverage of local, national, Mexican, and international news; a Borderland section that covers metro, neighborhood, New Mexico, and Texas news; a Sports section with local and national sports and an emphasis on high-school and UTEP coverage; a Business section; and a Living section, which has local and national feature stories including rotating sections covering seniors, religion, pop culture, the arts, books, health, home decor, entertainment news, local music, and fashion. *Tiempo* is a weekly entertainment supplement published on Fri that includes concerts, movies, galleries, restaurant reviews, and other entertainment-related stories. The *Eastside Reporter* is a small publication specifically covering events and stories about businesses and people making a difference on the Eastside of El Paso.

WEEKLIES

EL PASO INC.
120 Porfirio Diaz
(915) 534-4422
www.elpasoinc.com
This weekly newspaper covers El Paso business climate and business makers in the news, including current business developments, industrial parks, and other related issues. *El Paso Inc.* began publishing in September of 1995 and it is a unique, Sunday morning, paid-circulation, weekly newspaper widely read by business managers, professionals, business owners, philanthropists, and their families. Some 8,200 copies are home delivered to subscribers, and it is sold at more than 150 locations and mailed around the country. Yearly subscriptions are available for $52.

El Paso Inc. is divided into four sections: Main News, which focuses on business, economic, and financial news of local interest; Lifestyle, which covers civic, charitable, philanthropic, social, and lifestyle events; Border Business, which covers events and issues of interest to people doing business in Mexico as well as national economic news plus comprehensive stock and mutual fund tables of local interest; and the Personal Finance section, which has one goal—to help its readers navigate the increasingly complex world of personal finance by giving readers advice and information presented in a way that's easy to understand. It includes local reporting on personal finance issues, columns from industry experts, and coverage of personal finance issues.

FORT BLISS MONITOR
5959 Gateway Blvd. West, Suite 450
(915) 772-0934
www.fbmonitor.com
A small, 40- to 60-page free weekly newspaper covering Fort Bliss and overseas news for those stationed on or from Fort Bliss. Sections include some classifieds, ads directed at military clients, and some discounts for military personnel. Every Thursday 20,000 issues of the *Monitor* are published, and the more than 80,000 readers (both on and off post) represent active and retired military, civilian employees, and their families. The *Monitor* is the only authorized newspaper on post and the only newspaper that saturates the military market in El Paso.

THE PROSPECTOR

UTEP Campus
105 Union East
500 West University Ave.
(915) 747-5161
www.utepprospector.com

The Prospector is the official University of Texas at El Paso college newspaper, published twice a week during the school calendar year. The paper, which is written and edited primarily by students, covers UTEP campus news and events and includes a classifieds section with job and housing listings aimed at students. The Sports section provides coverage of all the UTEP sports teams and standings. It is available for free from kiosks and distribution stands around the UTEP campus.

SPOTLIGHT

11385 James Watt, Suite B-12
(915) 595-2492
www.spotlightepnews.com

This Hispanic-interest newspaper provides articles in English and Spanish on local entertainment, community news, family-oriented entertainment articles, movie and concert reviews, health-related stories, and a regional calendar of events. It also includes Lifestyles, Just Kidding, Pet Connection, Golf Digest, and NASCAR Insider sections. A free publication, it can be picked up at a variety of outlets around El Paso and Fort Bliss.

WHAT'S UP

120 Porfirio Diaz
(915) 534-4422
www.whatsuppub.com

An entertainment-focused, free weekly publication that covers El Paso, Las Cruces, and Juárez. *What's Up* circulates around 30,000 copies that are distributed in more than 600 locations throughout the area and covers events from Wed through Tues. The paper's content includes calendar listings, concert reviews, band profiles, celebrity interviews, CD reviews, movie reviews, art exhibits, sports, hobbies, and other entertainment and lifestyle topics geared for the 20 to 40 age range.

MONTHLIES AND MAGAZINES

EL PASO VISITORS GUIDE

444 East Robinson Dr., Suite A
(915) 533-4711
www.pinatapublishing.com

This glossy-cover magazine is published by the El Paso Convention and Visitors Bureau and provides plenty of visitor information about El Paso in several sections that include: Places, Events, Shopping, Dining, Lodging, History, and Mexico. The magazine is printed quarterly and is available for free from the Convention and Visitors Bureau, as well as at many hotels and tourist attractions across town. You can also view the full edition online.

THE EL PASOAN

www.theelpasoan.com

The El Pasoan, launched in 2006, is a free, glossy magazine that showcases the business, culture, and people of El Paso's downtown area. The magazine includes extensive coverage on the Downtown Revitalization Plan; monthly columns written by the mayor, among others; and reviews of galleries, hotspots, and restaurants located downtown. *The El Pasoan* prides itself on being the only "city lifestyle magazine" about El Paso. The publication is available at a variety of locations downtown for free.

EL PASO MAGAZINE
416 North Stanton St., Suite 300
(915) 351-0605
www.epmediagroup.com
This 124-page monthly urban lifestyle magazine began publication in 2007. The aim of the magazine is to offer readers a chance to explore the cosmopolitan side of El Paso, and thus *El Paso Magazine* is known for its sleek design and comprehensive editorial on the business and community leaders of El Paso. The magazine sells for $2.95 an issue at some 200 newsstands in West Texas and Southern New Mexico.

EL PASO SCENE
316 Arboles Dr.
(915) 542-1422
www.epscene.com
Founded in 1993, *El Paso Scene* is a free monthly community newspaper dedicated to upcoming cultural and recreational events. With an average of 60 pages and more than 120 advertisers, the paper prints 40,000 copies each month. Each issue is dedicated to upcoming events in El Paso and the surrounding region, from rock concerts and street festivals to chamber music and art openings. Each issue also contains a feature story and a variety of columns, as well as listings for local events and shows. *El Paso Scene* is distributed at nearly 200 locations throughout El Paso, Las Cruces, Juárez, and the surrounding region and is the best place to find out about local artists, community entertainment, recreation, and culture.

RIO GRANDE CATHOLIC
499 St. Matthews St.
(915) 872-8414
www.riograndecatholic.org

The *Rio Grande Catholic* is a monthly newspaper produced by the Diocese of El Paso to communicate to local parishioners the events and themes of the faith life of the local and universal church through news reports, features, columns, and photography. *The Rio Grande Catholic* is available at local Catholic parishes and through subscription.

RADIO
AM Stations
KAMA 750
(915) 544-9797
Tejano/Spanish

KHEY 1390
(915) 351-5400
www.khey1380.com
ESPN Sports Radio

KROD 600
(915) 544 9550
www.krod.com
News/Talk/Sports

KTSM 690
(915) 351-5400
www.ktsmradio.com
News/Talk/Sports

FM Stations
KBNA 97.5
(915) 544-9797
Spanish Adult Contemporary

KELP 95.9
(915) 779 0016
www.kelpradio.com
Christian

KHEY 96.3
(915) 351-5400
www.khey.com
Country

KLAQ 95.5
(915) 544 9550
www.klaq.com
Rock

KPRR 102.1
(915) 351-5400
www.kprr.com
Top 40/Hip Hop/R&B

XHTO 104.3
(915) 541-1043
www.hitfmradio.com
Top 40/R&B

KTSM 99.9
(915) 351-5400
www.sunny999fm.com
Adult Contemporary

KTEP 88.5
(915) 747-5152
www.ktep.org
National Public Radio/News/Classical

TELEVISION

KVIA ABC CH. 7
4140 Rio Bravo St.
(915) 496-7777
www.kvia.com

KTSM NBC CH. 9
801 North Oregon St.
(915) 880-9629
www.ktsm.com

KFOX FOX CH. 14
6004 North Mesa St.
(915) 833-8585
www.kfoxtv.com

KDBC CBS CH. 4
2201 East Wyoming Ave.
(915) 496-4444
www.kdbc.com

KINT UNIVISION CH. 26 (SPANISH)
5426 North Mesa St.
(915) 581-1126
www.univision26.com

KCOS PBS CH. 13
9050 Viscount Blvd., Suite A-440
(915) 590-1313
www.kcostv.org

INDEX